THE
REGENCY YEARS

The Prince Regent, engraved by A. Heath

THE
REGENCY
YEARS

*During Which Jane Austen Writes,
Napoleon Fights, Byron Makes Love,
and Britain Becomes Modern*

ROBERT MORRISON

W. W. NORTON & COMPANY
INDEPENDENT PUBLISHERS SINCE 1923 / NEW YORK • LONDON

For information about permission to reproduce selections from this book,
write to Permissions, W. W. Norton & Company, Inc.,
500 Fifth Avenue, New York, NY 10110

For information about special discounts for bulk purchases, please contact
W. W. Norton Special Sales at specialsales@wwnorton.com or 800-233-4830

Manufacturing by Lake Book Manufacturing, Inc.
Book design by Brooke Koven
Production manager: Julia Druskin

Library of Congress Cataloging-in-Publication Data

Names: Morrison, Robert, 1961– author.
Title: The Regency years : during which Jane Austen writes, Napoleon fights,
Byron makes love, and Britain becomes modern / Robert Morrison.
Other titles: Jane Austen writes, Napoleon fights, Byron makes love, and Britain
becomes modern
Description: First edition. | New York ; London : W. W. Norton & Company,
[2019] | Includes bibliographical references and index.
Identifiers: LCCN 2018053659 | ISBN 9780393249057 (hardcover)
Subjects: LCSH: Great Britain—Civilization—19th century. | Regency—Great
Britain. | Arts—Great Britain—History—20th century. | Great Britain—Social
life and customs—19th century. | Great Britain—Social conditions—19th century.
Classification: LCC DA533 .M775 2019 | DDC 941.07/3—dc23
LC record available at https://lccn.loc.gov/2018053659

W. W. Norton & Company, Inc., 500 Fifth Avenue, New York, N.Y. 10110
www.wwnorton.com

W. W. Norton & Company Ltd., 15 Carlisle Street, London W1D 3BS

1 2 3 4 5 6 7 8 9 0

For Carole
Again and Always

CONTENTS

ACKNOWLEDGMENTS

My research for this book was generously funded by the Social Sciences and Humanities Research Council of Canada. I am deeply grateful for the council's support. I would like to thank the following librarians and archivists for providing extra information and guiding me to new sources: Rachel Foss at the British Library; Susan Halpert at the Houghton Library, Harvard University; Rachel Beattie at the National Library of Scotland; Kimberley Bell, Bonnie Brooks, and Jillian Sparks at the Queen's University Library; and Chris Sutherns at Tate Images. For his indispensable assistance on this project, I would especially like to record my thanks to Jeff Cowton of the Wordsworth Trust.

Writing this book has been a complicated and exhilarating task, and I have benefited enormously from the expertise and support of a number of scholars and friends. I am grateful to Chris Baldick, Peter Bell, John Berry, Benjamin Colbert, Roy Golsteyn, Roger Hamilton, Wendy-Lee Hamilton, Kanonhsyonne Janice C. Hill, Markus Iseli, Paul James, Kaveh Khanverdi, Larry Krupp, John Kulka, Grevel Lindop, Amy Loyst, Charles Mahoney, Robert McCullum, Johanna McLeod, Peter McLeod, Martha Paul, Nick Paul, Ian Reed, Bob Richardson, Sir Christopher Ricks, Daniel Sanjiv Roberts, Nicholas Roe, Patricia Meyer Spacks, Lee Spinks, Vinita Srivastava, Nancy Stokes, John Strachan, and Duncan Wu. I would like to thank Lyndon Bray, Randy Paskuski, and Neil Sheets for being my bandmates for all these years. Thank you, as well, to Michael Davie, who has been such a good friend for more than three decades, and who walked with me around the Brighton Pavilion and John Keats's house.

Anthony Holden and Alan Samson both believed in this project right from the start, and I am deeply grateful for their friendship and support. For invaluable assistance and advice, I would like to thank Guy Gavriel Kay and James Nightingale, as well as my literary agents, Julian Alexander and John Silbersack. At W. W. Norton, thank you to Nancy Palmquist and, in particular, to my editor Amy Cherry, who read the manuscript with such care, and who offered so many insightful suggestions.

For their love, friendship, and constant encouragement, I would like to thank Zachary and Alastair.

This book is for Carole.

Leigh House
Brewer's Mills

INTRODUCTION

The Regency began on February 5, 1811. King George III had been crowned in 1760, and had presided over both the loss of the American colonies and Britain's struggles against Revolutionary and Napoleonic France. But he was replaced as Britain's ruler because he suffered from some form of insanity, which struck him down several times during his long reign, and which in late 1810 cast him into darkness, clearing the way for the Regency of his dissolute eldest son, George, Prince of Wales, who ruled Britain as Prince Regent until January 29, 1820, when George III died and the Regent became King George IV. Despite its brevity, the Regency was a time of major events, from the Luddite Riots and the War of 1812 to the Battle of Waterloo, the explosion of Mount Tambora, and the Peterloo Massacre. And it had a glorious cast, including Jane Austen, Beau Brummell, Lord Byron, John Constable, John Keats, Walter Scott, Mary Shelley, Percy Shelley, J. M. W. Turner, the Duke of Wellington, and of course the Regent himself. But there were dozens of other figures who made a decisive contribution to the period, including athletes (Tom Cribb), artists (Mary Linwood and Thomas Rowlandson), engineers (Thomas Telford), explorers (John Franklin), inventors (Charles Babbage), journalists (Pierce Egan), novelists (Mary Brunton and Maria Edgeworth), poets (John Clare), reformers (Elizabeth Fry and Robert Owen), and scientists (Humphry Davy and Michael Faraday). While I recognize the deep continuities between the Regency and the decades that both preceded and followed it, I believe the Regency is perhaps the most extraordinary decade in all of British history. It is certainly the period that most definitively marks the appearance of the modern world.

In fiction, the Regency is brought most vividly to life in William Makepeace Thackeray's magnificent *Vanity Fair* (1847–48) and in the novels of Georgette Heyer, including *Regency Buck* (1935) and *An Infamous Army* (1937). Popular studies began with William Cobbett's *History of the Regency and Reign of King George the Fourth* (1830–34), continued through a number of nineteenth- and early-twentieth-century accounts, and culminated in the 1970s and 1980s in a spate of shorter surveys, including those by Joanna Richardson, Donald Low, and Carolly Erickson. There have been a host of books on individual aspects of the Regency, including its architecture, art, fashion, furniture, politics, prizefighters, and rakes. There have also been a number of studies that fold the Regency into a longer historical survey, including Paul Johnson's magisterial *The Birth of the Modern* (1991), or that see it variously as a part of the "Age of Atonement," the "Age of Elegance," the "Age of Improvement," the "Age of Revolution," or the "Age of Wonder." Several studies, too, have been devoted to an examination of the "Regency world" of individual authors, including, most prominently, Austen and Byron.

Yet despite the wealth of interest, this book is the first in more than three decades to focus solely on the Regency years, and in its account of the period's remarkable diversity, upheaval, and elegance, it pushes well beyond the scope of any previous work on the decade. It builds on the key sources about the Regency, including the memoirs and journals of Frances Burney, Joseph Farington, Rees Howell Gronow, and Henry Crabb Robinson. More importantly, it taps the rich stores found in recent biographies of leading figures, including Percy Shelley and the Duke of Wellington, as well as in new editions of works by Regency authors, from well-known writers like Jane Austen to lesser-known figures such as the courtesan Harriette Wilson and the diarist Anne Lister, who during the Regency recorded in code her joyous experiences of same-sex love.

Above all, this book ranges across the decade to mark the moment when Thackeray and Charles Dickens were boys, Benjamin Disraeli and Thomas Macaulay were teenagers, and John Keats and Thomas

Carlyle (both born in 1795) were young men. It considers Britain at home and abroad, at war and at peace, at work and at pleasure. It brings the central figures of the period into dialogue with one another, as Turner chats with Constable, Lady Caroline Lamb pursues Byron, Wellington spies Napoleon across the battlefield, Keats watches Edmund Kean on stage, and Mary Russell Mitford enthuses over a lecture by William Hazlitt. In its dreams of equality and freedom, its embrace of consumerism and celebrity culture, its mass radical protests in support of parliamentary reform, and its complicated response to the burgeoning pace of industrial, technological, and scientific advance, the Regency signals both a decisive break from the past and the onset of the desiring, democratic, secular, opportunistic society that is for the first time recognizably our own.

THE
REGENCY YEARS

The Regent and the Regency

He burst into tears. It was May 1812, and his erstwhile friend Lord Moira had just explained to him that the country was in a "terrible state." The Prince Regent admitted ignorance. He had not received any news from his ministers in the last three or four weeks, and he did not know what was happening in the kingdom. How bad were things beyond the opulent confines of his home at Carlton House in London, or his seaside retreat at the Brighton Pavilion? The answer, as Moira undoubtedly informed him, was that things were very bad indeed.[1] In Ireland there were government crackdowns and bitter outbreaks of sectarian violence; in Scotland landlords were clearing their estates for sheep farming by forcing thousands of Highlanders from their homes; and in England there were riots in the industrial Midlands and widespread despair in the agricultural districts. And this was to say nothing of the monumental struggle Britain was waging in Europe against Napoleonic France, or the anger building between America and Britain that led less than a month later to the two countries descending into the War of 1812.

Long before Moira finished, the Regent was "very nearly in convulsions," and Moira suggested that he return the next day in order to allow the Regent time to compose himself.[2] Yet despite the stress these meetings caused him, and the turmoil that continued to sweep through the country, the Regent rarely took more than a sporadic interest in domestic politics. The result was repeated and often ferocious attacks on him by satirists, caricaturists, political enemies, and discarded friends, all of which created an image of him as self-indulgent, incompetent, and lachrymose that has endured from his day to ours.

Nonetheless, if widely despised and too often oblivious in matters of state, the Regent in matters of taste and style left a profound impact on his era, for in his love of both elegance and excess, violence and restraint, learning and lasciviousness, the low-brow and the high-minded, he embodied many of the extremes that have come to define his Regency, not only within court circles but also much further down the social hierarchies. His love of prizefighting, horse racing, and the theater set the tone for the age, as did his delight in consumerism. Gamblers bet wildly, like him, on cards and dice, losing far more than they could afford and racking up cripplingly high debt loads. The Regent's vast consumption of food and especially drink empowered male and female debauchees from across the social spectrum. His days and nights of committed libertinism inspired rakes of both sexes, who throughout his Regency enjoyed an unabashed revelry of promiscuity and pornographic obsession.

The Regent had passions, however, that extended well beyond the stimulations of sport, gaming, sex, booze, food, and shopping. His cultural, aesthetic, and literary judgments have proven remarkably sound. John Rennie was his engineer and John Nash his architect, and together their building projects transformed Regency London. In fashion, he was for many years an intimate of George "Beau" Brummell, who set new standards for sartorial elegance in male dress. In art, he commissioned portraits from Thomas Lawrence and genre paintings from David Wilkie. In prose fiction, he championed Jane Austen, who did not admire him but who dedicated *Emma* (1816) "to his Royal Highness the Prince Regent" and who was "read & admired" by him at a time when her work enjoyed only limited popularity. In poetry, the Regent, like so many of his contemporaries, thought Walter Scott preeminent until George Gordon Byron, sixth

Baron Byron, skyrocketed to fame in March 1812 with the publication of *Childe Harold's Pilgrimage*, whereupon the Regent asked to meet Byron, whom he "surprised & delighted" with his intimate knowledge of "poetry and Poets." In science, the Regent knighted Humphry Davy, the most eminent chemist of the day. "The works of scientific men," Davy declared, "are like the atoms of gold, of sapphire and diamonds, that exist in a mountain. . . . When sovereigns are at the expense of digging out these riches, they are repaid by seeing them gems in their crowns."[3]

The deep contradictions in the Regent's character both energized and undermined him, and were evident from an early age. Born August 12, 1762, and named George Augustus Frederick, he was the eldest of fifteen children of King George III and Queen Charlotte (eight brothers and six sisters followed). Given the title of Prince of Wales within a week of his birth, he was as a child actively involved in a rigorous education that—on his father's instructions—attempted to inculcate the virtues of honesty, hard work, and punctuality, and that eventually grew to include everything from lessons in boxing, fencing, and drawing to the study of mathematics, natural philosophy, languages, literature, music, agriculture, and the classics. George did well across this curriculum, but he sometimes showed an irritability and a lack of commitment that his father wanted beaten out of him. One of his sisters remembered how she had seen George and some of his brothers "held by their tutors to be flogged like dogs with a long whip."[4]

Prince George seems to have taken such discipline in his stride, and to have continued to develop his knowledge of art, architecture, music, and literature. But by the time he was seventeen, he was already "rather too fond of wine and women" and in open revolt against his father, whose industry, uxoriousness, and parsimony he utterly rejected, and whose expectations he seemed hell-bent on disappointing.[5] He took up with the brilliant Whig politician Charles James Fox, a bitter enemy of his father's and a renowned champion of both liberty and dissipation. He accumulated gambling and consumer debts at a rate that almost beggars belief. He entertained several mistresses, including the beautiful actress Mary Robinson. In

December 1785, after a tumultuous courtship, he secretly married Maria Fitzherbert, a Roman Catholic widow six years his senior, but the union was unlawful because members of the royal family needed the king's consent to marry if they were under the age of twenty-five. The prince was twenty-three years old.

Three years later, the king became seriously ill with what appeared to be insanity, throwing the country into the so-called "Regency Crisis," during which time George relished the thought of the money and influence that would be available to him should he become sovereign de facto, and he and his Whig friends engaged in pleasant games of "cabinet-making." But in February 1789 the king unexpectedly recovered, and George went back to boozing and betting and womanizing and weight gain. Only a few months later, the French Revolution broke out. Though he had pushed hard for many years to be allowed to join the army, and though he was fascinated by military costume and strategy, George was always denied the opportunity to fight for his country because he was heir to the throne and his father forbade it. The decision humiliated him and meant that he was forced to sit on the sidelines while his brothers (with the exception of George III's sixth son, sickly Augustus) served as high-ranking officers on the land or at sea. Byron later imagined George in 1791 as "full of promise" and "[a] finished gentleman from top to toe." But well before that date, as one observer put it, George was "a man occupied in trifles, because he had no opportunity of displaying his talents in the conduct of great concerns."[6]

Britain went to war against Revolutionary France in February 1793, while George ran up such a mountain of new debt that—his secret marriage to Maria Fitzherbert notwithstanding—he agreed to marry his cousin, Caroline of Brunswick, in exchange for a settlement that would make him solvent again. The couple met for the first time just a few days before their wedding. Neither was impressed. "I am not well," said George on first seeing Caroline. "Pray get me a glass of brandy." When he left the room, Caroline declared, "I think he's very fat and he's nothing like as handsome as his portrait."[7] On their wedding day, April 8, 1795, George was drunk and collapsed in the evening by the fireplace of their bridal chamber, though he clearly managed to revive himself the next morning, for exactly nine months later a daughter, Charlotte, was born. Shortly thereafter Caroline moved out of Carlton House and into a separate residence. The brief, stormy marriage between the Prince and Princess of Wales was unofficially at an end.

George returned to the arms of Mrs. Fitzherbert, and then a new series of mistresses, while Caroline, warmhearted but light-headed, and famously disinclined to ablutions, embarked on her own career of sexual licentiousness. Her conduct—certainly no worse than his— prompted him to order what became known as the "Delicate Investigation," in which a committee quietly looked into the salacious rumors surrounding her private life but determined that there was no conclusive proof of adultery. Husband and wife by now thoroughly despised each other. Public opinion was decidedly on her side. "I shall support her as long as I can, because she *is* a Woman, & because I hate her Husband," Austen stated flatly. The welfare and upbringing of the couple's daughter, Charlotte, provoked especially bitter disagreements between them. "My mother was wicked," Charlotte later wrote, "but she would not have turned so wicked had not my father been much more wicked still."[8]

The death in November 1810 of George III's youngest and favorite daughter, Amelia, was a severe blow from which he was unable to recover, and by the end of the year it was evident that the madness that had afflicted him before had now returned in an even more virulent form. Forced to take action, Parliament introduced the Regency Act, and on February 5, 1811, the forty-eight-year-old Prince of Wales was sworn in as Prince Regent. One day earlier he had confounded many by announcing that he had decided to retain his father's Tory ministers rather than appoint a new government from among his Whig friends. His decision was based in part on his fear of what his father would do if he recovered his senses and discovered that he had a Whig prime minister. But there were other factors as well. He no longer felt the same loyalty to the Whig party, especially after the death of Fox in 1806. He also disagreed with several leading Whigs over their support of Catholic emancipation, a campaign to remove the numerous political and civil restrictions that harassed Roman

Catholics living in Britain, and an issue on which the Regent had no intention of giving any ground despite his love for Maria Fitzherbert. More decisively, he abhorred their willingness to abandon the fight against Napoleon and leave continental Europe to him, a pusillanimous policy that the Regent rejected in favor of unstinting support for the Duke of Wellington and a vigorous pursuit of the British war effort. The government imposed a one-year restriction on the powers of the Regent, but in February 1812 he assumed the full authority of the crown, and "might now, therefore, be regarded as virtually king," as the essayist and opium addict Thomas De Quincey remarked.[9] This made the Regent not only the most powerful man in Britain but also the man at the head of the wealthiest, strongest, most ambitious, vibrant, and productive country in the world—though Britain in the Regency was at the same time a country of strikingly paradoxical attitudes and experiences, and a country that was almost torn apart by radical anger and anguish.

CHAPTER ONE

Crime, Punishment, and the Pursuit of Freedom

I

John Bellingham spent the sunny afternoon of Monday, May 11, 1812, with his landlady, a widower named Rebecca Robarts, and her young son. Together they walked the two miles from 9 New Millman Street, where Bellingham had been a lodger for about four months, to King Street, next to St. James's Square. Here they visited the European Museum, an institution devoted to the promotion of the fine arts, where they wandered for more than two hours, and Bellingham pointed out a sketch of the Last Judgment by the great Flemish master Peter Paul Rubens. Sometime shortly after four o'clock they left the museum to begin their journey home, but when they reached Sidney's Alley, off Leicester Square, Bellingham announced that he had to go and buy a prayer book, leaving Mrs. Robarts and her son to return to New Millman Street, while he headed off in the direction of Westminster. In under thirty minutes he made his way down crowded Whitehall, into Parliament Street, across Palace Yard, and up the broad steps of St. Stephen's into the lobby of the House of Commons. He stopped, caught his breath, and positioned himself by the door. Just a few minutes behind him in the London streets was the evangelical Tory prime minister, Spencer Perceval, a devoted husband and father of twelve children who had assumed the premiership in October 1809 and who was then at the height of his political power. Scheduled to attend the 4:30 P.M. session, he had left 10 Downing Street (the home of prime ministers) late but decided against traveling by carriage. It was almost quarter past five before a brisk walk brought him to the doors of the House.[1]

Bellingham was waiting for Perceval, armed—as he had been throughout the afternoon—with two primed-and-cocked pistols. He had not wanted it to come to this, but what choice did he have? Eight years earlier, he had sailed from Liverpool to Archangel in Russia on a mercantile venture, but things had soon gone terribly wrong, and he found himself in prison for a debt that he insisted he did not owe. Confused and increasingly angry, he appealed to the British authorities for help, but they repeatedly informed him that his case was under the jurisdiction of the Russian government alone. After five dreadful years trying to prove his innocence, he was finally released in October 1809, and two months later he was back in England, where he immediately began to lobby the authorities for redress. His pleas, including one to the Prince Regent and one to Perceval, again fell on deaf ears.

Bitter and by now obsessed, he decided to take matters into his own hands. In his early forties, with his wife and three children living in Liverpool, he relocated to London. After two months he fell behind in his rent to Mrs. Robarts, though she found him a kind and polite lodger and especially appreciated his willingness to escort her to church services. On about April 21, Bellingham spent four guineas on a brace of seven-inch steel pistols that he bought from the celebrated London gunsmith William Beckwith. Over the next few days he took them to Hampstead Heath, where he practiced firing at trees. Shortly thereafter he hired a tailor to alter one of his coats by sewing into it a nine-inch-deep inside pocket on the left-hand side that could hold one of the pistols and that he could access conveniently with his right hand. Bellingham also began during these weeks to attend Parliament regularly, sitting in the Strangers' Gallery and peering down through the gloom at the government benches, while frequently asking those seated around him about the identity of different ministers.

Soon he put the name "Spencer Perceval" to the face, and Bellingham's rage honed in on him as the leader of an oppressive and brutally indifferent government.[2]

Tall and large-boned, with a thin face, aquiline nose, sunken eyes, and sallow complexion, Bellingham was intensely aware of the pistol concealed in his dark brown coat, while the backup gun protruded awkwardly in the pocket of his nankeen trousers. Perceval, a much smaller man, with a pale face and wide eyes, now entered the lobby, wearing a blue coat, white waistcoat, and charcoal breeches. Bellingham knew him instantly, walked calmly and directly up to him with pistol drawn, and fired at point-blank range. The large bullet tore into the prime minister's chest, creating a wound at least three inches deep as it passed over the fourth rib on the left-hand side and then downward toward the heart. "I am murdered!" Perceval screamed as he reeled backward against the door and then, staggering forward, collapsed facedown on the floor. It was only when two horrified bystanders turned him over that they recognized who had been shot, and the enormity of what had just happened broke upon the people in the lobby, before spreading quickly into the rooms beyond. Several men assisted in picking up the prime minister and carrying him into the Speaker's apartments. Blood leaked from the corners of his mouth and seeped from his chest into his shirt and waistcoat. Gently the men seated him upright on a table, but he did not speak again, and within a few minutes he was dead, the first and only British prime minister to be assassinated. Bellingham made no attempt to flee. When he was seized by lobby onlookers, there were large beads of sweat running down his face, and his body heaved as if a "billiard-ball . . . were choking him." In the chaos, witnesses demanded to know why he had done such a thing. "I have been denied the redress of my grievances by Government," he replied; "I have been ill-treated."[3]

Reaction to the murder was swift, and—more than any other single incident—it exposed the bitter class divisions within Regency society. Many people, both within the government and far beyond, deeply admired Perceval, not only for the virtuousness of his private life but for his political stance, which was anti-French, anti-Catholic, anti-slavery, and fiercely anti-reform. The House met the following

THIS PRINT by George Cruikshank depicts the events of May
11, 1812, when the deranged merchant John Bellingham assassinated the prime minister, Spencer Perceval, in the lobby of the
House of Commons.

day to pay tribute to their fallen colleague, and several members—
from political allies like Lord Castlereagh, through rivals like George
Canning, to opponents such as Samuel Whitbread—were overcome
with emotion. "Mr. Perceval . . . I am singular enough to regard as
the best and wisest minister of this reign," wrote the poet Samuel
Taylor Coleridge.[4]

Outside the House, however, the mood could hardly have been
more different. An immense crowd of "from fifty to a hundred
thousand persons" gathered in the hours following the murder,
and—surprisingly, even shockingly—they were jubilant. What for
Bellingham had been a personal vendetta became in the public mind a
political assassination in which, on behalf of the angry, the impoverished, and the reviled, someone had finally hit back with lethal force.
An anxious Coleridge heard exultant agitators toasting the event with
"more of these damned Scoundrels must go the same way," while the

diarist and socialite Frances Calvert reported that "there were printed placards put on the House of Commons . . . stating that Mr. Perceval's ribs were only fit to broil the Regent's heart on. How horrible!" The poet William Wordsworth, in London at the time, came across a woman who was selling "the life of Bellingham" and who was glorying in the "good deed he did." "Nothing can be more deplorably ferocious and savage than the lowest orders in London," he reported, "and I am sorry to say that tens of thousands of the Middle class and even respectable Shop-keepers rejoice in this detestable murther." Meanwhile, celebrations spread north to the manufacturing towns, where people rang bells, lit bonfires, and showed "the most savage joy." From Kegworth in Leicestershire, the Irish poet Thomas Moore declared, "You cannot imagine what a *combustible* state this country is in—all the common people's heads are full of revolution."[5]

The government sent troops into the streets, awarded Perceval's widow Jane an annuity of £2,000 (about $200,000 US today), supplemented by a still more lavish grant of £50,000 (about $5,000,000 today) for the support of her children. Then it set its sights on making an example of Bellingham, who was formally charged with murder and dispatched to Newgate Prison amid throngs of supporters. "What were the people to do who were starving?" demanded one commentator. "Not murder people," snapped Wordsworth, "unless they mean to eat their hearts." Bellingham was tried at the Old Bailey on May 15 and contended throughout the day that he was perfectly justified in killing Perceval. "What he had done was a mite to a mountain, compared with what Government had done to him." The trial lasted eight hours, after which the jury withdrew for fifteen minutes and returned with a verdict of guilty. On Monday, May 18, 1812, one week after he had assassinated the prime minister, Bellingham emerged from Newgate into an early morning rain, calm and dignified, and ascended the gallows as "a score of persons in the mob set up a loud and reiterated cry of 'God bless you! God bless you!'" Lord Byron looked on from a rented window. As the clock tolled eight, he and thousands of others watched as Bellingham was "launched into eternity."[6]

The radical William Cobbett was a prisoner in Newgate at the time, and he too witnessed the execution. The people's enthusiasm for Bellingham, he concluded, did not mean that they were blood-thirsty. "Their conduct upon this occasion only shows, and it does show in the most striking light, the deep discontent that they felt at the terrible laws that had been passed . . . to abridge their liberties." For some, it was possible to accept these disadvantages and restric-tions, which extended from tight controls on the price and content of newspapers, through legislative measures that kept the price of food artificially high, to brutal laws that punished even minor transgres-sions. But many others simply could no longer tolerate a system in which power was consolidated in the hands of a privileged few, while consigning the vast majority to lives of want and despair. Driven var-iously by hunger, greed, boredom, and anger, tens of thousands of people turned—like Bellingham—to crime, which had a tighter grip on London in the Regency than in any previous or subsequent period, as criminals exulted in one last lawless spree before the government finally responded in the 1820s to repeated calls for legal, penal, and police reform. More broadly, throughout Britain the laboring classes assembled in unprecedented numbers to demand political reforms such as universal suffrage and annual parliaments. In response, the government enacted ferocious crackdowns, including the infamous Peterloo Massacre at Manchester, when British soldiers armed with axes and swords charged into a crowd of peaceful protesters, kill-ing eleven and wounding hundreds. Above all, the Regency's most important radical, Percy Bysshe Shelley, looked directly at contempo-rary suffering and responded by championing not only political but also, and more urgently, moral and spiritual reform. In his finest writ-ings, Shelley imagines a dramatic transformation in which human-kind's creative spirit is unbound, and "Love, hope and self-esteem" heal the divisions both within and between us.[7]

II

Crime was a pressing issue across the country. Contemporary assess-ments of it are marred by exaggeration, extenuation, and denial, but there is no question that the situation in the capital was especially acute because of its size. In 1811, London had around one million inhabitants, giving it ten times the population of other major centers, such as Glasgow (100,749), Manchester (98,573), Liverpool (94,376), and Birmingham (85,753).[8] Further, while the rural poor flooding into British cities often drifted into unemployment and criminality, it was only in London that they could find "rookeries," long-established, densely populated criminal districts occupied by tavern owners, lodging-house keepers, moneylenders, and beggars, all crowded together with criminals of every description. Whereas in other urban centers people might take to crime on their own, in the London rookeries they were recruited by hardened professionals, who taught them the best ruses, the fastest escape routes, and the surest hideouts before sending them into the streets to practice their trade.

The most notorious rookeries lay just outside the affluent square mile of London known as "the City," enabling thieves to plunder its centers of wealth and commerce and then go to ground only a street or two beyond its boundaries. Just across London Bridge in the borough of Southwark ran Tooley Street, its gin shops and proximity to the Thames long making it a favorite haunt of river pirates. To the northeast, in the Spitalfields-Whitechapel area, lay the seedy environs of Petticoat Lane. In Clerkenwell to the north was the slum located between "Whitecross-street, Golden-lane, the upper end of Bunhill-row, and the north end of Grub-street." "Do you conceive that a number of the public houses in Whitecross-street and the parts adjacent are supported by notorious thieves, prostitutes and other bad characters?" the 1817 Parliamentary Select Committee on the State of the Police asked the magistrate Samuel Mills. "I am afraid they are," he replied frankly.[9] Worst of all, to the west was the lair of St. Giles (known as the "Holy Land"), its inhabitants crammed together in filth and despair, and at its heart, the Rats' Castle, an infamous pub where criminals met, boasted, drank, and planned.

"Flash" language originated in the London rookeries, a mysterious and often humorous argot that reached the peak of its popularity in the Regency. A kind of "anti-language," it was spoken by everyone from the criminal and sporting classes all the way up to chic aristos and the Regent himself. "To speak *good flash* is to be well versed in cant terms," James Hardy Vaux explained in his *Vocabulary of the Flash Language* (1819), while Pierce Egan reported in his *Life in London* (1820–21) that "a kind of *cant* phraseology is current from one end of the Metropolis to the other." The Old Bailey judge John Silvester got so tired of the accused women and men in his courtroom speaking to and of one another in flash code that, in 1816, he drew up his own "list of cant words with their meaning" in order to decipher what was being said. Several terms from the flash lexicon have proven remarkably enduring, including "pig" for "a police officer" and "pigeon" for "a weak silly fellow easily imposed upon." [10]

Joseph Merceron was the Regency's most powerful gangland boss and, like many of the London thugs who followed in his footsteps, he was based in the East End at Bethnal Green, an impoverished parish run by an elected vestry, with drinking dens behind every fifth or sixth door. Merceron began life as a clerk in a lottery office, but through fraud, intimidation, political cunning, and shrewd investments, he rose to become the owner of eleven pubs, the treasurer of the parish funds, and a justice of the peace. With this kind of grip on local affairs, he was able to renew pub licenses for friends and criminal associates (no matter how noxious their establishments) and to stack vestry meetings with boisterous, sometimes malevolent, crowds of artisans and weavers who ensured that his nominations were carried and that it was business as usual with his criminal operations. In 1818, Merceron was finally arrested on fraud and corruption charges. He was sentenced to eighteen months in prison. When he emerged, he soon found ways of winning back most of his old power. [11]

Beholden to men like Merceron, or working further down the criminal ladder, were a vast series of gangs, small-time operators, highway robbers, petty thieves, and pickpockets who ran rackets of every conceivable kind in an attempt to get their hands on the food, money, clothing, and luxury items that they saw all around them. In the neat summation of the essayist and poet laureate Robert Southey: "More offences are committed in England than in other countries, because there is more wealth and more want." Stolen property typically made its way to a fence, who sold it on to other criminals or to members of the buying public who either did not know—or did not care—where it came from. Mrs. Diner of Field Lane traded exclusively in purloined silk handkerchiefs, which she kept in "a Cockloft through a Trap Door at the top of her house." Mrs. Jennings of Red Lion Market "has secret Rooms by Doors out of Cupboards where she plants or secretes the property she buys till she has got it disposed of." An unidentified woman in Gulston Street bought a whole range of stolen property, from petticoats to bread and cheese, stashing some of these articles "down her Bosom" and others in a barrow. Mr. Brand ran an old rag shop in Tottenham Court Road, but his special sideline was buying stolen pieces of lead.[12]

Children and adolescents were intimately involved in these criminal activities. Ringleaders sent them into recently completed homes to steal the doors, shutters, and brass knobs, after which they made their way across the rooftops to adjoining inhabited houses and looted them as well. Other youthful lawbreakers slipped into haberdashers' and linendrapers' shops on their hands and knees and made off with various items, or worked from outside the store, using a knife to remove windows and then grabbing whatever was within reach. If they were apprehended, their handlers hoped that, "in consideration of their youth," the magistrates would dismiss them. If they returned home empty-handed, they were usually flogged. The 1817 Select Committee on the State of the Police heard a great deal of testimony about young offenders. One, "*Q. R.* aged twelve . . . has a mother who encourages the vices of her son, and subsists by his depredations." Another, "*C. D.* aged ten . . . was committed to prison in the month of April 1815, having been sentenced to seven years imprisonment." A third, "*E. F.* aged eight," has been "in the habit of stealing for upwards of two years." In Covent Garden, between thirty and forty boys slept every night under sheds and baskets, and then awoke in the morning with theft as their only means of obtaining food. The MP (Member of Parliament) Henry Grey Bennet calculated that there were more than 6,000 boys and girls living solely on the proceeds of crime, and this number was, he added, a conservative estimate.[13]

The most notorious Regency thieves were the "resurrection men," who stole bodies from graveyards and sold them to medical professionals, who needed them to teach their students the techniques of surgery. One such was Astley Cooper, who ran a thriving private practice, but who was also a surgeon at Guy's Hospital (where one of his students was the poet John Keats), and a lecturer in anatomy at St. Thomas's Hospital, only a few minutes' walk away. Doctors like Cooper bought dead bodies because, legally, they had access only to the corpses of hanged criminals, and this supply, estimated at around 80 bodies each year, was nowhere near enough to meet the

DATED DECEMBER 31, 1815, this engraving by John Thomas Smith is part of his *Vagabondiana* collection and shows two boys selling matches.

demand, as there were 1,000 medical students in London and almost that same number in Edinburgh.[14] Cooper was unapologetic. Tens of thousands of British soldiers were in desperate need of life-saving or life-enhancing surgery, especially in the days and weeks following Waterloo. It was crucial that surgeons increase their knowledge of the human body and improve their operating skills. If that meant illegally purchasing corpses, so be it.

One of the most remarkable documents from the Regency is a diary kept by Joseph Naples, a member of the "Borough Boys," London's most successful gang of body snatchers. Led by the sharply dressed, pockmarked, ex-prizefighter Ben Crouch, and with a keen eye to business and convenience, these "sack 'em up men" or "shushy lifters" were based in Southwark and regularly preyed on the large burial ground situated to the south of Guy's and St. Thomas's that both of them used to dispose of their unclaimed dead, as well as on the three smaller cemeteries located nearby, though when circumstances demanded it the gang also traveled much farther afield. Different bodies sold at different prices, depending on size and age. In 1812, adult cadavers (or "subjects" as they were euphemistically known) of either sex brought the resurrectionists £4 4s (roughly $425 today) each, while corpses under three feet ("smalls" or "large smalls") were priced by the inch and, given the high levels of child mortality in the Regency, especially plentiful. Most of the corpses dug up and sold—it perhaps goes without saying—were those of poor people.[15]

Naples's diary covers thirteen months, from November 1811 to December 1812, and throws searching light on the brutish business of Regency grave robbing. A slight, civil man "with a pleasing expression of countenance," Naples's favorite activity was getting drunk, but on many nights he was out with the Borough Boys on raiding missions. December 12, 1811: "went to Bunhill row got 6, 1 of them . . . named Mary Rolph, aged 46." March 15, 1812: "went to St. John's, Got 1 Large and 1 Large Small, Burnt." October 22, 1812: "got 3 adults 2 M. 1 F. (left one behind us) 1 small & 1 Foetus."[16] The gang sold most of these bodies to the London hospitals—"1 for Mr. Cooper's Lectures"—but there was also brisk demand among medical practitioners elsewhere. "Sent 7 into the Country," Naples writes in

February 1812, while in December he is "packing up" 12 bodies for Edinburgh. The Borough Boys faced a number of problems, from bad weather, night patrols, and guard dogs to diseased corpses and competition from a rival Jewish gang led in all probability by Israel Chapman, with whom one night they "had a row." But Naples still made good money. The gang settled their accounts twice in February 1812: in the first instance, "each man's share £21 9s. 4d." ($2,200), and in the second, "each man's share £23 6s. 9d." ($2,375).[17]

III

Gun violence created a portion of these corpses. Dueling was illegal but commonplace. In Jane Austen's *Sense and Sensibility* (1811), Colonel Brandon describes his duel with John Willoughby as "unavoidable," and while Elinor sighs "over the fancied necessity of this," she presumes "not to censure it." Abraham Bosquett, the author of *The Young Man of Honour's Vade-Mecum* (1817), recounts his extensive experience of dueling, damns in particular the bloodthirstiness of too many seconds, and offers much useful advice: "due attention also should be had to the position of the body; the side, which is by much the narrowest, should carefully be given, the belly drawn in, and the right thigh and leg placed so as to cover the left." The Regency's most infamous duel involved the volatile Irish patriot Daniel O'Connell and a merchant named John D'Esterre, who belonged to the Corporation of Dublin (a Protestant stronghold) and who took umbrage at O'Connell's contemptuous criticism of it. The two men met twelve miles outside Dublin on February 1, 1815. D'Esterre fired first and missed. O'Connell replied with a bullet that ripped into the thigh of his antagonist. D'Esterre died two days later.[18]

Other, far less ritualized kinds of gun violence also flared across the Regency, as people, like Bellingham, sought vigilante justice to solve their problems or release their frustrations. Though the circumstances remain mysterious, Percy Shelley claimed that on the night of February 26, 1813, he "just escaped an atrocious assassination" when an attacker twice broke into his house in North Wales. Perhaps motivated by anger at Shelley's radical politics, the assailant in the first exchange allegedly shot at Shelley, who returned fire, driving the intruder off the property and into the surrounding woods. Later that same night the assailant or his agent returned to fire on Shelley a second time, and on this occasion the bullet passed through Shelley's flannel nightgown. Shelley escaped both attacks without injury, while the intruder, according to Shelley's first wife Harriet, may have received a bullet wound in the shoulder. On Saturday evening, February 17, 1816, the actress Frances Kelly was onstage at Drury Lane when George Barnett, an obsessed fan who had been sending her threatening mail, suddenly pulled out a gun and fired at her from the pit (or floor of the house), spraying shot across the stage but hitting no one. On Wednesday, April 8, 1818, Lieutenant David Davies, a mentally unstable half-pay officer who was demanding a military pension for a self-inflicted injury, fired at the secretary at war and future prime minister, Henry John Temple, third Viscount Palmerston, as he bounded up the first flight of stairs at the War Office. Palmerston groaned deeply when he was hit, but he escaped with only a severely bruised and burned back, while Davies was acquitted on the grounds of insanity and committed to the Bedlam asylum for the mentally ill. On Tuesday, January 28, 1817, the Regent was returning down the Mall to Carlton House after formally opening Parliament when an angry mob pelted his carriage with stones, and, it appears, bullets were fired from an air gun. He "*pretends* he was shot at," sniggered the Regent's liberal-minded brother, the Duke of Sussex. But Lord James Murray, who was in the royal carriage at the time, "spoke distinctly" of "two small holes . . . within one inch of each other through an uncommonly thick plate glass window; and the space between the two holes was not broken." [19]

Murder often dominated Regency headlines, but no killer fixed the public imagination like the Irish-born John Williams, the sailor presumed responsible for two horrendous acts of carnage in London's East End. Near midnight on Saturday, December 7, 1811, Williams slipped quietly into Timothy Marr's lace and pelisse warehouse at 29 Ratcliffe Highway, and, armed with a ship carpenter's maul and an iron ripping chisel, he ruthlessly dispatched Marr, his wife Celia, their three-month-old son, Timothy junior, and James Gowen, Marr's apprentice. Twelve days later, and scarcely a two-minute walk from the Marr home, Williams struck again, this time in the King's Arms pub, where he brutally murdered the owner John Williamson, his wife Elizabeth, and their servant Bridget Anna Harrington. On this occasion, though, two people inside the house survived, for Williams did not notice the Williamsons' granddaughter Catherine, who was asleep upstairs, or the Williamsons' lodger John Turner, who caught sight of Williams during the attacks, and who managed to escape by climbing out a third-story window, screaming as he descended down knotted sheets, "They are murdering the people in the house!"[20]

The public panicked. As news spread of the audacity, savagery, and inexplicability of the crimes, the Irish playwright and politician Richard Brinsley Sheridan was appalled at the xenophobia that surged to the surface, as rich and poor alike blamed foreigners, starting with the Portuguese and moving on to the Irish. Eleven-year-old Thomas Macaulay, who was in London at the time, vividly recollected "the terror which was on every face," as people barred their doors and armed themselves with blunderbusses. From three hundred miles away in Keswick, Robert Southey reported that "we in the country here are thinking and talking of nothing but the dreadful murders, which seem to bring a stigma, not merely on the police, but on the land we live in, and even our human nature." Urban overcrowding, mass social displacement, and the unpredictable rage of a solitary individual seemed to be behind the killing sprees, while extensive coverage in newspapers such as the *Morning Chronicle* and the *Times*, coupled with advances in print and travel technologies, meant that, for the first time, a local killing rose to the level of a national obsession. People everywhere felt vulnerable as never before. "Our houses are no longer our castles," announced the coroner after the second spate of killings; "we are no longer safe in our beds!"[21]

Circumstantial evidence against Williams started to mount soon after the Williamson murders, and on Christmas Eve he was committed to Coldbath Fields Prison, where three days later he was found hanged in his cell, an apparent suicide. The Regency's most celebrated portrait painter, Thomas Lawrence, who was fascinated by the faces of murderers, was allowed to see Williams shortly after he was cut down, and drew a haunting sketch of the dead man: "the forehead the finest one could see, hair light and curling, the eyes blue and only half closed; the mouth singularly handsome, tho' somewhat distorted, and the nose perfect."[22] The court decided to hear the evidence against Williams, but the circumstances of his death were widely interpreted as a confession of guilt (though several commentators raised substantial doubts regarding whether or not he acted alone, or even if he was involved). On the last day of 1811, amid a crowd that was estimated at over ten thousand people, Williams's body was publicly exhibited in a procession through the Ratcliffe Highway and then taken to the nearest crossroads, where a stake was driven through his heart and his corpse forced down into a narrow hole.

IV

Attempting to hold back the waves of crime that swept through London was a cumbersome, antiquated, and often bloodthirsty system of law and order. To be sure, the government had long been trying to control the mayhem and personal notoriety that flourished in the underworld. Back in the mid-seventeenth century, the City of London began to pay watchmen to patrol the streets at night calling out the time, checking that windows and doors were secured, and making the occasional arrest—though the crime-fighting abilities of these men were soon eclipsed by their reputation for drunkenness, decrepitude, corruption, and, especially, somnolence. A much more effective system was introduced in Westminster in the mid-eighteenth century, when officials established a small force that became known as the "Bow Street Runners," a professional unit of "thief-catchers" who were funded by the government and whose active investigation of crimes clearly distinguished them from the watchmen, who remained within the City and were essentially peacekeepers.[23]

Law enforcement continued to take important steps. The government exploited the latest technologies when it installed gas lighting in the streets of Westminster, an innovation that repelled—in Keats's words—"all the power of darkness" and that greatly curtailed the nocturnal activities of vandals and footpads. It struck a number of Select Committees to investigate various aspects of crime prevention, including three on the State of the Police. It consulted widely among magistrates and police officers, including John Townsend, the most famous Bow Street Runner of the day. Short and corpulent, but smartly turned out "with a flaxen wig, kerseymere breeches, a blue straight-cut coat, and a broad-brimmed white hat," Townsend "was said . . . to have taken more thieves than all the other Bow-Street officers put together."[24] Available for private hire as a bodyguard, detective, and security officer, Townsend had an unmatched reputation for discretion, cunning, and courage, while no one knew the criminal fraternity like he did. His known employers included Vauxhall Gardens, the Bank of England, and the Regent himself. Townsend was a principal witness before the 1816 Select Committee, where he answered questions on issues such as rewards, police salaries, horse patrols, and the conduct of jurymen.

Policing was not the only area of the Regency criminal justice system that needed thoroughgoing reform. The "Bloody Code" was the nom de guerre for England's notoriously severe system of punishment, in which more than two hundred major and minor crimes carried the death penalty. Moreover, many of these offenses related to property, so, in addition to its practical applications, the Code itself came to symbolize the vicious lengths to which the landed elites were willing to go to guard their possessions and stockpile their wealth. With policing so haphazard in the cities, and left essentially to magistrates and the militia (when they could be found) in the country, the idea was to create policies of punishment that terrified the populace into law-abiding behavior. The judge John Silvester and the attorney general Sir William Garrow, a brilliant barrister with more than three decades of experience in British courtrooms, were among those who defended the system, while there were others who saw the upsurge in crime as a reason to make the Bloody Code even bloodier.

Many political and legal activists, however, were deeply opposed to capital punishment, denouncing it as government-orchestrated, counterproductive barbarity, and campaigning indefatigably to have the number of crimes it applied to drastically reduced or eliminated altogether. Percy Shelley, in his "Essay on the Punishment of Death," described the abolition of capital punishment as "the first law which it becomes a reformer to propose and support." The Edinburgh medical graduate John Polidori argued in "On the Punishment of Death" that relying on capital punishment to deliver justice pointed to "some radical error in the very foundation of our criminal laws." The lawyer and MP Sir Samuel Romilly succeeded in 1808 in having the death penalty abolished for the crime of picking pockets, but his efforts during the Regency to enact further reforms met with limited success. "There is probably no other country in the world in which so many and so great a variety of human actions are punishable with loss of life as in England," he lamented in 1811.[25]

The greatest reason for reforming the Bloody Code was simply that it did not work very well, as Romilly and many others insisted. It did not act as a deterrent, as rising crime rates clearly demonstrated, and in some instances it seems to have incited criminals to additional acts of violence: a highwayman faced the death penalty if he was caught, so he had nothing to lose by killing his victim, and something to gain in terms of his own safety. Judges in many instances struggled to condemn a prisoner to death, especially when it was a child, who from the age of seven could be hanged for poaching a rabbit, or stealing a piece of lace, or cutting down a growing tree. Similarly, in many instances victims refused to prosecute, witnesses refused to testify, and juries refused to convict if they felt that the accused was going to the gallows. It was a set of laws, declared the great English philosopher and legal theorist Jeremy Bentham, that united "violence to feebleness" and that produced levels of capriciousness that greatly undermined public confidence in the judicial system. Human lives depended on the whims of judges, some of whom were ferocious, others of whom were merciful.[26]

V

Unsurprisingly, many judges and juries looked at other legal options in an attempt to steer a just course between the ruthless capital convictions mandated by the Bloody Code and the known realities of

Regency social and economic life, mindful, as William Cobbett maintained, that "poverty has always been the parent of crime." Some prisoners were pardoned, especially when family members or charitable
institutions pledged to take charge of them. Some were given lesser
physical penalties such as time in the pillory, where they were locked
helplessly into place for one hour while jeering crowds pelted them
with mud, rocks, fruit, vegetables, and dead animals. Thousands of
others, many of whom had had their capital sentences commuted, were
put on transport ships and sent halfway around the world to the British
penal colony in New South Wales, Australia—though conditions on
these vessels were so horrendous that many who had escaped the noose
at home died at sea long before their ship reached Botany Bay.[27]

Still other prisoners were packed onboard broken-down ships
known as "hulks." These had originally been used as a temporary
measure to house the surplus prison population, but by the Regency
they had become a standard part of the penal service. During the
day the convicts were sometimes taken ashore in work parties, but
for the rest of the time they were incarcerated on the ship and literally going nowhere. It was the closest thing the Regency knew to hell
on earth. "There were confined in this floating dungeon nearly six
hundred men, most of them double-ironed," wrote the convict James
Hardy Vaux; "and the reader may conceive the horrible effects arising
from the continual rattling of chains, the filth and vermin naturally
produced by such a crowd of miserable inhabitants, the oaths and exe-
crations constantly heard among them."[28]

Life in Regency prisons was an improvement on the hulks, but
boredom, overcrowding, disease, and aggression were endemic here
as well, while negligence and poor design led to the indiscriminate
mixing of male and female convicts, first-time offenders and hardened criminals, petty thieves and underworld bosses, the tried and
the untried, the sane and the insane. According to the journalist
John Badcock, there were in 1816 twenty-eight jails in London alone.
Newgate, one of the oldest, was notorious for fostering, rather than
correcting, criminality, for "no one can enter [its] walls . . . without
going out from thence more depraved and corrupted than when first
committed thereto," declared the 1814 Report from the Committee

on the State of the Gaols. One of the newest, the Surrey House of Correction (later Brixton Prison), was infamous as a champion of the treadmill, a form of punishment invented in 1817 as a way of using human labor to grind corn. Hailed as a new "corrective" measure, it was detested by prisoners as dangerous, exhausting, and soul-destroyingly futile, for most of the time it was attached to nothing and simply beat the air.[29]

Leigh Hunt, editor of the radical Sunday newspaper the *Examiner*, is the most famous prisoner of the Regency. From the founding of the paper in 1808, he and his older brother John, its publisher, lashed the government and the monarchy in its pages and evaded the various prosecutions mounted against them. But when in March 1812, as the Regent approached his fiftieth birthday, the Tory *Morning Post* hailed him as the "Glory of the People" and an *"Adonis in Loveliness,"* it was another stomach-turning piece of government tosh that the Hunts simply could not let pass. In reply they reached an apex of scorn that was clearly defamatory. The Regent "was a violator of his word, a libertine over head and ears in debt and disgrace, a despiser of domestic ties, the companion of gamblers and demireps, a man who has just closed half a century without one single claim on the gratitude of his country or the respect of posterity!"[30] Sir William Garrow acted for the government. Henry Brougham, the future Whig lord chancellor, defended the Hunts. It took the jury all of ten minutes to convict them of libeling the Regent. The brothers were sentenced to two years in prison, Leigh in Horsemonger Lane and John at Coldbath Fields.

Leigh entered his cell for the first time on February 3, 1813, and within days his health began to give way. Ruffian laughter and the constant clanking of chains badly unnerved him, as did the locking of all the doors and gates between him and the outside world. "I do not exaggerate when I say there were ten or eleven," he declared, and "every fresh turning of the key seemed a malignant insult to my love of liberty." His own arguments regarding his status as a political prisoner, coupled with the voices of influential Whig supporters, soon won him concessions, and within six weeks he had been moved from his initial cell into far more salubrious accommodations on the south side of the prison infirmary. Here his family joined him, and a carpenter and painter transformed the rooms into "a bower for a poet," the walls "papered . . . with a trellis of roses," the ceiling "coloured with clouds and sky," and the barred windows "screened with Venetian blinds." Hunt added bookcases, fresh flowers, busts, pictures, and a pianoforte. Further, outside there was a small prison yard that he converted into a garden, with green palings, a trellis, a narrow lawn, more flowers, and an apple tree, "from which we managed to get a pudding the second year."[31] It was one of the most extraordinary establishments in the whole of the Regency.

Hunt's cell became a fashionable rallying point for liberal and radical thinkers, and many came to call, including the editor John Scott, the essayist William Hazlitt, the novelist Maria Edgeworth, the philosopher James Mill, the painter David Wilkie, and the newspaperman Thomas Barnes. The essayist Charles Lamb and his sister, the children's writer Mary Lamb, came in all weathers. When Jeremy Bentham visited, he and Hunt played battledore (a precursor of badminton). Byron called on more than one occasion and dubbed Hunt "the wit in the dungeon." The painter Benjamin Robert Haydon arrived one morning before Hunt was out of bed, "calling for his breakfast, and sending those laughs of his about the place that sound like the trumpets of Jericho."[32]

The government had no doubt hoped that imprisoning Hunt would lead to the collapse of the *Examiner*, but the paper reached new heights of popularity during the brothers' trial, and it continued to appear throughout their time in prison, as a result of the efforts of loyal friends like Lamb, Barnes, and Hazlitt, who wrote articles for it, and the tireless commitment of the brothers themselves, who sent copy across town to each other and to the *Examiner* office. What is more, Hunt kept hope alive in the *Examiner* by championing Catholic emancipation, the freedom of the press, the abolition of slavery, and the reform of Parliament. He wrote in his small garden, while the noises of distress, fear, and anger were all around him. Yet he completed a drama, aptly entitled *The Descent of Liberty* (1815), as well as parts of his finest poem, *The Story of Rimini* (1816), which he dedicated to Byron (who supplied him with books), and which reflected his growing weariness ("Sad is the strain, with which I cheer my long

/ And caged hours"). When Hunt was finally released on February 3, 1815, Keats wrote a sonnet praising "his immortal spirit." But it was soon evident that the last two years had taken a terrible toll and that the pictures and visitors and flowers had ultimately been no match for the miseries of life in a Regency prison. Tired and ill, Hunt later recollected that his time in Horsemonger Lane had given him a "shock" from which he never fully recovered.[33]

VI

Prison reform during the Regency was spearheaded by Quakers and Evangelicals. Brave men such as William Allen, Henry Grey Bennet, Thomas Fowell Buxton, and William Crawford risked contagion from jail fever (a virulent strain of typhus) and the possibility of violence when they went inside London's prisons, and their horror at what they saw led them to push hard for fundamental improvements in the treatment of inmates. Rejecting tired eighteenth-century fulminations on the value of retribution, these men believed that prisoners were fellow human beings, and that the policies concerning them should be based on principles of justice and compassion. Typically, when examined by the 1817 Select Committee on the State of the Police, Crawford emphasized the need for humanity, and especially when dealing with so-called "juvenile depredators." "It is very easy," he told the committee, "to blame these poor children, and to ascribe their misconduct to an innate propensity to vice; but I much question whether any human being, circumstanced as many of them are, can reasonably be expected to act otherwise."[34]

Elizabeth Fry (née Gurney) is one of the most remarkable women of the Regency, and its most important prison reformer. A Norfolk-born Quaker with a lifelong commitment to philanthropic causes and religiously inspired service, she married the merchant and banker Joseph Fry in 1800, and their family eventually grew to eleven children. In February 1813, Elizabeth Fry stepped for the first time into Newgate and asked to see the female prisoners. Thirty-two years old and wearing the plain gray dress of the Quaker, she was, according to Maria

Edgeworth, "very handsome a delicate madona-looking woman." The prison's keeper, John Addison Newman, admitted to Fry that he was "reluctant to go amongst" the female inmates, and advised her to leave her watch in his office, as it would otherwise be torn from her wrist. Fry was then escorted to the notorious female quadrangle. Nothing prepared her for what she saw. Nearly three hundred female prisoners were crammed into a poorly supervised space intended to house no more than fifty. "The filth, the closeness of the rooms, the ferocious manners and expressions of the women towards each other, and the abandoned wickedness, which every thing bespoke, are quite indescribable," she stated.[35]

Family obligations and misfortunes prevented Fry from taking an active part in prison reform for much of the next four years, but she returned to Newgate around Christmas 1816, and with remarkable courage and kindness (one of her favorite words), she immediately set to work. Improvements had been made since her first visit—including more space for the women and mats to sleep on—but much remained to be done. Fry met with prisoners and prison authorities to establish objectives. She founded a school for the prisoners' children, which provided both religious and secular education. She introduced a series of basic reforms, including prison dress, the confiscation of alcohol, the separation of male and female inmates, paid employment such as needlework and knitting, and a ban on gaming, swearing, and dirty books and songs. Fry maintained, in addition, that female prisoners should be supervised, not by males but by female yard keepers, monitors, and matrons, for she believed passionately in women working on behalf of women, both within the prison and far beyond its walls, as she made clear in April 1817 when she and several of the Quaker women who had joined her founded the Ladies' Association for the Reformation of the Female Prisoners in Newgate.

Previous government investigations had exposed many horrors in the prison but removed very few. Fry, on the other hand, got things done. Thomas Fowell Buxton, an MP and Fry's brother-in-law, reported that in a few short months, the female side of the prison underwent "what, without exaggeration, may be called a transformation" and now "exhibited the appearance of an industrious manufactory, or a well regulated family." By 1820, the reforms Fry had implemented in Newgate were being introduced into prisons throughout Britain and across Europe. "I hope you will endeavour to be very useful, and not spend all your time in pleasing yourselves," she had written to her children after her first experience of Newgate in 1813. "Remember the way to be happy is to do good." Modern society is still not certain what it expects from its penal services, but there is a great deal to be learned from the compassionate spirit that shaped all Fry's efforts to reduce the levels of human misery in Regency prisons.[36]

VII

Robert Banks Jenkinson, second Earl of Liverpool, reluctantly became prime minister a month after the assassination of Spencer Perceval, and while always overshadowed by the greater political imagination of his foreign secretary, Robert Stewart, Viscount Castlereagh, he remained at the head of the Tory government for the rest of the Regency. Liverpool was learned and mildly evangelical with an interest in history and contemporary art. His composure, tact, and personal integrity were his greatest political strengths, and he used them to hold together cabinets that contained strong, often combative personalities, and that were at times under extraordinary pressure, pulled hard to the right by aristocratic interests, equally hard to the left by radical ultimatums, and dealing all the while with wars in Europe, North America, and India, the capricious interference of the Regent, and the incessant demands of various religious groups. Rarely has a single prime minister had to deal with so many diverse and volatile problems, and Liverpool fell back on sometimes vicious measures in an attempt to cow revolutionaries and contain dissent.

Ireland was in a calamitous state. A sudden spike in population at the close of the eighteenth century had pushed the Catholic peasantry to the brink of famine, and in June 1817 a full-blown crisis developed when the potato crop failed for the first time since the country had become reliant on that one food. The rural poor migrated in droves to Dublin, food riots broke out across the country, and a typhus epidemic ravaged areas of Munster, Connacht, and Ulster. In the summer of 1818, Keats traveled to Ireland and witnessed firsthand "the rags, the dirt and misery of the poor common Irish." One encounter, in particular, seemed to incarnate the country's despair. On his walk back from Belfast, he saw a kind of "dog kennel . . . upon two poles." In it "sat a squalid old Woman squat like an ape half starved . . . with a pipe in her mouth and looking out with a round-eyed skinny lidded, inanity—with a sort of horizontal idiotic movement of her head— squab and lean she sat and puff'd out the smoke while two ragged tattered Girls carried her along."[37]

Sectarian clashes further exacerbated the terrible conditions. Over the course of centuries, Britain had conquered Ireland many times, but never to the point of permanently subduing it. The result was a long and bloody tale of conflict in which the impoverished Irish Catholic majority fought to rid their country of the English Protestant elites who ruled it and who were in many cases demoralized and corrupt.[38] Robert Peel, the son of a cotton magnate and the future prime minister, was chief secretary in Ireland for much of the Regency and an outspoken supporter of the Protestant Ascendancy, as the ruling English clique was known. During his tenure Peel occasionally responded with compassion to the plight of the Irish poor. But he regarded Ireland as a primitive backwater; he did not question Britain's right to rule there; and he strenuously resisted all Catholic claims for political rights, a position grounded in the long-standing Protestant conviction that Catholic beliefs were at odds with "liberty."

Daniel O'Connell was Peel's arch antagonist, and smeared him with the sobriquet "Orange Peel," adding memorably that "Peel's smile . . . resembled the plate on a coffin."[39] A superb legal and political advocate, O'Connell was committed to the repeal of the 1801 Act of Union between Britain and Ireland, and though a firm believer in nonviolent resistance, he brought an intransigent anger to the Irish cause. Fluent in Gaelic, he appealed directly and countrywide to the priesthood and the poor, mobilizing them in support of Catholic emancipation, which he was certain would lead to upward mobility for the educated classes and an end to oppression for the peasantry.

Tensions between Peel and O'Connell reached the boiling point in 1815, when a duel between them was narrowly averted.

Numerous peasant confederacies and secret societies, however, had sprung up all over the country, and bloodshed between them was commonplace. Many of the battles pitted Catholic "Ribbonmen" (named for the green ribbon worn as a badge by members) against Protestant "Orangemen" (named for William of Orange, later King William III of Britain). In July 1813, at the so-called Battle of Garvagh in County Londonderry, several hundred Ribbonmen began to stone the King's Arms tavern to avenge a previous defeat at the hands of the Orangemen, but the Orangemen were waiting inside and replied with volleys of musket fire, killing three Ribbonmen and forcing the rest to flee. Commemorated in the Loyalist song "The Battle of Garvagh," the episode took hold in the popular imagination, but it was not very different from dozens of other Catholic/Protestant clashes in the north. Two and a half years later in County Tipperary, the British government ruthlessly suppressed sectarian conflicts. "We are . . . making a terrible but necessary example under the special commission we have sent there," Peel explained to Liverpool. "There have been thirteen capital convictions for offences amounting to little short of rebellion."[40]

Many of the worst atrocities, though, were acts of reprisal within, rather than between, Catholic or Protestant groups. Most infamously, in April 1816, Michael Tiernan, Patrick Stanley, and Philip Conlon broke into Wildgoose Lodge in County Louth. They were looking for guns and assaulted the occupants, Edward Lynch and his family, before being driven off. At trial, Lynch and his son-in-law Thomas Rooney identified the three invaders, who were convicted and hanged. In the early hours of October 30, the Ribbonmen exacted their revenge. Led by a weaver and parish clerk named Paddy Devaun, they massacred Lynch and seven others, including his daughter and grandchild. In the aftermath, Devaun and seventeen other Ribbonmen were executed. Summing up, Judge Fletcher noted that "religious bigotry had no part in producing these monstrous crimes. There were not here two conflicting parties arrayed under the colours of orange and green; not Protestant against Catholic, nor Catholic against Protestant—no, it was Catholic against Catholic."[41]

In Scotland, meanwhile, there was violent strife of another kind. For centuries in the Highlands there had been a Gaelic-speaking, semifeudal society based on the clan system, in which the laird, or clan chief, provided housing and grazing for tenants, most of whom lived on small subsistence farms known as "crofts," with goats and black cattle, potatoes and oats, rough beer and raw whisky. But by the latter stages of the eighteenth century, economic forces were exerting severe pressure on traditional notions of clanship. Lowland proprietors had become involved in impressively profitable sheep farming, while Highland lairds had uneconomical estates that were no longer able to support the alarming increases in the population of the crofters. It was time, the lairds argued, to bring the people and the estates of the Highlands into the modern world. Cheviot sheep would be moved onto the land in order to reap the benefits of large-scale commercial meat and wool production, while the tenantry would be resettled in small coastal crofts, where they would farm the sea rather than the earth. Such a relocation, many reasoned, was better for the tenants anyway. It would protect them from famine and give them more stable, comfortable lives, at least in the long run. To the families who had lived on the same allotment of land for generations, however, and who believed that they had an unwritten right to be there, being forced to turn over their territory to the great capitalist sheep farmers—especially those drawn from the Lowlands and England— was an unparalleled act of betrayal.[42]

Lady Sutherland and Lord Stafford authored one of the grimmest chapters in the story of these "Highland Clearances." Scottish-born Elizabeth Sutherland, as a teenager, inherited the estate of Sutherland in northern Scotland, and with it her family's contempt for the Highlanders. In 1785 she married English-born George Granville Leveson-Gower, who became second Marquess of Stafford in 1803, and together they were the greatest landowners in Britain. Like many of their wealthy aristocratic contemporaries, they caught the Regency rage for "improvement," and their massive investments in the Sutherland estate were designed to increase rental income, create employment for the displaced, and open up the entire region to trade and prosperity. They re-leased most of the inland territory and implemented a new management regime. They built roads, bridges, manses, inns, and harbors. They dramatically improved communications. They provided new housing. They installed fishing facilities. According to supporters, these changes were both necessary and inevitable, and they were introduced with benevolent intentions. James Loch, the Edinburgh lawyer hired by Stafford to manage the Sutherland estate, celebrated the success of the radical transformation in his 1820 *Account of the Improvements on the Estates of the Marquess of Stafford*.

On the ground, however, it looked very different. Those thousands among the Highlanders who fiercely resisted the "removals" were forced off their land, and their houses, barns, mills, kilns, and other buildings were destroyed to prevent reoccupation, usually by burning them. Lady Sutherland and Lord Stafford were kept well apprised of these events by Loch, but they never witnessed them firsthand, and as neither spoke Gaelic, the bitter protests of those being evicted would have fallen on ears already deaf to their plight. Patrick Sellar, one of several men hired to do the dirty work, embraced the role with gusto, furthering his own interests in sheep farming as he savagely enforced his employers' plans for progress. In the summer of 1814, he organized the brutal expulsions from Strathnaver, which lies in the valley of the river Naver, about twenty miles from the north coast of Scotland. Betsy MacKay was sixteen when Sellar and his men arrived. "Our family was very reluctant to leave," she recalled, "and stayed for some time, but the burning party came round and set fire to our house at both ends, reducing to ashes whatever remained within the walls. The people had to escape for their lives." Some starved. Some froze to death. Others fled into Scotland's central belt or across the sea. Sellar's tactics landed him in the dock in Inverness in April 1816, charged with acts of gross inhumanity, including culpable homicide. He was acquitted, however, and two years later retired from Stafford's service, but the burning parties—and the astonishing pace of the evictions during the Regency—continued. Strathnaver was ravaged again in May 1819, when the burners returned to drive two hundred more families from their homes. "Nothing but the sword was wanting to make the scene one of as great barbarity as the earth ever witnessed," declared Donald Macleod, a stonemason and journalist.

Lady Sutherland took all these events in her aristocratic stride. After looking one day at her half-starved tenantry, she observed to English friends that "Scotch people are of happier constitutions, and do not fatten like the larger breed of animals."[43]

Regency Highlanders were not alone in their despair, or in their resistance to modernity. In England, textile workers known as "Luddites" were also fighting to preserve a way of life that was being ruthlessly dismantled. Independent, traditionally trained artisans from the Midlands had for centuries been producing some of the finest woolen goods in the world, but new spinning and weaving technologies had steadily transformed the industry, and by the dawn of the Regency many of these men had been replaced by inexpensive, unskilled laborers (including children) who worked in large factories producing cheaper, inferior products that often brought the factory owners immense profit. Unemployed and angry, the artisans unsuccessfully petitioned Parliament for relief and then took matters into their own increasingly desperate hands. Equipped with sledgehammers, axes, muskets, and pistols, they practiced a masked and nocturnal vigilantism, marching in well-disciplined groups that broke into factories and smashed the machinery that had put them out of work. Their leader was the (probably mythical) Ned Ludd, better known as "General" or "King" Ludd.

The uprisings began in the Nottinghamshire village of Arnold in March 1811, and by the end of that year almost 1,000 stocking, spinning, cropping, and shearing frames (worth more than £6,000, or roughly $600,000 today) had been destroyed, and the vandalism had spread across the Midlands and north into Lancashire and the West Riding of Yorkshire. Worried by both the spread and the intensity of the violence, Perceval's government in February 1812 dispatched nearly two thousand soldiers to Nottingham. It was, the MP Richard Ryder told the House of Commons, the largest force ever used by the British government to quell a local disturbance. More menacingly, the government also introduced an act to make "frame-breaking" a capital offense. Byron, a Nottinghamshire landowner, used his maiden speech in the House of Lords to deplore the new measure. "Is there not blood enough upon your penal code?" he demanded. The actions of the Luddites were alarming, but they arose "from circumstances of the most unparalleled distress."[44]

Matters soon came to a head. William Cartwright owned a great mill at Rawfolds in Yorkshire and was one of the most vocal supporters of the new technologies. On April 11, 1812, about 150 Yorkshire Luddites advanced on his property. Cartwright—together with his family and some hired soldiery—was waiting for them, and when they were within range he issued the order to fire. Two Luddites were killed, and the raiding party failed to gain entry to the mill. A week later the Luddites tried to assassinate Cartwright, but he escaped. Another manufacturer, William Horsfall of nearby Marsden, was not so lucky. On April 28, George Mellor, William Thorpe, and Thomas Smith ambushed and murdered him in the name of Luddism. Public opinion, which for months had been firmly on the side of the Luddites, now began to soften. Government troops and spies flooded into the area and eventually got the information they wanted. Dozens of men were rounded up and tried at York for various crimes related to framebreaking. Seventeen of them were hanged, including Mellor and his two accomplices. The implacably conservative home secretary, Henry Addington, Viscount Sidmouth, was delighted with the news and confidently expected the executions to have the "happiest effects in various parts of the kingdom."[45]

Luddism never fully recovered from the Yorkshire purge, but it erupted again on several other occasions over the course of the next four and a half years. In June 1816 Luddites destroyed the bobbin-net lace machinery in John Heathcote's new Loughborough factory, and in April 1817 six young men swung off the gallows for their role in the attack. Yet the distress that lay behind the ongoing unrest was of little interest to the prime minister, who had a near-obsession with laissez-faire economics, and who—like many Tories—regarded working-class grief and anger as very much in the natural course of events. "Evils inseparable from the state of things should not be charged on any government," Liverpool maintained in 1819; "and, on enquiry, it would be found that by far the greater part of the miseries of which human nature complained were in all times and in all countries beyond the control of human legislation."[46]

The term "Luddite" today means someone who is opposed to technological change. This was not the position of the Regency Luddites. They rejected only those new pieces of equipment that were depriving them of their livelihood. To some extent, their protests were both naive and self-serving. But many Luddites seem also to have recognized the much larger and more threatening issues at stake. Their crushing, government-sponsored defeat enshrined the principle that industrialists in pursuit of huge profits are free to drive vulnerable people into poor-paying, dehumanizing factory work, and to impose—without consultation—up-to-the-minute technologies that may or may not be better for their employees and their customers. The Luddites launched the first well-organized, widespread fight against a new industrial system that was far more interested in profits than in people or social consequence. Their resistance anticipates twentieth-century unionization and the many modern campaigns against corporate greed, unfair labor practices, and the exploitative or squalid aspects of the twenty-first-century technological movement.

VIII

"War was a bitter scourge and curse; / Yet peace, is, somehow, ten times worse," declared the wit Henry Luttrell in 1820 of the politically riotous years that followed the defeat of Napoleon. The intensely patriotic enthusiasm generated within Britain by the demands and achievements of the war effort disintegrated under the pressure of economic stagnation, soaring unemployment, food shortages, and a massive influx of demobilized men (more than 300,000 in 1816 and another 32,000 in 1817). The government was soon worried by the scale of the distress, but in response it literally stuck to its guns, cracking down on the protesters, while at the same time maintaining its adamantine support of the traditional institutions of crown, aristocracy, and church. As the crisis deepened, and civil strife spread, the Welsh soldier, dandy, and memoirist Rees Howell Gronow was one of many observers who feared the political and economic center was giving way. "When I call to mind the dangerous state of the country at that time," he declared, ". . . I am astonished that some fatal catastrophe did not occur." The people were "driven to madness by every sort of oppression."[47]

It is not hard to trace the sources of their anger. The laboring classes constituted the vast majority of the population, yet the country was run by a small group of wealthy elites who had a stranglehold on land and political power, and who were determined to ignore radical demands for an extension of the franchise and a more representative political system. The only people eligible to vote were men over the age of twenty-one who fulfilled certain conditions of property ownership. This group amounted to less than fifteen percent of the adult male population, and it was a much smaller subset that actually wielded political power. On occasion, liberal-minded Whig MPs took up reform or even radical causes, but both the Tories and the Whigs were still profoundly aristocratic in their allegiances, and when unrest erupted in the lower orders, they promptly united in opposition to it. The political landscape in Regency Britain, asserted Cobbett, was best thought of as divided into two camps: a large group of reformers outside Parliament agitating for a fairer political system, and a much smaller group of Whig and Tory patricians sitting inside Parliament intent on the status quo in all its exclusivity.[48] For aristocrats and their many allies within the government, the situation was quite clear-cut. The House of Commons was not there to represent the people. That was a foreign and incendiary idea. Land was the historic foundation of the British constitution, and the House of Commons was there to guard and extend the interests of the men who owned it—those whose birthright, education, and affluence entitled them to be leaders among men. Anyone who thought otherwise was under a fundamental misapprehension. The masses did not partake in government. They submitted to government.

Various openly practiced forms of corruption had allowed this system to stay securely in place. Most notoriously, many landowners controlled "pocket" or "rotten" boroughs in which they bribed or browbeat an often tiny electorate into supporting their handpicked candidate, who of course once he became an MP felt far more beholden to his patron than to his constituents. The borough of

Dunwich on the Suffolk coast was essentially underwater, but that did not prevent it from returning two MPs. Old Sarum near Salisbury had fewer than a dozen voters, but it also returned two MPs. Robert Peel began his political career as MP for the corrupt borough of Cashel in County Tipperary. For most of the Regency, William Wilberforce was MP for Bramber in Sussex, a borough in the pocket of his wife's cousin, Lord Calthorpe, a wealthy Birmingham evangelical and landowner. In 1819, the economist and stockbroker David Ricardo became the member for Portarlington, where the sheep far outnumbered the roughly twelve electors. Meanwhile, people living in often appalling conditions in rapidly expanding industrial centers such as Birmingham, Manchester, and Leeds had no representation at all.

The glaring injustices of the system manifested themselves in the Regency in an especially harsh form when in early 1815 the landowning interests passed the notorious Corn Law, which was designed to keep the price of bread—the staple food of laborers—artificially inflated by banning the import of foreign grain until the domestic price had reached eighty shillings per quarter, or ten shillings per bushel of wheat. Selling at this price, which was more than triple the daily wage of the average worker, guaranteed that huge profits would flow to the propertied elites, and cushioned their agrarian interests against postwar difficulties. At the same time, the agricultural protectionists who steered the Corn Law through Parliament also aimed at mitigating the rise of the industrial sector, which they typically regarded as destabilizing and unhealthy. When Europe retaliated with tariffs against the new legislation, it inflicted a severe burden on British manufacturers, increasing the cost of production and restricting markets. In turn, workers were unable to purchase various commodities because most or all of their income was exhausted on food.

The government's hard-line approach in the years immediately following Waterloo attracted many ardent supporters. Among religious groups, the Anglican High Churchmen of the so-called "Hackney Phalanx" were Prime Minister Liverpool's soundest allies, especially concerned to defend the Church of England from popery, and the constitution from democratic reform. Samuel Taylor Coleridge, too, brought religious faith to bear on contemporary politics in his *Statesman's Manual, or The Bible the Best Guide to Political Skill and Foresight* (1816), where he argued that the privileged classes needed to thoroughly recast the way they understood their own power, but made it plain that he was content to leave the laboring classes unrepresented. The enormously influential *Quarterly Review*, edited by the combative satirist and classical scholar William Gifford, was widely perceived as the most reliable source for insider information on government strategy, and while it never tied itself to the agenda of the Liverpool administration, it shared with it a haughty tone and an often fierce commitment to the conservative principles of loyalty, piety, and order. Declared one commentator: "it comports itself as if it constituted a fourth estate of the realm—King, Lords, Commons, and The Quarterly Review."[49]

Radicals, reformers, and revolutionaries of all stripes hit back hard against the government and its allies, rejecting the deadening feudal world of God and King and Law, and fighting instead to bring into being a world that was more inclusive, commercial, democratic, and secular. Jeremy Bentham was the intellectual leader of the English reform movement, best remembered now as the chief exponent of the utilitarian axiom that the object of all government legislation must be "the greatest happiness of the greatest number." In 1817 he published his *Plan of Parliamentary Reform*, and in the following year his *Church-of-Englandism*, where he detailed his radical critique of religion and provocatively declared that the "remedy to all religious and much political mischief" is the "euthanasia of the church." Bentham was also the acknowledged leader of a group of Regency intellectuals known as the "Philosophical Radicals," among whom was the Scottish historian James Mill—father of the great philosopher and economist John Stuart Mill—who did more than anyone to spread the Benthamic gospel. In his most celebrated work, *Essay on Government* (1820), James Mill analyzes the problems with a political system that relies on a monarchy or an aristocracy and champions the benefits of representative government, which he calls "the grand discovery of modern times." Strikingly, though, even someone as politically progressive as Mill did not think it necessary to extend the franchise to women, "the interest of almost all of whom is involved either in that of their fathers or in that of their husbands."[50]

William Hazlitt, the hardest-hitting writer the political left has ever known, contributed regularly to the most significant liberal London daily, the *Morning Chronicle*, the Hunt brothers' *Examiner*, and the progressive *Edinburgh Review*, which was edited by the Scottish lawyer and literary critic Francis Jeffrey, and which set itself in direct opposition to the *Quarterly*, especially on issues such as Catholic emancipation, freedom of the press, and moderate parliamentary reform, all of which it championed. At the crux of Hazlitt's politics are the ideals of the French Revolution—*liberté, égalité, fraternité*—and his unwavering faith in Napoleon as the upholder of these ideals. So disillusioned, indeed, was he by the outcome of Waterloo—which to him marked the end of the cause of human freedom and the restoration of monarchical tyranny—that "he walked about unwashed, unshaved, hardly sober by day, and always intoxicated by night . . . for weeks," declared his friend Benjamin Robert Haydon. Hazlitt's prose—fierce, focused, and dramatic—is the product of a man bitterly disappointed in these early hopes. It is a prose of defiance that in its very form embodies the radical energy, creativity, and individuality that the government was trying to extinguish. It is a prose flexible enough to extend from sinuousness all the way to aphorism. "The love of liberty is the love of others," he wrote in the *Examiner* in 1817; "the love of power is the love of ourselves."[51]

Above all, Hazlitt was a "good hater." He hated censorship, arbitrary power, corruption, absolutism, and privilege. "He is your only good damner and if ever I am damn'd—damn me if I shoul'nt like him to damn me," asserted Keats, one of his greatest admirers. Hazlitt hated monarchy: "Any one above the rank of an idiot is supposed capable of exercising the highest functions of royal state." He hated the Duke of Wellington: "I cannot believe that a great general is contained under such a pasteboard vizor of a man." He hated his erstwhile friend Coleridge for discarding his youthful radicalism in exchange for middle-aged Tory orthodoxy: "He is the Dog in the Manger of literature." He hated the *Quarterly*: it "does not contain a concentrated essence of taste and knowledge, but is a receptacle for the scum and sediment of all the prejudice, bigotry, ill-will, ignorance, and ran-cour, afloat in the kingdom." He especially hated its editor Gifford: "You are the *Government Critic*, a character nicely differing from that of a government spy—the invisible link, that connects literature with the police."[52]

William Cobbett, according to Hazlitt, was "not only unquestion-ably the most powerful political writer of the present day, but one of the best writers in the language." In 1802, Cobbett founded the radical weekly *Political Register*, and in 1816 he began to issue it in a mass-circulation broadsheet edition, with a reduction in price from one shilling and a halfpenny to only two pence. His enemies quickly dubbed the new publication Cobbett's "Two-Penny Trash"—much to his delight. Per issue in the Regency, the *Quarterly* and the *Edinburgh* both sold around 13,000 copies, the *Examiner* peaked at around 7,500 copies, and the *Morning Chronicle* at around 3,000 copies, while the broadsheet version of the *Political Register* immediately sold between 40,000 and 50,000 copies, and may have gone as high as 70,000, mak-ing it far and away the most popular publication in garrets, stables, inns, coaches, taverns, camps, and factories across the country. The Lancashire weaver and author Samuel Bamford recalled that, in the years immediately following Waterloo, "the writings of William Cobbett suddenly became of great authority; they were read on nearly every cottage hearth in the manufacturing districts of South Lan-cashire, in those of Leicester, Derby, and Nottingham; also in many of the Scottish manufacturing towns."[53]

An autodidact, farmer, soldier, and publisher, Cobbett began his career as a trenchant advocate of conservatism, but his views grad-ually evolved into a decidedly paradoxical version of radicalism. His fundamental political creed in the Regency included freedom of the press, universal male suffrage, annual parliaments, the elimination of rotten boroughs, and equal electoral districts—and all to be achieved through disciplined, nonviolent popular agitation. He deplored facto-ries, industrial cities, and the rapid urbanization of London, which he scathingly referred to as the "Great Wen." He felt the same disgust for grubbing moneymen, bourgeois farmers, borough-mongering elites, and parasitic politicians. In several instances, his rabble-rousing prose style—emphatic, antagonistic, and deeply personal—alarmed even those who supported his political agenda. "A revolution in this country would not be *bloodless* if that man has any power in it," Mary Shelley asserted in 1817.[54]

Yet at the same time, Cobbett's urgent demands for far-reaching economic and political reforms were profoundly shaped by his attachment to the past, and his desire, not to prepare Britain for more of the nineteenth century, but to return it to the mid-eighteenth-century rural world of his imagination. It was an intensely nostalgic vision that held immense appeal for the great mass of people in both the agricultural and the industrial sectors of Regency Britain, many of whom felt disorientated by both the crackdowns and the upheavals of the modern world. Declared Cobbett: "The working people of England were, when I was born, well fed, well clad, and had each his barrel of beer in his house; and . . . if they be not thus again before I die, every one shall say, that the fault has not been that of William Cobbett." If the *Quarterly* was a kind of fourth estate for conservatives, Cobbett was, as Hazlitt observed, "a kind of *fourth estate*" for radicals and liberals.[55]

IX

The radical assault on Regency bastions of power was given humor and biting insight by a brilliant group of political satirists. The Regent was their favorite target, and remarkably easy to hit, not only because he was at the top of the political power structure but also because his weight, vanity, deceit, extravagance, and sexual incontinence provided them with endless opportunities. Charles Lamb produced an utterly transparent poetic lampoon in "The Triumph of the Whale," where he milks the "Whales / Wales" pun for all it is worth. The Regent is both loathsome and laughable, and Lamb singles out his alcohol consumption, his betrayal of the Whigs, his excessive use of creams for his complexion, and of course his girth: "By his bulk, and by his size, / By his oily qualities, / This (or else my eyesight fails), / This should be the PRINCE of WHALES." According to the barrister and author Thomas Noon Talfourd, when others criticized the Regent, Lamb used to smile and reply, *"I love my Regent."*[56]

Thomas Moore similarly despised the Regent, especially—as an Irishman—for his abandonment of the Catholics, and in a series of poetic satires he routinely reduced him to a butt: wigged, whiskered, drunken, and indiscreet. In 1813, Moore published *Intercepted Letters; or, the Twopenny Post-Bag*, a book-length collection of poetic epistles ostensibly written by the Regent and some of his associates, including his daughter Princess Charlotte and his private secretary John McMahon. Typically, in Letter III, the Regent writes to his boon companion Lord Yarmouth of a punch-sodden dinner that he attended the previous evening to celebrate the conviction of Leigh Hunt for libel, and while the Regent regards "H—t's condemnation" as *"my* brilliant triumph," it is clear that he is far more interested in the pleasures of the table laid on by his host, a hoary old sinner: "His soups scientific—his fishes quite *prime*— / His pâtés superb—and his cutlets sublime!"[57]

Moore also fixed the Regent at the crux of his finest satire, *The Fudge Family in Paris* (1818), another book-length collection of "intercepted letters" in which the poet adroitly combines engaging comedy with confrontational liberal politics. The fictional character Phelim Connor is by far the gravest of Moore's four letter writers. An Irish Catholic in faith and a Bonapartist in politics, Phelim thunders against the socioeconomic injustices of post-Napoleonic Europe, and repeatedly attacks kingship with men like the Regent in mind: "when wolves shall learn to spare / The helpless victim for whose blood they lusted, / Then, and then only, monarchs may be trusted!" More playfully, Bob Fudge, a second letter writer clearly based on a younger version of the Regent, is so preoccupied with fashion, nightlife, and *les plaisirs gastronomiques* that he is oblivious to the human misery all around him in war-ravaged Paris. In its review of the *Fudge Family*, the *Literary Gazette* damned its "unmeasured abuse of princes."[58] Moore undoubtedly took it as a compliment.

The editor, pamphleteer, and publisher William Hone produced a much bolder form of satire in which he cut to the bone, not of the Regent but of the Liverpool government more generally. Most notably, in early 1817 he issued three liturgical parodies. In the first, *Catechism of a Ministerial Member*, Hone imagines "a Placeman or Pensioner" brought before the minister to be confirmed. "What is your name?" the *Catechism* begins. "Lick Spittle" is the reply. "Who gave you this name?" "My Sureties to the Ministry, in my Political Change, wherein I was made a Member of the Majority, the Child of Corruption, and a Locust to devour the good Things of this Kingdom." In the second, *The Political Litany*, Hone exploits the call-and-response form to itemize the sufferings of the populace: "By the deprivation of millions—by the sighs of the widow—by the tears of the orphan—by the groans of the aged in distress—by the wants of all classes in the community, except your own and your dependents, *O Rulers, deliver us*." And in the third, *The Sinecurists' Creed*, Hone maligns Lords Castlereagh, Eldon, and Sidmouth in the form of the Book of Common Prayer's Athanasian Creed: "And yet they are not three Quacks: but one Quack." Hone's three parodies were cheap (two pence) and sold well (3,000 copies in six weeks), but government officials did not like people laughing at Church and State.[59] After first forcing Hone to withdraw the pamphlets, they arrested him in May, charged him with blasphemy, failed in their attempts to rig the jury, and finally brought him to trial in mid-December. Three trials—one for each parody— were held on three successive days. It was the Regency's most remarkable courtroom drama.

Hone appeared in his own defense. Raggedly clothed, in poor health, and deeply concerned about the privations facing his wife and children, he was everyman's David taking on the governmental Goliath. It was easy for him to explain why he was on trial: "I have ever been independent in mind," he told the court, "and hence I am a destitute man." But Hone also rose spectacularly above these circumstances. With dramatic flair and unflagging presence of mind, he cleverly exploited the government's ill-conceived decision to try him for blasphemy (rather than sedition). Reaching back to the sixteenth century, Hone introduced a slew of scriptural and liturgical parodies that established a clear tradition in Britain of lampooning authority with impunity: "Milton . . . himself was a parodist on the Scripture," he contended. What is more, Hone insisted that he had "not written for a religious, but for a political purpose—to produce a laugh against the Ministers . . . ha! ha! ha! he laughed at them now, and he *would* laugh at them, as long as they were laughing-stocks!" On several occasions, Hone seized the opportunity to extrapolate on passages from the parodies on trial, drawing gales of applause from the packed gallery and producing the very laughter that the government was bent on suppressing. Lord Chief Justice Ellenborough presided on days two and three of the trial, and he tried to rein Hone in, repeatedly complaining that he was wasting time. Hone was not having it. "Wasting time, my Lord!" he cried. "When I shall have been consigned to a dungeon, your Lordship will sit as coolly on that seat as ever. . . . I am the injured man. *I* am upon my trial *by those gentlemen*, my jury."[60]

He was found "not guilty" on all charges. Exultant shouts rang out in the courtroom, while thousands cheered for him outside the City's Guildhall where the trials took place. Elevated immediately to iconic status in British radical politics, Hone remains one of the most important champions not only of the rights of individuals but of freedom of expression. From the political left, the radical MP Francis Burdett lauded Hone's "ability and manly exertion" and claimed that "the scandalous conduct of the Government" had brought together "the whole British public." Even someone as far to the right as Coleridge "eloquently expatiated on the necessity of saving Hone, in order to save English law," though many other conservatives were disgusted with the outcome: "the acquittal of Hone is enough to make one out of love with English Juries," Dorothy Wordsworth protested. In the courtroom Hone had run circles around Ellenborough, who never emerged from the shadow of that humiliation. Keats contended that if Hone had been found guilty, it "would have dulled still more Liberty's Emblazoning—Lord Ellenborough has been paid in his own coin."[61]

Leagued with Hone on many of his publishing projects was the most outstanding visual satirist of the Regency and one of the greatest of all British graphic artists. Ambivalent, even opportunistic in his politics, George Cruikshank produced conservative-minded caricatures that bolstered patriotic spirits during the war years and that often took aim at Napoleon. But more forcefully and frequently, Cruikshank drew for the radical cause, battering the Regent, his

toadies, and his ministers with relentless ingenuity and satiric force. Cruikshank consolidated a picture of the Regent—fat, gouty, bespangled, bearded, and bacchanalian—that was continually plagiarized and repurposed by his fellow caricaturists. These prints, available in different formats and at various prices ("penny plain, tuppence coloureds"), were bought by those who could afford them, but masses of people also consumed them by crowding around print-sellers' windows to gaze at the latest installment.[62] Cruikshank's images became a rallying point around which all those who opposed the monarchy could instantly assemble, and for all their cleverness, they were invariably accessible even to the empty-headed and the coarse—in no small measure because they relied so heavily on the scatological, the phallic, and the monstrous. Cruikshank produced the most coruscating and vitriolic pictorial commentary on the contemptible activities

PUBLISHED IN the *Scourge* magazine in May 1812, this cartoon
by George Cruikshank mocks the lubricity and duplicity of the
Prince Regent, and is entitled "The Prince of Whales or the
Fisherman at Anchor."

of royals and politicians, and he created an indelible impression of the
Regent as a callous buffoon and inveterate sot. Two centuries have
passed, and our understanding of him is still shaped by the drubbing
Cruikshank gave him.

Only twenty-seven years old when the Regency ended, Cruikshank produced some of his greatest work during that decade. He
was inspired by Lamb's verses on "The Triumph of the Whale" in
his design for "The Prince of Whales or the Fisherman at Anchor,"
in which a blubbery leviathan with the disheveled head of the Regent
swims in the "Sea of Politics," spurting the "Liquor of Oblivion" over
former Whig friends like Richard Brinsley Sheridan (who is repre-

sented as a great clumsy beast), and the "Dew of Favour" over his new
Tory friends, including Prime Minister Perceval (figured as a fisherman who has hooked the Regent). In the foreground, the Regent's latest mistress, Lady Hertford, a curvaceous mermaid, plays the lyre and
draws the Regent's eye. Behind her is her husband Lord Hertford, an
angry merman horned to denote cuckoldry. Swimming in front of the
Regent is the bare-breasted Mrs. Fitzherbert, the woman he secretly
married in 1785 but whom he cast off long ago.[63]

Other caricatures by Cruikshank—equally damning and variously
grotesque—followed, all of which flailed the Regent and confirmed
for the dispossessed and the rebellious that he was absolutely incapa-
ble of leading the country or of putting its interests above his own.
"Merry Making on the Regent's Birthday, 1812" features an inebri-
ated Regent dancing and obliviously stamping on a petition to aid
helpless children, while behind him through a curtained entrance in
the palace appear two people hanging from the gibbet and a poor

THIS PRINT by George Cruikshank was published on December 4, 1819, and is entitled "Loyal Address's & Radical Petitions,
or the R——t's most gracious answer to both sides of the question at once."

family pleading for relief. "Gent, No Gent, & Re gent!!" is a three-paneled tale in which the Prince appears first as a handsome young officer, then as a fleshy dissolute out boozing with intimates, and finally as a bloated, soused, would-be king, Lady Hertford hanging on one arm, John McMahon on the other. In "Loyal Address's & Radical Petitions," the Regent stands on a dais facing to the left a group of obsequious "Lords & Gentlemen" who hold scrolls reading "Loyalty," while behind him to the right are a group of radical petitioners reeling backward from a powerful fart issuing from the Regent's large bum. In the legend, the Regent tells the sycophants that they may "Kiss my Hand" while "it will be easy to guess what the other side may Kiss!!" Before the dais is an open book authored by "F. Fartardo."[64] The Regent and his government contemplated legal action to try and stop Cruikshank and other caricaturists from so brazenly pouring scorn on them, but they wisely decided against it, especially after the Hone acquittal. Trying to put someone in prison for making a fart joke seemed far more likely to produce more courtroom laughter, more sensational acquittals, and a lot more fart jokes. The Regent had little choice but to endure the abuse in silence.

<h1 style="text-align:center">X</h1>

Popular unrest broke out in London in the spring of 1815, and in the years that followed it pushed Britain to the breaking point, as radical images and ideas reached ever-increasing numbers and people who had never been politically active started to protest their circumstances in forms that ranged from petitions with tens of thousands of signatures, through peaceful assemblies far larger than the country had ever seen, to open calls for violence, such as the radical handbill that urged "no rise of bread; no Regent; no Castlereagh, off with their heads." All the leading ministers of the Liverpool government had lived through the worst bloodbaths of the French Revolution, and as the protest movements built in London and then around the country, they began to fear that a similar revolution was being organized in Britain. It badly unnerved them, and they determined to eviscerate the threat long before they were driven to choose between social anarchy and military rule. Shall we "manfully . . . abate the nuisance of the state, or see the guillotine erected at Charing Cross?" foamed the Church of England clergyman George Croly in the truculently Tory *Blackwood's Magazine*.[65]

Two demonstrations at Spa Fields (near Clerkenwell in north London) in late 1816 confirmed for many that the insurrectionists were serious and gaining ground. The chief organizers, ultraradical Arthur Thistlewood, together with James Watson and his son of the same name, extended invitations to a number of the leading lights of reform, including Burdett and Cobbett, and planned to use the rallies to incite widespread disorder in London that they hoped might then touch off a general rising in the country at large. Encouraging their aspirations was the spirited radical network they had built up at convivial meetings in London barracks and pothouses, as well as their extensive correspondence with provincial centers where like-minded radicals—they believed—were ready and waiting to join them. The only national figure to accept their invitation, however, was Henry "Orator" Hunt (no relation to the Hunt brothers), a larger-than-life campaigner of Wiltshire farming stock, who had a bell-like voice that carried his message of reform for great distances, and who wore a white hat that became an emblem of his advanced opinions.

At the first Spa Fields rally on November 15, Hunt addressed a huge crowd of "Distressed Manufacturers, Mariners, Artisans, and others." He also circulated a petition addressed to the Regent calling for the secret ballot, annual general elections, and universal male suffrage. But he greatly disappointed the extremists by denouncing violence and successfully exhorting the people to disperse peacefully. Undaunted, Thistlewood and the Watsons organized a second Spa Fields assembly for December 2, and this time they got much more of what they wanted. Before Hunt had even arrived, they rallied a splinter group of about two hundred men that broke from the main assembly and marched toward the Tower of London in imitation of the French mob's march on the Bastille prison a generation earlier. On the way they ransacked a number of gunsmiths' shops, carrying

THIS PORTRAIT of the radical reformer Henry "Orator" Hunt is by George Cruikshank, and was published on December 4, 1816, just two days after Hunt had spoken for the second time at a protest rally on Spa Fields.

off fowling pieces, pistols, and other weapons, and there were several hours of fighting in the City—without, apparently, fatalities on either side—before at nightfall order was finally restored.[66]

As a spur to a countrywide rebellion, the assembly was a failure, but in response the government resolved on draconian measures, mistaking a small group of brute-force fanatics for a widespread insurrectionary movement. In February 1817, it struck the so-called "Green Bag Committee" to investigate sedition and revolutionary unrest, and the following month it took—with the support of many Whigs—the hugely unpopular step of suspending the writ of habeas corpus. John Cashman, a seaman, was tried and executed for his part in the Spa Fields riot. The older Watson was charged with high treason, but he was acquitted when the crown's lead witness—the Yorkshireman John Castle—was revealed as a fraudster and plausible *agent provocateur*. The younger Watson fled on a ship bound for America, after being smuggled on board disguised as a Quaker. The case against Thistlewood, who was also charged with high treason, was then withdrawn, and he returned to plotting against the government, still confident that there were 40,000 workers in London ready to back a revolution.[67]

The atmosphere in the provinces during these same months of 1816–17, meanwhile, had become equally overheated, as postwar distresses intensified, radical sentiment grew more uncompromising,

THE FARM LABORER

mobs targeted the homes and businesses of bankers, millers, grocers, and magistrates, and militiamen were regularly attacked by
the crowds they had been called out to disperse. About 2,000 protesters stormed the streets of Dundee, attacking every house that
contained articles of food and looting upwards of 100 shops. At Bideford in north Devon, rioters carrying bludgeons and other weapons attempted to prevent a shipment of potatoes from leaving the
harbor. In Essex, 200 people, armed with axes, saws, and spades,
descended on the village of Great Bardfield "with the avowed intention to destroy thrashing machines." Disorderly gangs in Norwich
broke streetlamps and windows, stole flour from the mills, and threw
stones and fireballs at the yeomanry. Near Bury in Suffolk, 1,500
insurgents, provoked by low wages and the high price of bread and
meat, destroyed houses, barns, and corn stacks. Most seriously, at
Littleport in Cambridgeshire, fen laborers ransacked the house of
a magistrate, after which they went on a rampage in nearby Ely,
drinking, smashing property, extorting money, and freeing confederates who had been jailed, before barricading themselves in different houses and firing "many shots at the military and civil power."
Two rebels were killed when the military returned fire, and by the
time order was restored the parish of Littleport "resembled in every
respect a town sacked by a besieging army." At trial, twenty-four
rioters were found guilty of capital offenses. Nineteen had their sentence commuted. Five others were executed.[68]

People rallied, too, in the industrial districts. About 400 men
"rose from their work at Tredegar iron-works" in Wales, gathering or
coercing supporters as they advanced, shutting down as many factory
furnaces as they could, and demanding bread and cheese. In Somer-
set, roughly 3,000 disaffected coal miners took possession of several
pits, crying "Bread or Blood; [Orator] Hunt for ever!" and informing
the magistrates and dragoons "that they were starving." On March 10,
1817, upwards of 5,000 demonstrators (most of whom were weavers)
met in St. Peter's Fields in Manchester intending to walk peacefully
to London to petition the Regent over the dreadful state of the Lan-
cashire textile industry. But the government was in no mood to allow
the protest to gather supporters and coherence as it moved south, and

it sent in the cavalry, which broke up the "March of the Blanketeers" (so called because many of the participants carried rugs and blankets). Most in the crowd dispersed without incident, but a determined band of about 300 made it to the bridge at Stockport, where the cavalry turned them back.[69]

Less than three months later, events took a much more violent turn when Jeremiah Brandreth, an unemployed stocking maker and almost certainly a former Luddite captain, spearheaded the ill-fated Pentrich Rebellion. Without a political program but keen to strike a blow at power, Brandreth gathered together as many as 300 laborers and artisans from several industrial villages in the Derby Peak and set off from Pentrich on the fourteen-mile march southeast to Nottingham, where, he had convinced his followers, they would be united with other revolutionaries as part of a much wider revolt. It rained incessantly as they marched, and when they stopped at a house to demand guns, Brandreth accidently shot and killed a servant.[70] Soaked and demoralized, the rebels eventually reached Nottingham, where a party of hussars was waiting for them, and the insurgency collapsed.

The government's most infamous spy, W. J. Richards (better known as "Oliver the Spy"), was shown to have been involved in the Pentrich uprising as either an informer or, more likely, an *agent provocateur* who fanned the flames of revolutionary feeling with exaggerated accounts of rebel cells across the Midlands ready to spring into action, before escaping at the last minute and leaving his collaborators to be prosecuted. Leigh Hunt damned the politics of entrapment in his *Examiner* essay on "Informers," while Hazlitt in the *Morning Chronicle* denounced the government for its belief that "morality, religion, and social order, are best defended . . . by spies." Arraigned for high treason, most of the Pentrich rioters entered a plea of guilty on the understanding that they would not be sent to the gallows, but Brandreth and two of his lieutenants were convicted of the charge and, on November 7, 1817, hanged and then decapitated on Nun's Green, in front of Derby Gaol. "Behold the head of Jeremiah Brandreth, the traitor," screamed the axe-wielding executioner, holding the head by its hair and exhibiting it to the crowd.[71] To the thousands who looked on, it was a horrifying reminder of the realities of Regency political power.

In the second half of 1817, a good harvest and improved economic conditions, together with some assistance from government measures, helped restore the country to a relative calm. But in early 1819, as the economy slumped and food prices rose again, radical leaders responded with plans for even larger open-air rallies. Designed to pressure the Regent and his government into accepting the justness of the reform cause and the determination of the British working classes to see their demands met, these demonstrations not only established civil disobedience as a new political tactic but also paved the way for the use of similar strategies by twentieth-century leaders such as Mahatma Gandhi and Martin Luther King, Jr.[72] After a spring in which tens of thousands of people gathered in industrial centers across the country, a meeting at St. Peter's Fields in Manchester on Monday, August 16, drew an unprecedentedly large crowd of 60,000 women, men, and children, who assembled peaceably and without arms to hear Orator Hunt and other pro-reform advocates.

As soon as the meeting began, however, the magistrates, taken aback by its size and prepared to see in it the insurgency they had long been predicting, ordered the newly formed Manchester yeomanry to arrest the speakers. Brandishing sabers, they charged into the crowd, seizing Hunt as part of a more general attack, and within minutes they were backed up by the Fifteenth Hussars, a cavalry regiment, many of whom had fought at Waterloo and whose involvement gave the incident its infamous nickname, "Peterloo." Samuel Bamford was in the crowd and watched in horror as the confused cavalry attempted to "penetrate that compact mass of human beings" with their sabers "plied to hew a way through naked held-up hands, and defenceless heads; and then chopped limbs, and wound-gaping skulls were seen; and groans and cries were mingled with the din of that horrid confusion. . . . Then, 'Break! break! they are killing them in front, and they cannot get away.'"[73] In ten minutes it was over. Eleven people were dead. More than six hundred were wounded. After years of fighting to defend Britain from Revolutionary France, British soldiers were now killing British citizens. Civil strife had turned the country upside

IN THIS print by George Cruikshank, the horrors of the Peterloo Massacre are brought luridly into view, as British soldiers
axe their way through defenseless women, men, and children on
St. Peter's Fields in Manchester on August 16, 1819.

down. Peterloo was the final and bloodiest episode in the internecine
violence that scarred the Regency.

Liverpool's government was unrepentant. It tried, convicted, and
imprisoned several radical leaders, including Bamford, Burdett, and
Orator Hunt. It passed the notorious Six Acts, which introduced
harsh measures of control over assembly, the popular press, and the
bearing of arms. At Viscount Sidmouth's request, the Regent wrote
to the Manchester magistrates to commend them for their decision
to send in the troops, while ministers such as Castlereagh and Canning vigorously defended the government's actions, as did conservatives across the country. The Duke of Cambridge fulminated that
"nothing but firmness" could quell the "abominable revolutionary
spirit now prevalent in England." The Duke of Wellington declared
that it was "very clear" to him that the demonstrators would not "be
quiet till a large number of them 'bite the dust,' as the French say,

or till some of their leaders are hanged." *Blackwood's Magazine* scornfully berated the protesters "who, had they their wills but for a single day, would drench in blood the beautiful fields of England." Walter Scott was even angrier, and in his pamphlet *The Visionary* (1819) he produced a series of semi-hysterical "dreams" in which, following a "great revolutionary war," civilization in Scotland collapses and the country falls into the hands of a radical electorate composed of "all the refuse of a corrupted population." Even Byron—ardently progressive in many instances but a lord first and virulently anti-mob—responded to Peterloo with a snobbish horror that extended as far as the wish that Hunt had been among those massacred: "I think I have neither been an illiberal man nor an unsteady man upon polities—but I think also that if the Manchester Yeomanry had cut down *Hunt only*—they would have done their duty."[74]

Passions, it need hardly be said, were equally inflamed on the other side of the deep political divide, while among those who occupied the middle ground Peterloo aroused sympathy and drew opinion toward the radical cause. Its atrocities notwithstanding, Orator Hunt regarded it as a great moral victory, and when he returned to London on September 13, " 30,000 people were in the streets waiting for him," as Keats—an eyewitness—reported. Unintimidated, the radical leadership went ahead with a series of massive rallies, including a September demonstration in Westminster that drew as many as 50,000 people, as well as simultaneous meetings in November in the industrial north and in Scotland. Reacting to the great waves of grief and outrage engulfing the radical community, Leigh Hunt asserted in the *Examiner* that "thousands and thousands of Englishmen" were on the edge of rebellion, while Richard Carlile published an open letter in his *Republican* newspaper condemning the *"atrocious Murders"* and issuing a frank warning to the Regent: "Your future fate, and that of your family likewise, depends on the line of conduct you now pursue."[75]

Peterloo was also the subject of the best-selling radical satire of the Regency. *The Political House that Jack Built* is William Hone's mocking exposé of the government in which he attacks ministers, lawyers, clergymen, and soldiers in verses that imitate the popular children's chapbook "The House that Jack Built"—a maneuver that enabled Hone to make his contempt for the government highly accessible to a vast popular audience while at the same time protecting him from legal action, for he knew from experience that no one would try to imprison him for publishing nursery rhymes. Hone extols the peaceful Manchester protesters who "Were sabred by Yeomanry Cavalry," and damns in particular the self-absorbed Regent, "Who, to tricksters and fools, leaves the State and its treasure, / And, when Britain's in tears, sails about at his pleasure." Cruikshank produced thirteen

GEORGE CRUIKSHANK created this unforgettable image of the Prince Regent for *The Political House that Jack Built*, published in the month following Peterloo. In the text that accompanied the portrait, William Hone described the Regent as "The Dandy of Sixty."

woodcuts to accompany *The Political House*, including one with "tatter'd and torn" people in the foreground and the massacre of Peterloo going on behind them, and another of the Regent as a posturing, potbellied peacock squeezed into a ludicrously overdecorated military uniform from which hang medals, orders, and a corkscrew, an accessory that seems to account for his glassy-eyed stare. *The Political House* closes with a quotation from William Cowper's *The Task*, a long, introspective poem published in 1785, four years before the outbreak of the French Revolution, and used by Hone in 1819, four years after the British victory at Waterloo, to summarize why dissidents before and especially during the Regency fought so hard to dismantle political tyranny and social injustice: "'Tis Liberty alone, that gives the flow'r / Of fleeting life its lustre and perfume / And we are weeds without it."[76]

XI

Percy Shelley was the most inspiring and impassioned radical of the Regency. He dedicated his gothic tale *The Wandering Jew* to Francis Burdett, his satire *Peter Bell the Third* to Thomas Moore, and his tragedy *The Cenci* to Leigh Hunt, one of his dearest friends. He traveled to Ireland in 1812 and again in 1813, where he championed religious tolerance and the revocation of the Act of Union. He was incensed by the government's handling of Luddism: "The military are gone to Nottingham—Curses light on them for their motives if they destroy *one* of its famine-wasted inhabitants." He found that William Cobbett "still more & more delights me, with all my horror of the sanguinary commonplaces of his creed." In *An Address to the People on the Death of the Princess Charlotte* (1817), Shelley deplores, not the death of a member of the royal family, but of liberty as a result of the execution of Jeremiah Brandreth and the two other Pentrich rebels, and he condemns public sentiment that extravagantly mourns the death of a princess while routinely ignoring the thousands of abandoned and mistreated women who share her fate. Shelley believed fervently in the fundamental freedoms of speech, press, and assembly, as well as in large, peaceful protests as the best means of compelling change. He abhorred human callousness: "People say that poverty is no evil; they have never felt it, or they would not think so."[77]

Shelley's most outstanding political essay is "A Philosophical View of Reform," which he began to write in late 1819. In it, he argues provocatively that there is a "secret sympathy . . . between monarchy and war" as well as an "inevitable connection" between, on the one hand, "national prosperity and freedom" and, on the other, "the cultivation of the imagination and the cultivation of scientific truth." Convinced as he was that the literary could renovate the political, Shelley in the same essay also famously describes "poets" as "the unacknowledged legislators of the world"—"legislators" because they are the first to inscribe ways of thinking and modes of being that will eventually gain broad political and cultural acceptance, and "unacknowledged" because most audiences do not realize the role poets play in imagining and then driving social transformation. Long before public opinion or legislative agendas accept or even recognize the need to change, poets—by which Shelley means "creators" in the fullest sense—have anticipated the moral and spiritual possibilities for humankind, and in their writings they have brought those possibilities into being. "Until the mind can love, and admire, and trust, and hope, and endure," Shelley declares in a different essay from 1819, "reasoned principles of moral conduct are seeds cast upon the highway of life, which the unconscious passenger tramples into dust, although they would bear the harvest of his happiness."[78]

Shelley's radical idealism is clearly evident in his first major poem, *Queen Mab* (1813), which his cousin and biographer Thomas Medwin described as "a systematic attack on the institutions of society." "To Wordsworth" is a sonnet in which Shelley laments the older poet's desertion of the radical cause and remembers with grief how the young Wordsworth "In honoured poverty . . . did weave / Songs consecrate to truth and liberty." In "Mont Blanc," Shelley's experience of gazing on the great mountain convinces him not of a Christian deity but of an enigmatic power within nature that is involved in an "unremitting interchange" with the human mind and that can inspire within us the creative energies needed to repeal institutionalized forms of oppression or what in the poem Shelley calls "[l]arge codes of fraud and woe."[79] "Ode to the West Wind" is a secular prayer in which Shelley imagines that the change of seasons in the natural world is mirrored by similarly inevitable changes in the political world, for as winter gives way to spring, so must the despondency and brutality of post-Napoleonic Britain give way to a new season of hope and revitalization. What is more, though "chained and bowed" by personal dejection and the failure of his poetry to reach a contemporary audience, Shelley finds strength in the transformative powers of the wind, which will "Be through my lips to unawakened Earth / The trumpet of a prophecy!" "England in 1819" describes the tumultuous state of the country in that momentous year. George III is "[a]n old, mad, blind, despised and dying King." His sons, especially the Regent, are "the dregs of their dull race." "The Mask of Anarchy" is Shelley's unforgettable response to Peterloo. One of the most powerful protest poems in the English language, it is a call to the downtrodden to "Rise like Lions after slumber," as well as a blistering indictment of the Liverpool government: "I met Murder on the way— / He had a mask like Castlereagh."[80]

Prometheus Unbound (1820) is Shelley's poetic masterpiece. Subtitled *"A Lyrical Drama,"* and written in four acts, it is an astonishing tour de force in which Shelley weaves together many diverse political, mythological, personal, philosophical, scientific, and literary influences to produce a vision in which despotism is overthrown and love regenerates the world. The drama opens with the arch-rebel Prometheus bound to an icy rock, where on the instructions of the autocratic Jupiter he suffers daily torture for having brought humankind the gifts of creativity and freedom. Through a curse Prometheus has tied himself to Jupiter in mutual hate, but he now recalls his "words . . . quick and vain" and forgives his enemy: "I wish no living thing to suffer pain."[81] In rejecting retribution, Prometheus breaks the vicious cycle of one tyrannous regime being ousted by a rebellion that promptly installs its own tyrannous regime. More importantly, he prepares himself to be reunited with his beloved partner Asia, who embodies a transcendent form of love and whose separation from Prometheus has generated epochs of injustice and repression.

In Act II, Asia, together with her sister Panthea, embarks on a dizzying descent to the cave of Demogorgon, a gnomic power that Shelley clearly associates with the vast, chaotic multitudes of Regency Britain ("demos" is "the people"). During a poignant conversation about the nature of the cosmos, Demogorgon confirms that it was Jupiter "who made terror, madness, crime, [and] remorse," and that it is "eternal Love" alone—as represented by Asia—that can defy "Fate, Time, Occasion, Chance, and Change." Act III depicts Demogorgon's defeat of Jupiter and Prometheus's reunion with Asia, after which the two lovers retreat to a cave where they dwell with beauty and devote themselves to propagating "the progeny immortal / Of Painting, Sculpture, and rapt Poesy."[82] Prometheus instructs the Spirit of the Hour to travel around the world spreading the news of redemption, and on her return she reports on the miraculous changes she has seen. "Thrones, altars, judgment-seats, and prisons" stand, "not o'erthrown, but unregarded now," while humankind is "Equal, unclassed, tribeless and nationless." The final act is a celebration of a rejuvenated universe in which love "folds over the world its healing wings," and freedom and creativity reign both within and among people. Demogorgon reappears at the end to declare that if despotism rises again, humankind can reinstate liberty by embracing the same revolutionary faith that guided Prometheus, who in order to achieve his victory had

> To suffer woes which Hope thinks infinite;
> To forgive wrongs darker than Death or Night;
>   To defy Power, which seems omnipotent;
> To love, and bear; to hope, till Hope creates
> From its own wreck the thing it contemplates.[83]

In *Prometheus Unbound*, Shelley transmutes the fierce Regency conflicts between the agents of progress and the defenders of order into a modern version of an ancient myth in which human consciousness undergoes a radiant expansion, and the self-serving tyrannies of ambition, envy, and revenge that have subjugated humanity for centuries are finally thrown off by a rebellion founded in forgiveness, compassion, and hope.

Prometheus Unbound turns the page on classical and Christian mythologies and gives humankind a new start. One of Shelley's favorite Keats poems was *Hyperion*, written like *Prometheus Unbound* in 1818–19, and also like it an account of a moral and political revolution. The inequalities of Regency society were evident everywhere, from the Highland Clearances in Scotland and the sectarian strife in Ireland, through the industrial unrest in Wales and the English Midlands, to the anger and despair that festered in the rookeries and prisons. Great swaths of the populace were caught up in or overtaken by these injustices. Others exploited them. Some belligerents— like John Bellingham—took matters into their own hands. Many among the privileged simply ignored the turmoil or, worse, blamed the poor for being famished, ill, or outraged, and then allowed the Bloody Code to do its work. These circumstances turned hundreds of thousands of people across the country into protesters who cried out, petitioned, campaigned, gathered in violence and in peace, in small groups and in large numbers, and in some instances gave up liberty or life for the personal freedoms and political reforms that are now at the heart of our modern democratic states. During the Regency, radical orators, politicians, novelists, satirists, caricaturists, philanthropists, poets, and journalists assailed the entrenched hierarchies of Church and State from every available angle, and focused in particular on the trumped-up, tricked-out Regent as a symbol of all that was wrong with Britain. Their strategies loosened the grip of Regency intolerance. Their courage and insight remain as an inspiration to those who seek to carry on their work and to move us beyond the dead-end brutalities and self-interested ideologies that continue to plague our own age.

CHAPTER TWO

Theaters of Entertainment

I

It is Christmas, 1819. Thomas Carlyle spends the festive season away from his family studying law at the University of Edinburgh and writing an unsolicited article on gravitation that he hopes will be published in the *Edinburgh Review*. Walter Scott is bowed by grief as he deals in mid-December with the deaths of an uncle and an aunt, and then on Christmas Eve with the death of his mother. The Rev. Sydney Smith is ensconced in his living at Foston-le-Clay near York reading Scott's latest *Waverley* novel, *Ivanhoe*, which has been published just in time for the Christmas market. Dorothy Wordsworth reports "intense frost and deep snow" at Rydal Mount in the Lake District, while Christmas minstrels under the eaves inspire William Wordsworth to write stanzas addressed to his younger brother Christopher. In the south, the foreign secretary Lord Castlereagh is passing the Christmas recess at his beautiful estate in Kent, so exhausted by the tumultuous political events and grinding parliamentary sessions of the autumn "as to require being refitted."[1]

For others, too, this is a memorable festive season. John Keats is in north London with an ominously sore throat, but after ordering a warm coat and some thick shoes, he feels well enough on Christmas Day to dine with friends. The American author Washington Irving, who has lived in England for the past four years, publishes four essays on Christmas as the fifth installment of his *Sketch Book of Geoffrey Crayon, Gent.*, an enormously successful collection of whimsical essays and satiric short stories. Perhaps most remarkable of all, seven-year-old Charles Dickens is taken this year on the thirty-five-mile journey from his home in Chatham to Covent Garden Theatre in the heart of London to behold "the splendour of Christmas Pantomimes." The show he sees stars Joseph Grimaldi, "in whose honor I am informed I clapped my hands with great precocity." Dickens later regretted that his memories of Grimaldi's acting were "shadowy and imperfect," but he never forgot the thrill of attending the pantomime that December evening.[2] It deepened his fascination with audiences, actors, theatrical spectacles, and comic performances—to say nothing of his belief in the magic of Christmas.

In addition to Christmas and holiday shows, the theater offered an extraordinary range of other entertainments, from farces, ballets, operas, and dramas to magic acts, aquatic spectaculars, translations of foreign plays, and adaptations of fashionable novels. Some of the finest creative minds of the Regency were drawn to the theater, from successful playwrights such as Joanna Baillie, Samuel Taylor Coleridge, and Charles Robert Maturin, through avid theatergoers like Jane Austen, John Keats, and Lord Byron, to brilliant reviewers such as Charles Lamb, William Hazlitt, and Leigh Hunt. Leading comedians, including John Liston, Charles Mathews, and Dorothy Jordan, generated gales of laughter and provided playgoers with an often much needed diversion from the tedium or drudgery of their workaday lives. The transformational figure on the Regency stage was the tragedian Edmund Kean, who electrified audiences, but whose booze-fueled recklessness off the stage reads like a parable on the toxic nature of fame.

Covent Garden and Drury Lane were the only two theaters in London licensed to stage "legitimate" or "serious" drama, though a third, the King's Theatre in the Haymarket, was authorized to do so in the summer months when the other two stages were closed. In

THE COVENT GARDEN Theatre burned down on September 20, 1808. It was rebuilt in record time and opened its doors again on September 18, 1809. Thomas Rowlandson and Auguste Charles Pugin produced this print of the "New Covent Garden Theatre."

theory, these theaters were committed to upholding the higher ideals of British drama, but in practice they invariably offered audiences a hodgepodge of the classical and the popular. The most successful of the "illegitimate" theaters included Sadler's Wells, the Surrey, the Coburg, and the Lyceum. Brazenly commercial, and in fierce competition both with one another and with the major venues, they featured a revolving array of light entertainment, but plays involving sexual conquest and vulgarity were especially popular, as were female travesty dancers in skintight breeches.

Audiences were typically composed of a remarkably broad cross-section of the public, for while Regency society was built on strict hierarchies, playhouses were great levelers, as indeed were entertainment venues of many different kinds. The Regent's long-standing love affair with the theater helped heighten its popularity, as did his own well-known talents as a singer, a raconteur, and a mimic, not to mention his love of ceremony, costume, and make-believe. In the words of his erstwhile friend, the dandy Beau Brummell, "if his lot had fallen that way, he would have been the best comic actor in Europe." Many elites went regularly to the theater, where they sat in the expensive boxes to the right and left of the stage. Middle-class patrons, including professionals, businessmen, and skilled craftsmen, usually crowded into the pit. That left the cheap seats in the lower and upper galleries, which were filled with the burgeoning and unlettered urban masses and brought within their reach both the excitement of live entertainment and the sight of the privileged and the stylish.[3]

These evenings were often raucous affairs. Fine performances were enthusiastically applauded, but catcalls damned dull or poorly acted shows, while fistfights and shouting matches routinely broke out in audiences that had lost interest. Working girls circulated among the crowds selling oranges and apples, which provided refreshment for those who chose to eat but ammunition for those who decided instead to launch the fruit or the peels at the stage as a mark of their displeasure with the actors or the show. "I think there is not in the world so stupid or boorish a congregation as the audience of an English playhouse," Thomas Moore snarled in 1811.[4] Scarce wonder that many, particularly among the respectable and the pious, regarded the theaters as dens of iniquity that openly promoted dangerous levels of intimacy and display—on the stage, in the audience, and between the sexes.

The theater was not the only venue that attracted Regency funseekers. Sporting events, especially prizefighting, drew huge crowds. People gambled, often to the point of obsession, and on everything from impromptu dares between friends to horse racing, cards, and dice games. Shopping was a major source of entertainment, as consumer culture moved from bustling markets to sleek new urban spaces. Elites gathered at Almack's to dance, dine, gossip, and charm, while crowds from across the social classes flocked to holiday resorts, pleasure gardens, and public fairs. The Regency's delight in wit was on full display at these events, as was its love of food and alcohol, both of which were consumed in jaw-dropping quantities.

There were more sober pleasures as well. Museums, menageries, and panoramas abounded. Art enthusiasts crowded into private galleries and public exhibitions. Popular public lecture series were delivered by leading experts, while prose fiction reached new and far higher levels of respectability and sophistication, driven by the innovations of Jane Austen, Maria Edgeworth, and, of course, Walter Scott, whose *Waverley* novels were the publishing sensation of the Regency. Lord Byron was the first modern celebrity, and his life, art, and image were voraciously consumed worldwide by men and women who were hungry for glamour and originality, and who both glorified and damned him as part of what we would now call "celebrity culture."

II

Dorothy Jordan was the reigning queen of British comedy. In her professional life, she was widely celebrated for her spontaneity, charm, timing, and beautiful voice. In her private life, she was notorious as the longtime mistress of the Duke of Clarence (later William IV). Born in Ireland, she was on the Dublin stage in her mid-teens, before moving to the York circuit and then to London, where she worked in the major theaters and—like many of her fellow performers— supplemented her income with lucrative but exhausting tours in the provinces. Jordan was admired especially for Rosalind in *As You Like It* and Viola in *Twelfth Night*, as well as for her portrayal of Hippolita— the lively Spanish heroine who dresses as an army officer—in Colley Cibber's *She Would and She Would Not*.

When the Regency began, Jordan was near the end of her career, almost fifty years old, increasingly corpulent, often ill, beleaguered by debt, and soon to find that—after bearing him ten children— the scattergood Duke of Clarence was ending their relationship to become a fortune hunter. Yet she still commanded the stage. The painter Charles Robert Leslie saw her at Covent Garden in the spring of 1813. "I had been taught to expect an immensely fat woman, and she is but moderately so," he declared. "Her face is still very fine. . . . Her performance of Rosalind was in my mind perfect." A year later, Byron was in the audience when she played Miss Hoyden in Richard Brinsley Sheridan's *A Trip to Scarborough*, and he judged her performance "superlative." In January 1815, Leigh Hunt contended that Jordan was "not only the first living actress in comedy," but "the only actress . . . who can any way be reckoned great and original." Seven months later, Jordan concluded a tour of the provinces with ten performances at Margate, after which she went into exile in France, where she died the following year. Charles Lamb, one of her greatest admirers, observed that she seemed "a privileged being, sent to teach mankind what it most wants, joyousness."[5]

Jordan was not the only Regency performer to fill Lamb with joy. He praised several other actresses closely associated with comedic roles, including Frances Kelly, to whom he unsuccessfully proposed marriage in 1819 ("what a lass that were . . . to go a gipseying through the world with"). Among male comedians, Robert William Elliston was one of Lamb's particular favorites. He could play tragic roles such as Hamlet and Othello, but he excelled in the portrayal of comic heroes like Benedick in *Much Ado About Nothing* or Charles Surface in Sheridan's *The School for Scandal*. Hunt liked him especially as the lover: "No man approached a woman as he did,—with so flattering a mixture of reverence and passion." William Beckford saw Elliston in January 1819 in William Thomas Moncrieff's *Rochester*, an example of Regency musical comedy at its exuberant best. "How divine he is," Beckford enthused.[6]

Elliston went beyond acting to lease or own no fewer than ten different Regency theaters, and in 1819 he became the manager of Drury Lane. He had a high regard for several of his fellow comedians, including Joseph Grimaldi, whose innovations with makeup and costume, extraordinarily expressive face, and demonic levels of energy made him not only the first modern clown but also the most illustrious and enduring representative of the kind of bawdy, violent, slapstick humor so beloved by Regency audiences. The tears of the clown, however, were never far from the surface, and all the kicks, beatings, pratfalls, sword fights, and dangerous stunts took a terrible toll on his body. "It is absolutely surprising," declared the *Times* in 1813, "that any human head or hide can resist the rough trials which he volunteers." Joseph Ballard, an American businessman, saw Grimaldi in a packed house at Sadler's Wells in 1815 and reported that his "fame has certainly not been over-rated." A year later, after enjoying a show at Covent Garden, Hazlitt described him as "a man of genius."[7] Grimaldi transformed the range and emotional depth of the clown, and he exerted a powerful influence on show business that reached its peak a full century later in the "little tramp" character of Charlie Chaplin, the world's first movie star and still one of our best comedians.

John Bannister was a more traditional comic actor who often performed on the same bill as Grimaldi and who was best known in the Regency for roles such as Sir Anthony Absolute in Sheridan's *The Rivals* and Tony Lumpkin in Oliver Goldsmith's *She Stoops to Conquer*. Lamb discerned in him the ability to "strike up a kind of personal friendship" with the audience, and found him especially funny when he played the craven, for through "a perpetual sub-insinuation" he managed to convey to the house, "even in the extremity of the shaking fit, that he was not half such a coward as we took him for." Hunt appreciated his versatility. Bannister could make you laugh heartily at some "yeoman or seaman in a comedy" and then "bring the tears into your eyes for some honest sufferer in an afterpiece."[8]

John Liston was regularly compared to Bannister, though he produced a much less genial brand of humor that relied on hilarious facial contortions, especially when he took the stage as a conceited Cockney or affected provincialist. According to Benjamin Robert Haydon, "Bannister's . . . forte was what might be called the Pathos of Peasant's life," while "Liston is more broad humour, though always native." Both actors played Tony Lumpkin to great acclaim. Hunt preferred Bannister in the role, but Keats's close friend John Hamilton Reynolds championed Liston: "He is the bumpkin squire to a nicety." The painter David Wilkie, a great lover of the theater and personally acquainted with Liston, incorporated him—or at least a version of him as he frequently appeared on stage—into his painting of the *Village Holiday*, dated 1811: "Liston came, and sat for an hour: I went over part of his face, and put a little more drunkenness into the looks." In 1817, Hazlitt saluted Liston as "the greatest comic genius who has appeared in our time."[9]

Other commentators, however, gave that palm to Joseph Munden. He was, declared Thomas Noon Talfourd, "by far the greatest comedian we ever saw." Lamb lauded Munden for the way he turned the ordinary into the extraordinary: "A tub of butter, contemplated by him, amounts to a Platonic idea." Hunt delighted in Munden's ability to milk a funny situation. "I have seen him," he smiles, "while playing the part of a vagabond loiterer about inn-doors, look at, and gradually approach, a pot of ale on a table from a distance, for ten minutes together, while he kept the house in roars of laughter by the intense idea which he dumbly conveyed of its contents, and the no less intense manifestation of his cautious but inflexible resolution to drink it." Mary Cowden Clarke saw Munden in the same role and laughed as hard as Hunt. "The tipsy lunge with which he rolled up to the table whereon stood that tempting brown jug; the leer of mingled slyness and attempted unconcernedness with which he slid out his furtive thought to the audience—'Some gentleman has left his ale!' then, with an unctuous smack of his lips, jovial and anticipative, adding, 'And some other gentleman will drink it!'"[10]

Perhaps the most remarkable Regency comedian of all, though, was Charles Mathews. Byron called him "this modern Proteus." Coleridge added simply, "I define him as a comic poet acting his own poems." Mathews played many of the standard roles in the Regency comedy repertoire, but he also developed his own one-man shows, which were popularly known by 1817 as "At Homes," and which he performed in three parts. In the first, he stood or sat at a cloth-covered table and, under a title such as *Mail-Coach Adventures during a Journey to the North* or *A Trip to Paris*, he took his audiences through an amusing series of escapades while exhibiting his gifts for mimicry, anecdote, malapropism, and comic song. The second part relied less on narrative and was mainly composed of comic sketches and impersonations, as when in 1818 he recited Hamlet's speech to the players in the guise of several contemporary actors, including Bannister and Munden. Mathews coined the term "monopolylogue" for the closing part, in which he played several different characters and further exploited his skills in storytelling and improvisation. Several British comedians performed successful one-man shows before Mathews, but his intuitive sense of what would make people laugh, coupled with his ability to create unique and strikingly dissimilar male and female characters in rapid succession, set him far ahead of the competition and produced what the London *Courier* in April 1818 described as an "attraction beyond all precedent."[11]

III

Tragedy passionately engaged audiences as well, and with perhaps even greater reason, for in the Regency the presentation of serious drama suddenly and exhilaratingly gave way to a far more modern mode of performance. For almost three decades, the Welsh-born Sarah Siddons had dominated British theater as its greatest tragic actress. But on the evening of June 29, 1812, the fifty-six-year-old bid an emotional farewell to the stage in a performance of Lady Macbeth, her most famous role. Joseph Farington was in a box that night and recorded that, after she left the stage at the end of the sleepwalking scene, the audience was so affected that they refused to let the play continue, and when at length the curtain was drawn up, Siddons was "dressed in White Sattin" and "sitting at a table in Her own character."[12] She curtsied and bowed until the audience finally calmed down, delivered an eight-minute farewell speech during which there was profound silence, and then withdrew to the loudest clapping of all. Friends and admirers soon succeeded in coaxing her back onto the boards, and she appeared in a succession of benefit shows before permanently retiring on June 9, 1819.

Siddons faced serious competition across the Regency. After years of success as a young actress in the theaters of Belfast and Dublin, Elizabeth O'Neill made her London debut at Covent Garden in 1814 in the role of Juliet. Hazlitt almost immediately hailed her as "by far the most impressive tragic actress we have seen since Mrs. Siddons," but went on to point out key differences in their approach, for whereas

THIS PORTRAIT of the great tragedian Sarah Siddons was
engraved by William Say in 1810, after the 1804 painting by
Thomas Lawrence.

Siddons combines "passion . . . with lofty imagination and commanding intellect," O'Neill "owes everything to extreme sensibility." Percy
Shelley saw O'Neill several times and was "deeply moved by . . . the
graceful sweetness, the intense pathos, and sublime vehemence of
passion she displayed." Not everyone, however, was impressed. "We
were all at the Play last night, to see Miss O'neal in Isabella," Austen
wrote in 1814. "I do not think she was quite equal to my expectation. . . . I took two Pocket handkerchiefs, but had very little occasion for either."[13] O'Neill performed for the last time in July 1819,
just one month after Siddons bid her absolute farewell. That Christmas she married a wealthy Irish landowner and retired to County
Cork, fiercely proud to have her reputation for virtue unblemished
and not yet thirty years old—an acting phenomenon who belongs to
the Regency alone.

John Philip Kemble was the leading male tragedian of his generation. Two years younger than his sister Sarah Siddons, he was studious
and prickly in his approach to his profession, acclaimed for his playing of the title roles in *Hamlet* and especially *Coriolanus*, and dogged
throughout his long career—like Elliston and many others—by his
fondness for drink. Byron saw him as Coriolanus in late 1811 and
thought "he was glorious," even at fifty-four years old. Six years later
in Bath, the novelist Frances Burney watched him in the same role.
"I never saw a more truly noble performance—the air, mien, height,
stern beauty, Age, All were in Unison with the character." Yet there
had always been naysayers. Kemble, they grumbled, was too grand,
too precise, too labored, too controlled. Hunt could never admire
him. He was "rather a teacher of elocution than an actor." When
Kemble said goodbye to the stage at Covent Garden in June 1817,
Hazlitt praised him for his "*intensity*," which had "not fallen off a jot"
and which had made him "the most excellent actor of his time." In the
same review, though, he could not refrain from carping that Kemble
"had always something dry, hard, and pedantic" in his manner. He
failed especially as Hamlet. He played it "like a man in armour."[14]

Enter Edmund Kean. Born into a theatrical family, and having
survived a childhood of isolation and bitterness, he spent more than a
dozen years on the margins of the entertainment world as a strolling

player and frustrated member of provincial companies. On January 26, 1814, however, he transformed his own fortunes, as well as those of Drury Lane, when he exploded onto the stage in the role of Shylock. Five feet four, with a thin face and dark hair, Kean was neither classically trained nor classically handsome. But audiences found it virtually impossible to take their eyes off him. Scornful, impulsive, and sexually charismatic, he was light on his feet, with powerfully expressive eyes and a harsh, commanding voice that "resembled a hackney-coachman's at one o'clock in the morning," as Hunt memorably put it.[15] Other actors projected control. Kean projected danger. His predecessors and rivals played their roles with discipline. Kean played his on the edge of irrationality.

Hazlitt broke the news. "Mr. Kean (of whom report had spoken highly) last night made his appearance at Drury Lane Theatre in the character of Shylock," he wrote in his *Morning Chronicle* review for January 27. "For voice, eye, action, and expression, no actor has come out for many years at all equal to him." Hazlitt went to see Kean again in the same role six days later. He was even more impressed. "His style of acting is, if we may use the expression, more significant, more pregnant with meaning, more varied and alive in every part, than any we have almost ever witnessed." Comparisons with Kemble were as prompt as they were inevitable, and very much to Kemble's disadvantage. "Kean appeared and extinguished Kemble," was Hunt's admirably succinct recollection. Tickets to see the fiery new actor were soon very hard to come by, but Austen secured one, and on Saturday, March 5, she was in Drury Lane to watch him perform Shylock. Her verdict: "I cannot imagine better acting."[16]

Kean quickly appeared in a succession of other Shakespearean roles and was equally triumphant, despite the predictable caviling about his sudden success and unusual techniques. Percy Shelley walked out of his *Hamlet* after Act II, but just a fortnight later Haydon saw Kean in the same role and declared "that his whole conception . . . is perfect." Coleridge thought Kean "not a thorough gentleman enough to play Othello," but when Henry Crabb Robinson saw him in the part, he "could hardly keep from crying; it was pure feeling." Kean's Macbeth was "fine but unequal," according to Byron, yet as the villainous Iago

AN UNKNOWN artist produced this etching of Edmund Kean as Richard III, the role that made him one of the Regency's leading celebrities.

he was "perfection": "I was *close* to him (in the orchestra), and never saw an English countenance half so expressive."[17]

Kean's greatest role was Richard III. Joanna Baillie had misgivings about his interpretation—"sometimes he seemed to me to act . . . with too much effort and labour"—but others were in awe. The aging painter Benjamin West was stunned by the intensity of Kean's Richard and lay awake all night after watching his performance. Hazlitt found Kean the embodiment of his own ideal of imaginative "gusto," which in art was the "power or passion defining any object." Kemble's Richard, he declared, "wanted that tempest and whirlwind of the soul, that life and spirit, and dazzling rapidity of motion, which fills the stage, and burns in every part of it, when Mr. Kean performs this character." Keats saw Kean in a number of different roles and lauded his ability both to seize the dramatic moment and to blend the sensual with the spiritual. In his December 1817 *Champion* review of Kean's Richard, Keats observed that while "other actors are continually thinking of their sum-total effect throughout a play," Kean "delivers himself up to the instant feeling, without the shadow of a thought about any thing else."[18]

Living with unprecedented intensity onstage, little changed for Kean when he stepped off it. He was dependent on alcohol before he arrived in London, and when stardom hit he drastically overindulged, quaffing booze by the vat and slaking his insatiable sexual appetites with numerous affairs (Kean was married and a father), and even more often with prostitutes, who crowded into his dressing room to service him: "I always take a shag before the play begins," he snapped on one occasion when asked why he was late for the curtaining.[19] Kean fought with management. He sabotaged people and plays he disliked. He disappeared for weeks. He was openly contemptuous of the crowds—especially of the fashionables—who came in droves to see him.

Imitators and up-and-comers soon emerged to challenge him, as he had challenged Kemble. William Charles Macready made his Covent Garden debut as Orestes in Ambrose Philips's *The Distressed Mother* and immediately showed himself to be "by far the best tragic actor that has come out in our remembrance, with the exception of

Mr. Kean," as Hazlitt reported in September 1816.[20] Equally impressive was Junius Brutus Booth, who looked and acted a great deal like Kean, and who established his name in two of the roles most closely associated with him: Richard III and the rapacious Sir Giles Overreach in Philip Massinger's *A New Way to Pay Old Debts*. Booth first appeared at Covent Garden in 1816, but when he quarreled with management over salary, Kean convinced him to defect to Drury Lane and to play Iago opposite his Othello.

Staged on February 20, 1817, it was the theatrical event of the Regency. "Both tragedians, of course, exerted themselves to their utmost, and acted their finest; and the result was a triumph of performance," Keats's close friend Charles Cowden Clarke remembered. After the show, Mary Shelley's father William Godwin exclaimed "rapturously, 'This is a night to be remembered!'" It was also a night that turned out to be unique. Booth, who had been upstaged by Kean, returned to Covent Garden, before retreating to the provinces and eventually America, where years later one of his sons, the actor and segregationist John Wilkes Booth, assassinated President Abraham Lincoln. Kean, increasingly in the grip of alcoholism, sexual disease, and his own megalomania, was soon judged to be past his prime. By 1819, Walter Scott could lambast him as "a copper-laced, two-penny tearmouth, rendered mad by conceit and success."[21] When, however, he was at his zenith, no one in the Regency blazed like him. In the last two hundred years, many immensely talented entertainers have risen suddenly to fame and then destroyed themselves in excess and self-loathing. Each is a distant descendant of Kean.

IV

"The character of a people is to be sought for and found in their amusements," declared John Wilson in *Blackwood's Magazine* in December 1819. An avid angler, walker, and wrestler, Wilson was referring specifically to sports, and to the crucial role they played in many people's lives, then as now. Cricket was one of the most popular games of the Regency. Lord's Ground, known worldwide as the home of cricket,

moved to its present site, just west of Regent's Park in London, in
1814. Lord Frederick Beauclerk, the bad-tempered vicar of Kimp-
ton in Hertfordshire, took part in the first recorded match there, and
his obsession with the sport is memorably captured by the courtesan
Harriette Wilson, who described him as "a sly, shy, odd man, not very
communicative, unless one talks about cricket." Rivals of Beauclerk,
including George Osbaldeston and William Ward, distinguished
themselves at the new ground as well, extending the popularity of
the game among metropolitan audiences. In rural Britain, too, cricket
attracted more and more interest as a source of both competition and
community cohesion. "I doubt if there be any scene in the world more
animating or delightful than a cricket-match . . . between neighbour-
ing parishes," Mary Russell Mitford wrote in her nostalgic account of
Our Village.[22] Such descriptions turned the game into an indispensable feature in the myth of bucolic "Merry Old England."

Horse racing was a passion, not just for its traditional supporters
among the nobility and landed gentry but also for people much further down the social scale. Indeed, at some of the major races, sang
Charles Mathews in 1811, "A peer and a 'prentice now dress so much
the same, / You cannot tell the diff'rence, excepting by the name."
Newmarket in Suffolk was the long-established headquarters of the
sport, with other important courses at Doncaster, York, Ascot, and
Epsom. Tattersall's horse auction room at Hyde Park Corner in London was the gathering place for horse-mad sportsmen of all descriptions, and it gave "a *tone* to the *sporting* world, in the same way that the
transactions on the ROYAL EXCHANGE influence the mercantile part
of society."[23] The three classic races—the St. Leger, the Oaks, and
the Derby—were all established more than three decades before the
Regency began, but to them was added the Two Thousand Guineas
in 1809 and the One Thousand Guineas in 1814.

Field sports, including the hunting of foxes and the shooting of
game birds, were deplored by activists like Percy Shelley: "it will be
a contemplation full of horror . . . that beings capable of the gentlest
and most admirable sympathies, should take delight in the death-
pangs and last convulsions of dying animals." But many Regency men
of leisure, including Charles Musgrove in Austen's *Persuasion* (1818),

"did nothing with much zeal" except fishing, hunting, and riding, which legions pursued with that "neck-or-nothing" speed that tested the limits of their horsemanship and drove them through bogs, over hedges, and down steep hills in pursuit of their quarry. Melton Mowbray in Leicestershire was the most fashionable destination for hunters. Many set up establishments in and around the town; splashed out huge sums on stables, horses, hounds, and liveried servants; and were in the field six days a week. The amount of game on many family estates was staggering, especially given the levels of hunger and despair in the country at large. At Woburn in January 1820, the Duke of Bedford hosted a large hunting party that included the Dukes of York and Wellington, and that in five days "killed 835 pheasants, 645 hares, 59 rabbits, 10 partridges, and 5 woodcocks." It would appear "as if the chace were natural to man," enthused Lord John Russell, the future prime minister. It was not just men, though. The redoubtable Lady Salisbury was an avid sportswoman, and in the Regency she hunted constantly, "riding as hard and clearing the fences with as much ardour as any sportsman in the field."[24]

There were bloodier sporting pastimes, too, including cockfighting and badger-baiting, that took place everywhere from makeshift rural pits to specially designed urban arenas. In bullbaiting, a spectacle of ferocious cruelty, dogs attacked a bull that was tied to a ring, lacerating his nostrils as he tossed them aside, until they were exhausted and he was led to the slaughterhouse. Bears were baited with the same savagery. Robert Southey maintained that these matches were the entertainment of "the rabble," but another commentator reported a much more heterogeneous crowd at London pits, including "dustmen, lamplighters, stage coachmen, bakers, farmers, barristers, swells, butchers, dog-fanciers, grooms, donkey-boys, weavers, snobs, market-men, watermen, honourables, sprigs of nobility, M.P.'s, [and] mail-guards."[25]

Boxing was the sporting craze of the Regency, though its status as a national pastime provoked intense debate. Among the burgeoning proto-Victorian forces of civility and restraint, it was loathed as dehumanizing and profoundly un-British. For its many advocates, however, it inculcated the virtues of bravery, endurance, discipline, and fair play, and it was, above all, quintessentially British. Effem-

THE BROTHERS Robert and George Cruikshank supplied all the illustrations for Pierce Egan's *Life in London*, including this one of the Royal Cockpit. Tom, Jerry, and Bob stand to the right, Tom with his hand up to place a bet.

inate foreigners settled their personal differences with the stiletto or the sword. Not Britons. Their weapon of choice was their fists, and their method of resolving disputes generous and nonfatal. Practiced at its highest level, pugilism produced sporting spectaculars that—more than any other Regency entertainment—united huge numbers of people from across the social hierarchies and provided them with a blow-by-blow opportunity to see the British character at its finest—the character that, in the first half of the Regency, *would* defeat Napoleon, and that in the second half, *did*. In the kind of disarmingly paradoxical phrase so often employed by members of "the Fancy" (the name used to designate the fraternity of boxing devotees), the sport turned British boys and men into "good-natured conquerors of the world," both in the ring and in the service of empire. "Boxing," William Cobbett affirmed in 1816, tends to "produce great energy in individuals, and it is of the union of individual energy that national power principally consists."[26]

Regency prizefights were brutal, bare-knuckle affairs. Before the match, and regardless of the weather, both boxers stripped to their waists, leaving only drawers on their lower body and pumps (light, heelless shoes) on their feet. Each was allowed two seconds, one of whom provided his knee as a seat between rounds, and the other of whom carried a sponge and a bottle (of water or, more commonly, brandy). There were few rules that governed the actual method of fighting: throwing, tripping, butting, and hairpulling were all permitted, as was locking an opponent's head under one arm while the other fist pummeled him into a stupor. A round lasted until one of the fighters was knocked or thrown down, after which he had thirty seconds to return to the mark in the center of the ring. The winner was declared only when one of the boxers was unable to do so. There was no time limit as such, so a contest could last anywhere from ten or twenty minutes to four or even five hours. Many men continued to fight long after they had been blinded by blood and pain. "It is said of a pugilist that he *is game*, or *has bottom*, when he possesses in a high degree passive courage or fortitude," reported one commentator in 1811. "A nose beaten flat, —an eye out of its socket, —broken ribs, — the skin and flesh torn and streaming with blood, —and still to stand and make head, shews a man to be game."[27]

Unsurprisingly, prize matches had for several decades been proscribed by law, and they would probably not have survived without the patronage of royalty and nobility, whose presence at ringside was usually enough to deter even the most zealous officer of the law. Matches were rarely advertised in advance and usually took place outside of London. Once the time and location of a bout was determined, word would spread quickly among the various social tiers of the Fancy, who would then set out in carriages, in carts, on horseback, and on foot toward the appointed venue, visiting and drinking as they went, debating the merits of the two combatants, falling in and out of various like-minded or rival groups, and getting more and more geared up for the contest. By the time most Regency prizefights were about to start, a crowd of "not less than twenty thousand of *both sexes*" had gathered.[28] At that point, the two fighters entered the ring, engaged in often theatrical displays of their physiques, and then took

THIS SKETCH by Thomas Rowlandson is of the September 28, 1811, rematch between the English bare-knuckle champion Tom Cribb and the formidable African American prizefighter Tom Molyneaux.

their places a yard apart on opposite sides of the mark. The umpires called time. The battle began.

Tom Cribb was the English bare-knuckle champion for the entire Regency. His most famous antagonist, Tom Molyneaux, was a freed black slave from America. The two first faced each other at Copthorne Common in Sussex on a rainy, cold day in December 1810. Overweight and out of shape, Cribb was not expecting much of a fight from Molyneaux, but he soon found himself in trouble and in one instance had to rely on chicanery from his seconds, who distracted the umpire with sham objections in order to allow Cribb time to find his feet. He went on to claim victory after thirty-four rounds, but many in the Fancy accepted that the contest had been unfair. Molyneaux promptly demanded a rematch, and this time Cribb took him seriously, training hard in Scotland and then defeating him at Thistleton Gap, near Leicester, in September 1811. Racism unquestionably fueled support for Cribb, who was seen by many as having won a personal victory that was simultaneously national and, indeed, international. But John Wilson and William Maginn took a different and much broader view. They understood the match as a spectacle that united—rather than divided—people, and they championed the ways in which sport dismantles social and racial barriers, both within and between countries. "When we first saw Molyneaux knock down Cribb," they asserted in *Blackwood's Magazine*, "at once all distinction of colour was lost. We saw before us two human beings—and our hearts beat for the cause of liberty all over the world."[29]

The Fancy reveled in many other spectacular Regency prizefights. Ned Painter defeated J. Alexander, known as "the Gamekeeper," in 1813, but he lost the following year to Tom Oliver, "the Chelsea Gardener." "The Lancashire Hero," Jack Carter, took on Oliver at Gretna Green in 1816 before a crowd estimated at thirty thousand people, and beat him senseless in under fifty minutes. Cribb's protégé Thomas Winter—punningly known as "Thomas Spring"—battled Painter twice in 1818, winning in April and losing in August, before securing his reputation at Crawley Down in Sussex in May 1819 when he emerged the victor after seventy-one rounds with Carter. The Irishman Dan Donnelly was known as the "King of the Curragh" in County Kildare after defeating two Englishmen, Tom Hall in 1814 and George Cooper in 1815, but his greatest fight was against Oliver, whom he defeated at Crawley in July 1819. Most intriguingly, though they attended in separate parties, John Keats and Thomas Moore were among the huge crowd that gathered in December 1818 to watch "the Nonpareil" Jack Randall vanquish Ned Turner at Crawley. Keats was close enough to the action that he afterward described the rapidity of Randall's punches by tapping his fingers on the windowpane. Moore found the experience "altogether not so horrible as I expected—Turner's face was a good deal de-humanized, but Randall . . . had hardly a scratch."[30]

Pugilism and literature intertwined in the Regency as never before or since, as the presence of Keats and Moore at a prizefight clearly suggests. The seminal *Sporting Magazine*, which featured contributions from reporters such as John James Brayfield, as well as from many of its readers, gave extensive coverage to prizefighting, as did several morning newspapers, including the *Post* and the *Chronicle*. The satirist William Maginn was a passionate fan, as were the poet Bryan Waller Procter and the literary and theater critics Hazlitt and Hamilton Reynolds. Byron considered boxing of "truly national" importance and, like many elites, he took lessons at the school established by the former prizefighter John "Gentleman" Jackson, with whom he was sparring daily as late as 1814. Moore took the popular fascination with pugilism in new directions when he pressed it into the service of his liberal politics. In his poetic "Epistle from Tom Cribb to Big Ben," the Regent—a well-known lover of the ring—takes a "milling" from Cribb over his unsportsmanlike decision to refuse Napoleon sanctuary in Britain following his defeat at Waterloo. Moore drubs the Regent again in his much longer verse satire *Tom Cribb's Memorial to Congress*, which features Cribb addressing the 1818 meeting of European sovereigns. In its uproarious "Grand Set-To," the muscular Tsar Alexander I of Russia ("Long Sandy") throttles the obese Regent ("Georgy the Porpus").[31]

Pierce Egan is the pivotal figure in the Regency literature of boxing, and is frequently recognized as the first modern sports journalist. He reported on prizefights for the *Weekly Dispatch* and made pugilism a central feature of his picaresque novel *Life in London*, where the hero Tom is an amateur boxer, and he and his fashionable friends visit both the home of Cribb and the school of Jackson. It was, however, in *Boxiana*—the first volume of which appeared in 1812, followed by a second in 1818—that Egan elevated sports journalism to an entirely new level. Several features of his reporting stand out. No devotee of the ring had his detailed understanding of the history of the sport, or of its techniques and strategies. No one else was as well connected to the contemporary scene or reported with such a wealth of insider information. No one wrote with more confidence about the ways in which the sport inculcated the "principles of generosity and heroism."[32] And, though many tried, no one else could match the verve of his prose style, which at its most overwrought combined a blizzard of dashes, exclamation marks, *italics*, and CAPITALS with elaborate metaphors, truly awful puns, and an extensive use of contemporary ("flash") slang. It was a style that Egan both exploited and in part created, and it united the Fancy in the vitality of a shared jargon. Egan spoke their language, and no one brought them closer to the intensity of the action.

Here he is on the most celebrated prizefight of the Regency, when Cribb defeated Molyneaux at Thistleton Gap. Egan's prose style has not yet taken on all the typographical oddities and rhetorical extravagances that would later distinguish it, but his fondness for slang, drama, and graphic description are already clearly evident. The first round was relatively uneventful, but in the second, "the *claret* was perceived to issue first from the mouth of Cribb," and in the third, "the right eye of Cribb was almost *darkened*." But Cribb rallied, and in round six gave Molyneaux "so severe a blow in the body with his right hand, that it . . . appeared to *roll him up*." This time it was Molyneaux who fought back, but in round nine Cribb hit him so hard that he broke Molyneaux's jaw. Round ten: "The *Moor*, still *game*, made a desperate though unsuccessful effort." Round eleven: it was over. With "his senses having been completely *milled* out of him," Molyneaux received a "*floorer*," and Cribb was awarded the victory.[33] The fight had lasted less than twenty minutes. Members of the Fancy, though, were able to relive it—and indeed every other major bout of the Regency—over and over again in Egan's enormously popular and increasingly florid accounts.

V

Sporting events triggered often rampant betting. Lord Frederick Beauclerk claimed to make six hundred guineas a year wagering on cricket, while in 1811 two unnamed noblemen bet five hundred guineas each on a cricket match between two female sides, one from Hampshire and the other from Surrey. Boxing fanatics raucously weighed up the odds given on a prizefight, and then gambled on how long the bout would last, who would draw first blood, which man would triumph, and so on. Sometimes fans rushed the ring when the favorite found himself in trouble, and those who had backed him panicked at the thought of the money they were on the verge of losing. Punters flocked to the bookmakers and the turf to bet on the horses. Once the races were run, it was usually possible to settle up at the track, or at Tattersall's on what became known as "Black Monday." In 1816, the racing results from Epsom were reported to have caused no less than £300,000 to change hands at Tattersall's. Starting around 1813, Beau Brummell was a constant winner at the track, but then his luck turned, and by May 1816 he was financially ruined. The situation was even worse for Roger Brograve, a former captain in the 2nd Dragoons, who committed suicide in June 1813 after losing a large sum on the horses.[34]

Gambling's grip on the Regency extended far beyond sports, though, and is perhaps best revealed by the extent to which people were ready to wager on virtually anything. There were impromptu eating competitions. Could one man consume "nine pounds of bullock's heart roasted, three pounds of potatoes, half a quartern loaf, and drink a pot of porter" in forty-five minutes? There were trials of strength and stamina. Could one man "run a coach-wheel the dis-

THIS SKETCH by Thomas Rowlandson is of the cricket match that was held at Ball's Pond, Newington, in October 1811, and that featured two all-women sides.

tance of 30 miles in six hours"? Could one corpulent man walk half
a mile in less time than it would take a rival "to eat, without drinking, 24 red herrings, and two ounces of mustard"? There were wagers
involving the time it took to build or make something. In June 1811,
a gentleman bet one thousand guineas that he could have a coat completed in a single day, from the process of shearing the sheep through
to the tailor presenting the finished product. The gentleman won,
taking the coat from the judge in the early evening and then delight-
ing an assembled crowd of more than five thousand spectators by
wearing it before them.[35]

Dice and cards were a mania. For centuries, gambling on them had
been a vice associated primarily with the aristocracy, and while successive eighteenth-century governments had passed legislation that
sought to bring the practice under control, these efforts seem only to
have made matters worse by driving the games behind closed doors
or down into the criminal underground. In the Regency, patrician
gamblers played faster and looser than ever before with the family
money and, much more dangerously, the family property. Gaming,
too, ensnared many men much further down the social scale—in
part because of the lax system of credit, which allowed the Bank of
England, as well as the provincial banks, to print their own banknotes
and to loan money at very favorable rates to anyone who could exhibit
the veneer of respectability. This included leisured beaux, minor
nobility, jobbing professionals, bored ecclesiastics, and rash militiamen like George Wickham in Austen's *Pride and Prejudice* (1813), who
undoubtedly took advantage of the easily available credit to run up his
considerable gaming debts. Even people at the lowest ends of the economic order took avidly to gambling. "The *flue-faker* [chimney sweep]
will drop his *bender* [sixpence] with as much *pluck* as the *honourable*
does his *fifty*," Egan reported. The "spirit is quite the same."[36]

Three ritzy West End clubs dominated the gambling landscape.
The oldest, White's, had an elected membership in 1814 of 500 and
was loosely affiliated with the Tories. In addition to whist, the card
game that ruled the club, its famous betting book contained wagers
between members on anything from birth and marriage dates to
domestic politics and the unfolding events of the Napoleonic wars:

"Mr. Brummell bets Mr. Irby one hundred guineas to ten that Bona-parte returns to Paris (Decr 12th 1812)." Brooks's, a second and only slightly less fashionable club, was allied with the Whigs, had like White's an exclusive membership, and was known for dice games such as hazard (the forerunner of craps) and card games like faro and macao (a variant on *vingt-et-un*). Watier's, on the east corner of Bolton Street, was the greatest of the gambling clubs. The Regent (at the time still Prince of Wales) had impetuously suggested its found-ing when—after listening to guests at his dinner table complain about the bad food at White's and Brooks's—he rang for one of his personal chefs, Jean Baptiste Watier, and asked him if he would like to start a club. Macao reigned supreme at Watier's, but play there was much more reckless than at the other two establishments, and in 1819 it was forced to close after only twelve years in business, a high-profile casu-alty of an appetite for gaming that too often knew no limits.[37]

Byron, though not an avid gambler himself, understood why so many men of fashion and rank stooped hour upon hour, sometimes day upon day, over the green baize tables of the clubs: "women— wine—fame—the table—even Ambition—*sate* now & then—but every turn of the card—& cast of the dice—keeps the Gambler alive." Those who suffered heavy losses routinely had to seek the assistance of moneylenders like Howard and Gibbs, or of bankers such as Thomas Coutts, a man well known to the bet-loving Regent. Predictably, disagreements between club members, especially at the end of grueling, alcohol-fueled sessions, were one of the lead-ing causes of duels in the Regency. In 1819, the social and political diarist Charles Greville sounded a strikingly modern note when he explained how gambling was taking over his existence. "Amusement is the last object I have in view in playing," he confessed. "Play is a detestable occupation; it absorbs all our thoughts and renders us unfit for everything else in life. It is hurtful to the mind and destroys the better feelings."[38]

Beyond the main establishments, the more adventurous of the wellborn visited the nearby gaming "hells," where they gambled with the same rapacity, but where they were far more likely to lose money, especially if they were novices. At White's and Brooks's, there were committees of management, aboveboard policies on fair play, strict rules on admission, and traditional codes of honor that set exacting standards for gentlemanly behavior. The owners of the hells, by contrast, sought to give their establishments the look of comfort or even luxuriousness in order to tempt the wealthy, but the play at their tables was much more corrupt, and their clientele a far less exclusive mixture that included the ambitious, the cunning, the desperate, and the volatile. An 1817 pamphlet, *The Pigeons*, concisely summarized the range of what the hells had to offer. Behind the red door on Bennet Street was what was called "a topping house," where "all things are in a very high style." Mrs. Leach's, at 6 King Street, was a "snug and quiet shop," and the name of the proprietor "singularly appropriate." A *rouge et noir* table distinguished 77 St. James's Street, though many of its customers complained about the churlish attitude of the house toward winners. George Smith was one of the proprietors at 77 Jermyn Street, where there was a notoriously crooked hazard table. Half a dozen other hells were located close by, to say nothing of the seedier dens in Lisle Street, Panton Street, and Covent Garden, or of all the more informal gaming that took place in taverns, prisons, schools, coffeehouses, rural fairs, military camps, and private parties.[39]

VI

Though many elites enjoyed entertainments where the working masses could also go, more often they separated themselves out. Like their ancestors, they did much of their entertaining on their country estates, where large parties often came to stay for weeks on end, the gentlemen hunting and playing cards and billiards, while the ladies embroidered, sketched, visited, and played the harp or pianoforte. In the spring, though, these patricians decamped to their mansions in London, where they spent the next three or four months engaged in "the season," a social whirl of events that helped them stave off boredom and that included fêtes, dinners, masquerades, charity balls, major horse races, the sitting of Parliament, the latest theater productions, and endless matchmaking and backbiting. They called on one another. They drove round in their handsome carriages. They walked and rode in Hyde Park.

Wednesday nights at Almack's were a "must." The most exclusive of the Regency fashionable venues, it was presided over, not by men as in the other main West End clubs, but by several "patronesses," including the Ladies Jersey, Cowper, Sefton, and Castlereagh, as well as Countess Lieven (who was married to the Russian ambassador) and Princess Esterhazy (who was married to the Austrian ambassador). These women, strikingly different from one another in temperament and ability, came together to exert enormous influence on the aristocratic marriage market and on Regency high society more generally, including "*great* COMMANDERS, *great* STATESMEN, *great* COURTIERS, and . . . men possessing GREAT talents." Under their direction, an evening at Almack's involved, not gambling, drinking, and eating, but socializing, dancing, and display. A nod or smile from the right person could mean many new opportunities. The opposite was also true. A famous Regency snub or "cut" presaged ostracism and public disgrace, and hit the "poor *cuttee*" with the "*severity* of a paralytic stroke."[40]

There were strict rules. Only those women and men whom the patronesses had approved were eligible to buy annual, nontransferable tickets, and anyone who misbehaved was unceremoniously removed from the membership list. Latecomers were imperiously turned away at the door, while an exacting dress code meant that men had to wear knee breeches, a white cravat, and a *chapeau bras* (a flat, three-cornered silk hat often carried under the arm). When Wellington arrived one evening dressed in black trousers, he was told that he could not be admitted, "whereupon the Duke, who had a great respect for orders and regulations, quietly walked away." There was room at Almack's, nonetheless, for innovation and excitement. For decades, reels and country dances had featured at British balls and assemblies, but at some point around 1815 the fashionables at Almack's began to waltz. The introduction of the new dance was decried by many as a scandalously promiscuous foreign import that allowed far too much physical intimacy between partners (all that swirling and clutching), but its acceptance at Almack's ensured that it became the rage in polite and less-polished social circles across the country.[41]

Regency elites also shopped with a vengeance. It was Hatchett's for new vehicles; Tattersall's for carriage horses; Manton's or Beckwith's for guns; Papworth's for interior design; Foxall and Fryer for cabinets; Storr's for silverware; Chappell's for musical instruments; Gunter's for elegant catering; Berry Brothers and Rudd's for wine and spirits; Fribourg and Treyer's for snuff and tobacco; Weston's, or Schweitzer and Davidson's, for men's fashions; Mrs. Bean's or Mrs. Triaud's for women's fashions; Hoby's for boots; Lock's for hats; Rowland's for hair and beauty products; Rundell, Bridge, and Rundell's for jewelry and precious stones. The Burlington Arcade, a single, straight, top-lit walkway, opened in the spring of 1819 and revolutionized shopping, turning it into an opportunity to promenade and admire in a kind of magical urban space of consumption in which fashionables were protected from the weather and the bustle of large crowds, as well as from thieves and indecorous behavior, for liveried beadles enforced a strict code of conduct. The original "exclusive" shopping mall, the Arcade's seventy-two small shops displayed the wares of upmarket milliners, hosiers, glovers, drapers, shoemakers, case-makers, gold- and silversmiths, tobacconists, engravers, florists, and umbrella and cane merchants.[42]

Consumerism was not confined to the titled classes, though. Many among the nouveau riche sought to emulate their betters. "It is curious," Maria Edgeworth remarked in April 1813, "to see rich manufacturers growing into fine people with pictures and gildings and mirrors and democratic principles and aristocratic tastes!" Indeed, according to Robert Southey, shopping was a favorite diversion even among those with only very moderate levels of disposable income. "Luxury," he observed, ". . . fills every head with caprice, from the servant-maid to the peeress." The highborn of course splurged in the glamorous stores of the West End, but there was a good deal of "opulence and splendour" in other, far less fashionable areas of London, such as Cheapside, where buyers, window-shopping aspirants, and committed bargain hunters could find "drapers, stationers, confectioners, pastry-cooks, seal-cutters, silver-smiths, book-sellers, print-sellers, hosiers, fruiterers, china-sellers,—one close to another, without intermission, a shop to every house, street after street, and mile after mile."[43]

The first craze for a novelty item belongs to the Regency and marks a new stage in the unstoppable ascent of modern consumer culture. Around 1816, the Scottish physicist David Brewster invented the kaleidoscope, which he patented in 1817 and sold as a toy. Brewster's model was constructed using an expensive brass tube and plate-glass reflectors, but cheap imitations were almost instantly available and flew off the shelves, as the vast rank and file of shoppers demonstrated that for the first time they possessed enough buying power to create a new market almost overnight. "Had I managed my patent rightly, I would have made one hundred thousand pounds by it!" Brewster exclaimed in May 1818. "Infants are seen carrying them in their hands, the coachmen on their boxes are busy using them, and thousands of poor people make their bread by making and selling them."[44] Our society's addiction to consumption—to buying *stuff*—took hold in the Regency.

VII

The pursuit of excitement and diversion did not end there. Vauxhall, London's leading pleasure garden, offered a slightly illicit allure, in addition to a spacious rotunda, tree-lined walkways, elaborate illuminations, orchestras and regimental bands, singers and dancers, waterfalls and fireworks, and some well-known if reviled refreshments, including ham shavings, burnt wine, and arrack punch. At Astley's Royal Amphitheatre, audiences packed into the boxes and seats surrounding its large sawdust circus ring to watch swashbuckling equestrian extravaganzas, as well as harlequins, acrobats, magicians, strongmen, tightrope-walkers, sword-swallowers, fire-eaters, and ropedancers. Troupes of Indian jugglers took Regency London by storm, attracting Austen to one of their shows and astonishing Hazlitt. "Is it then a trifling power we see at work, or is it not something next to miraculous?" he asked, after watching one of the jugglers keep four brass balls in the air at the same time.[45] Portable box theaters on sticks known as "peep shows" or "raree-shows" were among the most popular street entertainments, and exhibited puppets, rarities, and pictures, louche in some instances, but more commonly elegant or patriotic.

Leading holiday destinations included the seaside resort of Margate in Kent, which Londoners reached by taking a hoy (a small ship) down the Thames, and which gave them the chance to breathe some fresh air. Margate appealed to the genteel and the upwardly mobile, but even fun seekers on much lower rungs of the social ladder could afford to make the trip, creating plenty of social awkwardness as the rich and poor, the high and low, the sick and sound all jostled onboard together. "The passage in the Margate-hoy, which, like the grave, levels all distinctions, is frequently so replete with whim, incident, and character, that it may be considered as a dramatic entertainment on the stage of the ocean," wrote John Feltham in his 1815 *Guide to all the Watering and Sea-Bathing Places.*[46] In Margate itself, though, the emphasis was on refinement and relaxation, and options for holiday-makers included fine hotels, beautiful walks, a theater, bathing rooms and machines, commodious shops, day trips to nearby resorts, and elegant assembly rooms.

Fairs drew large crowds and were the most exuberant form of mass entertainment. They were inexpensive, ran sometimes for days on end, and were full of diversions for women, men, and children alike. In the provinces, they were tied to the church calendar and attracted everyone from prostitutes, strolling players, and wounded veterans to poachers, counterfeiters, and vagrants. Drinking, dancing, and eating were central to these celebrations, as were games that tolerated gender reversals, and mock elections that overturned traditional hierarchies by elevating a shearer and a milkmaid into m'lord and m'lady for a day. In London, meanwhile, impromptu Frost Fairs had been held for centuries on the Thames every time it froze solidly enough for people to walk on it, and the last of these occurred in the bitterly cold winter of 1814 (after which demolitions and reconstructions along the riverbank improved the flow of the water and prevented it from freezing over). Immense crowds swarmed onto the ice that year, tired of the cold and ready to enjoy themselves. A pathway that ran from Blackfriars Bridge to London Bridge was dubbed "The City Road," and soon on either side of it there were tradesmen selling books, toys,

THIS SCENE of revelry at the 1814 Frost Fair on the Thames is based on a drawing by Luke Clennell. Young and old enjoy themselves. There is music, food, drink, shelter, and plenty to buy and do.

and trinkets, printers issuing souvenir tickets to commemorate the event, singers and musicians performing on makeshift stages, tents for food, drink, and gambling, and several amusements designed specifically for children. Bartholomew Fair in Smithfield was the premier summer fair in London. Founded in the twelfth century as a meat and cloth market, it later became much better known as a boisterous entertainment center that featured acrobats, pugilists, wrestlers, singers, musicians, actors, puppets, ropedancers, and much else. In the Regency, it remained "the City carnival—the delight of apprentices, the abomination of their masters—the solace of maid servants, the dread of their mistresses—the encouragement of thieves, the terror of the constables," as the *Gentleman's Magazine* reported in 1817.[47]

No fair in the Regency, however, surpassed the extravagance and debauchery of the Great Fair, which began on August 1, 1814. Organized to celebrate both the peace following the exile of Napoleon to Elba and, coincidently, the hundredth anniversary of the accession of the House of Hanover to the English throne, it was open to all and featured different events held in Hyde Park, Green Park, and St. James's Park. Tens of thousands of people reveled on what turned out to be a beautiful summer day, wandering between the different locations and an endless series of booths, stages, and marquees, sampling, shouting, shopping, drinking, marveling, gossiping, gambling, and eating as they went. Highlights of the day included a balloon ascent by James Sadler, a reenactment on the Serpentine River of Admiral Nelson's brilliant victory over the French at the Battle of the Nile exactly sixteen years earlier, and a dazzling fireworks display. Best of all, spectators gazed in amazement as a towering Gothic building called the "Castle of Discord" vanished in a blaze of cannon smoke and then magically reemerged as the brilliantly illuminated "Temple of Concord," a revolving classical building with a central dome, and a symbol of the peace that had finally come to Britain. It marked the close of the first day, but not of the Great Fair, which rioted on for almost two weeks despite the attempts of the home secretary, Viscount Sidmouth, to shut it down. Charles Lamb was one of many Londoners who appreciated Sidmouth's efforts. "The whole surface of Hyde Park is dry crumbling sand," he wrote to Wordsworth on August 9. Booths and drinking places "go all round it," and "the stench of liquors, *bad* tobacco, dirty people and provisions, conquers the air."[48]

VIII

Food accompanied most entertainments, but it could also be one all on its own. In the best houses, it was served on a gargantuan scale. Dining at a rich man's table with just one other person, Harriet, Countess Granville was served "soup, fish, fricassee of chicken, cutlets, venison, veal, hare, vegetables of all kinds, tart, melon, pineapple, grapes, peaches, [and] nectarines." Rees Howell Gronow vividly recollected the meals at larger gatherings, where "mulligatawny and turtle soups were the first dishes placed before you; a little lower, the eye met with the familiar salmon at one end of the table, and the turbot, surrounded by smelts, at the other. The first course was sure to be followed by a saddle of mutton or a piece of roast beef; and then you could take your oath that fowls, tongue, and ham, would as assuredly succeed as darkness after day." Dessert favorites included trifles, custards, cakes, and biscuits, as well as gingerbread, plum pudding, candied fruits, and ice creams in an extraordinary range of flavors.[49]

The Regency was a hard-drinking age, and convivial evenings at every social level were heated by sometimes astonishing amounts of alcohol. It was wines (chiefly port, sherry, hock, claret, and Burgundy) among the upper orders, whiskey in Ireland and the Scottish Highlands, cider in the agricultural districts, grog (rum cut with water) for sailors, and gin among the lower urban classes, where slack licensing laws and a proliferation of hole-in-the-wall establishments made it possible to drink around the clock. In this, as in a great deal else, the Regent led the way, quaffing so much booze during one all-nighter in 1814 that he almost died of alcohol poisoning ("he was literally dead drunk," Greville reported), while among the privileged classes there were many four-, five-, and even six-bottle men, the number indicating how many bottles of wine the individual could consume at one sitting. At fashionable gatherings, "a perpetual thirst seemed to come over people, both men and women, as soon as they had tasted their soup," Gronow asserted; "as from that moment everybody was taking wine with everybody else till the close of the dinner; and such wine as produced that class of cordiality which frequently wanders into stupefaction." Fashionable young men who styled themselves "Corinthians" or "bucks" stayed up all night "drinking, swearing, and singing," before being sent home "in a hackney-coach, senseless, speechless, and motionless." Edmund Kean founded the Wolves Club for professional men of the theater, and while ostensibly devoted to philanthropic causes, its meetings quickly degenerated into drunken orgies. Poorer members of the Fancy established the Daffy Club, which sought to promote the sport of boxing, and which met in a number of different London pubs to knock back endless glasses of "White Wine, Old Tom, Max, Blue Ruin, a Flash of Lightning, Jacky, Stark

Naked, and Fuller's Earth"—all of which were "flash" terms for gin. According to the Duke of Wellington, men enlisted in the British army "from having got bastard children—some for minor offences— many for more drink."[50]

Wit was nowhere more in demand than at fashionable dinner parties. In England, "the agreeable man gets more reputation, more eating, and more drinking, in return for his talk than anywhere else," observed Lord John Russell in 1820. Much of this humor belongs to the "you had to be there" moment and has long since gone stale, especially when read on the printed page, but at its finest it still reveals the kind of intellectual agility and esprit so highly prized by Regency men-about-town. Byron thought Scrope Berdmore Davies "one of the cleverest men I ever knew in Conversation." Beau Brummell once bought a grammar book to help him learn French, and when Davies was asked what progress his friend had made in his studies, he replied that Brummell "had been stopped like Bonaparte in Russia by the *Elements*." Walter Scott praised Henry Luttrell as "the great London wit." When Thomas Moore commented on the dark complexion of a former hatmaker named Sharpe, as though "the dye of his old trade . . . had got engrained into his face," Luttrell responded, "Yes . . . Darkness that may be *felt*." The poet Samuel Rogers was among many who especially relished the wit of the bon vivant clergyman Sydney Smith. "Whenever the conversation is getting dull, he throws in some touch which makes it rebound, and rise again as light as ever," Rogers recollected. Of Luttrell, Smith declared: "[His] idea of heaven is eating *pâté de foie* to the sound of trumpets." Of his friend Mrs. Grote when she entered the drawing room wearing an enormous, rose-colored turban: "Now I know the meaning of the word grotesque." To that same Mrs. Grote: "Go where you will, do what you please, I have the most perfect confidence in your *indiscretion*." Smith could be scholarly: when he heard two women shouting at each other across an alleyway, he observed that they would never agree, for they were "arguing from different premises." He could also be crude: if the name of his friend Miss Alcock was translated into Latin, it would be "*Domina omnis penis*."[51]

Fittingly, the most famous dinner party in English literary history took place in the Regency. On Sunday, December 28, 1817, Benjamin Robert Haydon hosted a get-together at his home at 22 Lisson Grove in London. The party began at three o'clock in the afternoon, and Haydon's intention in organizing it was to bring together Wordsworth and Keats, as well as to give them, Charles Lamb, and a few other guests the opportunity to see his new painting, *Christ's Entry into Jerusalem*, which Haydon had already been working on for more than three years and which eventually featured the heads of Wordsworth and Keats in the crowd. Conversation at dinner sparkled. "Wordsworth was in fine and powerful cue," Haydon recorded. "We had a glorious set to on Homer, Shakespeare, Milton, & Virgil. Lamb got excessively merry and witty." Once the formal part of the meal was over, two more visitors arrived, an officious deputy comptroller at the Stamp Office, John Kingston, and a young doctor named Joseph Ritchie, who was about to travel to Africa in search of the source of the Niger. Lamb delivered the best line of the night. Well into his cups, and apparently not paying attention to the after-dinner conversation, he had fallen asleep, but he suddenly opened his eyes and, with the dangerous African expedition of Ritchie in mind, turned to the company and asked quizzically, "Pray, who is the Gentleman we are going *to lose*?" Haydon sat down to his diary as soon as his guests had gone home and found there was "no describing this scene adequately." Wine, Lamb's wit, Keats's "rich fancy," and Wordsworth's recitations, set against the backdrop of his own towering picture of *Christ's Entry*, had made this an "Immortal Dinner," the name by which the gathering is now known. "How one ought to treasure such evenings," Haydon added later, "when life gives us so few of them."[52]

IX

"An extensive knowledge is needful to thinking people," Keats declared in 1818; "—it takes away the heat and fever; and helps, by widening speculation, to ease the Burden of the Mystery."[53] Keats's desire to debate, explore, and apprehend was shared by many of his Regency contemporaries, who—like the Regent himself—were involved in both a headlong pursuit of excess, laughter, and consumption and an equally serious-minded commitment to refinement, learning, and beauty. In these social circles, it was commonplace to spend the afternoon viewing art, artifacts, antiquities, and curiosities, before devoting the evening and early morning to dissipations.

Londoners like Keats, Lamb, and Haydon were spoiled for choice. Robert Barker's Panorama in Leicester Square was a kind of forerunner to the modern movie theater and featured a series of huge cylindrical canvases that offered the illusion of looking at real cityscapes, landscapes, and battle scenes. Stephen Polito's—and then Edward Cross's—Menagerie was housed at Exeter Change in the Strand, where it was possible to see tigers, lions, monkeys, a sloth, and a five-ton elephant named Chunee, whose behavior was so good when Byron visited that he said he wished Chunee was his butler. William Bullock, a consummate showman, stuffed the Egyptian Hall in Piccadilly with "upwards of Fifteen Thousand Natural and Foreign Curiosities, Antiquities, and Productions of the Fine Arts," and outdid himself in 1816 when he staged an immensely popular exhibition of Napoleonic memorabilia that included the emperor's magnificent bulletproof carriage, complete with a folding camp bed and a traveling case of nearly one hundred pieces, most of them solid gold. More than 10,000 people a day flooded the exhibition, and when Bullock took the show on the road he did equally well, attracting across England, Scotland, and Ireland upwards of 800,000 people, for "old and young, rich and poor, clergy and laity, all ages, sexes, and conditions" were eager to examine "the spoils of the dead lion."[54]

Art galleries reached a new cultural prominence, extending their hold on noble patrons and attracting the upwardly mobile in ever-increasing numbers. During the Regency, the annual exhibitions of the Royal Academy and the British Institution featured paintings by an extraordinary collection of living artists, including John Constable, Edwin Landseer, Thomas Lawrence, Samuel Palmer, Henry Raeburn, J. M. W. Turner, Benjamin West, and David Wilkie. And this is to say nothing of the work exhibited in these same shows by three of the finest British sculptors: Francis Leggatt Chantrey, John Flaxman, and Joseph Nollekens. Tellingly, it was during the Regency that the

THIS PORTRAIT of the master embroiderer, Mary Linwood, was engraved in 1806 by Peltro W. Tomkins, after an unknown artist.

Dulwich Picture Gallery, the earliest public art gallery in England, opened with a small but excellent collection housed in a beautiful, top-lit building designed by John Soane.

The British art establishment usually managed to keep female artists on the margins of public recognition at best, or out of the picture entirely at worst. Mary Linwood was a remarkable exception. An artist in needlework, she specialized in producing full-length imitations of the paintings of past masters using both materials specifically designed for her (such as wools dyed to her requirements) and a series of innovative techniques, including stitches of varying lengths that looked like brushstrokes. Linwood established her own gallery in Leicester Square, where she displayed between sixty and seventy of her finest pieces. It was, according to *The Picture of London* for 1813, "undoubtedly the most unique and most interesting exhibition in the metropolis." Joseph Ballard visited two years later and was even more impressed: "Miss Linwood's gallery of needlework is perhaps the most extraordinary exhibition in the world."[55]

There were also private galleries, as wealthy or civic-minded patrons opened their homes to the public. The Marquess of Stafford and George O'Brien Wyndham, third Earl of Egremont, had magnificent collections of paintings, as did the insurance broker J. J. Angerstein and the banker Alexander Baring. At Lincoln's Inn Fields, John Soane steadily converted his home into a museum, which (then as now) was open to the public and ingeniously displayed all manner of models, drawings, prints, paintings, and antiquities. At 3 Soho Square, Richard Payne Knight housed his superb collection of coins, cameos, and small bronzes in a purpose-built gallery, while at 32 Soho Square Sir Joseph Banks painstakingly assembled a natural history museum where he welcomed all serious naturalists. Thomas Hope exhibited his exquisite collection of paintings, sculptures, and, especially, classical vases in both his London mansion in Duchess Street and his country house in Surrey. At Fonthill Abbey in Wiltshire, William Beckford collected on a scale that beggars belief: old masters, antique glass, furniture, precious and semi-precious stones, lacquer, statuary, ceramics, and much else. Walter Scott made

Abbotsford, his home on the banks of the River Tweed, a shrine to Scottish culture and history.

Public lecture series reached unprecedented levels of popularity. In many instances, they were delivered by the foremost authorities of the day, and arranged by learned societies like the Royal Institution where, for a subscription, members could gather to enjoy fine dining, the library, and the newsroom, in addition to the guest speaker. John Flaxman lectured on sculpture, John Soane on architecture, Charles Babbage on astronomy, John Dalton on chemistry, and William Lawrence on comparative anatomy. Byron and Lamb heard Coleridge lecture on Shakespeare and Milton in 1811, and Wordsworth was in attendance the following year when Coleridge was again at the rostrum, this time to speak on European drama. The *New Monthly Magazine* applauded J. M. W. Turner for his 1816 Royal Academy lectures on perspective, but damned the vulgar manner and coarse Cockney accent with which he delivered them. "Mathematics, he perpetually calls 'mithematics,' spheroids, 'spearides,' and 'haiving,' 'towaards,' and such like examples of vitiated cacophony are perpetually at war with his excellencies." Hazlitt gave lectures on the English poets before full houses that included Godwin, Moore, Keats, Turner, Soane, and Mary Russell Mitford, who declared that "Hazlitt . . . on modern poetry was amusing past all description to everybody but the parties concerned—them to be sure he spared as little as a mower spares the flowers in a hayfield." Added Mitford: "I never so thoroughly thanked heaven for the double blessing of being nobody and being a woman as at this lecture."[56]

X

The novel was at the heart of Regency culture, as well-established formulas reached ever-expanding audiences, while strikingly new levels of intensity and subtlety elevated its status and cleared the way for an understanding of it as the most important literary form of the modern world. For decades, prose fiction had been sneered at as unworthy of the kind of critical respect accorded both to other literary genres such as drama and poetry and to other prose forms like devotional tracts and scholarly essays. Eighteenth-century novelists like Samuel Richardson, best known for *Pamela* (1740) and *Clarissa* (1747–48), and Oliver Goldsmith, celebrated for *The Vicar of Wakefield* (1766), were significant exceptions to the rule, but by the beginning of the nineteenth century fiction was widely regarded as a shamelessly commercial assault on time-honored classical culture, and a particularly bad influence on the young, in whom it fostered immoral and rebellious desires. Worse still, women were the main consumers of novels, and they had easy access to them, for while priced high enough to be considered luxury items, novels could be borrowed at very reasonable rates from lending or "circulating" libraries, which had sprung up all over the country from the mid-eighteenth century onward and which catered to a female clientele by stocking items such as stationery, perfume, and jewelry in addition to a plentiful supply of popular books.[57]

The Minerva Press was the leading publisher of what we would now call "trashy" fiction, and it specialized in the bulk sale of cheap volumes that offered various combinations of the sentimental, the sensational, and the gothic, all wrapped around a highly predictable plotline in which young lovers of unequal rank must overcome several social and economic obstacles, and in which the woman in particular is driven through a series of picturesque landscapes and harrowing adventures before being reunited with her suitor and achieving the happy ending that has for so long been in jeopardy. Women wrote the vast majority of these novels, and in the Regency they were led by authors such as Emma Parker, Maria Roche, and Ann Julia Hatton, a younger sister of Sarah Siddons, who produced a steady stream of novels with trendy titles such as *Conviction, or, She is Innocent!* (1814), *Secret Avengers* (1815), *Secrets in Every Mansion* (1818), and *Cesario Rosalba* (1819). Elizabeth Meeke, the stepsister of Frances Burney, was as popular as Hatton and generated novels at an ever faster rate, including *Stratagems Defeated* (1811), *Matrimony, the Height of Bliss, or, The Extreme of Misery* (1812), *Conscience* (1814), *The Spanish Campaign* (1815), and *The Veiled Protectress, or, The Mysterious Mother* (1819). The teenage Thomas Macaulay became one of Meeke's biggest fans, though he considered her novels "incurably vulgar," and he agreed with his sister that they were all the same, "turning on the fortunes of some young man in a very low rank of life who eventually proves to be the son of a Duke."[58]

Regency prose writers, however, were also involved in a thorough-going reassessment of the novel and introduced fresh approaches and highly innovative techniques that steadily transformed the range and complexity of even its most derivative traditions. The Irish clergyman Charles Robert Maturin revitalized many of the tired conventions of the gothic novel in *Melmoth the Wanderer* (1820), which features a Faustian pact and an interlinking series of tales within tales, and which elaborates on the terrors of incarceration, insanity, persecution, and hopelessness, all at new levels of poetic intensity. The "evangelical" novel—the most important literary manifestation of the wider evangelical revival that began in Britain in the latter decades of the eighteenth century and that emphasized pious improvement and middle-class respectability—reached the height of its influence in the Regency, as seen in leading examples such as Mary Brunton's *Self-Control* (1811) and *Discipline* (1814), both of which brought a greater degree of psychological complexity, geographical specificity, and moral seriousness to the novel. *Glenarvon* (1816) by Lady Caroline Lamb (no relation to Charles and Mary Lamb), and *Florence Macarthy* (1818) by Sydney Owenson, Lady Morgan, count among the earliest of the so-called "Silver Fork" novels, which were written by elites for elites about elites but also held immense appeal for parvenus and determined social climbers who desperately wanted insider knowledge of highlife in all its elegance and emptiness.[59]

Jane Austen was both an astute critic and a brilliant writer of novels, and—as in many other instances—she was well ahead of her time in her recognition of the power of the form, especially in the hands of her favorite practitioners, such as Richardson and Burney. Revealingly, this clergyman's daughter found the religiosity of the "evangelical" novels off-putting, and she dismissed Brunton's *Self-Control* as "an excellently-meant, elegantly-written Work, without anything of Nature or Probability in it." Much more to her taste was Eaton Stannard Barrett's epistolary novel *The Heroine* (1813), a pastiche of sentimental and gothic fiction that diverted her "exceedingly." Indeed, in her brief, manuscript satire, "Plan of a Novel," Austen herself takes aim at the notion of what characters and plots are supposed to be like. "Heroine a faultless Character herself," she remarks, her tongue lodged firmly in her cheek, "—perfectly good, with much tenderness & sentiment, & not the least Wit." Elsewhere, Austen is more to the point on her "ideas of Novels & Heroines": "pictures of perfection . . . make me sick & wicked."[60]

On one level, Austen is not nearly as subversive as these comments make her sound. Her six published novels are broadly similar and

CASSANDRA AUSTEN produced this pencil and watercolor sketch of her younger sister Jane Austen. It is the only reasonably certain portrait from life of the novelist's face.

in many ways conventional, even predictable. All six are poised and tightly constructed comedies of manners that trace a young woman's errant but ultimately successful journey to self-discovery. All six center on a plot of unexceptional, apparently trivial, events in the lives of " 3 or 4 Families in a Country Village," with courtship as the foremost interest and marriage as the highest ambition. Austen herself made very limited claims for her artistry. Though she knew directly of the war and revolution that swirled around her, especially from the firsthand reports that came to her from her two brothers in the British navy, she described herself when writing novels as toiling on a "little bit (two Inches wide) of Ivory . . . with so fine a Brush, as produces little effect after much labour." Austen's novels can now seem to encapsulate a world of beauty and decorum that is far removed from the much more sordid realities of today, but what many contemporary readers found most remarkable about them was their ordinariness, as Walter Scott was at pains to point out in his famous *Quarterly* review of *Emma*. Austen, he asserted, wrote a new kind of novel, one that eschewed improbable mysteries and imaginary adventures, and that was characterized instead by "the art of copying from nature as she really exists in the common walks of life."[61]

Yet just beneath the domestic comedy and romantic love that shimmer across the surface of all six novels, Austen explores disturbing questions—especially concerning the fate of women—with an arch and amiable irony that only partially conceals an unflinching moral anger.[62] Men in her novels are in short supply, for tens of thousands of them are away on the Continent fighting in the Napoleonic wars, and those who are in Britain and eligible to marry have plenty to occupy them, as they command, spend, travel, and carouse. Women, in the meantime, wait and hope, and hope and wait, their shadowy lives only becoming more substantial and coherent when a man enters or returns. Spinsterhood haunts many of Austen's women, as do the very real threats posed by loss of reputation, abandonment, poorly paid employment, and poverty—to say nothing of the small number of years they have to attract a partner before they are deemed too old and forced onto the shelf by younger rivals. Better than anyone else either before or since, Austen wrote novels that combine romance with satire, and wish fulfillment with social realism. There are enormous depths within her narrow domestic settings, and rebellious passions within characters that are governed by polite restraint. Austen knew that our biggest hopes sometimes rest on the smallest events, and that tragedy can be played out not just on a national stage or a foreign battlefield but also in a drawing-room conversation or on a country walk.

Darcy's first proposal to Elizabeth in *Pride and Prejudice* is the most famous moment in Austen's most famous novel and a superb example of the way in which she blended passionately felt private emotion with much larger political and cultural concerns in order to drive the novel in dramatically new directions. Darcy fell in love with Elizabeth, not at first but at second sight, and his relationship with her to this point has been full of slights and misunderstandings. But when he proposes to her, he is entirely confident of success, and what he says to her is, at least in his own mind, very romantic. Yes, he knows he should not be making this proposal. Her situation in life is so far below his own as to be a degradation to him, while her family is an acute embarrassment, from her crass mother down to her vacuous younger sisters. Yet how deeply gratifying it must be for her to learn that he cannot help himself. His love for her is overwhelming. It has swept aside all his reservations. He wants her to become his wife. This is the gist of what he says to her.[63]

The comeuppance she gives him in response is unforgettable, though part of what gives the scene such energy is the fact that both of them seem to be in the right. Darcy can hardly be expected to rejoice in the thought of uniting himself to the vulgarity and indolence of the Bennet family, but Elizabeth is understandably repulsed at the idea of marrying into his family, given both his arrogant presumption and that of his aunt, Lady Catherine de Bourgh, who is—from much higher up the social ladder—perhaps even more tasteless and scheming than Elizabeth's mother. Darcy's acknowledgment of his role in separating Elizabeth's sister Jane from his friend Bingley further upsets Elizabeth, and she is unimpressed by his ironic observation that, in terms of marrying into the Bennet family, he has been kinder to Bingley in warning him away than he has been to himself in pursuing his suit. Elizabeth also blames Darcy for his supposed mistreatment of George Wickham, which she genuinely believes shows him to be a vindictive man, though it is clear that in the dispute between the two former friends, she sides with Wickham because he flattered her when they first met, whereas Darcy was inexcusably rude. Elizabeth's rejection stuns Darcy. No one has ever spoken to him like that. Yet it also reveals how thoroughly he engages her. Firm, tactful refusal would have been enough, as it was when she declined an earlier offer of marriage from the fatuous clergyman Mr. Collins. But the exchange between Elizabeth and Darcy becomes heated because he attracts her, and she is trying to get through to him, to make him see the extent to which he has misunderstood both her and himself. Darcy botches the proposal, but he matters enormously to Elizabeth, even as she furiously protests otherwise.

There are as well much bigger issues at stake in Elizabeth's rejection of one of the most eligible men in Regency England (and all of literature). In the eighteenth-century novel, class usually constitutes an unquestioned given. That ends with Austen, who in *Pride and Prejudice* serves notice that traditional notions of aristocratic privilege are now up for debate and open to scrutiny. Darcy has an adamantine belief in his own status as an English "gentleman," and he has all the trappings of wealth and social position to prove it. His problem is that he has fallen in love with a woman who simply does not accept that land, money, and rank equal respectability or that because of them he is entitled to think of himself as her superior. When she tells him that she might have felt more concern in refusing his proposal had he "behaved in a more gentleman-like manner," those words literally stagger him.[64] They signal a powerful collision between his elitist assumptions and her bourgeois aspirations. Darcy believes that he was *born* a gentleman. Elizabeth hopes that someday he might *become* one. She makes it disarmingly plain, though, that "gentleman" is a title he needs to earn, not one that he can simply inherit. Ultimately, of course, Elizabeth marries him and becomes part of the privileged clique that she had previously deplored. But in *Pride and Prejudice* she also ushers in the modern world, for she believes in meritocracy over aristocracy, individual preference over dynastic alliance, and female desire over male presumption. Elizabeth is Darcy's future, and ours.

XI

"I have made up my mind to like no Novels really, but Miss Edge-worth's, Yours & my own," Austen wrote to her niece Anna, an aspiring novelist.[65] Austen's admiration for Maria Edgeworth was widely shared. A member of the Protestant Ascendancy, Edgeworth was born in Oxfordshire but spent the vast majority of her long life on the family estate in County Longford in Ireland, where she pursued her fascination with the rural economy and with the dialects, manners, and humor of the Irish peasantry. Well established by the advent of the Regency as a novelist, educationalist, and author of children's stories, she consolidated her reputation with novels such as *The Absentee* (1812), *Patronage* (1814), and *Ormond* (1817).

A pervasive commitment to pedagogy meant that Edgeworth was determined to use fiction as a means of moral instruction, with the result that didacticism often burdened her plots and characterizations, though this same quality was singled out for praise in several contemporary reviews. It distinguished her novels from the many run-of-the-mill publications in the gothic and the sentimental traditions, and it imbued them with a "more serious importance than much of the true history and solemn philosophy that comes daily under our inspection," as Francis Jeffrey observed in the *Edinburgh Review* for 1812. At a time when the standard print run for a novel was 1,000 copies, Edgeworth's *Patronage* reportedly sold 8,000 copies on the first day of publication alone.[66]

Her greatest achievement was the founding of the so-called "regional" novel. Beginning with *Castle Rackrent* in 1800, she presented "the most accurate and yet the most diversified views that have ever been drawn of a national character," as the Irishman John Wilson Croker declared in the *Quarterly Review* for 1812.[67] Her finest novel, *The Absentee*, was clearly designed to draw the attention of her English readers to the plight of contemporary Ireland, and it concerned the economic and social havoc wreaked when Protestant landowners abandoned their Irish estates and moved to England. The novel opens in London, where two absentees—the dissolute Lord

Clonbrony and his ambitious, Anglophilic wife Lady Clonbrony—are recklessly draining the coffers of their Irish property in order to fund a fashionable lifestyle that she wants much more than he does and that far outstrips what they are able to afford. After learning of their various embarrassments, the Clonbronys' Cambridge-educated son Lord Colambre travels incognito to the family estate in Ireland, where he witnesses firsthand the duplicity of his father's land agents and comes to appreciate the good sense and openhearted decency of the Irish tenantry. In the end, the Clonbronys return to Ireland, embracing their role as members of the Protestant Ascendency and seeking to restore the fortunes of their estate. It is a conclusion in which Edgeworth gestures toward a reconciliation between the Irish and the Anglo-Irish, even as she raises much darker issues concerning colonialism, nostalgia, history, and race. The outlines of the Irish "Troubles" in the late twentieth century are clearly visible in *The Absentee*.

Walter Scott, like Edgeworth, rose to fame in the decade before the Regency, and across it he continued to make important contributions as a poet, editor, and reviewer. Far and away his greatest impact, though, came as a novelist, where—for all the innovations and achievements of other Regency novelists—it is no exaggeration to say that Scott changed virtually everything, from the compass and complexity of the novel to the immense increase in esteem with which it was regarded by the reading public. *Waverley*, his first novel, was, according to his own account, begun in 1805 and conceived by him as an attempt to represent the people and customs of his native Scotland with the same vitality that his friend Maria Edgeworth had achieved for Ireland. His early work on the novel, however, was unsuccessful, and after only six chapters he abandoned, and then lost, the manuscript, only to rediscover it in the autumn of 1813 when he was hunting around in his lumber garret for fishing tackle (or so he claimed).[68] With characteristic alacrity, Scott completed the rest of the first volume within a matter of weeks, and the other two volumes within a matter of months. Archibald Constable, his Edinburgh publisher, issued *Waverley; or, 'Tis Sixty Years Since* on July 7, 1814. Scott did not put his name to it—as was customary at the time—though in his case (and many others) his authorship was soon an open secret.

Waverley is widely regarded as the first "historical" novel, and it launched a worldwide craze for historical fiction. In it, Scott tells the compelling story of the 1745–46 Jacobite rebellion, a military uprising that began in Scotland under the leadership of Charles Edward Stuart (variously known as "Bonnie Prince Charlie," or "The Young Pretender," or "The Chevalier") and that was the last major effort of the Catholic Stuarts to remove the Protestant Hanoverians from the British throne. The novel's vacillating hero, the aptly named Edward Waverley, is raised in part by his Hanoverian father, Richard Waverley, but spends much of his secluded youth reading romances on the English estate of Sir Everard Waverley, his Jacobite uncle. As a young man, Waverley obtains a commission in the Hanoverian army and heads north to Dundee in the Scottish Lowlands, where the pace of the novel picks up considerably, and Scott begins to display his

THIS PORTRAIT of Walter Scott was engraved by W. and D. Lizars, after the 1808 painting by Henry Raeburn.

flair for dialogue and dialect, unforgettable minor characters, and the dramatic and picturesque details that bring historical events to life. Shortly after arriving in Dundee, Waverley takes leave to visit his uncle's Jacobite friend Lord Bradwardine at his Perthshire estate, where he also meets Bradwardine's daughter Rose.

Events, however, soon conspire to draw him even farther north and into the company of the Highland chieftain Fergus Mac-Ivor and his sister Flora, both of whom were educated in France at the court of the exiled Chevalier, and both of whom are fiercely committed Jacobites. Intoxicated by the life of the Highlanders, so much more vigorous than anything he had known in England and so much closer to the chivalric worlds of war and love that he had read about as a boy, Waverley soon falls in love with Flora and aligns himself ever more decisively with Fergus and the Jacobite cause. When a letter arrives from his Hanoverian regiment informing him that he will soon be considered absent without leave, Waverley abandons his commission in pique, oblivious to the dangers of the company he has been keeping, and to the ways in which he is being manipulated by the charismatic Fergus. After a meeting at Holyrood Palace in Edinburgh with Bonnie Prince Charlie himself—one of the many times that Scott in his novels uses a fictional character like Waverley to bring vividly into view the aspirations of a historical figure like Charles Edward Stuart—Waverley becomes radicalized, donning with Mac-Ivor and Bradwardine the emblematic white cockade (a ribbon or rosette worn in a hat) of the Jacobites and taking up arms against the British redcoats.

At Prestonpans outside Edinburgh, the rebels are victorious in the first important conflict of the uprising, but Waverley's loyalties are already in question—as seen especially when he saves a brave English officer, Colonel Talbot, who draws Waverley's sympathies despite being unknown to him, and who without Waverley's timely intervention faced certain death at the hands of the Jacobites. Flushed by their success, the insurgents rashly press down into England as far as the Midlands, but there is burgeoning dissension in their ranks, while the brutalities of hand-to-hand combat divest Waverley of his romantic illusions about the Highlanders and the Stuart dynasty, and force upon him the realization that the world is far more complicated than the single-minded fantasies of his youth had allowed. As the rebel army turns around at Derby and retreats back up to Scotland, Waverley is separated from Mac-Ivor during a skirmish and eventually takes refuge in a farmhouse, before setting off for London and a reunion with Colonel Talbot, who—despite the Hanoverian blood on Waverley's hands—is able to secure him a pardon. Shortly thereafter, reports reach Waverley of the horrendous conclusion of the Jacobite rebellion, when British forces slaughter the badly outnumbered Highlanders in the Battle of Culloden. At Carlisle, where Mac-Ivor has been imprisoned, Waverley is unable to prevent his execution, or the impaling of his head over the Scottish gate in the town wall, but later he succeeds in securing both the restitution of Bradwardine's property and Rose's hand in marriage. Waverley emerges from these events remarkably unscathed. He has compromised himself, to be sure, but he has also helped to effect enduring and beneficial compromises. His pragmatic reconciliation of Jacobitical and Hanoverian allegiances presages his future happiness with Rose and, more searchingly, the stability and prosperity of Regency Britain, a modern, revitalized country that has exorcised some of its bloodiest historical demons, and that has succeeded at last in peacefully uniting the kingdoms of Scotland and England.

With its romance, its action-packed historical sweep, and its confidently reassuring pro-Union politics, *Waverley* captivated readers, women and men alike. "The unexpected newness of the thing . . . struck us with an electric shock of delight," declared the Edinburgh advocate Henry Cockburn. The Edgeworths—like many Regency families—read aloud to one another in the evening, and when *Waverley* appeared they sat together as it seized hold of them. "I wish the author could have witnessed the impression it made," Edgeworth wrote directly to Scott. "We were . . . possessed with the belief that the whole story and every character in it was real." Austen did not want the competition of *Waverley* in the same year as she published *Mansfield Park*, but she too fell under the spell of the so-called "Wizard of the North." "Walter Scott has no business to write novels, especially good ones," she declared. "I do not like him, & do not mean to like Waverley if I can help it—but fear I must."[69]

It was just the beginning of what became the biggest publishing phenomenon of the Regency (and one of the biggest publishing phenomena ever). For having achieved great success with his first novel, which had the standard print run of 1,000 copies, Scott produced a torrent of others, now known collectively as the *Waverley* novels. *Guy Mannering*, followed by *The Antiquary* and *The Black Dwarf and the Tale of Old Mortality*, sold in ever-increasing numbers, and by the time *Rob Roy* and *The Heart of Mid-Lothian* appeared in 1818, the initial print runs had surged to 10,000 copies, and it was almost certainly the same number for *The Bride of Lammermoor* and *A Legend of the Wars of Montrose.*[70] Across broad and colorful canvasses, these novels centered—like *Waverley*—on Scottish history, and in various combinations they featured everything from dark heroes, brave women, and broken families, through lawyers, merchants, innkeepers, soldiers, fanatics, aristocrats, bailiffs, robbers, and servants, to fabulous landscapes, galloping horses, blazing hearths, drinking songs, battlefields, bagpipes, castles, abbeys, and prisons. After the humiliations of Culloden, these novels rehabilitated Scotland, promulgating an idea of the country that made it fashionable and romantic.

By 1819, however, Scott evidently felt it was time for a change, and in *Ivanhoe*, his final *Waverley* novel of the Regency, he began to mine English history as well, in an attempt to keep up with the voracious public demand for historical fiction that he himself had initiated. *Ivanhoe* was "received throughout England with a more clamorous delight than any of the *Scotch novels* had been," J. G. Lockhart reported. Even Scott himself was taken aback. "Are you not astonished at the success of these things?" he asked his literary agent John Ballantyne. "Egad— I am."[71] Bolstering his popularity still further was the immense entertainment industry that had sprung up around his production of the *Waverley* novels. Translations, redactions, imitations, and parodies rushed from the press; operas and plays based on the novels packed the theaters; and pictures of scenes from Scott filled the windows of printshops across the country, throughout Europe, and far beyond.

Three key factors lay behind this vast popularity. The first is that in *Waverley* and its successors, Scott made the novel respectable. He brought together the disparate and often denigrated techniques of contemporary fiction writing, and he turned them into a serious and expressive medium that melded romance with realism and that enabled him to reveal complex characters, localized settings, regional experiences, and long-forgotten lore. Book purchasers, library patrons, and reviewers who looked down on the novel at the beginning of the Regency looked up by its end to Scott as the writer who had shown the world that prose fiction, pushed through experimentation and renovation to the peaks of its potential, was the dignified equal of much older literary genres.

Scott's popularity was also directly linked to his appeal to male audiences. Following decades in which fiction was intimately associated with a female readership, Scott was the first to produce novels that gained wide acceptance from both women and men. Better than any other contemporary reader, Scott understood how much Austen and Edgeworth were achieving in their respective depictions of domestic and village life. But he also succeeded in supplanting them, in wresting the novel away from them—and from the many other Regency women writers who had adopted it for their own cultural purposes—in order to fix it firmly in the recognizably masculine realms of history, erudition, and adventure. Reading the *Waverley* novels was akin to the excitement of the hunt, declared John Scott, where men and animals are "all at full cry," the scenery is "fresh and invigorating," and "health and manliness are made to circulate through our frames." The satiric novelist Thomas Love Peacock declared in 1818 that Scott's novels were read, not by some or many, but by "all ranks and classes of men, from the peer to the peasant, and all orders and degrees of mind, from the philosopher to the man-milliner." As soon as a new *Waverley* novel was published, he added, "the scholar lays aside his Plato, the statesman suspends his calculations, the young lady deserts her hoop, the critic smiles as he trims his lamp . . . and the weary artisan resigns his sleep for the refreshment of the magic page."[72]

The final reason for Scott's unparalleled success was that, in a decade so often caught up in the turmoil of the present, his novels looked decisively to the past, though Scott's attitude toward that past was profoundly ambivalent. The *Waverley* novels celebrate the noble qualities of Scotland's history, and especially of the Jacobite clans—their courage, loyalty, integrity, and intense love of family, country, and tradition. Yet Scott was also acutely aware that there was a much darker side to the clans and that they belonged to a barbarous past of rooted bigotries and long-standing campaigns of murder, plunder, and persecution. The "secret of the success" of the *Waverley* novels, Hazlitt declared, was that "as we read, we throw aside the trammels of civilization" and "the wild beast resumes its sway within us."[73]

Scott's novels were enormously popular for more than just illuminating the past, however, for they also threw intense light on the present, though here again his attitudes were sharply divided. After the bloody Jacobite rebellion of 1745–46, thoroughgoing modernization had transformed Scotland into a commercial and industrial society that brought many benefits, from much greater safety and stability in areas that had long been untamed to new levels of cultural achievement in literature, architecture, art, education, scholarship, and publishing, including the development of the sophisticated reading audiences that were capable of appreciating, and had the disposable income to buy or borrow, the *Waverley* novels. Yet Scott was also deeply unnerved by the astonishingly rapid pace of these developments and the ways in which it had taken only a few decades to decimate a way of life in the Highlands that had been in existence for centuries. In the *Waverley* novels, he extols the past as a romantic place of valor, hospitality, and freedom even as he deplores the savagery of clan warfare. At the same time, he welcomes the present as a civilized society of commerce and technological advance while simultaneously lamenting the disorientating extent of the change and the much more prudent world it has introduced.

The clash of these complicated allegiances across the *Waverley* novels fascinated readers as they variously sought to come to terms with their own sense of nostalgia for a recent past that was already gone forever, and an ambivalent affinity for the modern world that promised more wealth and opportunity but that drastically reduced the possibility of imaginative feeling and heroic endeavor. Scott's detractors would later accuse him of inventing a version of his country's traditions and cultural identities based on his own political and imaginative loyalties rather than on historical fact and, worse, of launching a gaudy tourism industry of glossy brochures and spurious clan tartanry. Such criticisms both underestimate and misjudge Scott's achievement. In his writings, he moved Scotland beyond the violent political strife of its past, and gave it instead a repurposed set of symbols, myths, and memories around which to cohere. Deeply committed as he was both to the Union and to Scotland, he enabled his country to uphold the idea of nationhood while acknowledging that its future lay with England. His vision of Scotland as an independent cultural entity within a larger political structure has proven remarkably resilient and continues to exert a profound influence on modern debates about Scotland's place in Britain, Europe, and the world.

XII

"I awoke one morning and found myself famous," Byron declared following the hugely successful appearance on March 10, 1812, of the first two cantos of his poetic travelogue, *Childe Harold's Pilgrimage*. But Byron was not just famous. He was what we would call "a celebrity." There was no Siddonsomania, Keanomania, Cribbomania, or Scottomania. But there was what Byron's future wife Annabella Milbanke in 1812 labeled "Byromania." For centuries, authors and readers had connected in a variety of ways, from court culture and aristocratic patronage, through manuscript circulation and subscription publishing, to friendship networks, literary coteries, and political associations. *Childe Harold* signaled the passing of these traditional forms and the dynamic rise of celebrity culture, a new mode of literary and artistic exchange that was far more democratic, that capitalized on the advancing technologies in the publishing industry, and that involved collaborations between artists, entrepreneurs, and mass readerships. It was, moreover, a multinational and multimedia phenomenon that exploited the often unruly production of literary, visual, theatrical, and commercial representations, and that sought to exalt supremely talented individuals into secular divinities and to transform consumers into fans who bonded together in sometimes frenetic attachment to the object of their shared adoration.[74]

Byron was ideally suited to—and the partial creator of—this new commercial model of cultural exchange and production. He was young (twenty-four years old when *Childe Harold* was published) and very handsome. He was an aristocrat, with all the authority and allure that entailed, though his close alliance with the opposition Whig party meant that, in political terms, he was associated with defiance rather than power. He kept himself continually in the public eye by following up the dramatic success of *Childe Harold* with a string of verse tales, including *The Giaour* (1813), *The Bride of Abydos* (1813), *The Corsair* (1814), *Lara* (1814), and an additional two cantos of *Childe Harold* (1816, 1818), all of which sold in astonishing numbers. *The Corsair* went through nine editions and sold 25,000 copies in the first year alone. What is more, all of these poems featured a version of the proud, melancholic outcast who became known as "the Byronic hero," a character Byron derived from John Milton's portrait of Satan in *Paradise Lost*, as well as from the moody, isolated villains that populated the late eighteenth-century gothic novel. The Byronic hero mesmerized the public, not only because he "laid open darker recesses in the bosom than were previously supposed to exist," as Byron's friend and biographer John Galt observed, but because of the widely held belief that he was a spectacular self-projection of Byron himself—an impression that only grew stronger as Byron's personal life descended into chaos, and grim rumors of perversion and excess seemed to confirm that poet and poetic anti-hero were one and the same.[75]

This intense combination of moods, ideas, and postures overwhelmed his audience, as Byron united personal notoriety to much older and nobler notions of poetic fame, and steadily eroded the lines between creative genius and meretricious celebrity in order to fashion a public persona of unprecedented international appeal. He fixed the attention of male readers. During the Regency the preteen Alfred Tennyson was "an enormous admirer of Byron, so much so that I got a surfeit of him." Walter Scott, a good friend, noted Byron's "mysterious charm," which arose from "the sombre tone of his poetry, and the occasional melancholy of his deportment." For the Scottish memoirist Pryse Lockhart Gordon, Byron "looked the inspired poet," for he possessed "a beautiful, mild, and intelligent eye, fringed with long and dark lashes" and "an expansive and noble forehead, over which hung in thick clusters his rich dark natural curls." In America, the literary critic and novelist John Neal lauded *Childe Harold* as "full of deep philosophizing sadness." In Canada, the essayist James Irving found in Byron's poetry "a populous world of the human heart," for "there would be many Giaours, and Corsairs, and Laras, were the opportunity given." In Germany, the septuagenarian poet Johann Wolfgang von Goethe praised *Don Juan* (1819–24) as "a work of boundless genius."[76]

Female interest in Byron was even more intense. Teenage girls and young women besieged him with fan letters asking for his autograph, a signed copy of one of his books, a lock of his hair, or a place in his thoughts. His most hysterical fan, Lady Caroline Lamb, famously described him as "mad, bad, and dangerous to know," a phrase that enshrined his "bad boy" image and that succinctly captured his rakish appeal. Samuel Rogers knew "two old maids in Buckinghamshire who used to cry" over a particular passage in *Childe Harold*, while one sixty-five-year-old woman fainted when he came into the room. In the spring of 1816, following rampant gossip-mongering and widely publicized accounts of his notorious private life, Byron fled to the Continent, where he took up residence at the Villa Diodati on Lake Geneva, and where the mania continued, as well-wishers, groupies, and detractors gloried in his scandalous celebrity, waylaying him on his evening drives, and watching his house through telescopes from the opposite side of the lake. Byron, declared the Duchess of Devonshire after the publication of *Childe Harold*, "is really the only topic almost of every conversation—the men jealous of him, the women of each other." Almost a decade later, John Scott observed that Byron has "awakened, by literary exertion, a more intense interest in his person than ever before resulted from literature" and that he is "thought of a hundred times, in the breasts of young and old, men and women, for once that any other author is,—popular as are many of his living rivals."[77]

Byron was the first modern celebrity, however, not just because of his legions of far-flung and devoted readers. What elevated and dis-

tinguished him were the many ways in which his art and his image
were used by others in a flurry of different contexts that proliferated
far beyond his control. Everything he published was widely quoted,
imitated, transcribed, and parodied. His reputation as a handsome,
brooding, antisocial elite stands clearly behind Austen's portrait of
Darcy in *Pride and Prejudice*. Byron is the eponymous reprobate in
Lady Caroline Lamb's "kiss and tell" romance, *Glenarvon*; the cynical
"Maddalo" in Percy Shelley's poem "Julian and Maddalo: A Conversation," written in 1819; the self-pitying misanthrope "Mr. Cypress"
in Thomas Love Peacock's philosophical satire, *Nightmare Abbey*
(1818); and the bloodthirsty predator in John Polidori's tale of terror,
The Vampyre (1819). Further, Edmund Kean brought the Byronic hero
vigorously to life night after night in packed London and provincial
theaters with his portrayals of gloomy, energetic villains. Byron himself revealingly compared Kean to Conrad, the anti-hero in *The Corsair*: "There was a laughing Devil in his sneer, / That raised emotions
of both rage and fear." Many others saw a clear link between the leading poet and the leading actor. "How magnificent Kean's countenance
is!" exclaimed the Countess Granville. "Sometimes he looks like Lord
Byron." Most notably, prints, engravings, and souvenirs of scenes
from Byron's works filled shops, marketplaces, and malls, as did portraits of him, which were variously reproduced, altered, transformed,
and enhanced, and which were "sold in every town t[h]roughout the
Kingdom." Indeed, smirked J. G. Lockhart in 1821, images of Byron
were prized by his fans around the world, for "every boarding-school
in the empire still contains many devout believers in the amazing
misery of the black-haired, high-browed, blue-eyed, bare-throated,
Lord Byron. How melancholy you look in the prints!"[78]

The modern stereotype of the passionate, sexually charismatic,
died-too-young rebel is indebted primarily to Byron, who forged
it in dialogue with the broad fan base that responded so intensely

both to him and to his poetry. Enduring through the nineteenth century, Byronism reemerged in an especially powerful form in the mid-twentieth century, when it left a deep impression on youth and popular culture, as seen most clearly in the glamorous, smoldering anti-heroism of Marlon Brando, James Dean, and Elvis Presley, as well as a decade later both in the sneering, satanic flamboyance of self-destructive rock stars and in the striking number of ways in which Byromania anticipates Beatlemania. Confronted variously by ennui, ill-health, wartime atrocities, and economic injustices, Regency audiences flocked to entertainments and idolized entertainers as a means of escaping, however briefly, the wear and tear of their lives. In vast and often highly diverse social groups, they pursued stimulation and leisure in all its available forms, from theaters, sporting events, gambling halls, and boozy outdoor fairs, through fashionable clubs, holiday resorts, dinner parties, shopping centers, lecture halls, and art galleries, to the practice—both private and intensely social—of reading novels, in traditional as well as in much newer forms. Byron—as poet and pugilist, artist and showman, aristocrat and insurgent—was the brightest star of the Regency. More than any other figure in an age of great individual talent, he cast a complicated spell over his audiences both pre- and post-exile and set the stage for our ongoing fascination with personal notoriety, violent spectacle, creative genius, and celebrity culture.

CHAPTER THREE

Sexual Pastimes, Pleasures, and Perversities

I

In Jane Austen's *Pride and Prejudice*, all five Bennet sisters are under pressure to find a husband, but each has a different idea about how to interact with men and what constitutes proper female behavior. At one end of the spectrum is Mary, the middle daughter, who is devoted to the cult of chastity and who warns her sisters "that loss of virtue in a female is irretrievable—that one false step involves her in endless ruin." At the opposite end of the spectrum is Lydia, the youngest sister, who ignores all the injunctions to guard her reputation and who is a "most determined flirt." In between them is Elizabeth, the second eldest sister, who lifts up her eyes "in amazement" when Mary moralizes, but who is increasingly aware that Lydia needs to be contained. "She is lost forever," cries Elizabeth when she learns that Lydia has eloped with the predatory George Wickham, the consequences of which—as Mary had prophesized—come close to ruining Lydia, and by extension her sisters.[1]

Sexual censorship and oppression were commonplace across the Regency, as various political, legal, medical, and religious forces gathered momentum and sought to punish, deny, or thwart sexual gratification. These forces, however, were not enough to prevent—and indeed in some instances seem to have caused—a simultaneous outburst in passionate expressions of individual desire and erotic longing, as seen especially in the love stories of Jane Austen, the love poems of Percy Shelley, and the love letters of John Keats. Moralists and evangelicals who sought to inculcate higher levels of self-respect in women, and far more decorous codes of behavior in men, were particularly angered by the deep-rooted traditions of libertinism, which enjoyed its last great flourishing among the male and female rakes of the Regency and which prompted a host of different reactions, from the terror of John Polidori's *The Vampyre*, through the hedonism of Pierce Egan's *Life in London*, to the comedy of Byron's *Don Juan*. The same ravenous and defiant appetite for sexual pleasure also produced a booming trade in both prostitution and pornography.

As the Regency staged the fiercest collision between the eighteenth-century powers of rakery and the proto-Victorian forces of modesty and restraint, so too it witnessed both the highest peak of government-sanctioned, mob-based homophobic violence and the first sustained exploration of alternative sexual identities. Same-sex attraction took a striking number of different forms in the Regency, from romantic friendships between adolescent males to long-term relationships between female couples such as Lady Eleanor Butler and Sarah Ponsonby, who lived openly together in Wales and were widely known as the Ladies of Llangollen. Anne Lister detailed her extensive experience of same-sex love in a series of diaries, as did William Beckford in his private correspondence, while Jeremy Bentham defended homosexuality as harmless, especially when compared to the miseries too often visited upon women by heterosexual encounters. There was, too, a deep engagement with a series of other sexual topics and practices, from masturbation to flagellation, as well as with sexual deviancies such as necrophilia and incest, both of which are given disturbing expression in Mary Shelley's tale of terror, *Frankenstein* (1818).

II

Regency women were badly hemmed in. For centuries it had been assumed that women were far more libidinous than men, but in the middle decades of the eighteenth century the opposite conviction began to take hold. Women were regarded, not as lustful beings whose interest in sex could make them unmanageable, but as delicate, passive receptacles devoid of a libido and only interested in sex within the confines of marriage and for the God-ordained purpose of procreation. This dramatic volte-face in sexual attitudes was driven by a number of factors, but none more important than the emergence of female "conduct books" such as James Fordyce's *Sermons to Young Women* and John Gregory's *A Father's Legacy to his Daughters*, both of which were rooted in religious doctrine and both of which insisted that not only were women *naturally* elegant, chaste, and domestic, but that these virtues were the best way to secure a man's affection. The highly oppressive consequence of these strictures was that men and women came to occupy distinctly separate spheres, endlessly reinforced by a multiplicity of religious, legal, and social conventions. Men got a dynamic public world of politics, war, business, and adventure. Women got an airless private realm of purity and obedience in which their individual identities were submerged in their responsibilities as daughters, wives, and mothers.

In the Regency, the hectoring of Fordyce and Gregory could still be clearly heard (the former's *Sermons* reached a fourteenth edition in 1814), while a flurry of new publications variously recycled, stepped up, and diversified the conduct-book crusade against female agency and, especially, female sexuality. Mary Brunton gave the so-called "evangelical" novel its finest expression in her aptly titled *Self-Control*, where through "the power of the religious principle" the beleaguered heroine, Laura Montreville, is able to resist the temptations of a highly permissive society and to curb her own enduring sexual attraction to the man who betrayed her. Eaton Stannard Barrett based his best-selling poem "Woman" (1818) on the seven key self-denying virtues that defined appropriate female behavior and that allowed women to preside "over national morality": devotion, chastity, modesty, charity, good faith, forgiveness, and parental affection. Perhaps most revealingly, in 1818 Thomas Bowdler published his popular *Family Shakespeare*, a ten-volume edition in which he expurgated "whatever is unfit to be read aloud by a gentleman to a company of ladies" and in which he systematically targeted Shakespeare's sexual references, many of which "are of so indecent a nature, as to render it highly desirable that they should be erased."[2] Such editorial whitewashing was of course soon known notoriously as "bowdlerizing."

The women and men who belonged to these prudery brigades, and who raised their often clamorous voices on behalf of the dogmas of the separate spheres, made deep and sometimes salutary inroads into Regency culture. Their desire to effect social "improvement," and to inculcate moral "respectability," gradually transformed relations between the sexes, not only because they insisted that women behave with modesty and earnestness but also because, more urgently, they demanded greater civility from men, whose unbridled puerility and testosterone-fueled callousness had so frequently in the past gone without any sanction at all. Their initiatives were sometimes irrelevant, frivolous, or even irrational, but cumulatively they produced a burgeoning force of conservative reaction that claimed ever-widening circles of support and that soon brought the middle-class proprieties of the Victorian age clearly into view. Evangelicalism "is making way amongst us with increasing strength," declared Walter Scott in 1818, and one day, he predicted, it will "have its influence on the fate perhaps of nations."[3]

The strident sexual proprieties of the Regency did not prevent its authors from writing about sex, but they did force on them a series of strategies to ensure that they stayed within the bounds of respectability. Austen was the great master of the technique that used social constraint to heighten rather than reduce sexual tension. *Pride and Prejudice* is the finest love story of the era—perhaps of any era—and it continues to exert an enormous hold on the popular imagination, for to "fall in love" today still means in many ways to fall in love *like* Elizabeth and Darcy. Yet their story is very different from what we might expect. Austen does not describe them as caught up in heated embraces or secretive trysts in the manner of so many romances both before hers and since. Instead, she conveys their passion for each other in fleeting moments that fall well within the confines of correctness but that carry a sexual charge that is all the more potent for being intermittent and so understated. Like Darcy and Elizabeth themselves, Austen makes us wait, interpret, agonize, and wonder. Nonetheless, their sexual attraction to each other is clear when they stare across the room, or touch hands, or dance, or even verbally spar, and eventually it proves overwhelming, both to them and to us.

Other authors used code words to denote but not explicitly name sexual desire. Thus in the Regency there are large numbers of young women and men "swelling," "swooning," "panting," "blooming," "blushing," "burning," "glowing," "pouting," "throbbing," and "heaving." Thomas Moore specialized in this kind of titillation, as seen in particular in his Oriental epic *Lalla Rookh* (1817), which is full of veiled sexual references: "Every thing young, every thing fair / From East and West is blushing there." John Keats left less to the imagination in poems such as "The Eve of St. Agnes," where "young Porphyro, with heart on fire," steals up into the castle bedchamber of his beloved Madeline, watches unseen from the closet as she undresses and crawls into bed, and then appears before her "Ethereal, flush'd, and like a throbbing star." Percy Shelley went further still in several poems in which he produced evocative descriptions of the physical act of making love, as in "Alastor" (1816), where the poet dreams of a passionate encounter with a beautiful maid. "He reared his shuddering limbs and quelled / His gasping breath," Shelley enthuses: " . . . she drew back a while, / Then, yielding to the irresistible joy, / With frantic gesture and short breathless cry / Folded his frame in her dissolving arms." Passages such as this one led Keats's parson friend Benjamin Bailey to damn "that abominable principle of *Shelley's*—that *Sensual Love* is the principle of *things*," and to fret that Keats himself was too inclined to the same principle.[4]

Private letters contain some of the most impassioned thoughts of the Regency. The painter John Constable had to wait seven long years to marry Maria Bicknell, for her family would not consent to

IN 1816, Benjamin Robert Haydon drew this pen and brown-ink sketch of his friend John Keats. The inscription below the image reads, "Copied by B. R. Haydon from his original Sketch after Life."

the match until he had achieved a reasonable level of financial security. "I will submit to any thing you may command me—but cease to respect, to love and adore you I never can or will," he wrote to her in February 1816. In early June 1812, the forty-two-year-old William Wordsworth had been in London for several weeks and was missing Mary, his wife of nearly ten years, to the point where his body ached. "The fever of thought & longing & affection & desire is strengthening in me," he told her. "Last night I *suffered*; and this morning I tremble with sensations that almost overpower me." He was thinking of her all the time and urged her to "find the evidence of what is passing within me in *thy* heart . . . in thy own involuntary sighs & ejaculations, in the trembling of thy hands, in the tottering of thy knees, in the blessings which thy lips pronounce . . . and in the aching of thy bosom, and let a voice speak for me in every thing within thee & without thee."[5]

Keats is one of the great letter writers in the English language, and he wrote often and adoringly to his fiancée Fanny Brawne, although as tuberculosis tightened its death grip on him, he frequently collapsed into jealousy and despair. "A few more moments thought of you would uncrystallize and dissolve me," he wrote feverishly to the nineteen-year-old Fanny in August 1819. By the following summer he was even more emotional: "You are to me an object intensely desirable. . . . I cannot live without you, and not only you but *chaste you; virtuous you*." And five months later, as he lay dying in Rome, thoughts of her tormented him: "Every thing I have in my trunks that reminds me of her goes through me like a spear," he shuddered. "The silk lining she put in my travelling cap scalds my head. My imagination is horribly vivid about her." Why had he not made love to her? "I should have had her when I was in health," he snapped crudely.[6]

III

Unlike writers, royal and aristocratic rakes did not attempt to work within or around sexual strictures. They merely ignored them. To be sure, they needed to marry respectably, to sire a legitimate heir, and to behave with courtly refinement to ladies in salons or wives in domestic settings, and while many privately sneered at these obligations they nevertheless retained a deep social commitment to them. Once they had stepped outside polite circles and posturings, however, they frequently reveled in almost unfettered sexual freedom. According to the libertine creed, they were allowed—indeed entitled—to sow their wildest oats, and they proceeded to do so without guilt, guile, or the slightest intention of paying heed to the working-class radicals who despised them or the evangelical Christians who were working hard to raise the standards of male chivalry. "In the company of many of our fashionable women the greatest libertine need be under no restraint, except in guarding himself from the use of a few broad expressions," lamented one commentator in 1812.[7]

The Regency was the last great brazen huzzah for rakes before the sobering and much stricter mores of the Victorian age took at least some of the wind out of their sails. The Regent himself retained his deep weakness for women, and in 1812 Leigh Hunt launched his libelous assault on him as "a libertine" and "a despiser of domestic ties." The slovenly and often unwashed Charles Howard, eleventh Duke of Norfolk, married twice, fathered six children with his mistress, and took lovers "without delicacy and without number" right up until his death in 1815, aged sixty-nine. According to the *Scourge* magazine, George Hanger, soon-to-be fourth Baron Coleraine, remained at sixty-one years old a "Paragon of Debauchery" as well as the Regent's "*Confidential Friend.*" The Earl of Egremont, art patron and philanthropist, had eight children with his wife Elizabeth Ilive (seven of whom were born before their marriage and therefore illegitimate), four with Elizabeth Fox, and—allegedly—two (or possibly three) with Elizabeth Lamb, Viscountess Melbourne, leading the diarist Thomas Creevey to write of "my Lord's Seraglio." When a lady asked the Duke of Wellington if it was true that, following his victory at Waterloo, he had enjoyed the attention of many women, he replied briskly, "Oh yes! Plenty of that! Plenty of that!" Among the younger Regency men, Wellington's nephew, William Pole-Tylney-Long-Wellesley, the future fourth Earl of Mornington, was an irreclaimable womanizer, while Viscount Palmerston (nicknamed

"Cupid") fathered children with the married Lady Cowper, paid a regular allowance to a woman calling herself "Emma Murray," and in private diaries from 1818 and 1819 kept meticulous records of his sexual assignations ("visits"), referring to them as "fine days" and "fine nights" and occasionally adding a proud figure " 2," presumably as an indication of his virility.[8]

Perhaps the most notorious Regency dissolute, though, was Lord Yarmouth, later third Marquess of Hertford. William Makepeace Thackeray used him in *Vanity Fair* as the model for the malignant Marquess of Steyne, while Nicholas Suisse, Hertford's valet, left a scabrous account of what he saw and heard in his lordship's house-

RICHARD DIGHTON etched this 1818 portrait of Francis Charles Seymour-Conway, Lord Yarmouth, a notorious dissolute and a favorite of the Prince Regent's.

hold. In one case, asserts Suisse, the marquess supported "a lovely girl of about eighteen" named "Julia B——," who introduced him to her mother and then returned one evening from the opera to find the two of them "engaged in a most violent game at *all Fours*." On another occasion, Suisse claims he located a hiding place above the marquess's private pleasure dome—"the walls of which were entirely composed of looking-glass"—and then gazed down as the marquess took pleasure in the company of Angeline, Clara, and Henriette, whose "full-developed beauties" were "multiplied in endless succession in the mirrors which surrounded them."[9]

John Polidori put aristocratic libertinism at the heart of *The Vampyre*, which he composed as part of the same ghost-story competition that prompted Mary Shelley to create *Frankenstein* and which tells the story of the voracious Lord Ruthven and his consumption of beautiful young women. Traveling with Lord Byron in 1816 as his personal physician, Polidori gained firsthand knowledge of his employer's sexual practices: "As soon as he reached his room, Lord Byron fell like a thunderbolt upon the chambermaid."[10] In *The Vampyre*, Lord Byron is clearly the model for Lord Ruthven, as the two share wealth, good looks, mobility, callousness, high rank, and keen sexual appetites. Yet Ruthven is also unlike any other previous rake. He is immortal—apparently dying of a gunshot wound and then coming back to life—so that his sexual desires, as well as his opportunities to slake them, are unending. What is more, he is, not figuratively as in earlier representations, but *literally* a "lady-killer" who hunts down his victims and sucks their life away. In transforming the stock figure of the upper-class rake into the modern vampire, Polidori produces a potent male fantasy in which Ruthven penetrates and devours women without the constraints of guilt or even of time, and in doing so he exposes the vampire as both enthralling and appalling. Polidori took the libertine tradition to the level of myth and launched a vampire craze that still shows no signs of subsiding.

Pierce Egan moved further down the social scale in his hugely popular picaresque novel *Life in London*, but he too put libertinism at the core of a narrative that he suggestively subtitles *The Day and Night Scenes of Jerry Hawthorn, Esq. and his Elegant Friend Corinthian*

Tom, Accompanied by Bob Logic, the Oxonian, in their Rambles and Sprees through the Metropolis. George and Robert Cruikshank produced thirty-six plates that accompanied—and perhaps preceded—Egan's text, which like his *Boxiana* derives a great deal of linguistic verve from its use of fashionable slang terminology, and which is punctuated throughout by a cheerfully erratic use of *italics* and CAPITALS. It is commonly thought that the three creators of the book also serve as models for its three main characters, with George Cruikshank as Tom, Robert Cruikshank as Jerry, and Egan as Bob. All three men are womanizers, but Tom, a man-about-town who has only recently come into independent wealth, is more successful than his rustic protégé Jerry, and the tale moves effectively between his knowing presentation of urban delights and Jerry's less sophisticated responses to them, especially when they venture into the pleasure dens. Tom's "great . . . liberality of disposition" might perhaps "be attributed more to a defect in nature than any radical system of depravity," but "be that as it might, his character was not exempt from the term of a LIBERTINE."[11] In Egan's much more benign understanding of this word, however, Tom is represented, not as a hardened sensualist but as a healthy young man out on the boil with his friends looking for some fun, and the sexual hedonism he embraces is exciting and essentially warmhearted, both for him and for his partner(s).

In terms of social rank, Tom is a "Corinthian," a chic Regency designation that revealingly implies that he is both elegant and lewd, and that places him in the "highest order of swells," which in the "flash" vocabulary of the day signifies that he is "a gentleman" or "well-dressed person." "Corinthians" like Tom and his two friends reside comfortably in the middle tier of the social hierarchy, as the Cruikshank frontispiece makes plain. Above the three friends are the royal court, the "Noble," and the "Respectable," while below them dwell the "Mechanical," "The Tag, Rag & Bob tail," and "The Base." In the pursuit of pleasure, however, Tom and his friends easily and unashamedly cross over these class barriers, moving with remarkable fluidity along the social spectrum and united with both the "UPS" and the "DOWNS" by their shared interest in public enjoyment and sexual fulfillment.[12]

THIS IS the frontispiece created by Robert and George Cruikshank for Pierce Egan's *Life in London*. Within the strict social hierarchies of the Regency, Tom, Jerry, and Bob hover suggestively between the "Ups" and "Downs," and the "Ins" and "Outs."

Egan dramatizes this point most effectively by having the friends visit two clubs, fashionable Almack's in the West End and downtrodden All-Max in the East End. During their evening at the former, Jerry in particular relishes "the exquisite *beauty* of some of the female faces," "the *interesting* features of others," "the *diamond* eyes of many," and "the numerous lovely *busts*," and at one point he hopes to pursue his "fair incognita," the aptly named "LADY WANTON." But he is not free to do as he wishes. In the graceful and highly mannered world of Almack's, as Tom cautions him, "we must be on our P's and Q's," so that, far from discussing or following their sexual bents, the two spend much of their time monitoring each other's conversation to ensure that it remains free of vulgarity and on a tightly decorous track. Tellingly, their friend Bob does not accompany them to Almack's. He "does not like *etiquette*," Tom reports. "He is too fond of *fun*: he could not have carried on any *lark* here."[13]

When, however, the friends travel eastward to All-Max, not only is Bob their raucous partner, but Tom and Jerry are only too happy to throw off the straitjacket of Regency refinement in order to "slum it" among London's lower classes. All-Max is a dirty, gas-lit basement that attracts a "motley" group of patrons, including "lascars, blacks, jack tars, coal-heavers, dustmen, women of colour, old and young, and a sprinkling of the remnants of once fine girls." Freedom reigns, especially sexual freedom: "The parties *paired off* according to *fancy*; the eye was pleased in the choice, and nothing thought of about birth and distinction." Tom has his arm around the portly landlady. Jerry pours gin down the throat of a fiddler. Bob has the attention of two women, as "*Black* SALL" is perched on his right knee and "*Flashy* NANCE" on his left, surrounding him with "*Fields of Temptation*" to which he obligingly succumbs. Compared with the claustrophobically stylish respectabilities of the West End, Bob says to Tom, "the LOWER ORDERS of society . . . really ENJOY themselves."[14]

It is a highly romanticized version of libertinism in which Tom and his friends enjoy mobility, fraternity, and sexual adventurism, and in which their experience of "real life" offers readers—from the fashionable and the outwardly respectable down to the insecure and the isolated—a tantalizing view of what was on offer in London if they

ROBERT AND GEORGE Cruikshank produced these two illustrations for Pierce Egan's *Life in London*. In them, Tom and Jerry
run the gamut of what the city has to offer pleasure-seekers,
from "Highest Life" to "Lowest Life" in London.

knew how and where to look. But of course in order to achieve this utopia of sexual liberation, Egan has to leave out or minimize a great deal that is disturbing, or relegate his anxieties to footnotes in order to ensure that the trio in the main text enjoy their binges without the encumbrances of guilt or sorrow. Transgressing and exploiting social boundaries in the pursuit of sexual pleasures, for example, is a privileged one-way affair in *Life in London*. The haves are free to travel east, but the opposite is inconceivable. More distressingly, the potential for sexual savagery runs just beneath the surface of Tom's and Jerry's merriment, as Egan himself concedes when Bob points to a rich old lecher who is considered "the most *systematic* debauchee on the town" and who has "injured the peace of mind of *lots* of most interesting girls," though "he was never *injured* in his life." It would be "utterly impossible," Egan declares, to relate the manner in which "MARIA was *deceived*—BETSY *decoyed*—PAMELA *entreated*—AGNES *persuaded*—CHARLOTTE *inveigled*—LOUISA *cajoled*—NANCY *tricked*—FANNY *amused*—CAROLINE *played with*—POLLY *shuffled*—KITTY *cheated*—SUSAN *imposed upon*—JANE *hummed*—SALLY *deluded*—ELLEN *seduced*—LUCY *betrayed*—PEGGY *debauched*—SOPHIA *duped*—RACHEL *frightened*—and EMMA *coaxed*." [15]

By 1817, Austen had had enough of the many narratives in which a potent male seducer ensnares and then discards female quarry, and in her unfinished novel *Sanditon* she hit back with her portrait of the wannabe rakehell Sir Edward Denham, whose plans for sexual conquest are risible rather than menacing, and whose vacuous self-importance signals both the mounting moral contempt for libertines and the growing ability of women to assert their own preferences. "Sir Edward's great object in life was to be seductive," Austen reports. Indeed, "with such personal advantages as he knew himself to possess, and such talents as he did also give himself credit for, he regarded it as his duty.—He felt that he was formed to be a dangerous man." None of this matters to the elegant but impoverished Clara Brereton, however, as she sees through Sir Edward and has "not the least intention of being seduced." Earlier, in an 1814 letter to her niece Fanny on the subject of one of Fanny's admirers, Austen herself declared, "I am by no means convinced that we ought not all to be Evangelicals, & am at least persuaded that they who are so from Reason & Feeling, must be happiest & safest."[16]

IV

It was not just men. Rakery in the Regency also involved many women, who embarked on sexual careers every bit as enterprising as their male counterparts and who were often aided in their pursuits by their remarkably relaxed husbands. Contrary to the prevailing sexual doctrine of the separate spheres, libertinism held that "every woman is at heart a rake," enabling male profligates to claim—occasionally with justification—that the women they targeted were as hungry for sex as they were, and allowing female rakes to acknowledge that their sex drives were as strong and "natural" as men's, a liberating proposition, but one that in practice often promoted only an equally avid embrace of vulgarity and mean-spiritedness in both sexes.[17] At the same time, behind the Regency's breezy attitude toward promiscuity—it perhaps need hardly be said—lay a deep double standard that enabled men to emerge from their liaisons unscathed or even more widely admired while women were routinely punished for the same behavior, through either the loss of reputation, an unwanted pregnancy, or, worse, an illegitimate child that they loved but could not acknowledge as their own.

Infidelity in aristocratic circles was rife, and women were as active as men. Married at seventeen, Lady Melbourne went through slews of lovers and money but managed to hold on to her good name through adroit combinations of usefulness, charm, and discretion. Her son described her as "a remarkable woman, a devoted mother, an excellent wife—but not chaste, not chaste." Other equally reckless women were less able to parry scandal, or less interested in doing so. Jane Harley, Countess of Oxford, had children with so many different men that her brood became known as the "Harleian Miscellany," after her husband's library. Princess Esterhazy and Lady Cowper were, in Creevey's assessment, two of "the most notorious and profligate women in London." Byron was even harsher about Henrietta Frances Ponsonby, Countess of Bessborough, smearing her in 1820 as "the hack whore of the last half century." Lady Frances Wedderburn Webster could list Byron and Wellington "among her lovers," declared Thomas Moore in 1819, adding: "her manner to me very flattering & the eyes played off most skilfully—but this is evidently her habit—the fishing always going on, whether whales or sprats are to be caught."[18]

Lady Caroline Lamb was the most infamous woman of the Regency (though the Regent's estranged wife Princess Caroline might have challenged her for that title had she not gone into exile in 1814). The daughter of Lady Bessborough and daughter-in-law of Lady Melbourne, nineteen-year-old Lady Caroline married William Lamb, the future second Viscount Melbourne and the future prime minister, in June 1805, but the marriage was soon in trouble, and three difficult pregnancies in four years added to the strain. Charming, with large hazel eyes and hair cut in short golden curls, Lady Caroline met Lord Byron in the spring of 1812, and at the high point of their short affair, he thought her "the cleverest most agreeable, absurd, amiable, perplexing, dangerous fascinating little being that lives." But her near-complete disregard of social convention alarmed him, and Byron the roué took to lecturing her on "prudence," which is "tiresome enough but one *must* maintain it." In August she sent him a letter together with a clipping of her pubic hair. "I asked you not to send blood but yet do—because if it means love I like to have it," she told him. "—I cut the hair too close & bled much more than you need—do not you the same." By that point, however, his interest in her was waning, and even the intensity of her sex drive disturbed him: "you thought of others *even while with me*—of that I am sure," she later wrote to him, "—& the remembrance of that night and your accusation of wildness are disagreeable to me."[19]

Byron broke off their turbulent affair and in the autumn of 1812 moved on to the quieter attractions of the older and more voluptuous Lady Oxford, a situation that Lady Caroline essentially refused to accept. In early July 1813, she and Byron were both in attendance at a waltzing party thrown by Lady Heathcote, where Lamb made several attempts to attach herself to Byron and then seems to have tried to stab herself with (depending on the version) scissors, a dessert knife, or a broken jelly glass, "to the consternation of all the dowagers, and the pathetic admiration of every Miss, who witnessed or heard of the rapture," as John Galt put it. Two years later, following Waterloo, Lamb was in Brussels, continuing to flout convention and turn heads. Frances Burney saw her crossing the Place Royale "dressed, or, rather, *not* dressed, so as to excite universal attention, & authorize every boldness of staring from the General to the lowest soldier . . . for she had one shoulder, half her back, & all her throat & Neck, displayed." In 1816, Lamb published her gothic romance *Glenarvon*, which featured Byron as the eponymous villain and Lamb herself as the long-suffering Calantha. A *succès de scandale* that drove her from polite society and provoked her husband to initiate and then withdraw a legal separation, the novel rehearses in fictionalized terms the sexual tensions and libertinous desires at the core of her relationship with Byron. Demands Glenarvon of Calantha: "when passion is burning in every vein—when opportunity is kind—and when those who from the modesty of their sex ought to stand above us and force us from them, forget their dignity and sue and follow us, it is not in man's nature to resist. Is it in woman's?"[20]

For Claire Clairmont, the answer was no, and though on a much lower rung of the social ladder than Lamb, she too pursued an affair with Byron, and with equally disastrous results. Locked for nearly two years in an often fractious love triangle with Percy Shelley and her stepsister Mary Godwin (the future Mary Shelley), Clairmont decided in the spring of 1816 that there was more than one scandalous poet in the world, and that if her relationship with Shelley was permanently stalled, she would take the initiative and find another one. A tall and vivacious brunette with dark eyes and a beautiful singing voice, the seventeen-year-old Clairmont sat down and wrote to Byron. "An utter stranger takes the liberty of addressing you," she began tentatively, before moving on to confess "with a beating heart" that she had loved him for "many years."[21] Byron responded, the two agreed to meet, and Clairmont had sex with him on April 20, five days before he left England for good, and exactly one week before her eighteenth birthday.

It marked the start of a good deal of suffering for Clairmont, who nine months later in Bath gave birth to a daughter, Allegra, but who was often separated from her, to her great distress. When Byron received the news of Allegra's birth, he was indifferent. Of Clairmont, he shrugged, "I never loved nor pretended to love her—but a man is a man—& if a girl of eighteen comes prancing to you at all hours—there is but one way." Of the child, he asked with a sneer, "is the brat *mine*?" Clairmont later accused both Shelley and Byron of a particularly nasty form of hypocrisy in which they passed off their unrelenting desire for sexual conquest as a high-minded pursuit of "free love," a term that brought together the ideals of communal passion, nonpossessive interaction, and the collective sharing of bodies and minds. It sounded good in theory. In practice it was diabolical. "Under the influence of the doctrine and belief of free love I saw" Shelley and Byron "become monsters of lying, meanness cruelty and treachery," Clairmont asserted; "—under the influence of free love Lord B became a human tyger slaking his thirst for inflicting pain upon defenceless women who under the influence of free love ... loved him."[22]

Byron refused to take these claims seriously. More often than not, he declared, it was women who assailed him, not the other way around, as his involvement with both Lamb and Clairmont demonstrated. "I should like to know *who* has been carried off—except poor dear *me*," he protested in 1819. "—I have been more ravished myself than anybody since the Trojan war." What is more, his searching and often ironic understanding of the sexual appetites of both men and women thoroughly shaped his great comic epic *Don Juan*, one of the most important poems of the Regency as well as a remarkable compendium of its fascination with sexuality. "It may be bawdy—but is it not good English?—it may be profligate—but is it not *life*, is it not *the thing*?" Byron demanded jocularly of his boon companion Douglas Kinnaird in October 1819, following publication of the first two cantos. "Could any man have written it—who has not lived in the world?—and tooled in a post-chaise? in a hackney coach? in a Gon-

dola? against a wall? in a court carriage? in a vis a vis?—on a table?—
and under it?" The poem abounds with sexual longing: "Youth's hot
wishes in our red veins revel." It contains vulgar innuendo, sexual
slang, and lewd puns, together with accounts of "Philo-genitiveness"
(a "love of sex" and "a word quite after my own heart"). There are
scenes of nudity, seduction, premarital sex, extramarital sex, and rakery: "I saw the prettiest creature, fresh from Milan, / Which gave me
some sensations like a villain."[23]

Above all, Byron packs his poem with audaciously contradictory
references to female sexuality. Sometimes he mocks women, sometimes he seems to fear them. Sometimes men dominate women, but
much more often—lustful and in "juicy vigour" (rhymes with "men
much bigger")—they dominate the men. Sometimes Byron speaks
of women with great respect, as when they openly resist the ruling
separate-spheres ideology and insist on being themselves: "headlong,
headstrong, downright she, / Young, beautiful, and daring—who
would risk / A throne, the world, the universe, to be / Beloved in
her own way." Sometimes—the coldhearted actions of his private life
notwithstanding—he clearly sympathizes with women, as when they
are victimized by the same separate-spheres ideology. Most movingly,
the young and beautiful Donna Julia is trapped in a dead-end marriage with a much older (and philandering) husband, and in the letter that closes Canto I she compares her monochromatic existence
to the colorful world open to Don Juan. "Man's love is of his life a
thing apart, / 'Tis woman's whole existence," she tells him. Men have
many options and many resources at their disposal, women "but one,
/ To love again, and be again undone." Outrage—from friends and
enemies alike—greeted Byron's poem. He was unapologetic. For
more than one hundred and fifty years Milton's *Paradise Lost* had
been the most important epic poem in English. But the Christian
world it sought to justify, Byron knew, was unraveling. In *Don Juan*
he could see the consuming, desiring, sexual, secular modern world
coming clearly into view. "You have so many '*divine*' poems," he told
his publisher John Murray in April 1819, "is it nothing to have written
a *Human* one?"[24]

THIS PORTRAIT of Lord Byron was engraved by Henry Meyer in 1818, after the 1815 miniature by James Holmes.

V

Nothing reveals the vicious and competitive side of the Regency like its thriving trade in prostitution. In 1811, the novelist James Lawrence announced that within the last few years the total figure for London prostitutes had increased from "fifty . . . to seventy thousand: so that every eighth female that we meet in the streets is a prostitute." Two years later, Percy Shelley declared that prostitutes "formed one tenth of the population of London." In between these two dates, the silk merchant William Hale placed the number at 50,000, as in a separate account did the author of *Letters on Marriage*, Henry Thomas Kitchener, who added that there was "not a city or large town in the kingdom that does not abound with them."[25] Kitchener also broke down his London total. Of the 50,000 females working in the city as prostitutes, he conjectured, about 2,000 of them were well-educated; another 3,000 came from "the class composed of persons above the rank of menial servants"; a further 20,000 probably worked as servants at some point, or were "seduced in very early life," and now lived wholly by prostitution; and a final 25,000 lived partly by prostitution, laboring during the day as servants and shopgirls, or at trades such as silk manufactory, the straw-hat business, fruit selling, and slop-making (slops were cheap garments supplied to seamen), before going out in the evening in search of custom in the city's taverns, darkened lanes, and crowded pleasure grounds. Some of these women cohabited with laborers without matrimony. A number were married but separated, or had husbands fighting far away in the Napoleonic wars. Brothels housed thousands of sex workers. Others lived with their families. At this lower end, they were known as "flash mollishers." Many were horrifyingly young. "*Prostitution*," reported Egan, "is so profitable a business, and conducted so openly, that hundreds of persons keep houses of ill-fame, for the reception of girls not more than *twelve* and *thirteen* years of age."[26]

The preeminent center of the trade was Covent Garden, which in Keats's words contained "twenty thousand punks" ("whores"). But other main trafficking areas included the Haymarket in St. James's, as well as across the river in Southwark. To the north, in Smithfield, the men who worked in London's great stock market finished their day and then stopped into a convenient bordello, gin shop, or "house of resort" to take their pleasures. In the east lay the greatest dockland in the world, and into it sailed tens of thousands of men who had been without female companionship during their time at sea, and who wandered up the streets and alleys that led away from the river and into the bawdy houses of Shadwell, Limehouse, and the Ratcliffe Highway. In 1817, the Guardian Society reported that in just three London parishes there were " 360 brothels and 2,000 prostitutes, out of 9,925 houses and 59,050 inhabitants." "The City swarms with prostitutes, who now pick up men, in the most public streets . . . in the middle of the day," the *Anti-Jacobin Review* stated in 1816.[27]

For these girls and women, it was misery. The standard payment for services was one shilling, and it no doubt forced on them a wide variety of sexual practices. "I have good reason to believe . . . that the mouth is even sometimes prostituted to lustful purposes," Kitchener wrote in 1812. Occasionally, lone girls were preyed upon. A chambermaid might be confronted in the workplace and comply with a demand for sex rather than face the possibility of losing her job. Others—unemployed and hungry, out running an errand, standing in an entryway, huddled beneath a bridge—might be accosted by a man and agree to sex because the alternative was physical violence. More commonly, male and female "keepers" pimped them as part of a much larger sex-trafficking operation that kept the girls impoverished but brought their handlers a very comfortable livelihood. Egan maintained that there were "thousands of men" in London "who *exist* entirely on the *prostitution* of women." One witness called by the 1817 Select Committee on the State of the Police confirmed that a great deal—and in some cases the whole—of the money these sex workers earned was paid to "procuresses," who watched their girls closely, attending them on their daily and nightly walks, ensuring that they were drunk most of the time, and keeping an especially keen eye on the newer recruits in order to prevent the possibility of flight or reformation. If they did not bring home enough money, they were sent to bed without food and frequently beaten. Large numbers ended up homeless. Reported Joseph Ballard in April 1815: "Many of them have not where to lay their heads, and pass the night in the streets in any corner which will afford them a shelter."[28] Needless to say, sexual conquest in these circumstances was often not about physical pleasure but about the grimly misogynistic exercise of power over social inferiors.

There are numerous accounts of Regency men out whoring. The poet John Clare went to rural fairs, where "profligate companions" easily coaxed him into the "bad houses." The dandy Scrope Berdmore Davies had "intrigues with milliners who scratch his face and make him look unseemly." The politician John Cam Hobhouse regularly sought comfort in the arms of "ladies of the town," recording in his diary that he paid anywhere from the standard one shilling all the way up to "£1—5—." Benjamin Robert Haydon struggled routinely against sexual temptation, which one morning in April 1813 took the form of "an almost irresistible inclination to go down to Greenwich and have [a] delicious tumble with the Girls over the hills." On this occasion, he fancied "a fine creature in a sweet, fluttering, clean drapery, spotted with little flowers, a slight, delicate, muslin, white scarf crossed over her beating bosom, with health rising her shining cheeks, & love melting in her sparkling eyes, with a soft warm hand & bending form ready to leap into your arms, confiding & loving!"[29]

Byron took a frequently chilling view of sex workers. In Italy he spent a lot of time and money on "promiscuous concubinage," sleeping with hundreds of different women: "some of them are Countesses—& some of them Cobblers wives—some noble—some middling—some low—& all whores," as he himself summarized it in January 1819. On at least one occasion Lady Caroline Lamb pimped for him. Two girls—"Antoinette and Georgine"—were available. "The Father and Mother really hope you will hire one, but they say the younger one is the healthiest, and sweet and affectionate like nobody else," she informed him. "Please take one . . . and send back to me the one you don't want to keep." In another instance, Byron himself made the sexual recommendation. "*Try her*," he wrote to Kinnaird; "—you will find her a good one to go—and she is—or was uncommonly *firm* of *flesh*."[30]

Prostitution flourished in public places of entertainment and leisure, including playhouses, operas, circuses, and masquerades. In these lucrative and highly organized operations, girls who were "generally kept as dirty as *sweeps* all the day" were "decked out at night like *Duchesses*," a transformation that elevated them from lower-class mollishers into middle- and upper-class "Cyprians" or "Cythereans" (in evocation of the ancient worship of Venus, or "Cytheriea") or, most tellingly, "fashionable impures," an oxymoronic term that neatly encapsulated the way in which these girls were seen as both classical and debased—though there is of course in these titles an element of facetious contempt as well. On any given night, the young females were forced into rented wardrobes specifically designed to enhance their shape; painted to the nines; adorned with trinkets, muffs, plumes, flowers, and jewelry; and then sent out in groups. Once inside a theater, for example, they were trained to fan out, some into the auditorium itself and others into the lobbies, salons, and foyers, where they sent out "lures," such as leaning forward to flaunt their breasts, or lifting dresses that already concealed very little to expose still more naked flesh. For an appropriate tip, women selling fruit acted as go-betweens, carrying messages from the clients to the girls and back again. Crucial to any madam's success was her ability to keep up "her stock of beautiful females." Girls who turned solid profits were given "the pleasure and enjoyment of an elegant carriage, and livery servants to attend upon them to all the public places of resort."[31]

Harriette Wilson was the leading Cyprian of the Regency and worked almost exclusively in aristocratic circles, where she was well beyond the reach of grubbing madams and enjoyed a great deal of social, sexual, and financial independence. Born Harriette Dubouchet in Mayfair in 1786, she was one of fifteen children of an irascible Swiss watchmaker and his English wife, a silk-stocking mender who kept a shop in fashionable Queen Street. According to her own account, Harriette decided before she was ten years old that she was going "to live, free as air, from any restraint but that of my conscience," and in her early teens she would sit with her sisters in her mother's shop window and watch young elites saunter by, or flirt with them when they stopped in. Before long, two of her older sisters, Amy and Fanny, entered the upper echelons of the London sex trade, smoothing the way for Harriette. "I shall not say why and how I became, at the age of fifteen, the mistress of the Earl of Craven," she later wrote. "Whether it was love, or the severity of my father, the depravity of my own heart, or the winning arts of the noble lord . . . does not now much signify." Over the next twenty years many lovers followed, including the Marquis of Lorne ("without any exception, the highest-bred man in England"), the Marquis of Worcester, the Duke of Leinster, Henry Brougham, Viscount Palmerston, and the handsome, dissolute Lord Ponsonby ("A very god!" Harriette cried, and her *grande passion*).[32]

Prostitutes in the East End were social pariahs who were frequently faced with the choice between going hungry or selling one-time sexual encounters. Women such as Harriette lived very different lives. They too were outcasts, but they inhabited a world that was a remarkable mirror image of the fashionable one that banished them. They sold, not just sex, but relationships of amusement, ease, and even emotional intimacy, and their roles as "mistresses" were elaborately bound up in courtly notions of loyalty, discretion, wit, beauty, and style. They were decadent accessories, used to round out a young man's education in the arts of love, or to enhance an older man's reputation for wealth or virility. One admirer "insisted on falling in love" with Harriette "merely to prove himself a fashionable man." Another told her, "Nothing is asked, but whether Harriette Wilson approves of this or that? Harriette likes white waistcoats,—Harriette commends silk stockings."[33]

Successful courtesans enjoyed many of the same privileges as aristocratic wives, including a furnished home, a generous income, a lavish wardrobe, and a raft of servants. But they were able to circulate only in spaces that were either open to the public or exclusively male, and not at all in those designated for "respectable" ladies and "society" entertainments. Thus, they rode in carriages in Hyde Park, walked up to Marylebone Fields and Primrose Hill, strolled through the pleasure grounds at Vauxhall, flirted from boxes at the opera and the theater, and attended soirees and routs in private rooms or in gentlemen's clubs like White's and Watier's. According to several commentators, leading courtesans also hosted an annual "Cyprian's Ball," which, in the account of the journalist Charles Westmacott, was first held in the Argyle Rooms in 1818. The event drew "almost all the leading *roués* of the day . . . including many of the highest note in the peerage, court calendar, and army list," and it gave these men the opportunity to ogle, assess, reconnect, and police, while courtesans like Harriette, dressed extravagantly in the sheerest muslins and silks, with empire waists and plunging necklines, assiduously plied their trade. "The eye of love shot forth the electric flash which animates the heart of young desire, lip met lip, and the soft cheek of violet beauty pressed the stubble down of manliness," as Westmacott frothily puts it. "Then, while the snowy orbs of nature undisguised heaved like old ocean with a circling swell, the amorous lover palmed the melting fair."[34]

By the time she was seventeen Harriette had gone into business with her amiable sister Fanny and their well-connected friend Julia Johnstone, a niece of John Joshua Proby, first Earl of Carysfort, and the daughter of the Honourable Elizabeth Proby, a former lady-in-waiting to Queen Charlotte. Celebrated as "the Three Graces," they were high-spirited young women who shared accommodation, gossiped about lovers, came and went as they pleased, laughed uproariously, talked wickedly, and laced their chatter with quotations from Shakespeare. No wonder so many men fell passionately in love with them. Their disrepute brought them freedom, even if it was clear from the start that it all came at a price and would end far too soon. At the peak of her popularity, Harriette maintained that it would have been easy for her to have secured "not less than a dozen annuities" from men who had ended their relationship with her and who were anxious to obtain her cooperation and silence.[35]

She was not beautiful, but she was sexy. Slim-waisted with large, voluptuous breasts, and dressed in her trademark white muslin, she was nevertheless a "tom-boy" (her words) who was appropriately nicknamed "Harry" and who was energetically at home in masculine realms like the club, the track, the hunt, the regimental parade, and the officers' mess.[36] But this was not all. She loved sex: "no woman, ever felt le besoin d'aimer, with greater ardor than I." She loved fun: "Harriette had certainly a bewitching method of making any one jocund against their inclination," recalled Julia Johnstone. She was a competitor: when her younger sister Sophia became the fourth Dubouchet girl to work as a demimondaine, and then achieved a spectacular social coup by marrying her protector Thomas Noel Hill, second Baron Berwick of Attingham, Harriette avenged herself by taking the box directly above Sophia's at the opera and spitting down at her head. Most of all, Harriette had self-confidence. She demanded respect: "I will be the mere instrument of pleasure to no man." She wanted to give and receive affection. "I was made for love," she confessed. "Nothing but the whole heart of the man I loved, could settle me."[37] At such moments she comes close to sounding like a heroine in an Austen novel.

Like many Regency women, Harriette had intense sexual fantasies about Byron: "I . . . think of you as a *man*, brilliant, *capricious*, voluptuous, *mad*, ill-tempered and delicious—for a moment a poet, the next a *devil*, the next a God!!" Her most celebrated *amour*, however, was the Duke of Wellington, who was still Sir Arthur Wellesley when he was introduced to her in the months preceding his ill-fated marriage in April 1806, and who "sighed over me, and groaned over me by the hour," she claimed. Harriette was not as keen on him, perhaps because he later refused to pay her hush money to cover up the details of their relationship, a threat that prompted his famous—and probably apocryphal—riposte, "Publish and be damned." Exclaimed Harriette: Wellesley was "now my constant visitor:—a most unentertaining one, Heaven knows! and, in the evenings, when he wore his broad red ribbon, he looked very like a rat-catcher." Unforgivably worse, he was bad in bed: he "possessed no . . . merit, for home service, or ladies' uses," was how she tactfully put it. They parted in 1808 when he left for the Peninsula, but—at least in her version of events— they met again in Paris in the months following Waterloo, when he paid a visit to her rooms, called her "a little fool," and kissed her "by main force."[38] She was by this time, however, nearing thirty and no longer the much-sought-after celebrity she had once been. When the Regency ended, Harriette was in financial and emotional straits, largely worn out by rash spending and nearly two decades of living off her charm and her body.

Women made up the vast majority of sex workers in Regency Britain, but men were involved in the trade as well. According to one authority, women in the higher circles of society were in the habit of "hiring foreigners for footmen" in the hope that one of them would be a eunuch "who would be *always* ready to satisfy their impure desires." Another report claimed that a woman named Mary Wilson was the proprietor of the *"Eleusinian Institution,"* a London brothel catering solely to women of rank and fortune. Secrecy was assured because it was located "between two great thoroughfares" and could be entered from each "by means of shops, devoted entirely to such trades as are exclusively resorted to by ladies." From the outside the bagnio looked like "a most elegant temple," while on the inside there were large saloons surrounded by boudoirs, where female clients stood behind darkened windows and viewed the male "inmates": "in one they will see fine elegantly dressed young men, playing at cards, music, &c.—in others athletic men, wrestling or bathing, in a state of perfect nudity—in short they will see such a variety of the animal, that they cannot fail of suiting their inclinations." Once a woman decided on the man she wished to bed, she simply pointed him out to the chambermaid, and he was immediately brought to her. "She can enjoy him in the dark, or have a light, and keep on her mask. She can stay an hour or a night, and have one or a dozen men as she pleases."[39]

These levels of promiscuity, both within aristocratic circles and down the social hierarchies, had a variety of consequences, the most serious of which was the rampant spread of sexually transmitted diseases, especially gonorrhea (the "clap") and, more critically, syphilis (the "pox"). In 1813, one commentator estimated that as many as 20,000 men in London were infected each year, as few of the female sex workers were free of disease, and five years later Thomas Harrison Burder announced in the inaugural issue of the *Medico-Chirurgical Journal* that it was "well known that many unfortunate prostitutes, although unconscious of being diseased, have infected numbers who have had commerce with them." Byron had "a *Clap*" in July 1811. Roughly two years later, J. M. W. Turner wrote out his "Cure for Gonorrhoea." John Clare contracted a venereal disease, or at least he believed he had: "Not only my health but my life has often been on the eve of its sacrifice by an illness too well known and too disgusting to mention."[40] Edmund Kean battled venereal disease, as did John Keats, who began taking mercury as the best-known remedy in the autumn of 1817, and who was still dosing himself with it a year later, probably for gonorrhea, but conceivably for syphilis. Thomas Bruce, seventh Earl of Elgin, almost certainly had syphilis. The same is true of Lord Castlereagh. Beau Brummell contracted syphilis in the Regency and later died of it.

VI

Female bodies were continually on display, and in a wide variety of more or less explicit forms. In the theater, attractive young actresses performed in risqué plays and revealed acres of alluring cleavage, while the beautiful, vivacious Lucia Vestris became a particular object of male fantasy, scoring her first success on the London stage in 1815 and repeatedly praised thereafter for her "pretty little figure," as William Hazlitt put it. Fashion trends, too, exposed female bodies and encouraged women—according to the *Sermonets* (1814) of Henry and Laetitia-Matilda Hawkins—to "degrade themselves, by not only offering to view, but forcing on the view of their very servants, as much of their persons as they think will be endured." Corsets were so tight they squeezed the hips "into a circumference little more than the waist," while shoving the bosom "up to the chin, making a sort of fleshy shelf" on which the "gross Epicurean" may "feast his imbruted gaze."[41]

"Lewd" publications (the word "pornography" was not in use in Britain until the 1840s) sold in huge numbers. There was something for everyone's taste and budget. At the upper end of the market, wealthy smut connoisseurs with private collections purchased expensive books containing color copperplate engravings with images "as indecent and obscene as can possibly be imagined," in the words of one observer. But cheaper versions of these pictures were also widely available, together with a highly diverse assortment of other print materials targeted for sale and circulation among the middle and lower ranks: profane chapbooks, scandalous travelogues, raunchy seduction stories, Bibles with "indecent . . . pictorial embellishments," scabrous priestly confessions from the French, erotic magazines like the *New Rambler*, salacious fictions wrapped around medical and legal satire, and topical broadsheet vulgarities.[42]

This under-the-counter material could be purchased from a number of Regency book and print sellers, including John Benjamin Brookes, George Cannon (alias the "Rev. Erasmus Perkins"), and William Benbow, whose Leicester Square business was damned by Robert Southey as "one of those preparatory schools for the brothel and the gallows; where obscenity, sedition, and blasphemy, are retailed in drams for the vulgar." Dirty books and dirty pictures were also available from iterant dealers and "women of the town, whose nightly attendance at taverns and the play-houses enables them to deal in this way with gentlemen." The literary forger William Henry Ireland reported in 1814 that it was commonplace to find "books and engravings of the most shameless description" in the library drawers of "deceased persons of *titled* as well as *plebeian* rank . . . whereas the late possessors were supposed during life to have nothing but *the fear of God before their eyes.*" In Mary Brunton's *Self-Control*, the libertine Mr. Warren has a back parlor where he keeps his collection of "amatory poems and loose novels," and where on the wall he has hung "prints and pictures . . . of the same licentious character." Meanwhile, outside London, a porn network estimated to have involved at least six hundred agents traveled the rest of Britain, working until "their stocks were exhausted" and then asking their "confederates in London" to send "fresh supplies by the waggons." Their biggest customers, according to the Society for the Suppression of Vice, were schools, "and chiefly those for females, into which they would contrive to introduce these articles by means of servants."[43]

Thomas Rowlandson was the prince of Regency erotica and obscenity. A comic satirist and painter who produced an immense and varied body of work, he began around 1811 to draw sexually explicit "diversions" that were designed primarily to amuse and arouse. Row-

landson sold these images privately or clandestinely, printing, publishing, and distributing them himself or working in partnership with
Thomas Tegg, a Cheapside publisher who specialized in remainders,
abridgments, and less expensive reprints. Highly adept at tailoring
his work for various audiences, Rowlandson produced both "public"
prints for the middle tiers of the market (popularly sold as "One Shilling, Coloured") as well as high-quality images for the private collections and portfolios of rich patrons, one of whom was the Regent,
who had several drawers full of pornography (euphemistically labeled
"Free prints and Drawings").[44]

Rowlandson's amatory illustrations champion youth, renewal, and
sexual delight, offering candid depictions of various sexual practices
(straightforward heterosexual intercourse, oral sex, group sex) and
a striking number of different positions (on the seat of a traveling
chaise, on the back of a horse, on a swing, on a table, on a fence, on
a military drum, and so on). He was particularly obsessed by voy-
eurism and seduction, and in picture after picture he presents relationships between ugly old men and voluptuous young women, or,
even more pointedly, between elderly grotesques and youthfully
eager lovers. His old men are almost invariably objects of ridicule—
poxed, bespectacled, sly, and desiccated husbands, doctors, parsons,
admirals, scholars, and musicians. Usually they are denied sexual
gratification, and often they are cuckolded. His young men are handsome officers, farmhands, and squires who engage in intense, if furtive, sexual adventures and who are impressively—even on occasion
implausibly—well-endowed. Rowlandson's women are at the center of
these images. Pretty, curvaceous, and enticing, they are the object of
the male gaze to be sure, both to the men within the picture and to
the men who purchased it. But they are also the creators of their own
sexual identities.[45] They initiate desire. They defy convention. They
glow with the pleasures of sex.

Humor informs many of Rowlandson's finest drawings, as he indi-
cates in the playful double entendres of titles such as "The Man of
Feeling," "The Finishing Stroke," "The Cunnyseurs," "The Country
Squire New Mounted," and "The Empress of Russia Receiving her
Brave Guards." "Out Posts of a Camp" features two full-blooded sol-

diers copulating with two women at a short distance from the tents. In "A Rage of Passion," two old dames are distressed at the sight of their household pets fornicating, while they fail to see their nubile female servants enjoying carnal pleasures with local farmers. "The Curious Wanton" depicts two nearly naked young women, one of whom holds a mirror while the other aligns herself in front of it in order to gaze on her reflected pudenda: "Is this the thing that day and night, / Make men fall out and madly fight," she asks in the accompanying caption; "The source of sorrow and of joy, / Which king and beggar both employ"?[46]

VII

For all his sexual outspokenness, Byron acknowledged in *Don Juan* that "Some truths are better kept behind a screen," and the very large truth that he kept screened in *Don Juan* was his own passionate homosexuality.[47] His discretion is entirely understandable. While the evangelical hostility to sexual delight was aimed primarily at heterosexuals, homosexuals provoked in them even deeper levels of disgust, and in this instance they were overwhelmingly on the side of popular opinion, for homosexuality was one of the most explosive topics in Regency Britain, and it united groups from every class and background in a common cause of loathing and rabid persecution.

For centuries in England, "sodomy" was the term used to describe sexual relations between two men, while "tribadism" (from the Greek root for "to rub") referred to a woman who engaged in sexual activity with another woman. A lively sodomitical subculture was first discernible in London in the late seventeenth century, and in the decades that followed a new vocabulary began to make itself known, including "molly" for an effeminate man and "lesbian" and "sapphist" in connection with female same-sex practice. By the end of the eighteenth century, what we would call a "homosexual" or a "gay" identity existed as a social category, with recognizably modern behaviors, personalities, psychologies, and even stereotypes—though the word "homosexual" was not invented for another one hundred years, and the term "gay" to describe homosexual men was not in use until the opening decades of the twentieth century.[48]

Regency London was home to a thriving male homosexual sub-culture with its own cruising grounds, clubs, networks, and social practices. Most of the men in these clubs came from the working classes, though they were often joined in their pursuits by elites who frequented known cruising areas or who met willing partners in preconcerted assignations. Homosexual encounters—planned or otherwise—took place in prisons, schools, navy ships, and churches, as well as in public toilets, parks, deserted buildings, and public houses, some of which had special rooms built for the trade and others of which catered exclusively to a homosexual clientele. In 1813, the lawyer and pamphleteer Robert Holloway reported that there were many "molly houses" in London, including one in the Strand, another in Blackman Street in the Borough, a third near the obelisk in St. George's Fields, and a fourth in the vicinity of Bishopsgate Street.[49]

Homosexual feeling in the Regency took many forms. As a "romantic friendship" between same-sex couples, it was a socially acceptable but also deeply ambiguous category, for the friendship could be maligned as unnatural or idealized to the point where sex was excluded altogether. For men, it was an emotion most often associated with adolescence—as it was for the future prime minister Benjamin Disraeli, who as a Regency teenager attended Higham Hall private school in Epping Forest and experienced intense same-sex attraction to at least one of his classmates. "It seemed to me that I never beheld so lovely and so pensive a countenance," Disraeli later wrote. "His face was quite oval, his eyes deep blue: his rich brown curls clustered in hyacinthine grace upon the delicate rose of his downy cheek." Elsewhere, Disraeli added that "at school friendship is a passion. It entrances the being; it tears the soul."[50]

For women, romantic friendship was understood within the context of female virtue. Heterosexual desire, it almost goes without saying, was fraught for them with multiple dangers and disadvantages, whereas when women were with other women it was possible to be far more uninhibited, sentimental, and trusting. "If any trait of the Lover appear, it is to each other," Coleridge noted in 1812 of his friends the

Brent sisters, adding, with more than a touch of envy, "In vain, shall the Husband or Lover or Brother or Friend expect from either the flush, the overflow, the rapture, after long absence." The Austen sisters, Cassandra and Jane, experienced a female friendship that was even more intense. They were, in the words of their mother, "wedded to each other," and when Jane died in July 1817, Cassandra was devastated: "She was the sun of my life, the gilder of every pleasure, the soother of every sorrow, I had not a thought concealed from her, & it is as if I had lost a part of myself." Several Regency women poets also wrote of romantic same-sex friendships. Matilda Betham addressed an impassioned "Song" to "Lucy," whom "I so truly love" that "but the shadow of a fear, / Wakes in my breast a pang sincere." In "To Miss Sophia Headle," Dorothea Primrose Campbell asked plaintively, "Wilt thou with fond remembrance turn / To her, that did thy pillow share?"[51]

Lady Eleanor Butler and Sarah Ponsonby were the most famous female couple of the Regency. After eloping from Ireland in 1778, they settled in northeastern Wales, where they were soon celebrated as the "Ladies of Llangollen" and where they lived for decades in apparently blissful rural seclusion. Eleanor's journal is full of references to Sarah as "my Beloved," "my sweet love," and "my Heart's darling," and as late as 1822 there were suggestions that the affection between them involved "something more tender still than friendship." As far as it is possible to tell, though, sex was not a part of their relationship. For envious women, the Ladies of Llangollen had managed to escape the burdens and duties of sex. For admiring men, they represented the acme of spiritual love and pure romantic friendship. Southey was one of many visitors during the Regency who enjoyed "the hospitalities of their delightful retirement."[52]

If, however, same-sex couples did decide on a physical relationship, they found themselves in starkly different situations, depending on whether they were men or women. Byron's good friend Charles Skinner Matthews had heard that there were "many" women "in the higher classes, who find in their own gender all that they wish for." But most people simply regarded the possibility of sex between two females as inconceivable, in line with the prevailing gender orthodoxies. No woman could come alive sexually without a man to arouse her, and no respectable woman could choose to participate in sexual activity that was not intended to produce a child, or perhaps to gratify a loving husband. Indeed, as paradoxical as it now seems, overt and intense displays of affection between two women were read as evidence, not of sapphic love, but of just the opposite—of an overmastering and pure love that by its very nature debarred the fiend of sexuality.[53] The result was that lesbians in the Regency could pursue their sexual interests opportunistically and virtually free of suspicion, for the rigid gender codes that bound women to the home and to the private sphere worked—at least in this one area—decidedly to their advantage.

One striking exception proves this general rule. In 1811, Lady Helen Cumming Gordon sued two Scottish schoolmistresses, Marianne Woods and Jane Pirie, for "indecent and criminal practices." Lady Helen's granddaughter, sixteen-year-old Jane Cumming, had been a student at the school run by Woods and Pirie and, as the oldest girl, she had slept in the same bed as Pirie in a dormitory they shared with several other girls, all of whom were similarly doubled up in beds, as was usual in Regency schools. Within months, though, Cumming was unhappy, particularly with school discipline, and in November 1810 she accused her two teachers of having sexual relations while she was in the same bed. At trial, Cumming testified under oath that on several occasions she had been awakened by the sound of the two schoolmistresses kissing. One night she heard Miss Pirie say, "'O do it darling,' and Miss Woods said, 'Not to night' . . . and then Miss Pirie pressed her again to come in, and she came in, and she lay above Miss Pirie: Then Miss Woods began to move, and she shook the bed, and she heard the same noise [like] putting one's finger in the neck of a wet bottle."[54] Cumming's shocking revelations led the panel of seven judges to find the two teachers guilty by a verdict of 4–3. Woods and Pirie appealed, however, and in February 1812 they were declared innocent by the same narrow margin. The case then went to the House of Lords, which in 1819 upheld the latter verdict.

Lord Meadowbank saw most clearly what was at stake. If the court acknowledged that Woods and Pirie had aroused each other, it raised the possibility that other—perhaps many other—respectable, God-fearing British women could be similarly aroused. Unthinkable. Literally unthinkable. For "the virtues, the comforts, and the freedom of domestic intercourse, mainly depend on the purity of female manners," Meadowbank insisted, "and that, again, on the habits of intercourse remaining as they have hitherto been,—free from suspicion." Lord Gillies agreed. He hoped that he never knew a woman "whose intimacies do not ripen into friendship, and whose friendship would not permit her to sleep in the same bed with her friend when necessary." Added Gillies: "I do believe that the crime here alleged has no existence."[55] Woods and Pirie were found innocent because, to a considerable extent, they *had* to be found innocent.

For homosexual men it was very different. The Regency was for them a time of terror, while at no place or period, "I suppose, since the creation of the world, has Sodomy been so rife," Skinner Matthews reported to Byron in early 1811. In theological terms, the sodomite was regarded as an insurgent hell-bent on overturning the established moral order, and his sin was the worst of sins because it could not lead to procreation, whereas even fornication, rape, and incest afforded that possibility. Homosexuality, moreover, was deeply aligned with foreignness and political radicalism at a time when the country was at war and highly intolerant of any suggestion that undermined traditional British values. Napoleon's refusal to make homosexuality a crime in France and the other European countries he controlled (except in cases involving violence or minors) only sharpened this conviction. In Parliament, Robert Peel referred to homosexuality as the crime "inter Christianos non nominandum" ("not to be named among Christians"), a reference that paradoxically designated its unspeakability with utter transparency. Warned a German traveler to England in 1818: "The kiss of friendship between men is strictly avoided as inclining towards the sin regarded in England as more abominable than any other." The punishment for a convicted sodomite was the pillory and then death by public hanging. The term "sodomy" was broadly used to cover all forms of nonprocreative sex. A man condemned to death in 1817 for fellatio with a boy, for example, was sentenced under the buggery laws.[56]

The trial and in many instances the execution of homosexuals was a routine feature of Regency Britain. The *Sussex Advertiser*, April 1, 1811: "William Clarke, aged 77, for sodomy, with Stephen Pentecost, at Isfield." The *Derby Mercury*, March 25, 1813: "Robert King alias Thomas Patrick, for sodomy . . . left for execution." *Trewman's Exeter Flying Post*, March 14, 1816: "Wm. Woodcock and Wm. Oatway for an unnatural crime." The *Newcastle Courant*, April 17, 1819: "The execution of Joseph Charlton, who was convicted at the late gaol delivery for Northumberland, of an unnatural crime, took place at Morpeth, on Wednesday morning, a little below the town."[57]

There were also a series of more high-profile cases, one of which concerned the navy, where sexual relations between men, and particularly across ranks, had long been seen as a threat to discipline. Prior to the Regency, naval trials for sodomy had typically involved one sailor engaged in private and usually consensual relations with one or more other sailors, but in the months following Waterloo a much larger homosexual network was brought to light. Rumors of sexual indecencies onboard the 38-gun frigate the *Africaine*, had reached the

IN THIS undated watercolor, Thomas Rowlandson depicts a crowd by a gibbet.

captain, Edward Rodney, as early as May 1813, but evidence was lacking, and he took no serious action until October 1815, when further tales of sexual transgressions surfaced and Rodney launched a more formal investigation. Initially, only three members of the crew were questioned, but their testimony quickly touched off an ever-widening inquiry involving charges, denials, pacts, and counterallegations.

Two months later, when the *Africaine* returned to Portsmouth, Rodney passed the information he had gathered on to the Admiralty, which conducted its own investigation and soon confirmed that there had been a stable, complex, and widespread gay subculture onboard the warship; that most of the sex had been consensual; that nearly all the men accused belonged to the ship's lower ranks; that crewmen looked for quiet times and secluded locations for their assignations but were not troubled if they were observed; and that several of the ship's boys partnered willingly, even enthusiastically, with older men. In total, some 50 of the roughly 225 crew members were involved in the investigation, and no fewer than 23 were charged or implicated in some kind of "unnatural crime." However, executing such a large number outstripped even the navy's appetite for punishing homosexuality, and so reasons were found to trim the list down to six men, two of whom were severely lashed while the other four were hanged for the "detestable sin of buggery."[58]

Commensurate levels of state-orchestrated homophobic violence were reached in the case of the so-called Vere Street coterie, which involved civilians and was far more widely known. Beginning in early 1810, James Cook and a man named Yardley operated a male brothel at the White Swan public house in Vere Street near Clare Market. The house featured the usual series of private and public areas, but it also contained three special rooms: the first, a ladies' dressing room, "with a toilette, and every appendage of rouge"; the second, a kind of Christian chapel for mock weddings; and the third, a celebration room where "two, three, or four couples" could consummate their union in "sight of each other." The Independent minister John Church officiated at some of these weddings, making him apparently the first ordained minister in Britain to help gay couples celebrate the rites of holy matrimony. On the upper floor of the White Swan, meanwhile, male prostitutes catered to more casual customers, including married men, men of rank, and priests. One popular client came from "a respectable house in the City," and "frequently . . . stayed several days and nights together," during which time he enjoyed himself with "eight, ten, and sometimes a dozen different boys and men." [59]

It did not take long for word to spread about what was on offer in Vere Street, and on the night of Sunday, July 8, 1810, the Bow Street constabulary executed a well-planned raid on the pub. The twenty-three working-class men detained included a coal merchant, a coal heaver, a grenadier, a blacksmith, a grocer, a butcher, a waiter, a bargeman, and a tire smith. They were better known to each other, though, by a series of campy code names such as "Miss Selina," "Kitty Cambric," "Black-Eyed Leonora," "Pretty Harriet," "Sally Fox," "Lucy Cooper," "Miss Sweet Lips," and "the Duchess of Devonshire." Sixteen of these men were eventually released. Of the seven that remained, the landlord James Cook was convicted, not of sodomy but of running a disorderly house. The other six men were found guilty of attempted sodomy and given prison sentences of between one and three years. Six of the seven convicted were also ordered to stand once in the pillory in the Haymarket. [60]

What followed was one of the most vicious unleashings of homophobic bigotry in British history. The six prisoners were loaded onto a caravan in the yard of the Old Bailey. Surrounding them was a force of roughly two hundred constables—half of whom were mounted and armed with pistols, half of whom were on foot. At exactly half past noon the gates were thrown open and a waiting mob surged forward, was pushed back, and then began pelting the slow-moving caravan with offal, dung, mud, fish entrails, rotten fruits and vegetables, and dead dogs and cats. Soon the prisoners "resembled bears dipped in a stagnant pool"; by the time their cart passed the Temple Bar they were so covered in filth "that a vestige of the human figure was scarcely discernible"; and before they had even reached the Haymarket "their faces were completely disfigured by blows." [61]

At one o'clock, four of the six men were tied into the pillory, and the punishment continued, led by upwards of fifty drunken women, who were allowed to stand right in front of the convicts and whose arsenal included rotten eggs and buckets of blood from nearby butchers. After one hour, the four men were removed from the stand and taken to Coldbath Fields prison, while the remaining two men—Cook and William Amos (alias "Sally Fox")—did their time in the pillory. "Cook received several hits in his face, and he had a lump raised upon his eye-brow as large as an egg. Amos's two eyes were completely closed up; and when they were untied, Cook appeared almost insensible." The two men were driven back to Newgate amid the same kind of bombardment that had followed them to the Haymarket. The French-born travel writer and businessman Louis Simond read of these events while visiting Coleridge and Southey in the north of England, and he laid blame on both sides, decrying the "wretches convicted of vile indecencies" as well as the mob that for hours indulged "in the cowardly and ferocious amusement of bruising and maiming men tied to the stake, and perfectly defenceless!"[62]

The prosecution of the Vere Street men did not end there. Thomas White, a sixteen-year-old drummer of the Guards, was a "universal favourite" at the White Swan pub and "very deep in the secrets of the fashionable part of the coterie." On May 27, 1810, he and John Newbolt Hepburn, a forty-two-year-old ensign, met by arrangement at the White Swan, ate dinner, and then had sex in a private room. Two weeks later, military authorities were tipped off about the tryst, and the two men were immediately arrested. In December, at trial, White and Hepburn were both found guilty of buggery and sentenced to hang. Several noblemen—including the Regent's crony Lord Yarmouth and his unsavory younger brother, the Duke of Cumberland—were among the large mob that jammed its way into the Newgate yard to see White and Hepburn put to death on the morning of Thursday, March 7, 1811. White appeared first at around five minutes before eight and "seemed perfectly indifferent to his awful fate" as he "continued adjusting the frill of his shirt." Hepburn came out about two minutes later and was immediately surrounded "by the clergyman, the executioner, his man, and others, in attendance." White "seemed to fix his eyes repeatedly on Hepburn." There were prayers for a few moments and then "the miserable wretches were launched into eternity."[63]

The brutalities involved in the White Swan convictions clearly demonstrate how gay men in the Regency made ideal scapegoats. Many women reviled them because these men seemed to spurn them and to reject their traditional roles as husbands and fathers. Holloway asserted that most of the White Swan coterie were married and that he found it "excruciating" to think "that a fine, elegant, perhaps beautiful woman, should be doomed to have her bed encumbered with a wretch" who "loathes her person." Many men, too, detested homosexuals both as a potential threat to their own sexual identity and as twisted "mollies" who were letting the entire country down by making love in Vere Street instead of war against Napoleon. Pillorying or executing members of the coterie thus became a kind of perverted patriotic act. People who were bitterly divided across economic and social lines—from a brother of the Regent down to drunken servants—were united in intensely cathartic moments of ritualized violence designed to purge the homosexual evil within and to affirm conventionally pious notions of British masculinity and loyalty.[64]

Faced with this kind of savagery, many gay men fled to the Continent, where their sexual preferences were not even illegal, let alone punishable by death. In Italy, as Byron wryly remarked in 1820, "they laugh instead of burning." Rumors had for many years swirled around the gothic novelist and dramatist Matthew "Monk" Lewis, who was "an effeminate looking man" with a "peculiar . . . namby-pamby" manner, declared Joseph Grimaldi. Lewis spent eighteen months in Europe in 1816–17, bookended by trips to his plantations in the West Indies, where he hoped to improve the conditions of his slaves but where he may also have traveled to pursue sexual pleasures. Byron thought as much: "Lewis is going to Jamaica to suck his sugar-canes," he quipped.[65]

Lewis kept his sexual life hidden well enough to avoid scandal. Others were not so discrete or fortunate. George Ferrars Townshend was a Cambridge undergraduate and "a very effeminate young man" who "sometimes . . . wore pink ribbons to His Shoes." When his father died in July 1811, Townshend succeeded to the peerage, but by that time he had already escaped to Europe, the victim of "flying rumours" and his own flamboyant behavior. William John Bankes, a politician and Egyptologist, was with Byron at Cambridge and intimately familiar with the university's gay set. He spent most of the Regency traveling before settling into a career as a Tory MP, but two trials for sodomitical misconduct eventually drove him into permanent continental exile. Richard Heber, MP for Oxford University, was a close friend of Walter Scott and devoted much of his adult life to an insatiable quest to buy rare books, including one trip to France, Belgium, and the Netherlands in the months following Waterloo. But later he was—in Scott's phrase—"detected in unnatural practices," and he absconded to Europe, which "the backwardness of the season renders . . . more congenial to some constitutions," smirked the *John Bull* newspaper.[66]

Percy Jocelyn, son of the first Earl of Roden, was a prominent member of the Society for the Suppression of Vice, as well as bishop of Ferns and Leighlin. In 1811, James Byrne brought charges against him for unnatural behavior, but Jocelyn was acquitted, after which he sued Byrne, who was convicted of criminal libel, flogged to within an inch of his life in the streets of Dublin, and then imprisoned for two years. Jocelyn was appointed bishop of Clogher in 1820. A few years later in London he and a twenty-two-year-old soldier named John Moverley were caught in the back parlor of the White Lion pub near the Haymarket. Both men had their trousers down around their ankles and were—as William Cobbett roared in his *Political Register*—"in the *actual commission* of that horrid and unnatural crime."[67] Moverley and Jocelyn were arrested but soon posted bail and fled, the soldier into obscurity and the "arsebishop"—as he was inevitably dubbed—to Belgium and then France.

VIII

The conviction that homosexuality did not exist in women, and must not exist in men, was vigorously enforced by the Regency courts, which inflicted all manner of shame, violence, and confusion on same-sex couples. Yet despite this barbarity—and also no doubt to some degree because of it—the Regency at the same time marks the crucial moment in British history when writers began a serious examination of the experiences, identities, and sensibilities of homosexuality, and fashioned in the process often strikingly diverse representations that continue to shape modern perceptions of same-sex love.

Commonly known as "the first modern lesbian," Anne Lister was born in Yorkshire in 1791 and educated at private schools in Ripon and York. Upper-middle class and snobbishly conservative, she was a keen walker, horsewoman, shot, and autodidact who was known among the inhabitants of Halifax as "Gentleman Jack" because of her masculine appearance and fiercely independent management of the family estate at Shibden Hall. At fifteen she began a private diary that she wrote partly in code and used to record her many lesbian adventures. "I love, & only love, the fairer sex," she declared in 1821; " . . . my heart revolts from any other love than theirs." Mary Belcombe was the great passion of Lister's life. The two met in 1812 and within months were lovers. When in 1816 Mary wed a wealthy landowner named Charles Lawton of Lawton Hall in Cheshire, a severely shaken Lister refused to give up on their relationship: "Mary, there is a nameless tie in that soft intercourse which blends us into one & makes me feel that you are mine."[68]

Yet Mary was able to return to Shibden Hall only occasionally after she became Lawton's wife, and Lister was far too hot-blooded to wait contentedly. She had a powerful sex drive, took a frequently rakish delight in seduction (in one instance she enjoyed relations with four sisters from one family), and experienced vivid sexual fantasies, in some of which she had male genitalia: "Foolish fancying about Caroline Greenwood, meeting her on Skircoat Moor, taking her into a shed . . . there & being connected with her. Supposing myself in men's clothes & having a penis." On other occasions Lister describes actual encounters in bawdy detail: "I had a complete fit of passion. My knees and thighs shook, my breathing and everything told her what was the matter. I then leaned on her bosom and, pretending to sleep, kept pottering about and rubbing the surface of her [vulva]." To Mary Belcombe's concern that their lesbianism was "unnatural," Lister tellingly replied that "my conduct & feelings" are "surely natural to me inasmuch as they were not taught, not fictitious, but instinctive." Throughout her diaries she writes with sophistication and largely without guilt, as she creates and then self-consciously embraces her own lesbian identity. "I know how to please girls," she declared in 1820.[69]

Samuel Taylor Coleridge dramatically altered the way female same-sex love was represented in his unfinished gothic ballad "Christabel," which he published in the year following Waterloo. Positioning himself as a male author voyeuristically enjoying a sexual encounter between two beautiful young women, Coleridge both exploits and transforms earlier pornographic and satiric traditions to produce an artful and highly evocative depiction of lesbianism as sinister, enigmatic, and sublime. When the poem opens, the ingenue Christabel (Christ/Abel) is outside at midnight, and beyond the gates of her father's castle, when she hears the moaning of the lamia-like enchantress Geraldine, who claims she has been abducted by evil men and abandoned in the forest. Anxious to assist, Christabel escorts Geraldine into the castle, and the two women quietly make their way up into Christabel's bedroom, where Christabel undresses and then watches in her turn as Geraldine removes "her silken Robe and inner Vest" to reveal a hideously deformed bosom. Geraldine joins Christabel in bed, embracing her and then casting a spell to prevent her from speaking about their night together. The next morning Geraldine wakes rested and more beautiful than ever, while Christabel stares at Geraldine's now clothed but "heaving Breasts" and is sure she has sinned.[70] Geraldine grows increasingly malevolent when the two are joined by Christabel's father, as she insidiously places Christabel in a trance in which the two become mirror images of each other, before consigning her—as the poem breaks off—to isolation and fear.

Byron recited "Christabel" one evening in mid-June 1816 at the Villa Diodati near Geneva, shortly after announcing the famous ghost-story competition for which Polidori produced *The Vampyre* and Mary Shelley wrote *Frankenstein*. Byron's own entry in the contest, the brief and unfinished fragment "Augustus Darvell," is most notable for its veiled references to Byron's homosexuality and for the way in which it invokes the plight of so many other homosexual men in the Regency, for Darvell is "prey to some cureless disquiet" as a result of having to develop "a power of giving to one passion the appearance of another." The fragment is only one of many instances in which Byron wrote about homosexual identity and experience. In June 1809, he contemplated producing a treatise entitled "Sodomy simplified or Paederasty proved to be praiseworthy." A week later, he embarked on a two-year tour of the Levant, where he fell in love with the young and volatile Eustathios Georgiou, whose "ambrosial curls" flowed down "his amiable back. . . . Our *parting* was vastly pathetic, as many kisses as would have sufficed for a boarding school." Byron fell even harder for Nicolo Giraud, a fifteen-year-old French national living in Athens with whom he had a passionate sexual relationship. In October 1810, he boasted to his friend Hobhouse of his sexual escapades with adolescent boys and claimed that he had "obtained above two hundred pl & opt Cs"—his coterie's code for "coitum plenum et optabilem" ("complete sexual satisfaction").[71]

When Byron sailed back to London in the summer of 1811, the icy homophobic winds blowing through Vere Street were a chilling reminder of how necessary it was for him to return to—and stay in— the closet, and for the next four years all his known intimacies were heterosexual. In early 1816, however, the jilted Lady Caroline Lamb began spreading vicious rumors about Byron's sexual interest in boys. "Even to have such a thing *said*," he shuddered, "is utter destruction & ruin to a man from which he can never recover." Within weeks, his marriage at an end and his finances in disarray, Byron left England for permanent exile on the Continent, where he recommenced same-sex involvements, including some with what appears to have been an effeminate—or perhaps transvestite—circle of Venetian homosexuals. As time passed, he grew more explicit about his homosexual desires. In an August 1819 letter to Murray, he described a Turkish bath as "that marble paradise of sherbet and sodomy."[72]

Percy Shelley was capable of damning homosexuality in the familiarly abusive rhetoric of the day, as when in the preface to his 1819 drama *The Cenci* he calls Count Cenci's homosexual acts "capital crimes of the most enormous and unspeakable kind." But elsewhere, such as in his 1818 manuscript *Discourse on the Manners of the Ancient Greeks Relative to the Subject of Love*, Shelley is far more insightful. Homosexuality, he explains, arose in Greece, and in part because the terrible degradation of women in that society led men to channel their passions toward other men: "beautiful persons of the male sex became the object of that sort of feelings, which are only cultivated at present as towards females." Greek men usually satisfied their sexual instinct with their wife or their slave, but when there was sexual contact between two men, the result was analogous to "certain phenomena connected with sleep, at the age of puberty." What Shelley cannot believe is that young Athenian men consummated their love with (the unnamed) anal intercourse, which he finds "disgusting" and "totally irreconcilable" with the "beautiful order" of Greek social life. In England, "a certain sentimental attachment towards persons of the same sex was not uncommon" two hundred years ago, and Shelley points particularly to the "impassioned" poetry of Shakespeare's sonnets, which commemorate male-male attraction and which are "wholly divested of any unworthy alloy." Most revealingly, Shelley tentatively defends modern homosexuality when he declares that sexual congress between men, while "sufficiently detestable," is no worse than "the usual intercourse endured by almost every youth of England with a diseased and insensible prostitute."[73]

William Beckford was a Regency byword for homosexuality and an exception to the rule that gay men needed to leave Britain if they were to live or love in safety, as Beckford's immense fortune—accumulated by the three generations of his family who owned sugar plantations in the West Indies—meant that he could make his own rules. Best known as the author of the fantastical Arabian tale *Vathek*, Beckford's life was overtaken by scandal in 1784 when he was discovered in the bedroom of a Westminster schoolboy named William Courtenay. It is unclear whether relations between Beckford and Courtenay ever reached sexual intimacy, and no charges were laid, but the infamy of the incident had a profound impact on both of them. In the years that followed, Courtenay refused to exercise caution regarding his sexual interests, and in late 1810 he was finally forced into permanent exile, after initially believing that he could brazen out the latest round of accusations, "saying that should He be accused before the Lords they, most of whom He said were like Himself, would not decide against Him," as Joseph Farington recorded it in May 1811.[74] Beckford, for his part, left England after his affair with Courtenay was exposed and spent the next eleven years in continental exile, before returning to live at his beautiful Fonthill estate in Wiltshire, where he engaged in endless building projects, including the construction of a six-mile-long, twelve-foot-high stone wall that was ostensibly designed to prevent fox hunters from coming onto his lands, but that was also undoubtedly intended to keep out homophobia and the law.

At Fonthill, Beckford surrounded himself with a retinue of beautiful young male servants, many of whom were recruited by his Portuguese factotum and lover, Gregorio Franchi, and some of whom seem to have inspired in Beckford a passion that was more sentimental than sexual. Beckford gave all these boys provocative nicknames: "there is pale Ambrose, infamous Poupee, horrid Ghoul . . . cadaverous Nicobuse, the portentous dwarf, frigid 'Silence,' Miss Long, Miss Butterfly . . . Countess Pox," and so on. Beckford's valet Richardson was known as "Mme Bion" and displayed "a certain kind of frigidity and insipidity" that annoyed his master. Yet after one assignation— or "flash," as Beckford liked to call it—he had to concede that "Bion always counts for something." Much more to his liking was an Albanian boy named Ali Dru, with whom he enjoyed bathing in the Fonthill lake. In 1819 Hester Piozzi gave an account of what was probably a typical dinner party at Fonthill: "*Four* Gentlemen only; Three Courses, and Fourteen Waiters, the handsomest Men who could Be seen or Selected."[75]

Though he did not circulate in high society—Byron called him "the Martyr of prejudice"—Beckford occasionally took pleasure trips to London. For much of the Regency, he rented a house in Upper Harley Street, but he often stayed elsewhere, perhaps in an effort to disguise his movements. On one evening he lodged at the Clarendon Hotel in New Bond Street but ventured out late at night "in search of a little amusement in an accustomed quarter." On another visit he waited for a lover in a hotel room in Leicester Square. "He is going to appear," wrote Beckford excitedly. "Ah, how my heart beats! For God's sake, be careful, risk nothing. Shall I kiss? No, for God's sake, not yet." Sometimes Beckford sent Franchi explicit instructions concerning men he wished to meet: "if it is at all possible, go to see an angel called Saunders who is a tight-rope walker at the Circus Royal and the certain captivator of every bugger's soul." There were other times, however, when even the allurements of Fonthill and London were not enough: "I'd like to run away, Heaven knows where, with some great Jock," Beckford sighed in 1813. He knew that he was lucky to be able to follow his passions while similarly inclined men fell victim to the ruthlessness of the British legal system. No case distressed him more than the September 1816 trial of John Attwood Eglerton, a waiter with a wife and children. Accused of sodomy by a stable boy, it took the jury less than ten minutes to find Eglerton guilty. Beckford was appalled. "I should like to know what kind of deity they fancy they are placating with these shocking human sacrifices."[76]

Jeremy Bentham shared Beckford's outrage. He deplored homophobic intolerance and was haunted by the face of a judge who had consigned two sodomites to the gallows. "Delight and exultation glistened in his countenance," he recalled; "his looks called for applause of the exploit he had achieved." As early as 1774, Bentham wrote an essay on "Paederasty," and during the Regency he produced a wide-ranging indictment of British attitudes toward homosexuality, including a twenty-two-page synopsis from 1817 that he addressed to Beckford. Like him, Bentham believed that England's sodomy laws brought "death to a human creature," "confusion, reproach, and anguish to an innocent family," and all to no purpose.[77]

Homosexuality was—in Bentham's memorable phrase—an "imaginary crime," and he systematically demolished the religious, legal, and historical claims of those who insisted that it was "unnatural," while striving at the same time to frame the discussion in terms that were more neutral, such as "improlific tendency" or "the improlific appetite." Popular belief held that homosexuality debilitated men, that it led to a reduction in population, and that it violated the teachings of the Bible. None of this was true. But Bentham did not stop there. Whereas early-nineteenth-century moral strictures were strongest against nonprocreative sexual acts, Bentham went so far as to suggest that the acceptance of homosexuality would produce social benefits. Heterosexuality, it was plain, created a number of very real social problems. Where was the harm in homosexuality? Many societies—

past and present—had accepted it. The British men who engaged in it did so willingly. They were not injured by the practice. They did not bother others. Most tellingly, as they risked the death penalty if caught, many of them clearly set a very high value on the pleasure and companionship it brought them. For Bentham, the evidence was unambiguous. Any pleasure without painful consequences was in itself "pure good," and punishing "pure good . . . will be not only evil, but so much pure evil." Punishing people for their sexual orientation was "pure evil."[78]

It was simply a matter of taste. The fact that homosexuals were in the minority, and that their sexual practices were unpalatable to the majority, did not justify punishing them, any more than it did punishing Jews, or heretics, or smokers, or people who ate oysters. Bentham conceded that he himself found homosexual practices "depraved." But that made no difference to the argument. When the British criminal justice system sentenced a man to die, "there should certainly be some better reason than mere dislike to his taste, let that dislike be ever so strong." Bentham did not publish his essays on homosexuality, as he knew the fierce opprobrium they would set loose would bring him and his entire reform agenda into unappeasable disrepute. But he hoped that his groundbreaking exploration of the issue might eventually contribute to open-minded debate and widespread acceptance. "When I am dead mankind will be the better for it," he reasoned.[79] In his writings Bentham put in place the central tenets of what we now regard as the modern gay rights movement.

IX

The Regency fascination with sex extended to a variety of other practices. Incest in some forms was broadly accepted and openly discussed, while in other forms, attitudes varied enormously, from enthusiasm all the way to disgust. Marriage between cousins had been legal since 1540 and was commonplace across the social spectrum. The Regent was married to his cousin, while his brother, the Duke of Cumberland, and his sister, Princess Mary, were similarly betrothed to cousins, as were a host of other Regency figures, including the boxer Daniel Mendoza, the political reformer Robert Waithman, the sculptor Francis Chantrey, the admiral John Jervis, and the scientist Mary Somerville (twice)—to name only a few. Revealingly, Austen viewed the marriage of cousins as romantic, even gratifying, because of what it suggested about the strength of family affection, and in her fiction close relationships of this kind feature prominently and unproblematically. Sometimes marriage to a cousin is rejected, overthrowing continuity and family expectation in favor of individual preference, as in *Pride and Prejudice*. In *Mansfield Park*, by contrast, Austen offers the possibility of outsiders as suitable marriage partners, but then firmly casts it off, as Edmund's brotherly affection for Fanny merges with the erotic to produce a union that is untinged by the prurient and that reconciles family aspiration and individual desire. "The happiness of the married cousins," concludes Austen, "must appear as secure as earthly happiness can be."[80]

The Byron-Shelley circle fixated on incest. Leigh Hunt based his long poem, *The Story of Rimini*, on the tale from Dante's *Inferno* of the quasi-incestuous love affair between Francesca and her husband's brother Paolo, which Hunt represents not as sinful but as the victory of "natural impulses" over the "authorized selfishness" of law and religion. More dramatically, in *Laon and Cythna* (1817), Percy Shelley transforms incest into a powerful symbol of an all-encompassing intellectual, imaginative, and sexual fusion that breaks through the gendered barriers thwarting women and desensitizing men, and that brings together two individuals in one ecstatic union, for the eponymous characters are brother and sister, and their passionate congress unites like in perfect harmony with like: "All thought, all sense, all feeling, into one / Unutterable power."[81]

On several other occasions, though, as in William Godwin's *Mandeville* (1817), John Polidori's *Ernestus Berchtold* (1819), Percy Shelley's *The Cenci*, and Mary Shelley's *Matilda*, incest is represented as a source of revulsion. Byron, too, often treated it in this way. Notoriously, he felt an intense passion for his half-sister Augusta that may or may not have reached sexual consummation and that was so bruited about that it hastened his departure from England. In several of his verse tales, Byron exploits the theme of forbidden love in ways that provocatively suggest his own feelings for Augusta. Most notably, his gothic drama *Manfred* (1817) centers on the love affair between the eponymous anti-hero and his virtual twin, Astarte: "her eyes, / Her hair, her features, all, to the very tone / Even of her voice, they said were like to mine." Together, and at some "all-nameless hour," Manfred and Astarte committed a crime which led to her death and which was almost certainly incest: "Thou lovedst me / Too much, as I loved thee," he tells a vision of her; "we were not made / To torture thus each other, though it were / The deadliest sin to love as we have loved." Asserted Benjamin Robert Haydon: "Byron, Shelley [and] Hunt . . . might have produced a revolution had they not shocked the Country by their opinions on sexual intercourse."[82]

While incest was met, at times, with equanimity, masturbation was regarded with horror. Manners might be improved. Seducers might be thwarted. Brothels might be closed. Books might be banned. Images might be destroyed. But how to stop a sexual activity that was typically carried out in secret, that virtually everyone denied, and that provided the solitary individual with irresistibly easy, all-hour access to an endless source of primal pleasure? Scaremongering seemed to campaigners the best available option. Theologians, clergymen, teachers, and parents pointed out that the Bible forbids it, at least according to the most generally accepted interpretation of Genesis 38: 8–10, where Onan spills his seed on the ground, and they vociferously condemned the practice as unnatural, nonreproductive, and antisocial. Doctors, too, damned "onanism" (as it was commonly called), not only because it encouraged overheated asocial fantasies that damaged the mind but also because it caused an excessive loss of fluids that severely and prematurely damaged the body. Masturbation, warned the eminent physician Benjamin Rush in 1812, "produces seminal weakness, impotence, dysury, tabes dorsalis, pulmonary consumption, dyspepsia, dimness of sight, vertigo, epilepsy, hypochondriasis, loss of memory, manalgia, fatuity, and death." Even Bentham—and there was no one more for sexual pleasure than Bentham—was convinced that masturbation was "the most incontestably pernicious . . . to the health and lasting happiness of those who are led to practice it."[83]

Unsurprisingly, shame took deep hold of many habitués. In 1818, the physician Alexander Peter Buchan recounted the story of a young man of "ardent imagination, whose athletic appearance offered the most satisfactory proof that his constitution had suffered no material injury from some improper habits acquired at school." At the age of about twenty, however, the young man happened to read *L'Onanisme*, the hugely influential denunciation of the practice published in 1760 by the Swiss physician Samuel Auguste Tissot. Horrified to learn that he may already have ruined his constitution, the young man considered it his duty to purchase all the copies of Tissot that he could find and distribute them among his friends, both female and male. Yet these actions did little to assuage his conviction that his teenage masturbating had made him "his own assassin."[84] After a year of living with the guilt and humiliation, he committed suicide.

Similarly, an appetite for flagellation was often acquired at school. Thomas De Quincey recognized it as a "peculiar and *sexual* degradation." The standard explanation was that many headmasters and headmistresses enjoyed the sadistic pleasure of flogging, and that many students embraced the corresponding masochistic appeal of witnessing or suffering these beatings, the toxic combination of which produced intense spectacles of mutually gratifying sexual perversion. Eton, Merchant Taylors', Rugby, Westminster, and Winchester were especially infamous for the frequency with which they meted out this widely accepted form of sexual savagery. "It is very true that there are innumerable old generals, admirals, colonels, and captains, as well as bishops, judges, barristers, lords, commoners, and physicians, who periodically go to be whipped," George Cannon reported. But, he added, "hundreds of young men" also enjoy the rod.[85]

Theresa Berkley, the most well-known of several so-called London "governesses," kept elaborately furnished apartments dedicated to flagellation. According to Cannon, she also possessed the primary quality needed to succeed in her line of work: "lewdness." For if a governess is not "positively lecherous," she cannot "long keep up the affectation of it, and it will be soon perceived that she only moves her hands or her buttocks to the tune of pounds, shillings, and pence." Berkley was a true professional, and she kept on hand an extensive inventory of rods, whips, straps, canes, battledores, and fresh bushes to accommodate every desire or caprice. "At her shop, whoever went with plenty of money, could be birched, whipped, fustigated, scourged, needle-pricked, half-hung, holly-brushed, furse-brushed, butcher-brushed, stinging-nettled, curry-combed, phlebotomized, and tortured till he had a belly full."[86]

Several Regency men spoke of their love of the lash. "I do declare, when next I see you, I will whip * * * * * * ," wrote Edmund Kean. "Be a good girl, and do not fret, or remember the whipping." William Lamb was flogged when he was a student at Eton, and as an adult he found flagellation highly arousing. "He called me Prudish," wrote his wife Lady Caroline Lamb in 1810, perhaps in reference to his fascination with the rod; "said I was straight-laced, amused himself with instructing me in things I should never have heard of or known." The anonymous author of *Venus School-Mistress: or; Birchen Sports* produced one of the most celebrated pieces of Regency pornography. An unrelieved flagellant fantasy, it concerns a young woman named—predictably—"Miss R. Birch," who at nine years old is launched on her career of depravity when she watches unseen as her mother's partner, Miss Smart, lashes a middle-aged letch: "Now, my pretty gentleman, nothing will save your bum; and by heaven, I'll whip, whip, whip, whip, whip, whip, whip you to-day, as you never was whipped before."[87]

The most infamous Regency flagellant was Eton-educated Sir Eyre Coote, a fifty-six-year-old general and sitting MP who in November 1815 entered the mathematical school at Christ's Hospital in London, sent the younger boys out of the room, and then paid the older boys to flog him, after which he paid again to flog them. Polly Robinson, the school nurse, entered the room just as Coote was buttoning up his breeches. He was arrested and brought before the lord mayor of London, Sir Matthew Wood, who dismissed the case. Rumors of the incident refused to go away, though, and in April 1816 military authorities decided to conduct their own investigation. Coote had powerful friends, but the evidence of the Christ's Hospital boys was decisive: Coote had been at the school on several previous occasions, he had used different aliases, and they knew he was there to flog and be flogged for money. The tribunal concluded that Coote was "fully sensible of the indecency of the proceeding."[88] He was dismissed from the army and stripped of his knighthood. In a fierce broadsheet called "A Peep into the Blue Coat School!!!!!!!!!!!!!!," George Cruikshank drew Coote as a pig in a military uniform, with its forefeet against the classroom wall and its bottom exposed, as three Christ's Hospital boys birch him.

Mary Shelley's *Frankenstein* brings together the Regency's darkest anxieties about sexuality in its lurid account of Victor Frankenstein's creation of a monster who eventually destroys him. Victor's relationship with his Creature is clearly necrophilic, as he lovingly constructs him from an assemblage of dead body parts. The process of creation for Victor is masturbatory, as he locks himself away in his solitary chamber for months on end and dreams of infusing life into a form whose features he had "selected . . . as beautiful." Victor and his Crea-

PUBLISHED IN the *Scourge* magazine for September 1816, this print by George Cruikshank offers "A Peep into the Blue Coat School!!!!!!!!!!!!!!" and exposes the sexual predations of Sir Eyre Coote, MP.

ture are—broadly speaking—same-sex, and their intense preoccupa-
tion with each other is at some level homoerotic. But at the same time,
they are from different races or perhaps even species, which means
that their connection is implicitly miscegenetic, or even bestial. They
are also linked incestuously as father and son, and their relationship
is at the crux of Victor's incestuous fantasies, for immediately after
he brings his Creature to life, he has an extraordinary nightmare
in which his kiss on the lips of his cousin and bride-to-be Elizabeth
transforms her into the decomposing corpse of his own mother.[89] In
Frankenstein, an irreconcilable and highly destructive combination of
fear and desire in both the Creator and the Creature produces a broad
range of sexually transgressive behaviors that haunted the Regency—
and that explain in large measure why the novel retains its power to
possess and appall.

Robert Peel was chief secretary for Ireland when he first met Julia
Floyd, an acknowledged beauty with a wide circle of admirers.
By 1818, Peel was deeply in love with her, but he wondered whether
she would be able to leave her glittering social sphere for the much
more demanding role as the wife of a working politician. "You are
my world," was her disarming reply, and the prelude to a happy marriage that lasted for more than thirty years.[90] It is a reminder that,
though the Regency public sphere was often a cacophony of, on the
one hand, strident evangelical calls for restraint and, on the other,
insolent libertinous promotions of vulgarity, in private there were
many couples—Julia and Robert Peel, Maria and John Constable,
Lady Eleanor Butler and Sarah Ponsonby, Mary and William Wordsworth—who steered clear of both these extremes and who were passionately and exclusively devoted to one another. At the same time, it
is difficult not to applaud the evangelicals for campaigning so ardently
to reduce the virile callousness and buffoonery that so often blighted
the lives of Regency girls and women, or to acknowledge that many

of the men and women avidly pursuing sexual pleasures were committed to virtues such as candor, fellowship, and fun, and were simply not prepared to accept the doctrines of the killjoys who insisted that sex was shameful. Though many of its attitudes, practices, and laws have long since been discarded, the Regency continues to exert a powerful influence on modern understandings of human sexuality, as is clearly evident in the enduring appeal of its most powerful love stories, its potent assaults on the separate-sphere ideology, its pioneering explorations of gay and lesbian identities, its fascination with vampiric predators, and its many exuberant tributes to the joys of sex.

CHAPTER FOUR

Expanding Empire
and Waging War

I

"It is for you to save the world again," Tsar Alexander of Russia told the Duke of Wellington after hearing the momentous news. Napoleon had escaped. Just one year earlier, his story had seemed to be over. After more than two decades of almost continual warfare in Europe and a series of dazzlingly successful military campaigns that took him to the height of his power in 1810, Napoleon launched a disastrous invasion of Russia in 1812 that turned his fortunes. In October 1813, his Grande Armée was decimated at the "Battle of the Nations," and in April 1814 Napoleon abdicated, after which the allied forces banished him to Elba, a small island off the western coast of Italy. King Louis XVIII, alive and well and living for the past seven years in Buckinghamshire, was restored to the French throne, while the allies, including Wellington and Tsar Alexander, met in September at the Congress of Vienna to start redrawing the map of Europe. Napoleon, however, was not done just yet. Restlessly tracking events from Elba, he sensed deep dissatisfaction in France with both the restoration of the Bourbon dynasty and the Congress of Vienna, and on March 1,

1815, he broke from Elba and returned to France, where he quickly set about trying to rally support and rebuild his empire.[1]

Better than anyone, Wellington knew what an unleashed Napoleon meant, personally, nationally, and internationally, as Tsar Alexander's comments to him clearly indicate. From 1808 onward, and initially as Sir Arthur Wellesley, Wellington played the leading role in that part of the Napoleonic conflict known as the Peninsular War, which was fought in the Iberian Peninsula between French forces on the one hand, and British, Spanish, and Portuguese fighters on the other. By the time Wellesley joined this part of the war effort, many had come to think of Napoleon as almost invincible. "Here in London everybody is so besotted with admiration of Bonaparte and 'the talents' of French Generals—that no one thinks of detecting contradictions &c. in French accounts," Thomas De Quincey growled to Dorothy Wordsworth.[2]

Wellesley, appointed to command in Portugal in April 1809, changed that perception. Known as "Nosey" to his men (Lord Byron uncharitably referred to his "eagle beak") and "the Beau" to his officers (for his piercing blue eyes, dapper dress sense, and discreet womanizing), he landed in the Tagus on April 22 and immediately began the task of winning over the hearts and minds of his own troops, as well as of the Spanish and Portuguese people.[3] In late July, he gained an imperfect victory in central Spain at the Battle of Talavera, for which he was created Viscount Wellington. Following a retreat back into Portugal, he commenced secret work on a system of defensive fortifications built by his engineers north of Lisbon. Known as the "Lines of Torres Vedras," Wellington fell back on them in October 1810, thwarting French attempts to drive the British into the sea.

His Portuguese base secured, Wellington now started actively, if unevenly, to claw back territory and momentum from the French. His forces won a bloody battle at Albuera in May 1811. "How horrible it is to have so many people killed!" Jane Austen wrote after reading accounts of the fighting. It was the following year, however, before Wellington's growing army was strong enough to capture the Spanish frontier garrisons of Ciudad Rodrigo and, 150 miles to the south, Badajoz, where it took more than forty separate attacks before British troops finally surmounted the fortress walls and tore down the French flag. Their victory triggered a rampage. "The shouts and oaths of drunken soldiers in quest of more liquor, the reports of fire-arms and the crashing in of doors, together with the appalling shrieks of hapless women, might have induced anybody to believe himself in the regions of the damned," one British soldier reported. The following day Wellington surveyed the carnage in the breaches and broke down in tears. His troops had shown great gallantry, he wrote to Lord Liverpool, "but I greatly hope that I shall never again be the instrument of putting them to such a test."[4]

Wellington then turned his attention north to Salamanca and, on July 22, won a brilliantly maneuvered victory with the assistance of his brother-in-law Edward Pakenham, who broke the French center. A few weeks later Wellington entered Madrid, where Francisco Goya produced his famous chalk sketch of him, a sketch in which the forty-three-year-old Wellington looks a haunted man. When news of Salamanca reached Britain, the Regent awarded Wellington a marquessate, while from Bristol Benjamin Robert Haydon reported that

THE SPANISH painter Francisco Goya drew this portrait of Arthur Wellesley, the future Duke of Wellington, shortly after the British general routed the French at the Battle of Salamanca in July 1812.

the "People were all rejoiced, all was bustle, longing for the gazette, cursing the French, & praising Wellington."[5] In September, Wellington launched an unsuccessful siege of the castle at Burgos in northern Spain, and then retreated back into Portugal again, harassed by bad weather and formidable French troops.

The final push began in May 1813. With an allied army of 78,000 men, Wellington swept strategically past Burgos and across the peninsula to Vitoria, where he routed 57,000 French troops and broke Napoleon's grip in Spain. Beethoven composed "Wellington's Victory" to commemorate Vitoria, complete with trumpets, cannon, tags from "Rule Britannia," and a dedication to the Regent. Following the battle, however, discipline among British soldiers broke down again, as they swarmed over large amounts of booty rather than doing their duty and pursuing the French troops who had left it behind. Wellington was furious, railing against a lack of discipline in some of his officers and famously condemning his "common soldiers" as "the scum of the earth." Order restored, he moved farther east to take San Sebastián and Pamplona, where there was "fair bludgeon-work," but, as he remarked with some wryness, "I escaped unhurt as usual, and I begin to believe that the finger of God is upon me."[6]

By October, Wellington had pressed across the Bidassoa and into southern France, while that same month—far away to the north—Britain's Austrian, Swedish, Russian, and Prussian allies converged on Napoleon at the Battle of the Nations at Leipzig, shredding his armies and driving him decisively from Germany and Poland. On April 10, 1814, Wellington stormed Toulouse, ending the Peninsular War. He had not heard that, four days earlier, Napoleon had surrendered. "Hurrah!" Wellington exclaimed when he learned the news, spinning "round on his heel" and snapping his fingers "like a schoolboy."[7] In May, the Regent made Wellington a duke, and feted him in London that summer, when there were endless parties to celebrate the peace, and Tsar Alexander and the king of Prussia paid ceremonial visits.

Wellington had less than a year to catch his breath before Napoleon's dramatic escape forced him back into command, this time of Anglo-Dutch-Belgian forces in the Netherlands—for if Napoleon did decide to strike first, it was most likely to be there. Leaving the still-ongoing Congress of Vienna, Wellington rode hard, covering almost 700 miles in less than a week, and arriving on April 4, 1815, in Brussels, the seat of the allied forces. He saw immediately that there was a great deal to put in order, sourly observing, "I have got an infamous army, very weak and ill equipped, and a very inexperienced Staff." And this was to say nothing of the many other obstacles he faced: shaky intelligence, vulnerable ports and supply lines, a lack of common training and equipment within a multinational and multilingual force of just over 92,000 men, disagreements between allied leaders about strategy, and British government objectives at odds with his own military and political instincts.[8]

Undaunted, Wellington put his stamp on his army. The timely dispatch of many of his peninsular generals and officers substantially improved the quality of his fighting force, and together they enhanced discipline, training, organization, and morale. He bonded his troops together by combining British and Hanoverian units and by placing raw recruits alongside hardened veterans. He established a good working relationship with the Prussian field marshal Gebhard Blücher, whose army totaled nearly 121,000 men. "By God! I think Blucher and myself can do the thing," Wellington told Thomas Creevey as they walked together in a Brussels park later that spring. Then, spying a solitary British infantryman, he offered an assessment of the character of his men that stands in stark contrast to his earlier condemnation of them as "the scum of the earth." "There," he exclaimed, pointing to the soldier. "There . . . it all depends upon that article whether we do the business or not. Give me enough of it, and I am sure."[9]

Concerned not to appear the aggressors, the allies waited. Despite private worries and the feverish anxiety building in Brussels, Wellington did his best to project calm. Life went on as normally as possible, with drills and meetings, dances and cricket matches, concerts and theatergoing, card games and trysts, and plenty of tobacco, Hollands gin, and pink champagne. On June 15 in the rue de la Blanchisserie, the Duchess of Richmond held what has often been described as the most famous ball in history. A coachbuilder's large workshop was transformed with wallpaper, draperies, and flowers into a fairy-tale-like palace, and in the evening European royals and British aristocrats mingled with almost every important officer in Wellington's army.

Wellington himself arrived around 10:30, and immediately confirmed the news that had reached him only hours earlier. Napoleon had struck into Belgium. "Ah! then and there was hurrying to and fro," writes Byron in Canto III of *Childe Harold's Pilgrimage*: "And gathering tears, and tremblings of distress, / And cheeks all pale, which but an hour ago / Blush'd at the praise of their own loveliness." Some men dashed away to ready themselves for battle, but others lingered with a drink or a loved one and had to march in silk stockings and dancing pumps. Wellington stayed. Those closest to him could see the "care and anxiety on his countenance," but he maintained an outward insouciance. Napoleon be damned. Wellington was not about to undermine the morale of his men, or give up the opportunity of speaking with his officers, or rush through his evening of lively music, good food, and beautiful women because of *anything* the French did, and that included marching on Brussels with an invasion force of 125,000 men.[10]

More unnerving news arrived during an early-morning supper. Wellington finished eating, visited with guests for another twenty minutes, and then, as he prepared to depart, whispered to the Duke of Richmond, "Have you a good map in the house?" The two retired to Richmond's study. "Napoleon has *humbugged* me, by God!" Wellington exclaimed as he examined the map that Richmond had spread out before him; "he has gained twenty-four hours' march on me."[11] Roughly five hours later, after a brief sleep and a light meal of tea and toast, Wellington galloped out of Brussels toward the vital crossroads of Quatre Bras, twenty-two miles to the south. When he arrived, the French were not yet in sight, and his Anglo-Dutch-Belgian forces were lying low until badly needed reinforcements joined them. Wellington seized the opportunity to dash southward another six miles to the Bussy windmill, near the village of Brye, to confer with Blücher about their joint strategy, and together the two climbed the windmill, from where they looked out through their telescopes and watched Napoleon moving among his staff. Wellington promised Blücher his aid if not attacked himself and then raced back toward Quatre Bras.

In his rear, he heard the boom of nine cannon shots. Napoleon was advancing. The Battle of Ligny had commenced.

It was already midafternoon by the time Wellington returned to Quatre Bras. In the intervening hours, the situation had deteriorated dramatically. Led by Marshal Michel Ney, the French subsidiary force of 20,000 men had launched a fierce assault on an allied army that was badly outnumbered. Wellington immediately took personal charge, forming his troops whenever possible into defensive "squares"—blocks of men brandishing bayonets—and steadying them in the face of sharpshooters, heavy cannon fire, and wave after wave of cavalry. At one point, among his men guiding, cajoling, and instructing, he was almost overwhelmed by a pack of French horsemen and forced to ride for his life.[12] The battle seemed lost on several occasions and then, just at the moment of collapse, fresh reinforcements arrived, which Wellington sent out either to shore up a weakened position or to check a French advance. By six-thirty he had seized the initiative, and at nightfall Ney withdrew.

Early the next morning Wellington learned that Blücher's army had been mauled at Ligny and was withdrawing northward toward Wavre. "As they have gone back we must go too," he declared, for it was crucial that he maintain contact with the Prussians and not allow Napoleon to smash the hinge between them. By noon, Wellington was in full parallel retreat toward the low ridge of Mont-Saint-Jean, which lay just south of the village of Waterloo and which his engineers had previously determined was the best defensive ground south of Brussels. Here he would wait for Napoleon. Wellington's entire front at Waterloo was about two miles long running roughly east to west, with boggy ground on his left flank, rolling fields of rye before him, and the road to Nivelles heading off at a forty-five-degree angle on his right. His greatest advantage lay in the three groups of buildings situated almost immediately in front of the ridge: the substantial walled enclosure of Hougemont on his right flank; the smaller farmhouse of La Haye Sainte in the center; and, smaller still, the farms of Papelotte and La Haye on his far left.[13] Wellington concentrated his troops on his vulnerable right flank and on the reverse slope of the ridge, while he sent crack riflemen forward to occupy the crucial garrisons of Hougemont and La Haye Sainte. Blücher, headquartered fourteen miles directly east, wrote to inform Wellington that at day-break he would lead two Prussian army corps in the direction of Wellington's left flank. In reply, Wellington pledged to hold his position until Blücher reached him.

On June 17, the French drew up across the fields at Waterloo. After two hot days, rain started to fall in sheets. Wellington slept briefly that night at an inn in the village of Waterloo and was thus spared the miseries of the cold and the wet, but the vast majority of his men, on the roads, in the fields and ditches, and along the ridge, were soaked to the skin, though tobacco, booze, and bonfires kept some of them reasonably warm. At six in the morning on Sunday, June 18, 1815, Wellington—wearing white buckskin breeches, a blue frock coat, and a black cocked hat—rode out of Waterloo village on his chest-nut charger, Copenhagen, to survey the sodden ground and speak to his bedraggled troops, whose morale was high despite the dreadful weather. "The very sight of him put heart into us all," reported the surgeon John Haddy James.[14] They waited. The rain ceased at around nine A.M. No advance from Napoleon. They drank tea, cleaned their weapons, dried their clothes, and ate what food could be found. Eleven A.M. Still no advance. Wellington had won many victories against the French in the Peninsular War, but he had never fought Napoleon. Finally, at eleven-thirty A.M., that changed. With a violent cannonade, the emperor launched his forces at the duke, and the most famous battle in British history began.

The allied soldiers occupying the farmhouses of Hougemont and La Haye Sainte were under pressure from the start, and they repulsed—in ferocious close-quarter fighting—repeated French attempts to capture these two strongholds. Early in the afternoon, Napoleon ordered a direct thrust at the center of the British troops lined up two and three deep along the ridge, but they held firm, and a subsequent cavalry charge sent the French columns into retreat. Wellington was everywhere, giving orders, rallying troops, adjust-ing strategy, punching and counterpunching as Napoleon sent his men forward. At three o'clock, while the French artillery continued to bombard the British front line, Napoleon demanded that another

PUBLISHED IN April 1816, this illustration of the farm compound of La Haye Sainte plainly shows the damage it sustained ten months earlier during the Battle of Waterloo.

attempt be made on La Haye Sainte. Wellington, with a close eye on both growing British casualties and gathering French momentum, ordered his troops to retreat behind the ridge. From across the bloody battlefield, Marshal Ney thought that French firepower had finally broken the British line, and he released his cavalry. But when the French charged up over the ridge, the British troops were waiting for them and, massed in tight red squares, they launched volley after volley of musket fire, cutting down and driving back the oncoming horsemen.

Time and again the French cavalry charged and was repulsed. Time and again the French artillery tore into the British squares, where dead soldiers were dragged to the center and piled higher and higher, while the next redcoat stepped forward to fill the gap in the line. "Hard pounding, this, gentlemen," Wellington remarked; "try who can pound the longest." By five o'clock there were massive casualties on both sides, and while the British squares continued to stand firm amid the relentless French onslaught, Wellington knew his side could not hold out much longer. "Night or the Prussians must come," he murmured.[15] At six-fifteen Napoleon unleashed yet another strike on La Haye Sainte, and this time—with the allied forces exhausted, badly outnumbered, and low on ammunition—he succeeded. The center of the battlefield at last belonged to him. With the day now hanging in the balance, soldiers were spotted to the east moving steadily toward the carnage.

It was Blücher and the Prussians, who had set off from Wavre early that morning and arrived exactly when and where Wellington needed them most. Napoleon ordered his crack troops—the "Old Guard"— to the front to break the British before the Prussians could join them. Wellington put a line of soldiers along the ridge, and then instructed the bulk of his men to lie down on its reverse slope. The French easily bested the British line, but as they approached the crest of the ridge, the remaining British infantrymen stood up and launched a salvo directly into the Old Guard. The surprise devastated the French assault. Within minutes it was in disarray. Wellington stood up in his stirrups, raised his hat in the air, and gave the order for his entire army to advance. The French, their willingness to fight for Napoleon finally shattered, turned and fled over the debris of previous assaults. The discipline and determination of the British soldiers, coupled with the crucial arrival of Blücher's men to siphon off French forces, had carried the day. But just. As the duke famously remarked, the battle of Waterloo was "the nearest run thing you ever saw in your life."[16]

News of the allied victory traveled fast, and before long thousands upon thousands of Britons flocked to Belgium to see Wellington's battlefield. John Scott was there soon enough to pick a "trophy" right off the ground (a twelve-pound cannonball), while many other early tourists bought mementos from local peasants who had scoured the fields and were doing a booming trade in caps, helmets, cuirasses, bayonets, feathers, brass eagles, empty cartridges, cannon-wadding, and so on. Robert Peel spoke directly to Wellington one month after his triumph, and then drove out in the pouring rain to see the scene of it. The writer Charlotte Anne Waldie visited when the effluvia rising up from the grave pits "was horrible." The smell of putrefaction still hung heavy in the air in August during a tour of the field by Walter

Scott, who in short order produced both *The Field of Waterloo, A Poem* and *Paul's Letters to his Kinsfolk*. Robert Southey was there in October, and commemorated both Wellington's triumph and his own journey to the site in *The Poet's Pilgrimage to Waterloo*, a book that bristles with anti-French sentiment, and which Austen read "generally with much approbation."[17]

Byron explored the battlefield in May 1816, but in a very different frame of mind than Scott and Southey. They regarded Napoleon as a warmongering tyrant and Wellington as an international hero. Byron scoffed at these assessments. In his view, Napoleon was a glorious if destructive self-made sovereign, while Wellington was an over-rewarded reactionary who was responsible for restoring despots to European thrones. J. M. W. Turner went to Waterloo in the spring of 1817, and the following year at the Royal Academy he exhibited *The Field of Waterloo*, a gloomy nighttime scene of slaughter and pathos that in its catalogue entry carried lines from *Childe Harold*: "Rider and horse,—friend, foe,—in one red burial blent!" By 1820, when Dorothy Wordsworth walked the fields of Waterloo, "there was little to be seen; but much to be felt;—sorrow and sadness, and even something like horror breathed out of the ground as we stood upon it!"[18]

Following their battle, Wellington and Napoleon went in opposite directions. Intimately involved in both socializing and the peace settlement, Wellington lived for many months in Paris before returning in 1818 to England, where he joined Lord Liverpool's cabinet as master general of the ordnance, a position from which he rose within a decade to become prime minister. Napoleon, meanwhile, abdicated for a second time, on June 22, 1815, and then surrendered to the British, who put him on board the *Bellerophon* and sailed with him to Plymouth Sound. Some in England wanted Napoleon to be allowed to live in the country under house arrest, as befitted the fair treatment of a mighty opponent. "After all," declared Charles Lamb, "Bonaparte is a fine fellow, as my barber says, and I should not mind standing bareheaded at his table to do him service in his fall."[19] But the government rejected the idea and, instead, sent Napoleon into permanent exile on St. Helena, a remote British colony 1,200 miles west of the southwestern coast of Africa.

II

As the battle against France entered its final phase, Britain found itself involved in a second international conflict. "A strange business this in America, Dr. Grant!—What is your opinion?" Tom Bertram asks in *Mansfield Park*, a reference—depending on the internal dating of Austen's narrative—to the War of 1812, or to the series of incidents that led up to it.[20] For more than a decade, tensions between America and Britain had been building over issues such as Britain's interference with American trade to Europe, the Royal Navy's impressment of American sailors to help fight in the war against France, and Britain's supply of arms to Indigenous soldiers in North America in an effort to thwart the expansionist plans of the United States congressmen known as "The War Hawks," who were calling for the conquest of Canada and the eradication of the Indigenous resistance. James Madison, fourth President of the United States, laid these grievances before Congress in early June 1812, and two weeks later the young nation of America declared war on Great Britain, the supreme naval power in the world. The conflict lasted for two and a half years, and was fought by relatively small numbers over a vast area of land, lake, and sea. The British army was allied with members of several different Indigenous nations, French-speaking and English-speaking Canadian colonists, American loyalists living in Canada, and a number of freed and escaped American slaves, including those who belonged to a militia company known as the "Coloured Corps."

The United States entered the war unprepared, but in the opening months its navy won three straight, stunning single-frigate actions over the British, including an August 19, 1812, battle in which USS *Constitution* sent HMS *Guerrière* to the bottom. British forces restored national pride the following year when Philip Broke, commander of the frigate HMS *Shannon*, defeated the USS frigate *Chesapeake* within sight of Boston. Farther to the south, Rear Admiral George Cockburn led a small British squadron that, seizing control of Chesapeake Bay, inflicted severe economic damage with a blockade and ravaged the vulnerable American shoreline in a series of raiding missions. The

FIRST PUBLISHED on September 1, 1813, this cartoon by George Cruikshank depicts the British boarding party from the HMS *Shannon* overwhelming the American crew of the USS *Chesapeake*.

American navy regained some of its momentum in September 1813 when it scored a major victory in the Battle of Lake Erie, destroying the British squadron and securing control of the lake—as British ships maintained their domination of the high seas and the American coastline—for the rest of the war.

On the land, meanwhile, American plans to invade Canada were repeatedly thwarted. The Canadian resistance was energetically organized by Guernsey-born soldier and administrator Isaac Brock, who commanded military forces in Upper Canada and had the daunting task of guarding roughly 1,000 miles of frontier. When in July 1812 American troops under the aging general William Hull pushed from Detroit into Upper Canada and then withdrew, Brock followed them back over the border, and then boldly marched on Fort Detroit, where he forced a terrified Hull into a quick and humiliating surrender. Among Canadians, the unexpected victory over their powerful neighbor sent confidence soaring, while in Britain the Regent, upon

THIS PORTRAIT of Isaac Brock was painted posthumously by John Wycliffe Lowes Forster, after the picture attributed to William Berczy, circa 1809. Brock worked closely with the Indigenous leader Tecumseh during the opening months of the War of 1812.

learning of the capture of Detroit, knighted Brock for his "singular judgement, firmness, skill, and courage."[21] Less than two months later, however, the New York State militia launched a predawn raid from Lewiston across the treacherous Niagara River into Canada, where they stormed the heights at the village of Queenston and captured a British gun emplacement. Brock, seven miles to the north at Fort George, was awoken by the sounds of the battle. Riding hard to the scene, he hastily organized an aggressive charge to retake the high ground, only to be killed by an American sniper. Indigenous soldiers led by the Scottish-born Mohawk leader John Norton, together with the Coloured Corps and British reinforcements, eventually retook the heights, forcing the surrender of nearly 1,000 American soldiers.

Brock's great ally in these early months of the land war was Tecumseh, leader of the Shawnee and, more importantly, of what was known as the "Indigenous Confederacy," which he founded to unite and rejuvenate opposition to American expansionism, and which he envisioned as a union of Indigenous nations living on the lands that stretched from the Great Lakes to the Gulf of Mexico. "A more sagacious or a more gallant warrior does not, I believe, exist," Brock declared of Tecumseh, who, with his men, appeared "determined to continue the contest" with the Americans "until they obtain the Ohio for a boundary."[22] Tecumseh was with Brock when the British marched on Detroit, and he played a key role in the hapless Hull's decision to raise the white flag.

Eight months later, in league with the far less inspiring British general Henry Procter, Tecumseh lay siege to Fort Meigs in Ohio. But when the offensive failed, he reluctantly agreed to withdraw on the understanding that he and Procter would soon engage the pursuing Americans, who were led by the major general and future president, William Henry Harrison. After eight days in retreat, the Indigenous and British fighters turned to face Harrison's forces on October 5, 1813, at Moraviantown (near present-day Chatham, in southwestern Ontario). Procter performed poorly at the battle, leaving his tired soldiers disorganized and vulnerable, and confirming Indigenous fears that their British allies lacked commitment and would abandon them in a crisis. The Indigenous forces, keen to confront the despised

Americans and push back into Ohio, fought fiercely, but when Tecumseh was killed their efforts disintegrated, and they fell into retreat. Harrison knew he had vanquished a formidable adversary. Tecumseh, he asserted, was "one of those uncommon geniuses, which spring up occasionally to produce revolutions."[23] With Tecumseh out of the way, the Americans were now firmly in control of the northwest. It was the end of the Indigenous Confederacy.

Neither British nor United States forces could gain the upper hand, however. Both sides struggled with sickness and desertion, with guerrilla warfare atrocities, and with cross-border invasions and counter-invasions. Most famously, on the morning of April 27, 1813, an American force of 1,700 regulars landed on the northwestern shore of Lake Ontario, withstood the fire of a small group of Indigenous fighters, and then, as the British resolve melted away, easily seized control of the town, fort, and dockyard of York (now Toronto), the capital of Upper Canada. Outnumbered by more than two to one, and facing almost certain death in battle, the American-born British commander Sir Roger Hale Sheaffe gathered his regulars and hastily retreated eastward to the British naval base at Kingston, leaving local militia and civilians to deal with the Americans, who looted homes, smashed the local printing press, and set fire to the Parliament buildings.

Humiliated, the British took their tit-for-tat revenge sixteen months later. Freed from their military commitments in Europe by the abdication of Napoleon in April 1814, they went on the offensive in America, appointing the Peninsular War veteran Major General Robert Ross to command an expeditionary force that grew to 4,500 regulars, and in August they sailed up the Chesapeake Bay and landed at Benedict, Maryland. The British strategy was to intensify attacks across the region in order to force America to divert its troops from the frontiers of Upper and Lower Canada. Ross soon set his sights on Washington, less than fifty miles away, and after British regulars routed a numerically superior force of American militiamen at the Battle of Bladensburg, he entered the capital on the evening of August 24, 1814.

James Madison and his administration had fled only hours earlier, but not before Dolley Madison, the president's wife, had organized the safe removal of government papers and precious holdings. When Ross and his advanced party entered the president's Executive Mansion, they found that Madison "had prepared a supper for the expected conquerors." Ross and his men "voraciously devoured" the meal instead, and "the health of the Prince Regent and success to his Majesty's arms by sea and land, was drunk in the best wines."[24] In the next twenty-four hours, the British put the torch to the Executive Mansion, the Capitol building, the Treasury building, and the State and War Department buildings, before riding out of Washington and back to their ships.

Baltimore was next. Landing at North Point, Ross led some 4,000 British soldiers ashore and started to march on the city, but the Americans had learned from the sacking of Washington, and this time they had in place a much stouter defense force of 3,200 militiamen. Skirmishes began as soon as the redcoats came into view. Ross, immediately involving himself in the action, was mortally wounded when a bullet slammed through his right arm and into his chest. The next morning, Vice Admiral Sir Alexander Cochrane, commander of the North American station, ordered the bombardment of Baltimore and the most important of its forts, Fort McHenry. The Americans had previously seized and sunk twenty-four ships in the harbor, however, which prevented Cochrane from sailing in and making a direct attack. His response was to stay out of the range of the fort's gunners and to launch a ferocious long-range shelling that lasted for almost twenty-four hours and that pounded American positions with between 1,500 and 1,800 shells, including approximately 400 that hit Fort McHenry directly.[25]

Francis Scott Key, a young American lawyer, spent the day pacing the deck of a nearby truce ship (a ship carrying a white flag which could be hoisted to signal to the enemy a wish to either confer or surrender) and watching the bombardment, which continued throughout the night. Would British firepower overwhelm the fort, or would American fighters successfully defend it? At dawn, Key saw the American flag still flying above Fort McHenry. He pulled an envelope from his pocket and, in a moment of intense pride and excitement, scribbled down the words and phrases that he would later polish in a Baltimore hotel room and that would become the poem, and then the song, and then the national anthem that we now know as "The Star Spangled Banner." America had won a resounding victory, and the British withdrew.

Both sides began looking for a way out, tired of winning individual battles but not the war. Peace talks were under way at Ghent (modern Belgium) by August 1814, but they dragged on through the autumn, and the fighting continued. Having failed at Baltimore, the British planned to capture New Orleans to stop the movement of American goods and soldiers along the Mississippi River, to gain access to the vast resources of the Louisiana Purchase, and to give themselves more bargaining power at the Ghent negotiations. On December 14, Vice Admiral Cochrane's fleet quickly disposed of a small American flotilla at the Battle of Lake Borgne, and in the week that followed, British troops pushed to within nine miles of New Orleans, where they paused to await the arrival of their commander, Sir Edward Pakenham, who had been delayed by adverse winds and who finally reached the British position on Christmas day. Two and a half years earlier, Pakenham had been with his brother-in-law, the Duke of Wellington, at the Battle of Salamanca and had played a crucial role in the British victory over the French. Now he found himself wedged onto a narrow strip of land in southeastern Louisiana, with the Mississippi River on his left and an impassable swamp on his right, preparing to lead roughly 6,000 British regulars and 1,000 black soldiers from two West India regiments into battle against the Americans.[26]

Andrew Jackson was ready for Pakenham. The commander of the U.S. Army of the Southwest, and a future president of the United States, "Old Hickory," as he was known, had found New Orleans ill-prepared for an attack when he reached the city on December 1. But over the course of the next three and a half weeks, he got the American side primed to fight, for he was a brave if ruthless military leader, and he loathed both the British and any talk of American capitulation. Building on his army of regulars and militia, Jackson accepted backwoods volunteers, black men, bayou pirates, Indigenous fighters, and French and Spanish mercenaries, all of whom he banded together into a single fighting unit of about 4,000 men. At the same time, he ordered the construction of a barricade across the field from where the British were readying themselves for battle. Made up of cotton bales, sugar barrels, and earth, it ran the three-fifths of a mile between the Mississippi River on Jackson's right flank and the swamp on his left, with a wide empty ditch stretching out in front of it and artillery pieces positioned behind it.

Pakenham struck in the early hours of January 8, 1815. It was a two-pronged offensive. Colonel William Thornton crossed the Mississippi with 500 regulars and, after advancing up the west bank to outflank the American position, drove off 800 Kentucky militiamen and occupied the deserted ground. His success, however, came far too late for the main assault. Pakenham, who was both full of misgivings about the British position and overconfident that the undertrained Americans would flee at the sight of the advancing British regulars, waited until daybreak and then, to the sound of drums and bagpipes, gave the order for his men to storm the American breastwork. Within minutes there was panic and blood everywhere. Far from bolting, the Americans stood up from behind their well-fortified positions and aimed volley after volley into the three British columns advancing across the open field. Pakenham, watching the massacre unfold, tried to rally his troops and was killed when grapeshot split his spine. In less than half an hour the battle was over. The redcoats had been torn to shreds, suffering as many as 1,800 casualties (including 300–400 killed), while the Americans had only 71 killed or wounded.[27] The campaign against New Orleans was finished. The British retreated once again.

One month later, the futility of the war was made painfully clear when word finally reached British forces that a peace treaty had been signed at Ghent on Christmas Eve 1814, meaning that Pakenham had led his troops into the blood-soaked Battle of New Orleans two weeks after the War of 1812 had officially ended. The Treaty of Ghent restored the status quo without resolving any of the issues that had caused the war in the first place. One British officer, Jersey-born Lieutenant John Le Couteur, aptly described the conflict as "a hot and unnatural war between kindred people." The British were happy to go home. "We . . . saw that neither fame nor any military distinction could be acquired in this species of milito-nautico-guerilla-plundering warfare," wrote the veteran Harry Smith.[28] If he and his fellow soldiers had hoped for a respite once they reached England, however, it was not to be. Napoleon had just broken from Elba. Wellington needed them again in Europe.

Yet if the numbers were small, and the battles themselves a kind of sideshow to the gigantic struggle being waged by Britain against Napoleon, the War of 1812 nevertheless forged the future of an entire continent. It established land and lake boundaries, it intensified a sense of national identity and purpose in both Canada and the United States, and it confirmed that in North America there would be two separate countries with two different versions of freedom and democracy. For the Indigenous nations of North America, however, the War of 1812 was a catastrophe that opened the way to western expansionism on both sides of the border that did not end until Canada and the United States reached all the way to the Pacific Ocean. Without the land they had lived on for centuries, Indigenous nations, spirits, and lives were broken. The War of 1812 set in motion the policies and land transfers that inflicted cultural genocide on the Indigenous peoples of North America, deepening old wounds and opening new ones that have bled in many instances from the Regency up to today, and that still have not begun to heal.

III

War was not the only reason Britons traveled abroad. Indeed, across the Regency and to destinations around the world, tens of thousands of women, men, and children left Britain, some for only a short time, others never to return. Many went willingly, as missionaries, philanthropists, entrepreneurs, mercenaries, fortune hunters, and empire builders. Others went as convicts on transport ships. Still others sailed as emigrants, from those who were forced from their homes in some way to those who simply believed that a better life awaited them elsewhere.

The Levant was the most popular destination for tourists and explorers. For centuries the entire region had been under the dominion of the Ottoman Empire, and its customs, peoples, landscapes, and antiquities were a source of fascination to many British travelers, including Byron's friend John Cam Hobhouse, the Scottish novelist John Galt, and the physician Henry Holland. However, the most celebrated Regency tour of the Levant is Byron's *Childe Harold's Pilgrimage*, a verse travelogue in which the poet details his experiences in Portugal, Spain, Malta, Greece, Albania, and Turkey. Galt, who traveled with Byron for several weeks, noted that in *Childe Harold*, the poet thrilled audiences by producing, not creative renderings of Mediterranean landscapes, but faithful copies of them. Similarly, according to Galt, Byron based one of the most famous figures of the Regency—the Byronic hero—not on himself but on his firsthand observations of Mediterranean adventurers whose courage and intensity lie behind not just the eponymous Childe Harold but behind all the magnetic heroes who followed in Byron's enormously successful series of "Turkish Tales," including *The Giaour*, *The Bride of Abydos*, *The Corsair*, and *Lara*. "The traveller who visits that region . . . will see there how little of invention was necessary to form such heroes as Conrad" of *The Corsair*, Galt states, "and how much the actual traffic of life and trade is constantly stimulating enterprise and bravery."[29]

In addition to sightseers and outcasts on journeys of discovery, British antiquarians and treasure hunters spread out across the Levant. Lady Hester Stanhope, the indomitable niece of the late prime minister William Pitt, had, as Byron observed, "a great disregard of received notions in her conversation as well as conduct." With her rich and much younger lover, Michael Bruce, she traveled in great style to Turkey, Egypt, the Holy Land, and Lebanon. Most daringly, in 1813, under the escort of a well-paid Bedouin cavalcade, she became the first European woman to reach Palmyra in Syria, where she was crowned "Queen of the Desert" and where she spent several days exploring the ancient ruins. Two years later, Lady Hester arrived in Ascalon, a coastal city north of Gaza, in search of buried treasure, which she had promised to turn over to the Ottoman authorities if found, for she was in pursuit only of excitement. When her team unearthed a headless, nearly seven-foot-high statue of what appeared to be a Roman emperor, she "ordered it to be broken into a thousand pieces that malicious persons might not say I came to look for statues for my countrymen and not for treasures for the Porte."[30] The digging continued fruitlessly for another ten days, and then Lady Hester packed up and left Ascalon—though not the Middle East, where she lived for the rest of her life.

William John Bankes was a wealthy thrill seeker who distinguished himself as both an art connoisseur and a serious scholar. Annabella Milbanke rejected his proposal of marriage in 1812, the same year that she refused his good friend Byron. Bankes decided to travel. He followed Wellington's armies across the peninsula, buying up art treasures as he went, and then journeyed in 1815 to Egypt, where he made important contributions to nascent Egyptology and the history of hieroglyphics. Twice he took exploratory tours up the Nile, collecting artifacts, taking detailed notes, producing meticulous site plans, and sketching monuments and inscriptions. Bankes's prize possession was a large obelisk that he discovered on the Nile island of Philae near Aswan in 1815, and that he had transported back to Kingston Lacy, the family estate in Dorset, where it can still be seen.

Like Bankes, the Italian adventurer Giovanni Belzoni arrived in Egypt in 1815, leaving behind his career in England as a renowned circus strongman. Three years later, Belzoni accompanied Bankes on his second trip up the Nile. At the ancient capital of Thebes, Belzoni skillfully engineered the removal of the damaged but monumental granite statue of the head and upper body of Ramses II ("the Younger Memnon"), which he shipped back to England and which is now in the British Museum. Close by, Belzoni rediscovered the tomb of Seti I, the grandest in the Valley of the Kings, enclosed within which lay a superb alabaster sarcophagus that is now housed in Sir John Soane's Museum in London. Several more outstanding discoveries followed before Belzoni left Egypt in 1819 and returned to London, where he published his remarkable *Narrative of the Operations and Recent Discoveries within the Pyramids, Temples, Tombs, and Excavations, in Egypt and Nubia* (1820).

The most extensive and controversial removal of antiquities, however, was the work arranged by Lord Elgin. Appointed British ambassador to Constantinople in 1799, Elgin obtained permission from the Ottoman authorities to study, measure, and sketch the surviving sculptures on the Parthenon at Athens—motivated by his desire to bestow "some benefit on the progress of taste in England" as well as by his knowledge of the terrible damage being inflicted on the monument by European souvenir hunters and by the Turkish garrison stationed on the Acropolis.[31] But Elgin's plans soon expanded into a much more invasive operation in which—with the full knowledge of the Turkish authorities, who were indifferent to the fate of Greece's cultural heritage—large sections of the Parthenon frieze were cut down, packed up, and shipped off to Britain, along with all manner of other treasure. The expense for the entire project, including artists, excavators, transporters, and various agents, fell almost exclusively on Elgin, and by the time the last shipment of the Parthenon Marbles reached Britain in 1812, he was financially ruined. Four years later, following a Parliamentary Select Committee investigation that cleared Elgin of any wrongdoing, the British government purchased the "Elgin Marbles" for £35,000, a price far below Elgin's expenses, and placed them in the British Museum. Still deeply in debt, and with a disease that was undoubtedly syphilis eating savagely into his nose, Elgin retired from public life.

To many, Elgin was responsible for saving some of the most significant sculptures of the ancient world, sculptures that transcended place and time and that inspired the British arts community as he had always believed they would. For John Keats, who lacked a formal knowledge of Greek, the Parthenon fragments revealed a vision of the ancient world that he commemorated in his sonnet "On Seeing the Elgin Marbles" and that he realized much more impressively in his "Ode on a Grecian Urn." Another poet, Felicia Hemans, believed that relocating the marbles would usher in a new dawn of British creativity and freedom. "And who can tell how pure, how bright a flame, / Caught from these models, may illume the west?" she asks in *Modern Greece* (1817). Benjamin Robert Haydon declared that the arrival of the marbles marked "an Aera in public feeling" and that it effected an "extraordinary . . . revolution . . . in England, as to what was the true high style."[32]

Byron was having none of this. Unlike virtually every other commentator, he had actually been in Athens when Elgin's crews were at work prying loose the Parthenon sculptures, and he damned an endorsement of the project like Hemans's *Modern Greece* as "Good for nothing—written by some one who has never been there." Elgin was not a rescuer. He was a plunderer. He had not saved the Parthenon frieze. He had looted it. In *Childe Harold*, Byron attacked the vanity, pettiness, corruption, and bickering that characterized the entire operation on the Parthenon, as Elgin hauled away "mouldering shrines" from "a bleeding land." More fiercely, in *The Curse of Minerva* (1812), Byron broadened his often personal assault on Elgin into a condemnation of the moral bankruptcy of Britain itself, not only for its failing domestic policies but for its colonial ambitions, which invariably involved tyranny and violence. With Hemans and Haydon on one side, and Byron on the other, Regency artists and writers defined the terms of the debate about the Parthenon Marbles that continues to inflame opinion today and that raises crucial legal and moral questions about history, museum stewardship, cultural commodification, and postcolonial restitution.[33] The Greek government has repeatedly asked for the return of the Parthenon Marbles. They remain in the British Museum.

IV

In pursuit of wealth and treasure, Britons also traveled far beyond the Levant. The British East India Company was the largest and most powerful multinational corporation in the world. Founded in 1600, it had by the time of the Regency transformed itself from a mercantile body into an empire builder, with a vast series of highly lucrative trade routes under its control and hundreds of thousands of people in its employ, including the soldiers of its own private army. India, with its rich stores of silk, cotton, tea, coffee, and spices, was the company's most prized possession, and from its base in Calcutta (as it was then known), it extended its influence across the subcontinent until, in the Regency, it achieved a stranglehold. In 1813, when the East India Company's charter was renewed, the British government granted Christian missionaries permission to proselytize throughout India, and a year later the

Church of England consecrated Thomas Fanshaw Middleton as the first bishop of Calcutta, a diocese that included the whole of India.

More decisively, the Regent used his influence to have Lord Moira appointed commander in chief of British forces in India. Arriving in Calcutta in the autumn of 1813, Moira soon extended British control in the region. In March 1816, after seventeen months of border warfare, he made an advantageous peace with Nepal, which ceded roughly one-third of its territory to British India. For the victory he was created Marquess of Hastings. An even greater triumph came a few years later when Hastings led his forces against the Maratha Confederacy, an alliance of powerful warrior families that controlled most of northwestern India. Britain had already fought two wars against the Confederacy (1775–82 and 1803–5), and in the third Maratha War (1817–18) Hastings finally destroyed it. The triumph increased the momentum of Britain's colonizing project and gave the East India Company unfettered access to the riches of India.

British life in British India comes most vividly into view in a series of journals, letters, and diaries. Edward Ellerker Williams, a gifted amateur artist and the future friend of Percy Shelley, served for more than six years in the East India Company army. In addition to producing many drawings of Indian ruins and landscapes, Williams wrote *Sporting Sketches during a Short Stay in Hindustane*, a remarkable travel diary in which he records his visits to the mosques and harems of Delhi, his adventures hunting big game in the jungles of Rhotuk, and his phrenological reflections on the people of the East. The author and illustrator Maria Graham traveled for two years in southeast India, sometimes with her husband, sometimes not, and she took a keen interest in the country's history, languages, literature, music, mythology, and religion. Yet, as she made clear in her *Journal of a Residence in India* (1812) and *Letters on India* (1814), she was also a committed imperialist, and she urged her fellow Britons, both in India and back home, to continue to "conduct the innovations necessary for . . . our own security" and for the "permanent improvement" of the Indians.[34]

Lady Maria Nugent spent three years in India with her husband Sir George Nugent, who served as commander in chief before the arrival of Lord Moira, and who accepted the position solely for financial reasons. Heartbroken at having to leave her four young children behind in England, Lady Nugent spent much of her time battling loneliness, extreme heat, and poor health. She recovered some of her wonted spirit when, beginning in July 1812, she and her husband embarked on a fourteen-month tour of the upper provinces, boating on rivers and marching overland with their vast retinue (consisting of 87 elephants, 355 camels, and upwards of 3,000 attendants) in order to check imperial borders and pay diplomatic visits to Indian rulers. She wrote insightfully on Anglo-India relations, deplored the lack of Christian reverence in her fellow colonists, and praised Hindus "for real feelings of religion." But through it all she retained—like Graham—her overweening confidence in the benefits bestowed by British rule. "I cannot help remarking," she declared in 1813, "how much . . . more prosperous and happy the people seem, in this part of India, which has been so much longer under the dominion of the British Government."[35]

Other parts of Asia also attracted British colonists. Robert Morrison was one of the first British Protestant missionaries in China, and the first major British sinologist. Ordained in 1807, he arrived in Canton (Guangzhou) later that same year, and in 1809 he was hired by the East India Company as a translator, though he remained tirelessly focused on promulgating his religious beliefs and completely mastering the Chinese language. His *Grammar of the Chinese Language*, and the first volume of the *Dictionary of the Chinese Language*, appeared in 1815, and the following year he accompanied Lord Amherst on his failed trade mission to Peking (Beijing), which Morrison describes in his *Memoir of the Principal Occurrences during an Embassy from the British Government to the Court of China*. Perhaps most intriguingly, in 1819, he published—in Chinese and at Canton—his *Brief Account of Things that I have seen and heard during a Voyage Westwards around the World*, a fictionalized travelogue in which a Chinese scholar seeks to demonstrate the geographical and historical interconnectedness of Asia and Europe.

William Milne, after studying—like Morrison—at the college of the London Missionary Society at Gosport in Hampshire, was ordained in 1812 and shortly thereafter joined Morrison in China, where he assisted him with his lexicographical and translation work, and where he edited and published the *Indo-Chinese Gleaner*, a quarterly magazine of miscellaneous articles that was designed to disseminate information to British colonists and to keep them up-to-date on initiatives under way in settlements across the region. Milne traveled widely, including a missionary tour through Java, before founding with Morrison the Anglo-Chinese College at Malacca in 1818, with "the reciprocal cultivation of Chinese and European literature" as its declared objective. The following year the two men completed their translation into Chinese of the Old and New Testaments. "Christianity, as revealed in the Holy Scriptures, is the only religion which is in all respects adapted to the moral state of the whole world," Milne declared with customary zeal in his *Retrospect of the first ten years of the Protestant Mission to China*, published in January 1820 at the Anglo-Chinese Press at Malacca; "hence it possesses an indisputable and unrivalled claim to supersede every other."[36]

Thomas Stamford Raffles was also on a mission in the East, though his was commercial and philanthropic rather than religious. Just fourteen years old when he began as a clerk in the service of the East India Company, he rose quickly through the ranks, distinguished by his agile intellect, his immense capacity for work, his enthusiasm for languages, and his fascination with natural history. Most East India Company agents were interested only in money and perhaps adventure, but Raffles had a vision of the world—colonialist at its crux, but also progressive and humane, especially on issues such as education, disease control, prison reform, slave emancipation, and religious freedom: "I am . . . inclined . . . to let people go to heaven in their own way," he declared.[37] Determined both to undermine the Dutch—who controlled the East Indies—and to improve the lives of millions of people native to the archipelago, Raffles first served in Asia at Penang on the Strait of Malacca and then as lieutenant governor at Java, where in September 1811 British forces occupied the island after expelling the French and the Dutch.

Raffles soon transformed the British presence in the region. On his orders, the military seized the nearby islands of Billiton and, more importantly, Banca, which was rich in the lucrative commodity of tin.

He also launched sweeping economic reforms, saw to it that local people were trained to administer the smallpox vaccine, and introduced measures designed to ameliorate the plight of the island's slave population. The government of Java, he believed, "should consider the inhabitants without reference to bare mercantile profits."[38] Such views on what we would now call "corporate social responsibility" were far ahead of their time and put Raffles decidedly at odds with a trading company fixated on making money. He compounded his problems by pushing so hard to implement his radical reforms of the land tenure system that he lost important sources of government revenue. When the island's paper currency began to depreciate, Raffles resorted to selling public lands without the proper authorization.

By 1816 the directors of the East India Company had had enough, and they recalled him. Broken in health and shattered by the death of his beloved wife Olivia, Raffles returned to England, where he threw himself into the task of writing a two-volume *History of Java*. Dedicated to the Regent, it brought him a knighthood in 1817 and dramatically reversed his fortunes. Remarried, and with his utopian aspirations as strong as ever, Raffles left again for the East in November 1817 to take up the lieutenant governorship at Bencoolen (Bengkulu), a pepper port in southwestern Sumatra. Horrified on his arrival at run-down, malaria-ridden, earthquake-damaged Fort Marlborough, Raffles moved swiftly to improve the situation. He banned gambling, reorganized the administration, increased pepper production, and emancipated the slaves who belonged to the East India Company.[39]

Next, he took his biggest step. Tired of watching the Dutch maintain control of the East Indies, and anxious to secure the safe passage of British ships through the Strait of Malacca and on to the trading ports of Japan and China, Raffles in late January 1819 landed on the island of Singapore, at that point home to approximately 150 people, covered in jungle, and part of the Riau-Johor empire. His actions were not sanctioned by London, and they ran the risk of serious repercussions from the Dutch, but Raffles knew that if the British were able to hang on to the island, "our influence over the Archipelago, as far as concerns our commerce, will be fully established." Within days he had successfully exploited a confused political situation between two half-brothers with rival claims to the Sultanate of Riau-Johor, and on February 6, 1819, he signed a treaty with Hussein, the elder brother out of favor with the Dutch, confirming the East India Company's right to found a British colony on Singapore.[40] The Dutch cried foul at the blatant British encroachment into their trading territory, but they mounted no military action.

Almost four months later, Raffles returned to the island to oversee the implementation of plans that would permanently alter the political and economic geography of Southeast Asia. He was delighted with the progress that had been made in his absence. Roads were being built, and the new township already had more than 5,000 inhabitants, most of whom seem to have come from Malaysia and China. More jungle was cleared. Maps were developed for the town, including the location of the garrison, the hospital, the botanical garden, the church, the mosque, the school, the warehouses, and the government buildings. Above all, Raffles established Singapore as a trading post where no duties were exacted from visiting ships, an initiative that quickly transformed it from a stopover point between India and China into a flourishing commercial hub that attracted traders of all kinds from across the entire region, and that gave rise—as Raffles had imagined—to Singapore as an international city of free trade. A statue of him now stands in the heart of the downtown core on the spot where he is reported to have come ashore. The plaque below it reads: "On this historic site Sir Thomas Stamford Raffles first landed in Singapore on 28 January 1819 and with genius and perception changed the destiny of Singapore from an obscure fishing village to a great seaport and modern metropolis."

V

It was an explosion that shook the world. On April 5, 1815, Mount Tambora, a volcano on the Indonesian island of Sumbawa, erupted. Raffles, nearly 800 miles away on Java, heard the explosion and mistook it for cannon fire. Five days later, Tambora erupted again, this time even more fiercely. Three massive columns of flame shot up into the air and merged briefly at their peak, blasting ash, debris, and molten rock everywhere, while lava poured down the mountainside and into the ocean, triggering firestorms, whirlwinds, and tsunamis. Almost all of the 12,000 people living in close proximity to Tambora were dead within the first twenty-four hours. Meanwhile, villages twenty miles away were covered in ash up to forty inches thick, and hundreds of miles away ten-inch layers of dust brought down houses, destroyed crops, poisoned water supplies, and killed birds, fish, and cattle. Famine, disease, and infection quickly followed for the human population, killing tens of thousands more and driving the death toll in Indonesia alone to almost 90,000 people. The entire eruption took as much as four thousand feet off the top of Tambora and propelled the finer black and gray particles of ash, soot, and dust up into the stratosphere, where winds gradually dispersed the cloud around the globe.[41]

In Britain, the consequences of the catastrophe were not felt until early the following spring. At a time when a series of postwar crises had placed the country under enormous strain, the almost invisible cloud of stratospheric ash began wreaking havoc on weather patterns, blocking out the sun, cooling temperatures, unleashing torrential rains, and seriously exacerbating an already volatile situation. What is more, no one at the time understood that the Tambora explosion was behind these changes, as it was not until the second half of the twentieth century that scientists were able to demonstrate conclusively that major volcanic eruptions cool the climate. J. M. W. Turner complained that he needed to be "web-footed like a drake" to cope with the "Rain, Rain, Rain, day after day." Jane Austen spoke to a neighbor "of its' being bad weather for the Hay—& he returned me the comfort of its' being much worse for the Wheat." Samuel Taylor Coleridge called it *"end of the World Weather."* James Mill prophesized bloody ruin. "There must now be of necessity a very deficient crop, and very high prices—and these with an unexampled scarcity of work will produce a degree of misery, the thought of which makes the flesh creep on one's bones—one third of the people must die—it would be a blessing to take them into the streets and highways, and cut their throats as we do with pigs."[42]

The mood of many in Europe was just as savage. Most famously, in Switzerland, the "wet, ungenial summer" of 1816 gave rise to the gothic horrors of John Polidori's *The Vampyre*, Mary Shelley's *Frankenstein*, and Byron's "Darkness," the work most closely associated with the disaster. Written at Geneva on "a celebrated dark day" when "the fowls went to roost at noon," the poem captures the fear of that terrible "year without summer," when it seemed that the sun was dying, that the earth was shriveling, that famine and deprivation were inescapable, and that supplications were mockeries. "I had a dream, which was not all a dream," Byron states:

> The bright sun was extinguish'd, and the stars
> Did wander darkling in the eternal space,
> Rayless, and pathless, and the icy earth
> Swung blind and blackening in the moonless air;
> Morn came, and went—and came, and brought no day,
> And men forgot their passions in the dread
> Of this their desolation.

Directly and indirectly, the eruption of Mount Tambora killed hundreds of thousands of people. Ten times more violent than the famous Krakatoa eruption of 1883, it remains the most powerful eruption in recorded history.[43]

VI

Beyond the volcanic ash that literally cast a shadow over Regency Britain, the East manifested itself in the country in a wide variety of other forms. Through the distorted lens of colonial conquest, it was variously sexualized, infantilized, and idealized by a host of writers who had—in the vast majority of instances—never been there but who created representations of it that both unnerved and enthralled Regency audiences eager to consume the foreign, the exotic, and the mysterious. The myths of ancient Greece were explored and updated in long poems such as John Keats's *Hyperion* and Percy Shelley's *Pro-*

metheus Unbound, and in novels like Mary Shelley's *Frankenstein; or, The Modern Prometheus* and John Polidori's *Ernestus Berchtold; or, The Modern Oedipus*. Percy Shelley set his revolutionary epic, *The Revolt of Islam* (1818), in Turkey and Greece. Byron's "Turkish Tales" generated scores of imitations, including John Hamilton Reynolds's *Safie: an Eastern Tale* (1814), and Edward Bulwer's first volume of poetry, *Ismael: an Oriental Tale* (1820). Polidori based *The Vampyre* on a "superstition . . . very general in the East," and one that did not "extend itself to the Greeks until after the establishment of Christianity."[44]

India, as the most profitable and populous of Britain's colonies, also drew a great deal of commentary. In 1817, James Mill published his monumental *History of British India*. Shaped throughout by his stern utilitarianism, the work reveals Mill's deep faith in the "civilizing mission" of British colonialism, a faith that led him to damn the East India Company for maladministration and that prompted in him even fiercer denunciations of the Indian people, who, Mill argued, needed British intervention to rid them of superstition, ignorance, and misogyny. Typically, Mill writes, "the Hindus," like "the Chinese," were "dissembling, treacherous, mendacious, to an excess which surpasses even the usual measure of uncultivated society." Percy Shelley took a more enlightened approach, maintaining that "the thing to be sought" is that the Indian people should do "as they would if they were free [to] attain to a system of arts and literature on their own." But he too accepts that the British imperial presence has brought the people of India substantial advantages. "*Revolutions* in the political and religious state of the Indian peninsula seem to be accomplishing," he notes, "and it cannot be doubted but the zeal of the missionaries of what is called the Christian faith will produce beneficial innovation there."[45]

Regency writers also produced many novels and poems on India. Sydney Owenson (the future Lady Morgan) set her novel *The Missionary* (1811) in seventeenth-century India amid various religious and sexual pressures that thwart both Luxima, a Hindu priestess of exquisite sensibility, and her lover, a Portuguese friar named Hilarion. Luxima does not renounce her religion, and she meets a tragic end, but the novel is highlighted by those moments when she and Hilarion acknowledge the superiority of love to religious dogma, and the possibility of a union between a Christian and a Hindu. "Silently gazing, in wonder, upon each other, they stood finely opposed, the noblest specimens of the human species, as it appears in the most opposite regions of the earth; she, like the East, lovely and luxuriant; he, like the West, lofty and commanding."[46]

Thomas Moore presented a more playful and enthusiastically exotic vision of India in his long poem *Lalla Rookh*. A runaway bestseller that benefited from the craze for Oriental verse tales initiated by his friend Byron, it recounts the journey of the eponymous princess Lalla Rookh (her name means "tulip cheek") from Delhi to Kashmir to meet her betrothed, and is composed of four distinct verse tales that range from the gothic through the pious to the tantalizingly sensual and that are presented to the princess as evening entertainments by her handsome minstrel Feramorz, who turns out to be her lover in disguise. Moore did not create his vision of the people, animals, customs, and sceneries of India from firsthand observations. Rather, he based *Lalla Rookh* on the information he gathered from the works of famous seventeenth- and eighteenth-century European writers who traveled to the East. The result is an engaging poetic fantasy that brims with mannerisms and stereotypes but that profoundly shaped popular conceptions of India in the Regency and far beyond. Moore, declared John Wilson in his 1817 review, has "imbued his mind with so familiar a knowledge of eastern scenery—that we feel as if we were reading the poetry of one of the children of the Sun."[47]

Orientalism permeated Regency culture in many other ways as well. Consumers filled their homes with Eastern decorations. "Every room is in masquerade," Mary Russell Mitford reported of one ornamented cottage: "the saloon Chinese, full of jars and mandarins and pagodas; the library Egyptian, all covered with hieroglyphics, and swarming with furniture crocodiles and sphinxes."[48] Sir Charles Cockerell, a wealthy banker and longtime employee of the East India Company at Calcutta, built Sezincote, a Mogul Indian palace, in the Gloucestershire countryside. Constructed of Cotswold stone stained red-orange to imitate Indian sandstone, Sezincote House features an extravagant weathered-copper onion dome and an elegant orangery, while the grounds include grottoes, temples, statues of Brahmin bulls, and a Persian paradise garden.

No British architectural tribute to the East, however, surpasses the Brighton Pavilion, the Regent's seaside home away from home. Originally a late-eighteenth-century farmhouse, it was expanded by the architect Henry Holland into a modest neoclassical villa, but plans to carry out further and more elaborate developments in an Indian style collapsed due to a lack of funds, and it was only in 1815 that—with the increased financial clout accorded to him as the sovereign de facto—the Regent was able to relaunch the project under the supervision of the brilliant architect John Nash, who steadily enlarged and transformed the building into an Oriental palace of dreams. On the inside, the decor had been predominantly Eastern for a number of years—"All is Chinese, quite overloaded with china of all sorts," observed one guest in 1811—but Nash added several new Eastern flourishes, including pillars entwined by serpents, lights in the shape of lotus flowers, and a series of large painted panels with Chinese domestic scenes. On the outside, too, Nash introduced a series of striking Eastern features, including four onion domes, two on either side of a gigantic central onion dome that was flanked by minarets. "How can one describe such a piece of architecture"? asked Countess Lieven. "The style is a mixture of Moorish, Tartar, Gothic, and Chinese, and all in stone and iron."[49]

The entire scheme provoked outrage, and to many the Pavilion quickly became the most potent example of how egregiously out of touch the Regent was. How could he be asking for large sums of public money to indulge his infatuation with chinoiserie when in the country at large there was so much suffering and so much anger? Ultra-Tories like John Wilson Croker called the project "an absurd waste of money," while there was equal contempt at the other end of the political spectrum, where satiric artists like George Cruikshank lashed the Regent in print after print as a grotesquely fat Chinese emperor, and radical journalists including William Hazlitt sneered at the Pavilion as "a collection of stone pumpkins and pepper-boxes."[50]

Nonetheless, against considerable aesthetic odds, the Brighton Pavilion is a dazzling success. Built though it was when the money was desperately needed almost everywhere else, it stands as a remarkable monument to the Regent and his vision of what the country was and could become. He wanted Britain—as the wealthiest and most powerful nation in the world—to be recognized not only for its military prowess and growing empire but also for its cultural accomplishments. In the planning and construction of the Brighton Pavilion, the Regent flouted the rules, ignored the critics, and pushed the project to the heights of imaginative extravagance without allowing it to tip over into confusion or vulgarity. The Pavilion is his shrine to the expertise, the originality, and the sheer bravado of his Regency, and it reveals the Oriental fantasies at the crux of the decade. Part homage and part pastiche, it is, remarkably, an Eastern structure that most spectacularly symbolizes the British Regency.

VII

A different export from the East was opium. Probably the oldest drug known to humankind, it is obtained by slightly incising the unripe seed capsules of the poppy plant, *Papaver somniferum*. The East India Company exported it from Bengal to China, and then used the revenue from the sales to buy Chinese luxury items like spices, ivories, porcelain, silk, and, especially, tea, all of which were in great demand in Regency Britain. Better, shorter, and more well-established trade routes, however, meant that Turkey supplied the vast majority of the opium consumed in Britain. Turkish opium was also a good deal stronger than the Indian variety. Opium pills were available, but most people consumed the drug as "laudanum," a tincture "made by pouring the best French brandy, or spirits of wine, upon crude Opium." The drug was an unremarkable part of daily life in the Regency. It was cheaper than beer or gin. It was legal, a very different situation from the restrictions and criminality that we associate with opiates today. And it was available everywhere, from chemists and general stores to bakers, grocers, publicans, tailors, street hawkers, market vendors, and country peddlers.[51]

Opium was a crucial part of Regency medicine. People of every age and class used it for self-medication in much the same way as aspi-rin is used today. Opium was also "the most common drug in medical practice," as the Edinburgh physician Robert Christison observed, and doctors recommended it for all manner of mental and physical ailments, from bronchitis, cancer, depression, diabetes, and hyster-ics to malaria, smallpox, sciatica, and venereal disease. Entrepreneurs, quacks, and pharmacists marketed it in a vast array of cure-alls. Mothers and nursemaids actively and unselfconsciously adminis-tered it to ill, wakeful, or unruly children in now sinister-sounding panaceas such as Atkinson's Infants' Preservative or Mother Bailey's Quieting Syrup. Other popular opium-based nostrums included Collis Browne's Chlorodyne, Dr. Dover's Powder, Godfrey's Cor-dial, and the Kendal Black Drop (rumored to be four times stronger than laudanum). Walter Scott took opium for intense stomach pains; Charles Lamb for a bad cold; Jane Austen's mother for travel sickness; Thomas Moore for cholera; Percy Shelley for headaches; Lord Byron for stress; Robert Southey for hay fever; and so on.[52]

Most of all, opium was highly prized by the medical community— as it had been for centuries—as the best available means of reduc-ing the agonies involved in the brutal business of surgery, when the development of safe and effective anesthetics was still decades away and when screaming patients usually had to be tied or held down by medical attendants while the surgeon sliced and sawed and the blood dripped steadily into the sawdust box below the operating table—to say nothing of the ongoing horrors of the Napoleonic wars and the emergency surgeries and amputations routinely taking place on ships and battlefields. "While the pain is exceedingly severe, opium should always be given, and in repeated doses, so as to keep the system under its influence," declared Samuel Cooper in *The First Lines of the Practice of Surgery*, a standard Regency medical textbook.[53]

The need for opium during surgery was vividly recorded by Fran-ces Burney, who in September 1811 had a mastectomy. Before the operation started, the doctor gave fifty-nine-year-old Burney a "wine cordial," which undoubtedly contained opium and soon induced a kind of "stupor," after which Burney mounted a bedstead and a cambric handkerchief was spread over her face, through which she saw "the glitter of polished Steel." Then, after "a silence the most profound," the "dreadful steel was plunged into the breast—cutting through veins—arteries—flesh—nerves. . . . I began a scream that lasted unintermittingly during the whole time of the incision . . . so excruciating was the agony." Briefly the surgeon withdrew the knife and then began a second incision, "describing a curve," and "cutting against the grain, if I may so say, while the flesh resisted in a manner so forcible" that the surgeon's hand grew tired. Again the knife was withdrawn, and this time Burney concluded the operation was over. But the terrible cutting began for a third time, as the surgeon worked to separate "the foundation of this dreadful gland from the parts to which it adhered." Finally the digging and scraping stopped. This time it was over. Burney had lost consciousness at least twice and was lifted to her bed "totally annihilated." The operation had lasted twenty minutes, including the treatment and the dressing. She had borne it all with immense courage, but it was months before she could even "*think* of it with impunity."[54] Confronted like her with the necessity of life-saving surgery, opium-induced stupors helped thousands of Regency Britons cope with similarly horrifying levels of trauma and pain.

Opium, however, was also widely consumed for other reasons. The Regency, indeed, marks perhaps the most decisive moment in the history of western drug use, for this is when English opium-eaters started to celebrate laudanum, not as belonging exclusively to medicine but as a recreational device that brought exquisite pleasures. It is a shift that has had an enormous and still-accelerating impact on our world and that has made opium and its various derivatives, including heroin, the drug of choice for millions upon millions of users and abusers seeking the euphoria described by some of the Regency's most powerful creative intellects. In *Lalla Rookh*, Moore has Falladeen, the tiresome Chamberlain of the Harem, refresh "his faculties with a dose of that delicious opium." Keats was consuming a good deal of laudanum in early 1819 and writes directly of his drug experience a few months later in the opening lines of his greatest poem, "Ode to a Nightingale": "My heart aches, and a drowsy numbness pains / My sense, as though of hemlock I had drunk, / Or emptied some dull opiate to the drains."[55]

Most famously, Samuel Taylor Coleridge inextricably linked drugs and imaginative rapture in his poetic fragment, "Kubla Khan," first published in 1816. Coleridge claims in the prose "Preface" that the poem was composed in a dream after he swallowed laudanum for medical reasons. In the poem itself, however, he writes about the drug's ability, not to assuage bodily torment but to unlock terrifying passageways into human creativity:

> And all should cry, Beware! Beware!
> His flashing eyes, his floating hair!
> Weave a circle round him thrice,
> And close your eyes with holy dread:
> For he on honey-dew hath fed,
> And drank the milk of Paradise.[56]

In these and other works, Regency writers moved opium out of the medicine cabinet and into the popular bloodstream. They invented recreational drug taking and permanently altered the way drugs are consumed and perceived.

There is of course much more to the story, for in the vast majority of cases, drugged raptures quickly gave way to what we now call "opiate addiction" (or what was then referred to as the "opium habit"). The Regent regularly dosed himself with large amounts of the drug to relieve a number of bodily ills as well as "a degree of irritation on his nerves nearly approaching to delirium." If, after decades of opium dependence, the abolitionist William Wilberforce forgot his nightly dose, he felt ill the next morning, forced "to lie in bed, great sneezing and other signs of spasm." The actor John Philip Kemble had been using opium for so long that Leigh Hunt thought it was evident even in the way he delivered his lines, for "really this artificial actor does so dole out his words, and so drop his syllables one by one upon the ear" that it is "as if he were measuring out laudanum for us." Coleridge told Byron of his "daily habit of taking enormous doses of Laudanum." Two years earlier, in 1814, he acknowledged that he had "in this one dirty business of Laudanum an hundred times deceived, tricked, nay, actually & consciously LIED." The stimulus of conversation temporarily suspended his guilt and anxiety, but "when I am alone," he confessed, "the horrors, I have suffered from Laudanum, the degradation, the blighted Utility, almost overwhelm me."[57]

Thomas De Quincey knew all about the blight of laudanum, as he details in his *Confessions of an English Opium-Eater*, the first modern drug memoir. After several years of recreational use, De Quincey in 1813 became "a regular and confirmed opium-eater" and spiraled toward rock-bottom, routed when he took too much of the drug, ill when he tried to renounce it, unable to hold down a job, increasingly isolated, and very often confined to his bed. Henry Crabb Robinson called on De Quincey in the autumn of 1816 and found him in a bad way, "an invalid . . . very dirty and even squalid." A proud imperialist with an uncle serving in the East India Company army in Bengal, De Quincey—like many of his contemporaries—was acutely aware that his drug of choice came from the East. Sometimes, in the lucid opium nightmares that descended on him in his addiction, it seemed a place of salvation, as in his elegiac Easter Sunday dream of June 1819, where he is reunited with a lost love after the scene changes from an English to "an oriental one; and there also it was Easter Sunday, and very early in the morning. And at a vast distance were visible, as a stain upon the horizon, the domes and cupolas of a great city."[58]

But on other occasions, the East terrified De Quincey, as in another dream of May 1818, when his xenophobic insistence on his own English superiority steadily gives way to lurid visions of contamination, persecution, and bestiality. In these dreams, De Quincey shudders, "I brought together all creatures, birds, beasts, reptiles, all trees and plants, usages and appearances, that are found in all tropical regions, and assembled them together in China or Indostan." But it does not end there. "From kindred feelings," he continues, "I soon brought Egypt and all her gods under the same law. I was stared at, hooted at, grinned at, chattered at, by monkeys, by paroquets, by cockatoos. . . . I was kissed, with cancerous kisses, by crocodiles; and laid, confounded with all unutterable slimy things, amongst reeds and Nilotic mud."[59] Regency society was literally soaked in opium, and De Quincey's elaborate nightmare captures the horror he feels as an undifferentiated East storms his dreaming mind, while laudanum tightens its grip on his deteriorating body. Modern ideas of drug "addiction" as referring to the physiological, psychological, and social effects associated with the habitual use of certain substances, including opiates, were not in place until the early twentieth century. But De Quincey, in common with thousands of his contemporaries, knew all about the terrors of the drug and its ability to trap people in endless cycles of loathing and despair.

VIII

Britain sent traders, builders, soldiers, administrators, and entrepreneurs to the East to exploit and enjoy its riches. It had a very different place in mind for the large part of its prison population that had been sentenced to be transported. Founded in the late eighteenth century, the British penal colony at Sydney in New South Wales was established on land seized from the Aboriginal people who had been living on it for centuries. By the time of the Regency, Sydney had grown from a grim dumping ground for criminals into a prospering, if still ramshackle, town that functioned as an open prison, with military, government, and civil districts and areas for shopping, shipping, recreation, and the trades.

It was, however, a town deeply divided between "emancipists" (former convicts) and "exclusionists" (including clergy, magistrates, free settlers, landholders, and wealthy merchants). The emancipists were denied legal and political equality. The exclusionists wanted it kept that way. Forgotten or ignored in these debates about rights and privileges were the Aboriginal people, who were forced to the very margins of society in Sydney, or who were driven out altogether as the government tightened its colonial grip on the town and took control of land that extended farther and farther into traditional Aboriginal territories. One of the most important early Aboriginal leaders, Bennelong, became a kind of ambassador for the British, but he ended up caught between colonial and Aboriginal cultures. Diminished in the eyes of both, he succumbed to alcoholism following the British introduction of rum and died in a tribal fight at

Kissing Point near Sydney in January 1813. "He was a thorough savage," the *Sydney Gazette* remarked in its scathing obituary, "not to be warped from the form and character that nature gave him by all the efforts that mankind could use."[60]

Lachlan Macquarie was the Scottish-born governor of New South Wales, a post he took up in 1810. Another colonialist intent on "civilizing" and "improving," he was despotic but much more productive and well-intentioned than many of his Regency contemporaries in the foreign service. In his view, he was the benevolent landlord of New South Wales, and he worked hard to take care of its people and the land they lived on. He brought greater clarity and coherence to the government. He improved banking, trade, and manufacturing as well as public order. He rewarded the friendlier Aboriginal people with more conciliatory policies, including annual meetings and attempts to establish them as farmers. But he also ordered the military to carry out brutal reprisals against "Hostile Natives" when they resisted his expansionism, while the school he founded for Aboriginal children in 1814 often traumatized them by forcibly removing them from their parents.[61] Unexpectedly for an old-fashioned Tory paternalist, Macquarie was a staunch supporter of the emancipists. Once convicts had served their sentence, he insisted, their slate was clean, and they should enjoy the rights of free women and men. This was a controversial belief that brought him the enduring enmity of the exclusionists, led by men like John Macarthur, a merchant and wool-grower originally from Devon, and John Thomas Bigge, an English judge who arrived at Sydney in September 1819 to conduct a review of Macquarie's administration and who was soon deeply at odds with him.

These conflicts notwithstanding, Sydney boomed under Macquarie. The population of the colony more than tripled to just under 40,000 people, while the number of acres of land cleared and in tillage more than quadrupled, from 7,615 to 32,267.[62] Most of all, Macquarie was determined to transform Sydney into a place of respectability and importance, and he built and built: barracks, hospitals, schools, churches, prisons, parks, roads, bridges, and towns. Francis Greenway, his favorite architect, assisted him on many of these projects. A former pupil of John Nash, and a convicted forger,

Greenway was transported to Sydney in 1814 but was soon able to take up his former profession, and between 1816 and 1820 he built Fort Macquarie at Bennelong Point, the Macquarie lighthouse, the stables at Government House, and churches at Sydney, Liverpool, and Windsor. Faced with increasingly successful opposition to his administration, however, Macquarie resigned in 1821 and returned to Britain, where he was further embittered by attacks on his reputation and rollbacks on his policies, but where he remained convinced that he had made an indelibly constructive contribution to the colony. He died only a few years later and was buried on the Isle of Mull, off the western coast of Scotland. The inscription on his tomb reads "The Father of Australia."

Like Greenway, William Charles Wentworth served under Macquarie. Born on board a ship harbored at Norfolk Island, Australia, to an Irish father and his mistress, Wentworth was sent when he was twelve years old to be educated in England, but at nineteen he returned to Australia, where in October 1811 Macquarie appointed him acting provost-marshal in New South Wales and granted him 1,750 acres by the Nepean River. Two years later, Wentworth and two friends crossed the Blue Mountains west of Sydney, opening up vast new tracts of grazing land for the colony. Wentworth sailed back to England in 1816 and entered the Middle Temple to study the law, determined to be "the instrument of procuring a free constitution for my country." His *Statistical, Historical, and Political Description of the Colony of New South Wales*, published in London in 1819, is the first book by a native-born Australian, and it launched Wentworth on his remarkable career in New South Wales as a leading journalist, lawyer, and politician. In his book, he championed emigration, attacked the present autocratic form of government, and urged reforms such as a House of Assembly elected on a small property franchise that included emancipists. Writes Wentworth: "Never was there a more humane and upright man that Governor Macqaurie," but even he has been propelled "beyond the bounds of moderation and justice" by the "demoralizing influence of arbitrary authority."[63]

Barron Field was a much harsher critic of Macquarie. A friend of Leigh Hunt and Charles Lamb, Field was a struggling lawyer in

England before accepting an appointment as a judge in the Supreme Court of New South Wales, where he and his wife arrived in February 1817. "Well, and how does the land of thieves use you?" Lamb wrote to him mischievously in August. "And what do they do when they an't stealing?" Field soon took sides in the ongoing conflict between the exclusionists and the emancipists. Attracted by John Macarthur's vision of the colony as a traditionally hierarchical society in which power rested with an elite group of wealthy landowners, Field adopted the mantra "Convict once, Convict forever."[64] That decision put him on the opposite side of men like Greenway, Wentworth, and of course Macquarie, who tried ineffectively to stop Field from using his courtroom to exacerbate the tensions between the free and the unfree.

All the acrimony, however, did not prevent Field from pursuing his literary interests. In 1819, he published *First Fruits of Australian Poetry*, the first book of poems printed in the colony and one that evoked for British readers the unfamiliarity of New South Wales:

> Kangaroo, Kangaroo!
> Thou spirit of Australia,
> That redeems from utter failure,
> From perfect desolation,
> And warrants the creation
> Of this fifth part of the earth.

Lamb reviewed the volume in Hunt's *Examiner* and was willing to augur from it the "dawn of refinement at Sydney," but others were far less impressed, and there were the inevitable puns about the "barren field" of Australia.[65]

IX

Another issue of emancipation was ongoing in Britain. In 1807, the country formally forbade the slave trade, but the fight against it was far from over. The leading abolitionists—religiously inspired men like

Thomas Clarkson, Zachary Macaulay, and William Wilberforce—
pushed hard during the Regency to ensure that every effort was made
to enforce the new legislation, that other countries were urged to follow Britain's lead, and that support mounted for the abolition of slavery itself. Under the auspices of the African Institution, which they
created in 1807 to replace the Society for the Abolition of the Slave
Trade, they also championed the intensification of the philanthropic
activities they were already sponsoring in West Africa, and the ame-
lioration of the condition of slaves in the West Indies.

For two decades, Freetown on the coast of Sierra Leone had been
a settlement for freed black slaves, including escaped slaves from the
West Indies ("Maroons") and American slaves from Nova Scotia

THIS PRINT by Thomas Rowlandson and Auguste Charles
Pugin shows several large trading ships moored alongside the
imposing warehouses of the West India docks and illustrates
the massive volume of trade that flowed into and out of Regency
London.

who had fought for the British in the American Revolutionary War. The Sierra Leone Company, a commercial enterprise sponsored by a group of wealthy abolitionists, ran the colony from 1792 until 1808, when the British government took direct control and quickly transformed Freetown into the center of British missionary and political power in the region as well as a base from which the Royal Navy suppressed the Atlantic slave trade. Britain extended its reach in West Africa even further in 1816 when its soldiers moved from Sierra Leone north to The Gambia, purchased St. Mary's Island from the chief of Kombo, and founded the town of Bathurst (Banjul). Named after the colonial secretary, Henry Bathurst, third Earl Bathurst, it became for Britain another power base from which its ships checked the slave trade, its merchants explored trade routes and opportunities, and its missionaries promulgated European ideals and the Christian faith.

In the West Indies, meanwhile, it was business as usual. British plantation owners had increased their numbers of enslaved people prior to the passage of abolition, and thus continued the frequently barbaric exploitation of black women, men, and children in order to produce two major Regency commodities: rum and sugar. The profits from these estates were enormous. In Austen's *Mansfield Park*, Sir Thomas Bertram, a Christian gentleman, travels to his slave-labor property in Antigua "for the better arrangement of his affairs," which toward the end of his stay are "prosperously rapid." William Gladstone, the future prime minister, and Elizabeth Barrett Browning, the future poet, both came from families that derived large incomes from West India sugar properties. The phenomenal prosperity of William Beckford—Byron called him "England's wealthiest son"—came from sugar plantations in Jamaica. In September 1813, Beckford's lawyer Richard Samuel White was "more jubilant than I've ever seen him—all sugar, all rum. He speaks only of thousands and tens of thousands."[66]

Most remarkably, in 1812, Matthew Lewis inherited his family's large Jamaican properties, whereupon he abandoned his successful literary career and devoted himself to his business interests. Concerned about the condition of 600–700 slaves on his estates at Hordley in the east and Cornwall in the west, Lewis made two separate visits to

Jamaica, the first in 1816 and the second in 1818, both of which he details in his *Journal of a West India Proprietor*. His firsthand accounts of slavery reveal him as deeply conflicted about his involvement in a system that benefits him financially but appalls him morally, and in his *Journal* he is by turns callous, vulnerable, uncertain, aggressive, sympathetic, self-deprecating, self-justifying, and self-important.

When he first visits, his colonial eyes see what they want to see. Jamaica is an enchanting land, and his slaves live in beautiful surroundings. But as time wears on, this Eden gives way to anguish, especially when he visits his eastern plantation at Hordley: "here I expected to find a perfect paradise, and I found a perfect hell." Lewis regards his slaves as his property, but when one of them refers to himself in those terms ("Massa . . . *me your slave!*"), he feels "quite humiliated." It is, he realizes, a question of human freedom. The lad seems to enjoy serving him, but "if he had detested me he must have served me still." Lewis says nothing to the boy, but the limits of his compassion are revealed when he is "tempted" to tell him, "Do not say that again; say that you are my negro, but do not call yourself my slave."[67]

At once patriarch and profiteer, Lewis seeks to improve the welfare, safety, and productivity of his workers. He builds a new hospital "entirely for the use of lying-in women," in part because he wishes to help them, but, more pressingly, because he is worried about the decline in his slave population, and with the slave trade now illegal, his only alternative is the avid promotion of motherhood. Lewis also institutes a series of humane reforms, including a ban on the use of the cart whip, a strict set of rules for punishments, and an elaborate program of rewards. His claim late in the *Journal*, however, that these schemes have been a "complete success" is undermined by the many occasions on which it is clear that little has actually improved. Lewis blames the slaves. They are lazy. They feign illness. They disappear for days or run away altogether. Rumors swirl of their discontent and of a possible uprising. It does not seem to dawn on him that the slaves are engaging in various forms of resistance to the fact of slavery itself—the terrible diet, the poor living conditions, the backbreaking work, the prevalence of disease, the abhorrent circumstances that brought them to Jamaica in the first place, and so on. In Lewis's view, their opposition has a separate and much more primal source. "As far as mere observation admits of my judging, there does seem to be a very great difference between the brain of a black person and a white one."[68]

He tries to remain upbeat, but violence is all around him, and reports of it soon start seeping into his account. His slaves sing a song about a former owner of a nearby plantation who used to save himself the expense of taking care of sick slaves by ordering that they be thrown into a gulley, where they were eaten alive by turkey vultures. Lewis himself "found on one of my estates a woman who had been kicked in the womb by a white book-keeper, by which she was crippled herself, and on another of my estates another woman who had been kicked in the womb by another white book-keeper, by which he had crippled the child." Such violence of course begets violence, as when a fifteen-year-old black girl named Minetta tries to kill her master by putting "corrosive sublimate" (mercuric chloride) into his brandy-and-water. By the middle of his second stay, Lewis's ameliorative fantasies are collapsing. "I felt strongly tempted to . . . leave all these black devils and white ones to tear one another to pieces." Less than two months later, as he prepares to leave the island for the final time, he concludes that it is simply too dangerous to set the enslaved free. "Every man of humanity must wish that slavery, even in its best and most mitigated form, had never found a legal sanction," he contends, "and must regret that its system is now so incorporated with the welfare of Great Britain as well as of Jamaica, as to make its extirpation an absolute impossibility."[69]

Slavery in the Regency, however, was not seen just as an issue that involved West Africa and the West Indies. Many writers also saw it at the core of all manner of social abuses taking place in Britain itself, though their comparisons between slavery at home and slavery abroad were often counterproductive, for they normalized the evil by making it seem as bad in Britain as it was in the West Indies, and rarely did they speak—like Lewis—with firsthand knowledge of the conditions in places such as Jamaica. In Austen's *Emma*, Jane Fairfax links the "slave-trade" and the "governess-trade," which are "widely different certainly as to the guilt of those who carry it on," but "as to the greater misery of the victims, I do not know where it lies." Prostitutes, according to another commentator, suffered a harsher form of the same abuse, for they lived in "a state of slavery . . . worse, much worse, than that of the African in the West Indies." Byron in *Childe Harold* framed the debate for religious liberties in similar terms: "The English have at last compassionated their Negroes, and under a less bigoted government may probably one day release their Catholic brethren." In Maria Edgeworth's *The Absentee*, Lord Clonbrony is an Irish estate owner who spends all his time in London, squandering the rents and indifferent to the fate of his tenants. "He might as well be a West India planter," declares a local innkeeper, "and we negroes, for any thing he knows to the contrary."[70]

William Cobbett regarded the miseries of the English poor as infinitely greater than those suffered by the West India slaves. A jaw-breakingly crude bigot, he used the issue of slavery as a means of exalting the English nation and its workers. To him, Wilberforce was the enemy, for he claimed—piously and from a position of great privilege—to care about the welfare of humankind. In Cobbett's view, this was vile hypocrisy. There was only so much public benevolence to go around, and rather than directing it toward assistance for the anguished masses in Britain, Wilberforce drew off large amounts of it in his tireless campaigns to highlight the plight of the West India slaves. Cobbett fought ferociously to reset the reform and relief agenda. What did it matter that Jamaican slaves were suffering under British colonial rule? The poor in Britain were in great distress, and they urgently needed as much aid as possible. On one level, Cobbett compared the two labor forces and insisted that the West India slaves "were better fed and less hardly worked than the people of England." But on another level, he damned such comparisons as in themselves injustices, for next to the "intelligent and ingenious people of England," the "grossly ignorant Negro . . . rises even in mental capacity, generally speaking, not many degrees above that of numerous inferior animals."[71]

Robert Wedderburn also compared Jamaican slaves with the English laboring classes, and while he was often as inflammatory as Cobbett, he was also a great deal more constructive. Wedderburn was born at Kingston in Jamaica to an African-born house slave named Rosanna and a Scottish doctor and plantation owner named James Wedderburn, who sold Rosanna when she was five months pregnant and whose new owners deemed that Robert was free from birth. He was rejected by his father and permanently separated from his mother after she was sold several more times, leaving him to be raised by his grandmother, "Talkee Amy," a Kingston slave who worked for her master as a market woman and who also traded as a smuggler. Robert witnessed her being flogged for witchcraft when she was seventy years old and he was still a child.[72] At seventeen, he joined the British navy and traveled to England, where he drifted into the St. Giles rookery in London and where, as a jobbing tailor, Unitarian preacher, and ultra-radical propagandist, he eked out a living.

Antislavery issues, and his eyewitness experience of the brutalities of the master-slave relationship, dominated his political activism. Working outside the formal emancipationist movement led by Wilberforce and Clarkson, and on a collision course with Cobbett and other radicals hostile to the slave cause, Wedderburn was a rabble-rousing orator and journalist who repeatedly linked the idea of slave revolution in Jamaica with working-class revolution in Britain. The threat of violence did not bother him. He wanted the current system overthrown, and he believed that oppressed Jamaicans, like oppressed Britons, were ready to act. "Before Six Months were over there would be Slaughter in England," he declared in the autumn of 1819, and he was confident that following the uprising there would be a comprehensive redistribution of property and that both West India slaves and British wage-slaves would soon "hail the Kingdom of Christ . . . and experience the new birth." In Cobbett, nationalism leads to bigotry. In Wedderburn, it leads to universalism. "The earth was given to the children of men, making no difference for colour or character," Wedderburn declared in 1817, anticipating the rhetoric of some of the most powerful black leaders of the next two centuries. "I am a West-Indian," he added, "a lover of liberty, and would dishonour human nature if I did not shew myself a friend to the liberty of others."[73]

X

John Barrow was a keen traveler, a powerful figure within the Admiralty as its second secretary, and a hugely prolific contributor to the Tory *Quarterly Review*. Chair-bound Regency explorers, eager for information about discovery and adventure, were often unable to afford the expensive travel books issued by publishers like John Murray. The *Quarterly*, however, fell within their budgets, and in its pages Barrow produced detailed geographical and ethnographical accounts in which he ranged from Africa, Asia, and the Mediterranean to Australia, the Americas, and the East and West Indies, and in which he repeatedly took Britain's imperial objectives and cultural superiority as his guiding themes. Most notably, when peace finally came in 1815, Barrow ensured that the Royal Navy resumed its interest in Arctic exploration, and especially in trying to find the almost mythical "Northwest Passage."[74] For naval men left idle by the conclusion of the wars, it was ideal employment, spurring on studies in cartography, science, and natural history, and renewing the possibility of a commercially viable Arctic sea corridor between Europe and Asia. The race to discover new worlds in the north involved harrowing tales of British

THE NAVAL officer and explorer Robert Hood accompanied John Franklin on his second polar expedition, and on September 19, 1819, he drew this view from Morgan's Rocks of Hill River, which is part of Hayes River in present-day Manitoba.

endurance and expertise and took tight hold of the Regency imagination, drawn as it invariably was to the remote and the exotic. Navigating the Arctic archipelago became an intense source of national pride, akin to the space race a century and a half later.

Two Arctic expeditions left London in late April 1818, both led by Scotsmen. Captain David Buchan, in command of the *Dorothea*, was instructed to find a route through the polar ice northwest of Spitsbergen (a Norwegian island in the Arctic Ocean). Accompanying him was Lieutenant John Franklin, who had been injured less than three years earlier at the Battle of New Orleans and who was placed in charge of a second vessel, the *Trent*. Buchan and Franklin were back in London six months later with little more to report than that the pack ice north of Spitsbergen was impenetrable. But their expedition fueled public fascination with the Arctic, and Barker's Panorama in Leicester Square added to the excitement when it staged a new exhibition depicting "the North Coast of Spitsbergen." Keats visited within the first week. "I have been very much pleased with the Panorama of the ships at the north Pole," he enthused, "—with the icebergs, the Mountains, the Bears the Walrus—the seals the Penguins—and a large whale floating back above water."[75]

The second 1818 expedition, led by Captain John Ross, was ordered to search for the Northwest Passage, Ross on the flagship *Isabella*, with its consort, *Alexander*, under the command of Lieutenant William Edward Parry. Captain Edward Sabine was assigned to the expedition to conduct a broad range of scientific experiments, from determining latitude and longitude, and measuring the intensity of the earth's magnetism, to collecting data on temperatures, tides, atmospheric refractions, and bottom sediments. Like Buchan and Franklin, Ross and Parry were back in London by late autumn, having turned around to avoid wintering in the Arctic. Benjamin Robert Haydon heard an account of the Ross mission from Lieutenant Henry Parkyns Hoppner, one of the junior members of the crew, and relayed it to Keats. "The Ship was sometimes entirely surrounded with vast mountains and crags of ice," he wrote. "Once they met with so vast a Mass that they gave themselves over for lost."[76]

Undeterred by the meager results of 1818, but dissatisfied with the performance of Ross, Barrow sent out two more expeditions in May of the following year. Franklin led an overland mission charged with exploring the northern shoreline of Canada eastward from the mouth of the Coppermine River. His party reached York Factory on the western shore of Hudson's Bay at the end of August, Cumberland House on the Saskatchewan River by October, and Fort Chipewyan on Lake Athabasca in March 1820, a westward trek of over 1,500 miles. But from the start the expedition was plagued by a shortage of men and supplies, and in the months that followed, exhaustion, starvation, and unreliable guides took a calamitous toll, as did bad weather and bad luck. One man murdered another and was then executed. There were rumors of cannibalism. In total, eleven men in a party of twenty died. Remarkably, Franklin, together with two other noted Arctic explorers, John Richardson and George Back, made it out alive and mapped in precise detail previously unexplored sections of the Arctic seaboard.

Parry, who had accompanied Ross in 1818, was in command of the second 1819 expedition, which was to continue the work originally assigned to Ross by searching for an entrance to the Northwest Passage from Baffin Bay through Lancaster Sound. It was the most important and successful Regency expedition to the Arctic. Pushing westward far beyond where Ross had reached, Parry named several geographical features, including Wellington Channel and Prince Regent Inlet. By the autumn of 1819 he had arrived at Melville Island, where he and his crew were the first to demonstrate how to winter productively and in relative safety in the high Arctic. They hunted. They carefully managed their supplies. They developed survival techniques. They conducted magnetic and meteorological observations. They charted the landscape. Officers entertained the crew with theater productions. Edward Sabine edited a weekly newspaper, the *North Georgia Gazette, and Winter Chronicle*. After sailing even farther westward in the summer of 1820, Parry returned to England, where he was promoted to commander.

Regency writers responded powerfully to the imaginative allure of the Arctic. Lady Morgan concluded her Irish novel *Florence Macarthy* (1818) with the disappointed Lord Aldem departing for the North

Pole. Eleanor Anne Porden, the future wife of John Franklin, celebrated *The Arctic Expeditions* (1818) as a source of national honor: "The barrier bursts—and Britain, first of all / Wherever perils threat, or duties call, / Sends forth her heroes." Keats exploited his fascination with the north in the opening of "The Eve of St. Agnes," with its "bitter chill," "numb . . . fingers," and "frosted breath," as well as in "La Belle Dame Sans Merci," where the knight-at-arms sees "starv'd lips in the gloam / With horrid warning gaped wide, / And I awoke and found me here / On the cold hill's side." Most famously, Mary Shelley frames *Frankenstein* with narratives of the north. In the opening chapter, the explorer Robert Walton explains the appeal of the Arctic to Victor Frankenstein and to so many others in the Regency: "I shall satiate my ardent curiosity with the sight of a part of the world never before visited." In the closing chapter, Frankenstein dies aboard Walton's ship in the Arctic. His Creature, after visiting him and briefly conversing with Walton, jumps from the cabin window onto a nearby ice raft and is "soon borne away by the waves, and lost in darkness and distance."[77]

XI

"So the wide waters," William Wordsworth declared in *The Excursion* (1814),

> open to the power,
> The will, the instincts, and appointed needs
> Of Britain, do invite her to cast off
> Her swarms, and in succession send them forth;
> Bound to establish new communities
> On every shore.

In the Regency, and especially after Waterloo, Ireland, Scotland, England, and Wales did "cast off . . . swarms" of people, the vast majority of whom ended up in either Canada or the United States. For tens of thousands of people, political violence and economic despair left them with little or no choice but to abandon their homes, sail across the Atlantic, and try to make new lives in the New World. Others were more fortunate. For them, emigration was a choice, an opportunity for social and economic advancement that far exceeded what was available to them in Britain, and it powerfully evoked the promises of what we would now call the "American Dream." "*Never, in the memory of man, was there any thing known like the emigration now taking place*," proclaimed the *Morning Chronicle* in 1816. Two years later, in *Sketches of America*, Henry Bradshaw Fearon observed that it was "no longer merely the poor, the idle, the profligate, or the wildly speculative, who were proposing to quit their native country; but men also of capital, of industry, of sober habits, and regular pursuits."[78]

Philanthropist, investor, and ambitious colonialist Thomas Douglas, fifth Earl of Selkirk, was the leading supporter of emigration to Canada. Shocked by the devastating impact of the Highland Clearances in his native Scotland, Selkirk sought to reshape British government policy on resettlement, convinced as he was by firsthand observation that the Highlanders were "a fine body of men" deserving of a better life, and that their desire to emigrate "in a body" should be respected, for only if they were "concentrated in one national settlement" could their language, rights, and manners as a cultural minority be preserved.[79] In 1809, Selkirk obtained a controlling interest in the Hudson's Bay Company of Canada, and two years later he signed an agreement with it under which, in exchange for establishing an agricultural settlement at the confluence of the Red and Assiniboine Rivers in what is now Manitoba, he received a land grant of 116,000 square miles. That is an area more than 20,000 square miles larger than the entire United Kingdom. The price was ten shillings.

There were problems from the outset. Arriving in the late summer of 1812, the first group of settlers soon found that—as they built the colony and worked the land and endured their first winter—they had traded a very hard life in the Scottish Highlands for a very hard life on the Canadian prairies, and in the spring some wrote home to tell their remaining family to stay in Scotland. Worse, the Red River Settlement was immediately caught up in the fur-trade wars between the Hudson's Bay Company and its bitter rival, the North West Com-

In addition to producing the text, Louis Simond drew a series of illustrations for his *Journal of a Tour and Residence in Great Britain, During the Years 1810 and 1811*, including this one of two Highland men.

pany, and before long the situation descended into violence, with both sides engaged in ransacking, kidnapping, ambushing, sabotaging supply lines, and murdering. Hostilities peaked in June 1816 when twenty Red River settlers were slain in a confrontation with a party of about sixty Métis (people of mixed Indigenous and European blood) under the leadership of Cuthbert Grant, a fur trader of Scottish heritage in the employ of the North West Company. Natural disasters, including an infestation of grasshoppers that devastated crops, further undermined the development of the colony. Selkirk died in 1820, worn out by travel, lawsuits, and ruinous financial decisions. Red River, he lamented during his final illness, was a place "where we had the prospect of doing so much good."[80]

Emigration to America at least seemed a rosier proposition. Morris Birkbeck, a fifty-three-year-old Quaker farmer in Surrey, pulled up stakes in 1817, as he details in his *Notes of a Journey from the Coast of Virginia to the Territory of Illinois* and its sequel, *Letters from Illinois*, both of which appeared in 1818. Like countless other liberal-minded Britons, Birkbeck was fed up with the state of the country—its political strife, its Established Church, its tiny electoral franchise, its parasitic aristocrats, and especially its taxes. America beckoned. "Think of a country without excisemen, or assessors, or collectors, or receivers-general, or—informers or paupers!" he exclaimed. There were problems, to be sure, including slavery, which Birkbeck abhorred, but they did not prevent him from representing America as a land of fertility and hope. "Liberty is no subject of dispute or speculation among us backwoods men," he stated; "it is the very atmosphere we breathe."[81]

Keats's younger brother George is Birkbeck's most well-known recruit. He had for a time worked as a clerk in a London counting house, but after reading *Letters from Illinois*, he quickly determined that his future lay in America. Keats approved of the decision. George "is of too independent and liberal a Mind to get on in trade in this Country," he declared. In May 1818, George married Georgiana Wylie, and a month later they traveled with Keats to Liverpool, bid him farewell, and set sail for America. The crossing took two months and brought the newlyweds to Philadelphia, from where they journeyed by horse and carriage to Pittsburgh, and then by boat down the Ohio River to Kentucky. Like so many of his Regency contemporaries, Keats thought continually of his loved ones far away. "Have you shot a Buffalo? Have you met with any Pheasants?" he asked George playfully in a letter of December 1818. On the cusp of the most superbly creative period of his life, Keats missed his brother terribly, but thinking of him also pulled his imagination further and further into the unknown, the strange, and the forlorn. "My Thoughts are very frequently in a foreign Country," he told George in the same December letter. "I live more out of England than in it."[82]

George found life in America far more complicated than he had hoped. Leaving a pregnant Georgiana behind in Kentucky, he visited Birkbeck on his "English Prairie" in Illinois but did not like what he saw. Despite Birkbeck's heady optimism and convincing sales pitch, his settlement was not thriving and would soon fail altogether, as perhaps George sensed. Conditions were primitive, even squalid, and George abandoned any notion of living there. Back in Kentucky, his affairs took an even bleaker turn when he invested in a business concern of John James Audubon, the soon-to-be famous artist and ornithologist, and lost all his money. In late 1819, George again left Georgiana behind and this time returned across the Atlantic to London, where he saw his brother often and hoped to obtain the money necessary to salvage his American business interests. "I cannot help thinking Mr. Audubon a dishonest man," Keats had written to him. "In truth I do not believe you fit to deal with the world; or at least the American world."[83] But George was already deeply committed to his life far away from England. He spent three hectic but productive weeks drawing together the various remittances due to him, which totaled approximately £700, before leaving London for Liverpool, and then—on February 1, 1820—the boat back to New York. Two and a half months later, Keats heard that George had arrived home safely in Kentucky. The brothers never saw each other again.

Georgiana and George Keats were not alone in struggling to adapt to their new life and new circumstances in America. But they stuck it out and eventually prospered, as did many other Regency Britons who had made the decision to leave. Angered at the capital, talent, and energy flowing out of the country, many supporters of the status quo reminded these unpatriotic migrants that what they thought was an opportunity was in fact an unbroken wilderness packed with brawlers, drunkards, gamblers, blasphemers, sharpers, and pimps. "With all our drawbacks . . . there is no country in the world where the mass of the people are so well fed, clothed, and lodged, as in England," Barrow chided in the *Quarterly*. It was all right for some. But for many others, emigration was worth the risk because America was already firmly established in the collective imagination as—in the words of Percy Shelley—"A land beyond the Oceans of the West, / Where, though with rudest rites, Freedom and Truth / Are worshipped."[84]

After winning Waterloo, Britain was the most powerful country in the world, and it dominated international affairs. For a wide variety of legal, military, political, and economic reasons, hundreds of thousands of people left the country during this period, and it is revealing that some of its most emblematic figures—including Princess Caroline, Byron, Wellington, and the Shelleys—spent a great deal of the Regency outside of Britain. At the same time, the country's immense maritime strength and brash confidence in the justness of its colonial mission meant that, in addition to taking control of enormous areas of land, goods from around the world flowed back to Britain, from ancient artifacts and modern chinoiserie, through sugar and rum, to tea and opium, for all of which Regency Britain had an unquenchable appetite. The defeat of Napoleon, for some a disaster that reinstated the tyrannies that had touched off the French Revolutionary Wars in the first place, was for the vast majority confirmation that the British character was sounder and stronger than ever before. Despite an uneven performance in the War of 1812, and a rash of contemporary evils that demanded reform, Waterloo in their eyes demonstrated that Regency Britain was out in front of every other country, and that its religious, martial, cultural, and financial superiority gave it the right and the opportunity to rule the world.

CHAPTER FIVE

Changing Landscapes
and Ominous Signs

I

"I sometimes wunder if it's the same waurld," exclaimed the Scots-woman Violet Macshake in Susan Ferrier's 1818 novel of manners, *Marriage*.[1] She was right to wonder. Britain in the Regency was still an agrarian nation, but the unstoppable momentum of the Industrial Revolution was driving the country into the modern age, produc-ing immense profits and opportunities for some and grinding mis-ery for countless others. In London, the commercial district thrived with dramatic increases in both domestic manufacture and imperial exploitation, while major infrastructure projects transformed the face of the city, though many of these changes treacherously rein-forced the divide between the impoverished working classes in the East End and the traditional elites and nouveau-riche businessmen in the West End. Edinburgh during the Regency was less than one-tenth the size of London, but it was a formidable rival as a center for the arts and publishing and the home of Walter Scott, the *Edinburgh Review*, and *Blackwood's Magazine*, which exploded onto the literary scene in October 1817.

Modernity was transforming the countryside as well. For decades, the nationwide practice of enclosure had been fencing in and closing off traditionally communal pastures and fields in favor of a system of private ownership that greatly increased food production but that forced tens of thousands of smallholders off the land and down into poverty. At the same time, amid lush green meadows and beautiful waves of fine trees, more and more factories, mines, and manufacturing districts sprang up belching smoke and chemicals on a scale that had never been seen before and that frequently inflicted long-term environmental damage.

The response to these changes varied enormously. Many rural laborers staged violent protests as industrial advance replaced people with machines. Others were even more deeply angered by the social, economic, and psychological consequences of enclosure. Still others left their towns and villages for roaring commercial hubs such as Manchester, where they quickly discovered that they had simply swapped despair in the country for despair in the city. In contrast, wealthy elites hired professional landscape gardeners to plan and oversee the aesthetic enhancement of their country estates. Tourists set off across Regency Britain in pursuit of the picturesque, an aesthetic quality that fell in between the sublime (or awe-inspiring) and the beautiful (or tranquil). Major writers and painters produced detailed accounts of provincial life that carefully excluded the despoliations of industry, that deepened the myth of rural Britain, and that induced a profound sense of nostalgia for traditional landscapes and occupations that were quickly becoming a thing of the past.

Many others looked decisively to the future, championing the wealth and influence that industrialism was bringing to Britain, and highlighting the achievements of the capitalists, engineers, scientists, and inventors who were making it all happen. Thousands of unemployed laborers were put to work building roads, bridges, and canals that spurred on trade and industry, that made domestic travel much faster and safer, and that opened up areas of the country that had for centuries been isolated. Robert Owen, a pioneer of socialist thought, ran factories in Lanarkshire in which he sought to demonstrate that it was possible to combine heady profits with the humane treatment of workers. Researchers such as Humphry Davy and his laboratory assistant Michael Faraday invented the miner's safety lamp, a device that drastically reduced the number of deaths in the pits and revealed Davy and Faraday's shared belief in the powers of science to alleviate human suffering. George Stephenson advanced railway engineering to its modern form in the design and construction of both the locomotive and the track. Charles Babbage conceived his "Analytical Engine" as the first modern digital computer. Electricity was the topic of heated debate in scientific, medical, and religious circles, and it provoked the "vitalist controversy" on the origins of life itself. More than any other figure of the Regency, Mary Shelley understood what was at stake in these disputes. Unleashing the powers of science and medicine had the potential to bring innumerable benefits to humankind, but these same forces, used unthinkingly or selfishly, could also produce monsters.

II

London was alive with invention, development, and experimentation, and by the start of the Regency it had become the power base for a new class of men who were hardworking and highly ambitious, and who owed their burgeoning wealth to trade and manufacture. As the capital of the richest and most economically dynamic country in the world, London had benefited enormously from the war economy, and while poor harvests, vested interests, and widespread radical anger had taken their toll, London had emerged from the French Revolutionary Wars much more affluent than ever before. In the slums and rookeries that sprawled to the north, east, and south of the city, there was little evidence of this prosperity, while in the West End old-money elites looked down contemptuously on trade and traders. But in the commercial district, located at the historic center of the City of London, business boomed and families built fortunes.

Regency Britain's wealth was founded on cheap labor at home and colonial conquest abroad. London's lifeline, the Thames, was crowded with ships "[f]reighted from every climate of the world," as William Wordsworth put it, while cotton and woolen goods, glass, china, brass,

bronze, and iron were among the many products transported around
the globe by British merchant ships. In the City, meanwhile, these
imports and exports fueled the profits of the Bank of England, East
India House, Ironmongers' Hall, and the Royal Exchange, around
which lay insurance companies, investment banks, brokerage houses,
and moneylenders, as well as booksellers, printsellers, linendrapers,
druggists, cheesemongers, confectioners, jewelers, stationers, and
many others. "Commerce, much-loved commerce, is the ruling principle, visible in every transaction of the English," declared John Badcock. "For this they go to war; to restore its activity, they make peace.
'Trade,' is toasted after dinner: and of its details, they talk to the latest
hour of night." Britain, Napoleon sneered with envy, was the "nation
of shopkeepers." In 1817, Samuel Taylor Coleridge attributed the
"immediate occasions of the existing distress" in the country to "the
OVERBALANCE OF THE COMMERCIAL SPIRIT."[2]

The face of London was changing to accommodate the modern
world of consumerism and trade. John Rennie was one of the leading civil engineers of the day, and in the Regency he crowned his
achievements with three new bridges across the Thames, all of which
were constructed to cope with the enormous increase in the volume
of people seeking to move back and forth across the river in pursuit of business and pleasure. The Thames was already crossed by
the Bridges of London, Blackfriars, and Westminster. Rennie added
Regent's Bridge, Southwark Bridge, and, most imposingly, Waterloo
Bridge, which cost just over one million pounds, and which—with
its nine elliptical arches and Doric columns at the piers—seemed
to embody the strength and solidity that had enabled the British to
defeat Napoleon. The Regent opened Waterloo Bridge on June 18,
1817, the second anniversary of the battle. A "Waterloo Fair" was
held on the riverbank, during which Waterloo veterans were cheered
as they arrived on an Admiralty barge amid a throng of sightseers
and revelers in small boats. The bridge itself was hung with allied
flags, and the Regent and his brother, the Duke of York, processed
across it on foot, followed by the Duke of Wellington. Benjamin
Robert Haydon witnessed the ceremonies on "that sunny lovely day,"
as did John Constable.[3]

Rennie's three large bridge-building projects combined utility with elegance and delighted the Regent, but they came nowhere near the imaginative sweep and grandeur of what he and his favorite architect, John Nash, were planning in London's West End. In 1811, the five hundred undistinguished acres of Mary-le-Bone Park reverted to the Crown. The development potential of this land intoxicated the Regent. More than any other British monarch, he was passionately interested in the greater glory of the capital city. In consultation with Nash, he immediately began pegging out a large-scale construction project that would transform not only Mary-le-Bone Park but also a good deal of the West End. Parliament approved Nash's plans in 1813 and building began, though private capital was to meet the main burden of the expense.[4]

Regent's Park, as it was soon renamed, was to be a garden playground for the aristocracy laid out on picturesque lines that emphasized charm, variety, and the artful management of vistas. At its center Nash planned a "national Valhalla" on elevated ground, while nearby the Regent would have his own private pleasure dome, or *guinguette*. Fifty-six handsome villas were to be built within the park, each set in its own grounds and screened by wooded groves to create the impression of uninterrupted parkland, while beautiful terraces were to run around the perimeter, their facades iced with gleaming stucco. On the east side Nash proposed a market that would provide the goods and services required by residents. An artificial and irregularly shaped lake was planned for the southwestern corner. The Regent's canal would run along the northern boundary.[5]

That was just the beginning. There was also to be a spectacular new road that would connect the park with Whitehall and the Strand to the south, demolishing in the process the best existing route, the winding and narrow Swallow Street, together with 741 homes that were now in the way. The proposed thoroughfare, known immediately as Regent Street, would dramatically reduce the time and effort it took exclusives to travel from their posh new homes in the environs of Regent's Park down to the seats of political power in Westminster, or out into the surrounding areas, where they might pursue various pleasures, from fashionable walks and rides, through upmarket shopping, to gambling, drink, and sex. Like his plans for Regent's Park, Nash based his designs for Regent Street on the picturesque principles of surprise, pleasing variety, scenic effect, and irregularity harmonized by grouping and composition. A hotel, a bank, a playhouse, and a church, along with shops, businesses, and private homes, were to be built along the road, which was itself to be highlighted by an impressively confident, colonnaded swerve to the east between Oxford Street and Piccadilly (known as the Quadrant).[6]

In theory, it could not have been a more exciting piece of town planning. In practice, the entire project soon came under immense strain, and without Nash's unending ingenuity and perseverance, alongside the Regent's unfaltering support, it simply would not have happened. Even in the tumultuous political climate of the Regency, and with London radicals protesting various social and economic injustices in the nearby streets, costs meant little to either the Regent or Nash—this development, after all, was about the splendor of Britain. But costs meant a great deal to others, and when private individuals were slow to invest and government officials balked at the escalating expenditure, Nash was forced to jettison various aspects of the Regent's Park project, including the princely *guinguette*, and 48 of the proposed 56 villas. Further issues arose along Regent Street, where Nash made controversial decisions (from his use of stucco to his rejection of the formalities of eighteenth-century street design) that set his critics baying, and where he tried to hold on to his original plan of a perfectly balanced thoroughfare, while individual investors who had chosen to build on the street naturally had ideas of their own about how they wanted their buildings to look and what that required.

In the end, though on a scale greatly diminished from the original conception, Nash and the Regent succeeded brilliantly, cajoling, redesigning, championing, and modifying as they went, and producing by 1820 one of the most beautiful and highly beneficial developments in the history of London. As early as February 1818, Henry Crabb Robinson drove through the new park in a gig and was mightily impressed: "I really think this enclosure, with the new street leading to it from Carlton House, will give a sort of glory to the Regent's government, which will be more felt by remote posterity than the

victories of Trafalgar and Waterloo." James Elmes, a writer on architecture, was similarly enthusiastic. Nash's achievements "metamor-
phosed Mary-le-bone park farm and its cow-sheds, into a rural city
of almost eastern magnificence." The project was utterly unlike anything else in London, and its impact on town planning and especially
on the development of the urban park has been felt from Nash's day
to ours. In response to the rapidly multiplying demands of an opportunistic, consumer-driven society, the Regent and Nash spearheaded
a highly imaginative transformation of the West End that stands as
a monument to the aesthetic tastes of both men. Without the spaces,
vistas, buildings, and thoroughfares of Regent's Park and Regent
Street, modern London is inconceivable.[7]

III

Behind the grandeur of Regent Street, however, there stands a much
darker purpose. Nash strategically used the road to reinforce the
sharp economic divide that already existed between those living in
the West End and those living everywhere else. In what amounted to
an insidious form of urban segregation, he put in place a broad and
dazzling barrier to demarcate the two Londons, a barrier that enabled
the rich to more easily ignore the sights, smells, and sounds of their
less well-born neighbors and that marked—in Nash's own words—a
"complete separation between the Streets and Squares occupied by
the Nobility and Gentry, and the narrow Streets and meaner Houses
occupied by mechanics and the trading part of the community."[8] As
construction proceeded, the privileged few went house shopping and
property developing, while thousands of poor but longtime residents
of the area were forced out of their soon-to-be-razed homes and into
the already overcrowded slums of St. Giles's, Lambeth, and beyond.

Nowhere are the two worlds that existed on either side of the
great West-East divide brought more vividly into view than in the
works of two very different artists. John Thomas Smith was a drafts-
man and engraver who during the Regency lived in Chandos Street,
a rather seedy purlieu just off Covent Garden. A longtime friend to

several other artists, including William Blake and John Constable, Smith in 1817 published an elegant collection of engravings entitled *Vagabondiana, or, Anecdotes of Mendicant Wanderers through the Streets of London*. In the text that accompanies the illustrations, Smith condemns beggary, which in the last six years has become "so dreadful in London."[9] Yet in the illustrations themselves, he tells a remarkably different story. The men, women, and children he places before us are individuals, not caricatures, stereotypes, or abstractions, and his representations of them are objective but full of compassion. Many of his beggars have been mutilated by war, disease, accident, or folly, but their powerful instinct for survival is etched deeply into their faces, and they have retained their dignity even after years on the margins of society. Some of these people have lived in London all their lives. Others have been drawn to the capital from across the British Isles. Still others are immigrants, including Indian lascars, displaced Europeans, and freed slaves from America and the West Indies.

There are musicians, strolling clowns, street sweepers, wayfarers, and vendors of matches, bootlaces, spoons, rattles, ballads, and religious tracts. There is a Jewish merchant who is unable to walk and is placed every morning in a wheeled cart in Petticoat Lane. There is Charles Wood, a blind man with an organ and a dancing dog. There is Priscilla, seated with her back against the wall sewing patchwork quilts. There is a blind beggar who sings obscene songs; a harmless shoemaker named Taylor who works on a stand in Tottenham Court Road; a father and son from Watford who make puzzles; and Joseph Johnson, a black man who wears "a model of the ship Nelson . . . on his cap" and who "by a bow of thanks, or a supplicating inclination to a drawing-room window" gives the "appearance of sea-motion."[10]

Life could hardly have been more different on the other side of Regent Street, where ennui rather than indigence was often the biggest blight, and where the serene faces of the elites were captured most famously by Thomas Lawrence, the leading portraitist of the era. Hopelessly extravagant in both his financial and amorous affairs, Lawrence used his immense charm and talent to produce highly flattering portraits that thrilled his rich and famous clients, and that

In his *Vagabondiana*, John Thomas Smith produced a series of evocative prints of the London poor, including the seamstress Priscilla of Clerkenwell and the former seaman Joseph Johnson.

created the image of Regency high society as beautiful and glamorous. Celebrated for his dazzling brushwork, his bold exploitation of color, and his use of external expressions to reveal inner, emotional states, Lawrence painted leading figures such as the actor John Philip Kemble, the history painter Benjamin West, the surgeon John Abernethy, and the scientist Humphry Davy. He loved to paint beautiful women, including Countess Lieven, Lady Elizabeth Leveson-Gower, Lady Selina Meade, and Mrs. Isabella Wolff, who had a close personal relationship with Lawrence and who was—Constable agreed—"very pretty."[11]

Lawrence painted several members of the royal family, including the Regent's estranged wife Princess Caroline (with whom he is rumored to have had an affair) and daughter Princess Charlotte. For the Regent, Lawrence executed several commissions and—like Nash in a different sphere—worked closely with him in pursuit of his highly ambitious creative vision. Most notably, Lawrence produced portraits of the allied leaders who had defeated Napoleon. This collection, which now lines the walls of the Waterloo Chamber in Windsor Castle, features pictures of the Prussian field marshal, Gebhard Blücher; the emperor of Russia, Alexander I; the British prime minister, Lord Liverpool; the British foreign secretary, Viscount Castlereagh; and, of course, the Duke of Wellington.[12]

Lawrence's most famous subject was the Regent himself. At a time when George Cruikshank and other brilliant caricaturists were skewering the Regent as a lecherous sot, an Oriental fantasist, and a self-centered simpleton, Lawrence—miraculously—painted images of him in which he appears handsome, regal, and without a hint of moral seediness. In 1814, Lawrence produced an unfinished oil sketch of the Regent in profile that was designed for a medal that was never struck. So delighted was the Regent with the picture that in 1815 he knighted Lawrence, who promptly outdid himself with a second, even more immaculate, portrait in which the fifty-two-year-old Regent is represented as a dashing, windswept soldier, his bloated figure elegantly encased within a field marshal's uniform. Thomas Moore damned the painting as "a lie upon canvas," but William Hazlitt could only laugh at the outrageousness of it. "Sir Thomas Lawrence has with the magic of his pencil recreated the Prince Regent as a well-fleshed Adonis of thirty-three," he reported.[13]

IV

George "Beau" Brummell was the foremost dandy of the Regency, and for nearly two decades he presided over the West End as its acknowledged leader of fashion. In the eighteenth century and across the Regency, some elites adopted an unpretentious or even a slovenly look, while others opted for a far more luxurious wardrobe that included silks, laces, diamonds, wigs, high heels, and perfumes. Still others followed various fashion trends, such as wearing the large turned-down collar that was popularized by Byron and that opened suggestively at the neck to reveal the throat and upper chest. Brummell imperiously rejected all these trends in favor of a new dress code that prized cleanliness, meticulous simplicity, and buttoned-up stylishness, and that revolutionized British fashion to produce a look that was highly structured and distinctly masculine. Day wear included a white shirt, a buff- or light-colored waistcoat (which hid his suspenders), a dark blue coat with tails, tight pantaloons (with a loop that fastened under the foot to prevent creasing), and plain black Hessians (riding boots that extended to just below the knee). Out for the evening, Brummell favored a white waistcoat, a blue coat, black pantaloons, and striped silk stockings.[14] Whatever the occasion, he completed his look with the indispensable, spotlessly white, well-starched cravat, which pushed his head up and gave him the desired air of superiority and exacting self-confidence.

Tying a cravat was no simple matter, and Brummell sometimes spent hours getting it just right. Robinson, his much-tried valet, was once seen carrying an armful of flowing cravats. When asked why his master wanted so many at once, Robinson replied, "These, sir, are our failures." Admiring or envious members of the *haut ton* crowded into Brummell's rooms in the late morning or early afternoon to watch him dress. His aim was to fit in, not to show off or stand out. "If John Bull turns round to look after you, you are not well dressed," he

IN THIS drawing of a ball at Almack's, supposedly from 1815, several couples waltz while to the left Beau Brummell stands talking to the Duchess of Rutland.

famously decreed. Lord William Pitt Lennox understood Brummell's secret. "Of all my acquaintances," he declared, Brummell was "the quietest, plainest, and most unpretending dresser.... He eschewed colours, trinkets, and gewgaws." Lord Byron agreed: there was "nothing remarkable" in Brummell's style of dress except a "certain exquisite propriety." [15]

Dandyism for Brummell, however, was always about much more than quality cloths and precise cuts and fits. His scrupulous sense of fashion was also at the core of much larger attitudes and patterns of behavior. Surrounded by excess, he drank and ate only moderately and kept his sexual appetites under tight control. In society he was charming and polite but invariably aloof. The upmarket courtesan Harriette Wilson perceptively declared that "many . . . wished to be well with him, through fear, for all knew him to be cold, heartless, and satirical." Brummell's wit, so often applauded and repeated in the Regency, was about style rather than substance. Hazlitt called it "the art of making something out of nothing." "Sitting one day at table between two other persons, Mr. Brummell said to his servant, who stood behind his chair—'John!' 'Yes, sir.' 'Who is this at my right hand?' 'If you please, sir, it's the Marquis of Headfort.' 'And who is this at my left hand?' 'It's my Lord Yarmouth.' 'Oh, very well!' and the Beau then proceeded to address himself to the persons who were thus announced to him." On other occasions, though, Brummell's humor took a nastier turn. In July 1813, when he and the Regent were in the midst of one of their increasingly frequent spats, Brummell cohosted a masquerade ball at the Argyle Rooms. The Regent was invited, and at his arrival he spoke to another one of the cohosts, William Arden, second Baron Alvanley. But he cut Brummell dead. Following a shocked silence, Brummell turned to Alvanley and demanded, "Who's your fat friend?"[16]

Above all, Brummell made dandyism about self-invention. He was a commoner, without a title or well-placed relations, and while his parents were wealthy, he did not possess a great fortune. Yet through impertinence and sheer panache he rose spectacularly to become one of the most famous men of the Regency. He based the dandy on previous male figures of fashion, including the "macaroni," the "fop," and the "exquisite." But he replaced the effeminacy and foolishness frequently associated with these types with the composure of the dandy and the shade of classical severity in his dress and behavior. The dandy was inspired by aristocratic ideals, as seen especially in Brummell's contempt for work, his commitment to metropolitan languor, and his powerful sense of exclusivity. Yet the dandy was also a profoundly democratic figure. Anyone could become one. Dandyism was not about being born into the right family. It was about a different kind of aristocracy, a new, modern version that was founded in individual talent, vision, and mettle. Brummell was on an intimate footing with some of the richest men in Britain. But he was also their nemesis. The traditional elites based their claims for superiority on blood, breeding, and education. Brummell showed them all up for shams. Social status, he demonstrated, was about performance rather than merit, and even someone from his much humbler origins could play the part as well as—or even better than—them.[17]

Brummell reached the zenith of his power in the opening year of the Regency, when he and other leading dandies, including Alvanley, Henry Mildmay, and Henry Pierrepoint, ensconced themselves in the newly installed bow window of the exclusive White's Club and, gazing out onto St. James's, pronounced on the passing scene. Their verdicts, prizing wit rather than accuracy, were often sour and petty, but they passed for law in fashion. Even Wellington acknowledged that he "had a high opinion of that mysterious and terrible tribunal 'White's Bow Window.'" Yet Brummell's reign as the *arbiter elegantiarum* of fashionable society was coming to an end. His most crucial supporter, the Regent, had once valued his opinion so highly that he reportedly "began to blubber . . . when he was told that Brummell did not like the cut of his coat." But the Regent's expanding waistline and love of peacockery were making the close-fitting simplicities of the dandy increasingly inaccessible, and Brummell's sharp-tongued narcissism eventually alienated him altogether. The Duchess of York, who had known Brummell for years, proved herself his firm friend after his intimacy with the Regent collapsed, but Brummell's mounting debts produced an increasingly desperate need for cash, and after a career of avoiding excesses, he fell prey to a gambling addiction. In May 1816, after a final run of bad luck, he slipped quietly out of England and into self-imposed exile. "I believe some public good, as far as the rising generation is concerned, will result from the downfall of such heroes as . . . Mr. Brummell," Robert Peel observed tersely.[18]

Dandyism in the Regency, however, continued to flourish even after Brummell's departure, its influence permeating down the social scale and far beyond London, though in variations that often strayed extravagantly from Brummell's original conception. The young Charles Dickens vividly remembered reading "picture-books about dandies" during "the time of the Prince Regent," including "satires upon that eminent personage himself." Joseph Grimaldi mocked the Regency dandy in his pantomime *Bang Up: or, Harlequin Prime!*, while in *Harlequin Gulliver* he transformed himself into a female dandy, a "dandizette." In 1816, George Cruikshank inaugurated his *Monstrosities* series, in which he pilloried the exaggerated fashions of the Regency and drew scores of dandies in gaudy colors, soaring collars, ballooning trousers, and corseted waistcoats cinched ludicrously tight. Thomas Moore went to a play at Leamington Spa in Warwickshire,

A DANDY stares contentedly at his reflection in the mirror as
he dresses for an evening out. He is wearing a high collar, frilly
shirt, jacket with tails, tight pantaloons, and pumps, and is slid-
ing a ring onto his finger.

where he saw a "Miss Ivers—dressed in the most exquisite extreme of
Dandyism, & looking as like a man as any of the brotherhood." [19]

Byron took a strikingly different view. In the midst of all the cross-
dressing and satire, he made it plain that he admired Brummell and
that he set an immensely high value on his achievement, not simply
as a rebel and an icon who had made his mark without Byron's own
aristocratic advantages, but as a man who broke new cultural ground,
who cast a spell across the social hierarchies, who dominated his so-
called "betters" through the force of his personality, and who pos-

sessed unparalleled powers of self-creation. When Byron ranked the "three great men of the nineteenth century," he placed "himself third, Napoleon second, and Brummell first."[20]

V

Edinburgh was the second city of the Regency, as the Scottish historian Archibald Alison explained in 1819. "While London is the Rome of the empire, to which the young, and the ambitious, and the gay, resort for the pursuit of pleasure, of fortune, or of ambition, Edinburgh might become another Athens, in which the arts and the sciences flourished, under the shade of her ancient fame." John Galt was similarly interested in the difference between the two capitals, and a year later he framed it in aesthetic terms. Edinburgh is a "picturesque and romantic" city, whereas London is a sublime and "stupendous pile of gloom."[21]

J. G. Lockhart provides the most comprehensive survey of Regency Edinburgh in his *Peter's Letters to his Kinsfolk* (1819), a fictitious travelogue in which Dr. Peter Morris, a Welshman on a visit to Scotland, sends lively letters home to his friends and relatives describing the beautiful places he has seen and the important people he has met. His letters range over a host of topics—from sport, religion, and business to architecture, politics, the Gaelic language, and the stage— and often reveal a Scottish bias. In Edinburgh, "they are, for the most part, a race of tall, well-formed people," and among them "a very fat man is stared at." But in London, "one of such bulk . . . is met with at every corner." In Edinburgh, "it is the fashion . . . for every man to lead two or three different kinds of lives all at once." But in London, "a lawyer is a lawyer, and he is nothing more." In Edinburgh, dandies "possess a finer theatre whereon to display their attractions than those of any other city in the three kingdoms. You have nothing in London which, as a promenade, can be compared to Prince's Street."[22]

Lockhart is equally sure that Edinburgh is home to superb artistic talent. In Henry Raeburn especially, he declares, the city enjoys "a portrait-painter, whose works would do honour to any capital in Europe. I really am not certain, that this artist is in any important particular inferior even to Sir Thomas Lawrence." Raeburn spent almost his entire career in Scotland, and in the Regency he produced a series of vigorous portraits that bring the culture and society of Edinburgh vividly into view. He painted some of the most famous Scots of the period, including Walter Scott, the civil engineer Thomas Telford, and the editor of the *Edinburgh Review*, Francis Jeffrey. Romantic longing suffuses his 1812 portrait of the Highland chief Alastair Ranaldson Macdonell of Glengarry, who stands proudly decked out in elaborate tartanry, his right hand grasping the barrel of a rifle, even as his thoughtful, sidelong gaze signals his knowledge that the traditional clan system has collapsed and that he has "lived a century too late," in the words of his friend Walter Scott. Raeburn's remarkable self-portrait of 1815 was intended for a London audience, and its romantic force hints at both the mind at work behind the artistry and his intense desire to be seen as producing portraits in Edinburgh that matched or surpassed what the leading English practitioners were achieving in London. Margaret (or Margaritta) Macdonald, who married the Edinburgh wine merchant Robert Scott Moncrieff, sat for Raeburn at some point around 1814. His beautiful portrait of her, dressed in a disheveled red cloak and a sensual white dress, with her head turned, her lips parted, and her eyes cast upward, is a fascinating combination of sensibility and sexuality, and one of the most enduring images of the Regency.[23]

The bookseller and publisher Archibald Constable turned Edinburgh into a "literary mart, famous with strangers, and the pride of its own citizens."[24] Nobody was better at selling books than him. Haughty and enthusiastic, he paid large sums of money to top-selling authors and then made back his investment through innovative advertising and robust marketing strategies, including different versions of the same book for different market sectors. In 1812 he purchased the *Encyclopaedia Britannica*, which had just appeared in its fourth edition, and over the course of the Regency he dramatically improved its size and quality with a series of supplements that contained new essays written by leading experts and that sold in huge numbers. Constable was also involved in a glorious, if often troubled, partnership with Walter Scott, and in 1814 he began to publish the *Waverley* novels, giving him a crucial role in one of the Regency's greatest success stories.

Constable's third major project was the liberal-minded *Edinburgh Review*. Founded in 1802, and ably edited by Francis Jeffrey, it featured a host of brilliant writers, including Henry Brougham, William Hazlitt, James Mill, Thomas Moore, and Sydney Smith. Constable paid generously for contributions, making it possible for the first time for literary men to earn a decent income publishing with the periodical press. "To be an Edinburgh Reviewer is, I suspect, the highest rank in modern literary society," declared Hazlitt in 1818.[25] Formidable competition soon arose in the shape of the *Quarterly Review*, which was published in London by Constable's chief rival, John Murray, whose home at 50 Albemarle Street became the greatest literary salon in the West End, and whose firm issued books in the Regency by Austen, Byron, Coleridge, and George Crabbe. Politically, the *Quarterly* was as far to the right as the *Edinburgh* was to the left. Its editor, William Gifford, counted Robert Southey, Walter Scott, John Barrow, and John Wilson Croker among his most prolific contributors. These two reviews slugged it out over all the key political, economic, and cultural issues of the day.

William Blackwood was the other great Edinburgh publisher. A long-standing enemy of Constable, in 1811 he became the Edinburgh agent for John Murray, which greatly strengthened his ties to the English book trade. In the years that followed he published several prominent Scottish authors, including Susan Ferrier, James Hogg, Lockhart, and Scott, who signed with Blackwood and Murray for two of his *Waverley* novels, *The Black Dwarf* and *Old Mortality*. More significantly, in 1817, Blackwood became the publisher and editor of *Blackwood's Edinburgh Magazine*, which appeared every month (rather than every three months like the major reviews) and established a new model for magazines by removing all the formal departments, mixing together fiction, reviews, essays, and correspondence, and infusing exuberance throughout. *Blackwood's* never acquired (or sought) the authority of the *Edinburgh* or the *Quarterly*, but it was a powerful alternative.

Unpredictable, scabrous, erudite, and bellicosely High Tory, *Blackwood's* came out swinging. Its first number of October 1817 contained the incendiary "Chaldee Manuscript," which was written by its three most important Regency contributors: Hogg, Lockhart, and John Wilson. A mock-biblical satire that told the story of the founding of the magazine, the "Chaldee" represented *Blackwood's* Whig enemies and Tory friends alike in the fictional guise of birds and beasts, and it took particular aim at Archibald Constable, "a man who was crafty in counsel, and cunning in all manner of working." The slashing derision, ad hominem attacks, and faux scriptural language caused outrage among Edinburgh Whigs and shocked even *Blackwood's* supporters. "The 'reading' or rather the talking 'public' is greatly beholden to the Author" of the "Chaldee," Thomas Carlyle announced. "He has kept its jaws moving these four weeks—and the sport is not finished yet."²⁶ Blackwood laughed all the way to the bank. Soon Coleridge, Galt, Thomas De Quincey, and William Maginn were publishing in his magazine.

Entertaining and informing an English readership was a priority, but *Blackwood's* was resolutely, indeed effusively, Scottish, and regularly featured contributions such as Anne Grant's "On Leaving the North Highlands," Felicia Hemans's "The Meeting of Wallace and Bruce," Hogg's "The Shepherd's Calendar," Lockhart's "On the Pulpit Eloquence of Scotland," Wilson's "A Day in Glen-Aven," and Scott's "Phantasmagoria," a supernatural tale involving a Highland ghost. *Blackwood's* constantly compared Scotland to England, and typically found the latter wanting. Edinburgh, it insisted, was a European seat of classical learning, high romantic feeling, and sound conservative principles, whereas London was an ill-defined and out-of-touch place in which people thought locally rather than internationally, and in which radicalism, effeminacy, and presumption had taken hold.

Most infamously, in the same inaugural number of the magazine that featured the "Chaldee," Lockhart published the first of his vicious assaults on what he labeled the "Cockney School of Poetry," a group of London writers that included Leigh Hunt, John Keats, and William Hazlitt. Snobbery and political animus surged through these articles. "All the great poets of our country have been men of some

rank in society, and there is no vulgarity in any of their writings,"
Lockhart sneered; "but Mr. Hunt cannot utter a dedication, or even
a note, without betraying the *Shibboleth* of low birth and low habits."
Keats had "never read any thing so virulent," and within months it
was his turn, as *Blackwood's* rounded on him in August 1818 in another
ferocious condemnation in which the Edinburgh reviewer heaped
scorn on the London poet. "If I die you must ruin Lockhart," Keats
seethed to his friend Charles Brown.[27] *Blackwood's* was unrepentant.
In the fierce competition between rival publications that overtook
the periodical press in late-Regency Britain, *Blackwood's* championed
Edinburgh as the pinnacle of cultural authority and derided London
as a plebeian place ideally suited to upstart, suburban mediocrities
like Keats and Hunt.

VI

Manchester, Liverpool, Birmingham, and Glasgow had all been
transformed in the eighteenth century by the Industrial Revolution
and its many promises of prosperity. By the Regency, however, it was
clear that urbanization and industrialization were coming at a terrible
social cost. Women, men, and children were working long hours in
mind-numbingly repetitive jobs amid dangerous machinery for low
wages, and when they were finally released from their shift in the
mine or the factory, they faced appalling living conditions, including undrained streets, filthy and overcrowded housing, and polluted
water supplies, all of which contributed to the spread of disease and
high death rates. In 1816, a parliamentary inquiry into the "State of
Children Employed in the Manufactories of the United Kingdom"
brought many of these abuses to light and prompted Robert Peel
the Elder to introduce his Cotton Mills and Factories Act, which he
steered through Parliament in 1819 and which paved the way for successive Factory Acts.

Manchester, the capital of the cotton trade, was a magnet for
employment and, during the Regency, drew to it tens of thousands
of people from towns and rural districts across the British Isles. The

influx of labor continually exacerbated the social ills that were already making life in the city wretched, but it was also a clear indication of how dire conditions often were in the countryside, where there was disease and squalor even in towns and villages with no direct connection to industry, and where manufacturing areas were sometimes decimated due to a depletion of raw materials or a temporary slump in demand. In 1814, one traveler visited Amlwch in North Wales, where he discovered that the "poisonous fumes from the copper-works" had inflicted widespread environmental degradation and that in the last few years the productivity of the mine itself had fallen by two-thirds, ravaging the local economy. Some families had fled the area in the hope of finding employment elsewhere, but there was still not enough work for those left behind. "This wretched town stands in the midst of a hideous scene of desolation," he notes; "the country round looks as if it had been blasted by a horrid pestilence."[28]

For Wordsworth, industrialism was "A new and unforeseen Creation" that had arisen "From out the labours of a peaceful Land," and in *The Excursion* he strove—like many in the Regency—to come to terms with the bewilderingly rapid and extensive changes it had introduced. The Industrial Revolution was the product of British inventiveness and expertise, and in this sense, Wordsworth acknowledged, it was a source of great pride to him. "I exult . . . to see / An Intellectual mastery exercised / O'er the blind Elements." Yet he also recognized that industrialism had generated immense turmoil and hardship, and he hoped that *The Excursion* would serve as a fount of spiritual strength for those having to fight against these debilitating forces. The crucial aim of the poem, as Coleridge understood it, was to foster a philosophy of "Life, and Intelligence" in place of that "philosophy of mechanism" meted out by industrialism, and to promulgate "a general revolution in the modes of developing & disciplining the human mind."[29]

Robert Owen also wanted a general revolution, though his was of a far more pragmatic kind. A self-made magnate from Wales whose fortune came from the Manchester cotton mills, Owen knew that Britain had benefited enormously from the Industrial Revolution, which had brought a "rapid increase" in "wealth, industry, popula-

GEORGE CRUIKSHANK drew this picture of Robert Owen lecturing, with his right arm curiously aloft and his left hand clutching a paper that reads, "New Views of Society by OWEN."

tion, and political influence" and had enabled the country to sustain a twenty-two-year war effort against Napoleon. But this had all come at an exorbitantly high cost, especially to the working classes. "Perish the cotton trade," Owen declared in January 1815, "perish even the political superiority of our country . . . if it depends on the cotton trade."[30] There was another way. It was possible, he maintained, to treat factory workers compassionately and still make money, and to seize the opportunities of industrialism to improve—rather than to debase—humankind.

In his most famous work, *A New View of Society* (1813–14), Owen addresses himself to the ruling classes, detailing how best to manage the laboring poor and mapping in his proto-socialist vision. There must be a national system of education in order both to enlighten children and to prevent penury and idleness, and it must be based, not on punishments and rewards but on presenting knowledge in a way that interested young minds. There must be an acknowledgment that character is formed, not by the will, but by the social environment. Instead of sprawling, ugly industrial towns, social progress was better served by a system of much smaller villages where cooperation rather than competition was emphasized. Factory hours must be reduced. Drinking, gambling, and unwanted pregnancies needed to be discouraged in order to improve output as well as the health and welfare of workers.

Tellingly, Owen dedicated *A New View* to the Regent and garnered a good deal of support from evangelically minded crusaders. Radicals—unsurprisingly—smelled a government rat. Owen's proposals presented no serious threat to the status quo, and they enabled him to keep a close eye on laborers while passing himself off as a philanthropist. "The lower classes," snapped Robert Wedderburn, "are pretty well convinced that [Owen] is a tool to the landholders and Ministers." Undeterred, Owen in the second half of the Regency expanded his socialist agenda, declaiming in the language of the millennium, and presenting himself as a kind of prophet whose ideas would lead inexorably, not simply to "the relief of the poor" but to "the emancipation of mankind." "A CHANGE of the most extensive magnitude the world ever contemplated, will be accomplished, without violence or confusion," he proudly announced. "THE WORLD APPROVES—AND NONE CAN RESIST!" Such grandiloquence convinced some, but it left Hazlitt cold. "Must the whole world be converted into a cotton-factory?" he demanded.[31]

Robert Southey was more sympathetic, but he too had deep reservations about Owen's utopian paternalism. Across the Regency, Owen was co-owner and chief operator of the New Lanark mills, where he worked hard to establish a model industrial village and where—for all the criticisms leveled at him—he spent large sums of his own money putting many of his most progressive theories into practice. Calling on Owen at New Lanark in September 1819, Southey found much to praise in what had become widely known as "The Happy Valley." There were rows of houses for the roughly 2,200 men, women, and children who worked there, together with lecture rooms and a store that supplied "all the necessaries of life," while the mills themselves were clean, well-ventilated, and "perfect in their kind, according to the present state of mechanical science." Yet Owen deceived himself, Southey asserted. Compelled by various motives, he sought to make his "*human machines* as he calls them (and too literally believes them to be) as happy as he can, and"—worse—"to make a display of their happiness." To be sure, his workers could leave New Lanark at any time, but ultimately there was little difference between a slave owner and him. Owen, Southey concluded, "keeps out of sight from others, and perhaps from himself, that his system, instead of aiming at perfect freedom, can only be kept in play by absolute power."[32]

VII

The Industrial Revolution left deep scars on rural England, but one of the most remarkable features of Regency Britain is how many areas of the countryside were virtually unaffected by it. Landed elites sought new ways to make their estates both more lucrative and more beautiful, while also taking steps whenever necessary to ensure that pollution, urban development, and radical unrest were kept well away from their doors. Humphry Repton was the premier landscape gardener of the age and an enthusiastic exponent of the picturesque, which he defined as a middle ground between the unruliness of nature and the rigidity of art. In order to explain his intentions to prospective clients, Repton produced his famous "Red Books," which contained both textual descriptions of his ideas and his own watercolors, and which often came complete with overlays so that "before" and "after" effects could be displayed. According to his own description in his *Fragments on the Theory and Practice of Landscape Gardening* (1816), a book he dedicated to the Regent, he was a "professional Improver."[33]

In his designs, Repton typically sought to match the style of the architecture (which should be uniform) to the character of the countryside, and to create a gradual transition from the main house out into the park by introducing some combination of terraces, balustrades, steps, conservatories, aviaries, arbors, cottages, lodges, and parterres. The approach to the house was crucial. It should be curved and smooth, and it should contain as many interesting objects and handsome "prospects" as possible. The grounds themselves should undulate, be thickly planted with artfully placed clumps of trees, and sweep down tastefully to features such as lakes, streams, bridges, gravel walks, shrubberies, statues, or mock ruins. In the Regency, by which point Repton was in the latter stages of his career, his clients included parvenus, small estate owners, and traditional elites such as John Russell, sixth Duke of Bedford, and John William Egerton, seventh Earl of Bridgewater.

The carefully planned informality of Repton's designs did much to promulgate the image of elegant living, but not everyone was impressed. In *Mansfield Park*, Austen gently satirized him as one of a number of landscape gardeners: "Repton, or any body of that sort." More severely, in the first of his comedic conversation novels, *Headlong Hall* (1816), Thomas Love Peacock lampooned Repton as the fawning Marmaduke Milestone. "The rocks shall be blown up, the trees shall be cut down, the wilderness and all its goats shall vanish like mist," Marmaduke assures the dilettante painter, Sir Patrick O'Prism, who immediately takes exception to the scheme. "Your system of levelling, and trimming, and clipping, and docking, and clumping, and polishing, and cropping, and shaving, destroys all the beautiful intricacies of natural luxuriance," he protests. "Your improved places . . . are nothing but big bowling-greens."[34]

The poet and Church of England clergyman George Crabbe shared Sir Patrick's contempt for "improvers" like Repton. "People speak with raptures of fine prospects, clear skies, lawns, parks, and the blended beauties of art and nature," asserted Crabbe, "but give me a wild, wide fen, in a foggy day; with quaking boggy ground and trembling hillocks in a putrid soil." Crabbe also took little interest in the impact of industrialism, though he knew of the "Men, Women & Children of all ages . . . breathing Contagion" in the factories, as he put it in a letter of 1818.[35] Instead, in long poems in heroic couplets such as *The Village* and *The Borough*, he produced unflinchingly realistic depictions of the suffering of the laborers who live in the countryside or in the old-fashioned coastal villages and who scraped out a living there. In the Regency, Crabbe continued to concentrate on rural life and to write in the tradition of heroic couplets that looked back to the eighteenth century, but his poetry is more varied, more disposed to tenderness and humor, and more interested in people of a higher social status than those who filled his earlier volumes.

Tales, Crabbe's most commercially successful poem, was published in 1812 and is composed of twenty-one narratives that range widely, dealing in the main with people such as farmers, merchants, pastors, tradesmen, intellectuals, and struggling professionals—people perched often uneasily "between the humble and the great," as Crabbe himself explained it. He had still not elevated his subject matter high enough to please the *Eclectic Review*, however, which complained that in his *Tales*, as in his previous work, Crabbe was far too inclined to "paint life, or rather the most loathsome and painful forms of life, in their true colours." John Murray paid Crabbe £3,000 for his existing copyrights and his next volume of poetry, *Tales of the Hall*, which appeared in 1819 and which concentrated on stories of marriage and love. Crabbe "seems to become more amorous as he grows older," Jeffrey observed in his *Edinburgh* review. John Wilson in *Blackwood's* declared that Crabbe now writes with "a gentler and more pitying spirit" of human follies and vices, and that "of all men of this age, he is the best portrait-painter."[36]

In these two collections of tales, Crabbe depicts rural England as a place full of passion, strife, isolation, and thwarted ambition, frequently using natural scenes to reflect remarkably varied states of mind and emotion. But in both volumes he also represents the country as a place of beauty, where people take pride in community, and where the land is both worked and enjoyed. "Aye, this is Nature," observes the squire in "The Lover's Journey" from *Tales*. "This ease, peace, pleasure—who would not admire? / With what delight these sturdy children play, / And joyful rustics at the close of day." In *Tales of the Hall*, two estranged half-brothers, the liberal-minded Richard and the prosperous, cynical George, meet out-of-doors one morning shortly after they have reconciled. "There is delicious quiet in this scene, / At once so rich, so varied, so serene," declares Richard. "No doubt," George replies, "the country has its charms!" But when he looks out across the fields he is interested not in aesthetics but in agricultural productivity. "My farm behold! the model for all farms! / Look at that land—you find not there a weed, / We grub the roots, and suffer none to seed."[37]

Austen was an immense admirer of Crabbe, in part no doubt because his representation of rural England as unmarked by industrial advance is so deeply congruent with her own, for in her imaginative world—as in his—there are no Luddite riots, no steam locomotives, no displaced families of factory workers, and no contaminated rivers. Revealingly, in *Mansfield Park*, Fanny Price includes Crabbe's *Tales* among her favorite books. Austen herself was even more fascinated with him. According to half-serious banter within her family, she "thoroughly enjoyed Crabbe; perhaps on account of a certain resemblance to herself in minute and highly finished detail; and would sometimes say, in jest, that, if she ever married at all, she could fancy being Mrs. Crabbe."[38]

The Scottish painter David Wilkie shared with Crabbe a deep interest in the traditional and the commonplace in rural society. Profoundly influenced by the seventeenth-century Dutch and Flemish genre painters, Wilkie produced lively scenes full of keenly observed detail, and while he painted interiors, "still you always connect them with the country," as Hazlitt shrewdly remarked in 1815. Lockhart deplored Wilkie's focus on rustic life. The proper subjects for art, in his view, were historical, biblical, and mythic. But Wilkie also had many admirers, and they came from a broad social spectrum. The Regent, guided in part by his taste for Dutch pictures, was among Wilkie's most loyal supporters and, in 1811, commissioned a picture from him that resulted in *Blind Man's Buff*, which shows a boisterous group of young people playing the game in a large kitchen where the furniture has been pushed back against the wall and which so pleased the Regent that he asked Wilkie for "a companion picture of the same size."[39] At the same time, urban audiences went in droves to see Wilkie's paintings, drawn to their humor, their remarkable gestures and expressions, their perceived Scottishness, and their imaginative re-creations of rural existence.

Wilkie was conservative minded, but some of his finest work

reflects poignantly on the plight of the exploited and the disenfran-
chised. In *Rent Day*, a landowner, or perhaps his agent, sits at a table
receiving visits from tenants who have come to pay their rent, and
who are in various states from prosperity to distress. In particular, a
woman with two young children sits somberly waiting to hand over,
not her rent, but her house key, for she has recently been widowed
and must now prepare to leave her home and cope with an uncertain
future. Reviewing an engraving of the picture in 1817, the *Examiner*
tried to "suppress the thousand thoughts and emotions respecting the
politically oppressed and their oppressors, which so immediately arise
from the first glance at the *Rent-Day*." More famously, in *Distraining
for Rent*, which Wilkie first exhibited in the year of Waterloo, harsh
economic realities burst into the domestic sphere as a humiliated
farmer and his large family face eviction over being in arrears on rent.
Neighbors argue vociferously in defense of the despairing household,
as the husband and wife have collapsed into isolated states of anguish,
unable to support or acknowledge each other, while a well-dressed
bailiff and his assistant prepare for a seizure of goods. The artist
Charles Robert Leslie went to see *Distraining for Rent* with the American author Washington Irving. "I remember that he stood before it
without saying a word," Leslie reported; "and, when he turned round,
tears were streaming down his cheeks."[40]

Like many of his Regency contemporaries, Wilkie sometimes
responded to current ills by retreating into the past, partly as a way
of throwing a more intense light on the present and partly in an
attempt to capture scenes and customs that were fast disappearing.
In this process of backward glancing, Walter Scott showed him the
way, as Wilkie devoured the *Waverley* novels and sought in his nostalgic paintings to combine diverting fiction and historical fact in a
manner highly reminiscent of Scott. Painted in 1817, Wilkie's *The
Veteran Highlander* depicts a former soldier who saw action at the Battle of Minden in 1759. Wilkie exhibited *The Reading of a Will* at the
Royal Academy in 1820, complete with a catalogue tag that referred
to an episode in Scott's story of *Guy Mannering*. Most memorably, in
The Penny Wedding, painted for the Regent as the companion piece
to *Blind Man's Buff*, Wilkie presented a type of traditional wedding

ceremony in Scotland, where everyone who attended paid a penny to enjoy the festivities. Among the crowd are historical figures as well as ordinary people, who dance, sing, feast, and gossip in a humble but joyous setting that is full of animated faces and half-told stories, and that fixes the details of a way of life that had once been common in Scotland. Aware of the kinship between his narrative art and Wilkie's, Scott made explicit reference to the painter in three of his Regency novels, including *The Antiquary*, which features a scene of mourning inside a cottage that "our Wilkie alone could have painted."[41]

Rural life in Regency Britain stirred John Clare as passionately as it did Wordsworth, Crabbe, and Wilkie, but his perspective on it was very different from theirs. Known as "the Northamptonshire Peasant Poet," Clare was from the agrarian working classes, and he communicated his understanding of the world in and around his native village of Helpstone, not as a socially superior, if sympathetic, observer of it but as a lifelong community member who was deeply embedded within it and who had developed an unrivaled knowledge of it during countless hours of laboring and wandering in the lanes, farmyards, woods, and fields of the area. Clare published his first and most successful collection, *Poems Descriptive of Rural Life and Scenery*, in January 1820. Composed of seventy-three titles, it is divided into three sections—"Poems," "Songs and Ballads," and "Sonnets"—and covers an extensive series of topics, from local traditions such as "The Village Funeral" to descriptions of different times of the day and all four seasons of the year. Throughout the collection, Clare presents highly personal evocations of the natural world and makes marvelous use of the Northamptonshire dialect, including words such as "bevering," "chelp," "cumbergrounds," "drowking," "kerchup," "proggling," "quawking," "sloomy," and "waterpudge."

Poems Descriptive reveals Clare as among the very first exponents of what we would now call "environmental activism." The volume opens with "Helpstone," a poem in which he writes of the trauma inflicted on rural England, not by machines and factories but by enclosure, the government-sanctioned process which enabled landlords to turn common or waste land into private property and which involved bringing down trees, diverting streams, planting hedgerows, digging ditches, putting up signs, and building straight fences. The practice led to greater agricultural productivity and profit, but it exacted a terrible price from the rural poor, who were deprived of the communal lands that had traditionally provided them with firewood and free grazing for their livestock. For Clare, enclosure was a violent imposition on the natural world that brought a profound sense of dislocation. "Accursed Wealth! o'er-bounding human laws, / Of every evil thou remain'st the cause," he writes in protest of the policy: "Victims of want, those wretches such as me, / Too truly lay their wretchedness to thee: / Thou art the bar that keeps from being fed, / And thine our loss of labour and of bread."[42]

What makes Clare such an important poet, however, is his knowledge that it is not just humankind that suffers when the earth is exploited. Clare is our first ecological poet because of his deep comprehension of both the human and the nonhuman worlds, and of the intricate interdependence of the two. In the finest work of *Poems Descriptive*, his achievement is not simply to write of woods and birds and meadows in economic or even aesthetic terms, but to view them as participants in a broader community of living things and to bring to consciousness the link between social and environmental injustice. Clare writes of insects ("To the Glow-worm," "The Ant"). He celebrates neglected beauty ("To an Insignificant Flower"). He displays a searching and respectful awareness of the habitat that he shares with the nonhuman world, as when he catches sight of some frogs—"And along the shaven mead, / Jumping travellers, they proceed"—or distinguishes between the calls of various birds:

> Crows crowd croaking over head,
> Hastening to the woods to bed.
> Cooing sits the lonely dove,
> Calling home her absent love.
> With 'Kirchup! kirchup!' 'mong the wheats,
> Partridge distant partridge greets.

Above all, Clare speaks of his connection to the natural world, a connection that both sustains and threatens him. He is especially moving on the destruction of trees and his passionate attachment to them: "Oh! who could see my dear green willows fall, / What feeling heart, but dropt a tear for all?"[43] In *Poems Descriptive*, Clare announces to the modern world his apprehension of ecological integrity and reveals how damage done to his environment is damage done to him and to us all.

VIII

John Constable, one of the greatest British landscape painters, produced many of the pictures that are widely thought to represent the quintessential English countryside. His favorite subject was the Stour Valley, located on the border of Suffolk and Essex, and now known worldwide as "Constable Country," where he lived until his early twenties and where as an artist he returned over and over again to tap into his intense childhood memories of the area. In the first half of the Regency, Constable met with very limited professional success and was given to bouts of melancholy that affected his work. "It is bleak," he wrote of one of his paintings in 1814, "and looks as if there would be a shower of sleet, and that you know is too much the case with my things." Distressing Constable especially at this time was his inability to marry the love of his life, Maria Bicknell, whose family was firmly opposed to her relationship with the struggling artist. But when in 1816 his father died and Constable received an inheritance, he finally had the financial independence needed to marry Maria, and thereafter he painted with much greater confidence. "All my hopes and prospects in life are included in my attachment to you," he had told her during their courtship, much of which they were forced to conduct clandestinely.[44]

Vitality, spontaneity, and comprehensiveness characterize Constable's finest Regency paintings. Admiring though he was of several of the great landscape artists who had come before him, Constable in his work nevertheless sought to emancipate himself from tradition and rule. He wanted to paint honestly, and to convey through his art what it was like, not to look at nature but to be in it. Driven by his desire to elevate the genre of landscape painting (which in terms of Regency aesthetic categories ranked below history painting and portraiture), Constable believed that the faithful representation of a landscape was a moral act that could communicate truths even more effectively than history painting. "Every tree," he wrote to Maria in May 1819, "seems full of blossom of some kind & the surface of the ground seems quite lovely—every step I take & on whatever object I turn my eye that sublime expression in the Scripture 'I am the resurrection & the life' &c, seems verified about me."[45]

Constable transformed British landscape art in several different ways. He committed himself to working outdoors, soaking up the atmosphere of the place as he painted it, and completing as much as possible of the picture with the landscape directly in front of him.

JOHN CONSTABLE exhibited this *Scene on the River Stour*, better known as *The White Horse*, in the spring of 1819, and its critical and popular success led directly to his long-overdue election as an associate of the Royal Academy.

His quest to capture the freshness and peculiarities of the English countryside meant he obstinately refused to give his works the glossy finish that contemporary taste demanded, leading critics to condemn his execution as rough and unsophisticated. To a much greater extent than previous landscape painters, Constable prized accuracy in detail, a passion that enabled him to imbue ordinary objects with extraordinary intensity. When he showed William Blake one of his sketches of an avenue of fir trees, Blake responded, "Why, this is not drawing, but *inspiration*." Constable studied a landscape systematically, sketching it from a variety of perspectives and at different times of the day and year. Finally, he was convinced that painters of the natural world should be aware of the latest advances in sciences such as optics and meteorology. The combination of these factors produced what Thomas Lawrence called Constable's "ferocious art."[46]

What is perhaps most remarkable about Constable's ferociousness, though, is that he used it to paint not sublime cliffs or violent storms but the peace and beauty of the Stour Valley, and to produce in his finest work the most cherished versions of a timelessly harmonious English landscape. These paintings are full of undulating hills carpeted with hardwoods, lawns covered in morning dew, fresh fields of hay, meandering lanes and rivers lined with flowers, and magnificent skies suffused in warm light, darkened by atmospheric cloud formations, or brightening under a rainbow. There are thatched cottages, windmills, manor houses, barns, and churches. There are bargemen, mill workers, and agricultural laborers. Children fish, ride, work, watch, and play. Farm animals graze. Rooks fly overhead. Constable pays special attention to the way the light casts shadows or plays on the water, the way the wind moves reeds or chimney smoke, the way the rain brings swooping birds looking for worms, and so on. His greatest painting of the Regency, *A Scene on the River Stour* (popularly known as *The White Horse*), was exhibited in 1819 and is the first in a series of grand canvases that Constable called his "six footers." It depicts, under a serenely blue-gray sky, a tow horse being ferried across the river, a skiff moored below Willy Lott's cottage, cattle feeding at the water's edge, and green fields stretching off into the distance. "What a grasp of everything beautiful in rural scenery!"

exclaimed the *Literary Chronicle* in its enthusiastic assessment of the painting.[47]

However, to achieve such untroubled visions of the English countryside, Constable had to reject or ignore a great deal, from the impact of factories, through the riots organized by artisans and agricultural laborers, to the tens of thousands of demobilized soldiers looking for work in the years immediately following Waterloo. Viewed from this perspective, his representations of rural England take on a highly charged political dimension. They reveal his pride in the ability of English farmers to feed the country during the Napoleonic wars, and they convey a patriotic message of stability and full employment in a bountiful countryside endearingly resistant to the disruptions of modernity. Constable was deeply committed to the direct and accurate study of nature, but he painted a world that was vanishing even as he immortalized it, and that he invariably viewed through the lens of memory and nostalgia. *The White Horse*, he told a close friend, was "one of the strongest instances" of his rendering as a picture what he had thought of as a child.[48]

J. M. W. Turner was Constable's great painting rival and the other preeminent figure in the history of British landscape art. The two had a good deal in common. Both painted with a new inventiveness. Both had a passionate interest in atmosphere, color, and light, and their combined effects on a particular place at a particular time. Both seized on contemporary discoveries in science to strengthen and refine their art, for both saw themselves as experimenters laboring—like their scientific contemporaries—to reveal the physical secrets of the earth. Both sought to elevate landscape painting to unparalleled levels of complexity and imaginative power, for both were convinced that the genre was capable of achieving the highest moral aspirations of public art. In June 1813, the two sat together at a Royal Academy dinner. "I was a good deal entertained with Turner," Constable wrote to Maria. "I always expected to find him what I did—he is uncouth but has a wonderfull range of mind."[49]

The differences between the two artists were even more pronounced. Turner was a prodigy who was elected to full membership in the Royal Academy at the remarkably early age of twenty-six, placing him at the summit of his profession, while Constable, equally ambitious and just a year younger, was not even elected to an associate membership until 1819, when he was forty-three ("the field of Waterloo is a field of mercy to ours," he remarked of his struggle for recognition). Turner drew inspiration from nature, history, and literature: Byron was his favorite contemporary poet. Only nature stirred the artist in Constable: Byron, he declared, had "deadly slime" in "his touch."[50] Turner was filled with restless energy and made annual sketching tours that included the West Country in 1811 and 1813, Yorkshire in 1816, Belgium and Holland in 1817, Scotland in 1818, and finally, in 1819, Italy. Constable rarely left the southeastern corner of England and never went abroad. Turner reveled in the sublime. Constable was unmoved by it. Turner painted industrialism with a mixture of excitement and anxiety. Constable disregarded it. Turner had a great deal of business savvy. Constable painted what mattered to him.

During the Regency, Turner's output was distinguished by the same technical mastery and astounding breadth that characterized his entire career. In several paintings he paid homage to his great predecessors in the tradition of marine and landscape art. At the annual Royal Academy exhibition in 1811, the Regent lauded landscape paintings that the seventeenth-century French painter Claude "would have admired," a reference that he seems to have made with Turner's extremely Claudian *Mercury and Hersé* in mind. Turner produced a second superb Regency tribute, this time to the Dutch master Cuyp, in his luminous *Dort, or Dordrecht, the Dort Packet-Boat from Rotterdam Becalmed*, exhibited in 1818. Constable, who could "remember most of Turner's early pictures," described the *Dort* as "of singular intricacy and beauty," depicting "a canal with numerous boats, making thousands of beautiful shapes, and I think the most complete work of genius I ever saw."[51]

Large paintings of Carthaginian subjects also preoccupied the Regency Turner, and these have frequently been interpreted as his exploration of the rise and fall of Napoleon. In *Snow Storm: Hannibal and his Army Crossing the Alps*, Turner ostensibly produced a historical painting of the kind much favored by the Royal Academy, but the work is dominated by an immense sky that is full of anger and flux and that dwarfs the struggling soldiers compressed down into the darkened foreground of the picture. Set against the overwhelming forces of nature, Hannibal's quest for military and imperial glory seems almost risible, and the clear implication is that the same may be said for the aspirations of Napoleon, whose expansionist campaigns against Britain, like Hannibal's against Rome, ultimately ended in failure. In the catalogue description that accompanied the painting, Turner appended lines from his own unfinished epic poem, *Fallacies of Hope*, for in *Snow Storm* he reveals, not the power of the individual but the vulnerability and transience of all human endeavor. Henry Crabb Robinson went to see the painting in May 1812 and said simply, "I can never forget it." In the *Examiner*, Robert Hunt (the elder artist brother of John and Leigh Hunt) described *Snow Storm* as "a performance that classes Mr. Turner in the highest rank of landscape painting," and noted in particular the "terrible splendour . . . in the shining of the sun" and the "terrible magnificence . . . in the widely circular sweep of snow whirling high in the air."[52]

In addition, Turner produced work for several wealthy clients and patrons, including Walter Fawkes at Farnley Hall in Yorkshire and the Earl of Egremont at Petworth in Sussex, and involved himself in a number of commercial ventures designed to display his versatility and augment his popularity and income. He published the *Liber Studiorum* (Book of Studies), his great series of mezzotint engravings, which he intended both as a demonstration of his own virtuosity as an artist and as a carefully conceived instruction manual that covered all the categories of landscape composition. He contributed illustrations for engraving to Walter Scott's *Provincial Antiquities of Scotland*, and while Scott griped that "Turner's palm is as itchy as his fingers are ingenious and he will . . . do nothing without cash," Lockhart in *Peter's Letters* marveled at the "exquisite representations of the old castles and romantic skies of Scotland, over whose forms and hues of native majesty, a new atmosphere of magical interest has just been diffused by the poetical pencil of Turner."[53]

Most business-minded of all, in *England: Richmond Hill, on the Prince Regent's Birthday*, Turner exploited an immense canvas to depict

J. M. W. Turner drew this picture of Borthwick Castle during his 1818 tour of Scotland. The picture was engraved by Henry Le Keux and published the following year in the first installment of Walter Scott's *Provincial Antiquities of Scotland*.

an idyllic English scene that he hoped would attract royal favor and gratify public interest in the monarchy. The painting is distinguished once again by its vast sky, this time of summer blue largely veiled in white cloud. In the foreground, an elegantly dressed crowd containing many women has gathered to celebrate the Regent's birthday, while below them a cricket game takes place in a meadow, and the Thames winds away through wooded fields into the distance. Exhibited at the Royal Academy in 1819, it is a rural vision of England unified under the crown, and at peace and play. Nonetheless, like Constable in *The White Horse*, which appeared in the same 1819 Royal Academy exhibition, Turner achieved the harmony of *England: Richmond Hill* only by overlooking the tempestuous political events that were taking place as he produced the painting, and that were soon to culminate in the carnage of Peterloo.

William Hazlitt, who had once harbored ambitions as a painter, was the finest art critic of the Regency, and in his assessments of Turner he typically blended admiration with forthright censure. Most famously, in the *Examiner* for February 1816, Hazlitt hailed Turner as "the ablest landscape painter now living, whose pictures are, however, too much abstractions of aerial perspective, and representations not so properly of the objects of nature as of the medium through which they are seen. . . . Some one said of his landscapes that they were *pictures of nothing, and very like*." Hazlitt here seems to be gazing into the future, as Turner in his later style often dissolves form into prismatic vapors or general abstractions of color and light that might well seem like "*pictures of nothing*." The fact that Hazlitt could write this commentary of the Regency Turner, however, indicates how thoroughly revolutionary Turner already seemed to his contemporaries.[54] He is probably the greatest painter Britain has ever produced, and the audacity and inventiveness of his work in the Regency era confirms his place at the fountainhead of the modern movement in art.

IX

Napoleon's rampage through Europe forced many who would otherwise have gone on a grand—or even a not-so-grand—tour through France, Switzerland, and Italy to stay at home, and to search instead for recreation, education, and inspiration in the sublime and picturesque landscapes of Scotland, Wales, or the English Lake District. And while British sightseers poured into Europe after Wellington's victory at Waterloo, tourism at home continued to thrive, as many travelers, constrained by time or money, or driven by a genuine desire to see more of Britain, fanned out on coach and packet-boat trips, walking and riding tours, and holiday excursions to inland spas and seaside resorts.

There was a great deal to experience and discover. In 1811, Lord John Russell took a tour of the manufacturing districts of England, where he saw firsthand the factories of Birmingham, Liverpool, Manchester, and Leeds, and where, as he noted enthusiastically, "every machine . . . is a part of the glory and a source of the prosperity of England." Like many sportsmen, John Wilson had a special fondness for angling, and in the spring of 1816 he went on one of his many fishing expeditions, walking and steamboating his way from Glasgow north to Inveraray, where on one Saturday he "fished up the stream . . . and killed eighteen dozen." Though unknown to each other, John Keats and Thomas Carlyle both went on walking tours of the English Lakes in the summer of 1818, Keats increasingly confident that he would "learn poetry" from the "countenance or intellectual tone" of the mountains and waterfalls, and Carlyle hopeful that climbing peaks such as "Scawfell & Helvellyn" would improve him "both in body & mind." Watering places drew not only vacationers but also those in search of better health. Ramsgate, on the north Kent coast, was especially popular. In 1819, Coleridge walked from the town along the shoreline to a secret cavern, where he stripped off all his clothes and had "a glorious tumble in the waves."[55]

There were scores of Regency pocket itineraries and traveler's companions designed to help tourists find the best views, the easiest routes, and the most important historical spots. There were also— much further upmarket—dozens of color-plate books on British topography, including William Daniell and Richard Ayton's *A Voyage Round Great Britain*, which began appearing in 1814 and which grew to eight volumes. Guided firmly by the aesthetic of the picturesque, Daniell produced more than 300 aquatints of beautiful, if undemanding, views. Ayton, however, took a starkly different approach in his composition of the letterpress, where he rejected Daniell's idealizations and instead inserted urgent social commentary on the dismal lives of so many of the people that he encountered on the journey.

Most strikingly, when they visited Whitehaven on the Cumberland coast, Daniell drew a picture of the harbor while Ayton descended into a nearby coal mine, where he witnessed conditions and heard reports that horrified him. "In consequence of the employment of women in the mines, the most abominable profligacy prevails among the people," he asserted. "One should scarcely have supposed that there would be any temptations to sin in these gloomy and loathsome caverns, but they are made the scenes of the most bestial debauchery." Children were also employed in the mines, though their "cries . . . have never, I imagine, reached the ears of their noble proprietor." Britain had recently abolished the slave trade. How could it still allow a system of "cold-blooded tyranny" in which a child was "dragged from the light . . . and buried in a dark solitude for thirteen hours a day"?[56]

Domestic travel fills Regency novels. In Frances Burney's *The Wanderer* (1814), the impoverished Juliet Granville moves from one job to another as she journeys from France to Dover, on to London, down to Brighton and Lewes, back to London, and then to Salisbury and Stonehenge. More happily, in Mary Brunton's *Self-Control*, Laura Montreville takes a boat from Edinburgh to London, gliding smoothly along the coast for five days and reaching London on the evening of the sixth. Making the same journey overland was also an option, for there were "numerous coaches . . . perpetually passing and repassing betwixt the capital of Britain and her northern sister," as Scott puts it in *The Heart of Mid-Lothian*.[57] Elizabeth Bennet hopes to travel to the Lake District in Austen's *Pride and Prejudice*, but in the end she takes an eventful tour of the Peak District in Derbyshire. George Wickham hastens to Ramsgate in the same novel, not for medical reasons but with the intention of seducing Georgiana Darcy.

The Tour of Dr. Syntax in Search of the Picturesque (1812) was a lighthearted and highly successful parody of the period's rage for landscapes or seascapes that exhibited the picturesque. A product of the partnership between William Combe, who wrote the verse letterpress, and Thomas Rowlandson, who supplied the illustrations, *The Tour* features a naive but lovable skin-and-bones schoolmaster and clergyman named Dr. Syntax, who decides at the start of the holidays to mount his old gray mare Grizzle and make a tour of England. A series of misadventures follow as, among other things, he attends the Covent Garden Theatre, visits his Oxford college, loses his money at the York race-grounds, watches a military review, inadvertently stays at a "Gentleman's House," and preaches a sermon. Most memorably, and unlike Elizabeth Bennet, he visits the Lake District. A local lord invites him to go hunting, but Syntax has other plans.

'Your sport, my Lord, I cannot take,
For I must go and hunt a Lake;
And while you chace the flying deer,
I must fly off to *Windermere.*
'Stead of hallooing to a fox,
I must catch echoes from the rocks;
With curious eye and active scent,
I on the *picturesque* am bent.'[58]

The following day Syntax travels on to Keswick, where he spends his time sketching the lake before falling into it.

Rowlandson's marvelous illustrations brim with life on the road—with dogs and cats, horses and ducks, crowded inns, rustic sports, amorous lovers, debauched aristocrats, and much else. In his picture of "Dr. Syntax Meditating on the Tombs," Syntax stands on a gravestone, his sketchbook behind his back, as he waits for his imagination to take fire at the gothic scene in front of him. "Dr. Syntax Copying

Thomas Rowlandson supplied the illustrations for *Dr. Syntax in Search of the Picturesque,* including this one of "Dr. Syntax Reading his Tour." Rowlandson's collaborator, the satirist William Combe, provided the lively letterpress.

the Wit of the Window" features a maidservant named Dolly, who is distracted by her lover as she prepares the tea, and who spills boiling water on Syntax's groin. In "Dr. Syntax Reading his Tour," Syntax sits on a bench in a country inn caught up in his own account of his adventures through England, while his audience sleeps soundly all around him, except for two young lovers in the background who are clearly pursuing other interests.[59]

X

Main roads in the Regency were almost all turnpike roads, which were fitted with tollgates at various intervals to help offset the costs of improvements and repairs, and which were administered by turnpike trusts, composed typically of prominent local gentry and nobility. The average speed of coach travel was around seven miles an hour.[60] Significant delays were possible, though, if a party arrived at a post station with tired horses and fresh ones were not available. Breakdowns, too, were regular occurrences, and so were accidents, as Austen suggests in *Sanditon* and Scott in *The Heart of Mid-Lothian*, both of which open with a carriage being overturned.

By the advent of the Regency, Britain had taken significant strides in establishing a countrywide system of roads. In rural districts, the "foot-path faintly marked" and the "horse-track wild" had "vanished," Wordsworth notes in *The Excursion*, "swallowed up by stately roads / Easy and bold, that penetrate the gloom / Of England's farthest Glens." Upgrades, too, were evident on the major routes, as Ferrier remarks in *Marriage*, where the journey Mary Douglas makes from Edinburgh to London is performed, "like most modern journies . . . in comfort and safety." Mail-coach roads, in particular, had been improved. "The post-office is a wonderful establishment!" Jane Fairfax enthuses in Austen's *Emma*. "The regularity and dispatch of it!" In *Pride and Prejudice*, Darcy is keenly aware that road building is dramatically altering British life. Elizabeth's friend Charlotte has recently married Mr. Collins and moved to the parsonage at Hunsford, which Darcy describes to Elizabeth as an "easy . . . distance" from Charlotte's family and friends. "An easy distance do you call it?" she asks, typically challenging him. "It is nearly fifty miles." "And what is fifty miles of good road?" he replies, driven by his desire to impress upon her that his own home in Derbyshire is much closer than she realizes. "Little more than half a day's journey. Yes, I call it a *very* easy distance."[61]

Darcy is exaggerating, as Elizabeth suspects. The condition of British roads was not nearly as advanced as he implies, as many other commentators pointed out. In 1813, Maria Edgeworth's father, Richard Lovell Edgeworth, published his *Essay on the Construction of Roads and Carriages*, in the introduction to which he declared that since writing the essay he had visited England and had found, "on a journey of many hundred miles, scarcely twenty of well made road." Edward Berens echoed these views seven years later in the *Quarterly Review*: "We would not be understood as contending that the roads of the kingdom are worse than they were ten or twenty years ago; on the whole, perhaps, they are better. It admits of no dispute, however, that they are, generally speaking, bad." In Maria Edgeworth's *The Absentee*, Lord Colambre is driven over a road in Ireland where "the jolting and bumping" is "past endurance." Innumerable other Regency travelers had terrible experiences on the roads as well, including Mrs. Norris in Austen's *Mansfield Park*. "If you had seen the state of the roads *that* day!" she exclaims to Sir Thomas. "I thought we should never have got through them. . . . And then the poor horses too!—To see them straining away!"[62]

The Scottish entrepreneur and inventor John Loudon McAdam realized that something needed to be done. Fascinated for years by road construction and management, and an inveterate traveler who had covered thousands of miles of British roads, he understood that the fundamental problem with contemporary roads was that the stones used in their construction were too large, and that it was only a matter of time before they were cracked and dislodged by the wheels of carriages—to say nothing of the reciprocal damage inflicted on the carriages by the protruding stones and flying fragments. McAdam's solution was to build roads using much smaller stones. He proposed beginning with an eight-inch layer of small, angular, hand-broken stones laid directly onto an elevated and well-drained subsoil, covering that base with a two-inch layer of gravel and smaller stones, and then allowing the whole to be compacted and strengthened—rather than destroyed—by the passing traffic. "Every piece of stone put into a road, which exceeds an inch in any of its dimensions, is mischievous," he told a House of Commons committee "on the Highways of the Kingdom" in 1811, before going on to develop his ideas in two subsequent books, *Remarks on the Present System of Road-Making* (1816) and *Practical Essay on the Scientific Repair and Preservation of Roads* (1819).[63]

In 1816, the sixty-year-old McAdam got the opportunity to put his theories into practice when he was appointed surveyor-general for the roads of Bristol, one of the busiest ports in Britain, and began to build and restore roads according to his own designs. He was able to remove, break up, and reuse the hefty stones that were already overburdening many mucky streets and ill-mended thoroughfares, and the result was new roads that were quick, easy, and cheap to make, and that were also far stronger and smoother. Within eighteen months, McAdam had repaired the Bristol roads that were in bad condition and introduced numerous improvements. By 1819 he was a national figure and had been "sent for and consulted by 34 different sets of commissioners, and as many different trusts, and in 13 counties, to the extent of 637 miles." Asserted Mary Russell Mitford: "the Macadamised roads . . . have so abridged . . . distance in this fair Island, that what used to be a journey, is now a drive." Thomas De Quincey, that great traveler of Regency roads, especially on the top of mail coaches, confirmed that, "within a few years" of Waterloo, McAdam had effected a "revolution in the system of travelling."[64] Indeed, McAdam is one of those select innovators whose name has passed into the English language, in "macadamize" and, more famously, in "tarmac."

Thomas Telford was McAdam's great rival in Regency roadbuilding. To some extent their methods overlapped, in their emphasis on drainage and the use of broken stones, for example. However, Telford was an engineer, unlike McAdam, and he insisted on a hard foundation of large stones, which meant that his roads took more time and money to build, but they were also cheaper to maintain and more durable. Among his main accomplishments in roadbuilding are the Glasgow to Carlisle road and the Holyhead roads, including Shrewsbury to Bangor, Bangor to Chester, and London to Shrewsbury, work on all of which began in the Regency. In addition, during the construction of the Holyhead roads, Telford exhibited his superb skill as a bridge builder, especially in the elegant, wrought-iron suspension bridge that spans the Menai Strait from Bangor to the island of Angelsey in Wales. Begun in 1819, and employing state-of-the-art technologies, it was the first modern suspension bridge and one of the crowning achievements of Telford's career.

Canals were another area of expertise. For decades, British engineers had been steadily linking them to one another, to rivers, and to the sea in order to transport the bulky materials associated with the Industrial Revolution. By the Regency they formed an extensive network that continued to stimulate old markets, create new opportunities, and accelerate the movement of goods and people. Telford, the last of the great British canal builders, played a leading role in several projects that put finishing touches on the system, including the Regent's Canal in London, the Thames and Medway Canal, and the Edinburgh-Glasgow Union Canal.[65]

Telford's remarkable versatility as a civil engineer was most fully on display in the work he carried out in the Highlands of his native Scotland, work that, in his own assessment, brought inestimable moral, economic, and social benefits, "advancing the country at least a century." Southey took a tour of inspection with Telford in the autumn of 1819, and while impressed with the Scottish scenery, he was much more interested in the grandeur and extent of Telford's plans, for already in the Highlands he had laid " 1,000 miles of the finest roads in the world" and constructed " 1,500 bridges great and small," and everywhere he continued "making roads, building bridges, forming canals, and creating harbours." Above all, Southey was struck by the number of men, horses, and machines at work on the Caledonian Canal, which cut sixty miles across the Highlands from Fort William on the west coast northeastward to Inverness on the east coast, and which was made possible by Telford's immensely innovative construction of twenty-eight huge locks. In putting in place these vast improvements in infrastructure, Telford transformed the entire region and brought Scotland into the modern world. "The times have changed in nothing more . . . than in the rapid conveyance of intelligence and communication betwixt one part of Scotland and another," Walter Scott avowed in 1818.[66]

XI

Meanwhile, in response to the transport needs of the burgeoning coal industry, other Regency engineers, innovators, and enthusiasts were at work on another travel revolution. British manufacture had been using steam engines for almost a century when, in 1804, the brilliant Cornishman Richard Trevithick built the first railway locomotive at Penydarren in South Wales. Four years later, near Euston Road in London, he exhibited a new locomotive, "Catch-me-who-can," on a circular railway. The enterprise was not a commercial success and ended in disaster when a rail broke and the engine flew off the tracks and overturned.[67] Thereafter, Trevithick lost interest in locomotives, and in 1811 he was declared bankrupt. Colliery owners, however, were still keen to investigate the potentials of locomotion as a means of cutting costs, for while horse-drawn railways were commonplace in their mines, the Napoleonic wars meant high prices for feed and a chronic shortage of horses.

Numerous inventors stepped forward with ingenious solutions to the many problems posed by railway locomotion. In March 1813, William Hedley patented his design for a smooth-wheeled engine that stayed on smooth cast-iron rails through simple friction adhesion, and later that same year his locomotive, *Puffing Billy*, successfully pulled coal wagons about five miles from the colliery at Wylam in Northumberland to dockside on the River Tyne. During the opening years of the Regency, too, William Brunton, William Chapman, and John Blenkinsop all designed engines with an adhesion system that involved a cogwheel working into a toothed rail. Though soon obsolete, each of their schemes introduced valuable innovations, and of the three, Blenkinsop's was the most successful. His locomotive, named the *Prince Regent* and built by the outstanding mechanical engineer Matthew Murray, made its inaugural run in June 1812, and within eighteen months three of his engines were in service hauling coal trucks over rack-rail transmission from the Middleton collieries to nearby Leeds.

Thomas Gray of Nottingham saw Blenkinsop's train in action and soon succumbed to railway mania. Locomotives, he prophesized in 1820, "would revolutionize the whole face of the material world," superseding canal boats and road vehicles and alleviating the terrible suffering inflicted on the half-million horses pushed hard over Britain's turnpike roads by coach drivers determined to stay on schedule and ahead of the competition. Richard Lovell Edgeworth shared Gray's confidence that locomotives would transform travel everywhere. He had been experimenting with railways for more than four decades when, in 1813, he wrote to the renowned Scottish inventor James Watt, whose improvements to the steam engine had powered the Industrial Revolution in the final third of the eighteenth century. "I have always thought that steam would become the universal lord, and that we should in time scorn post-horses," Edgeworth told Watt.[68]

George Stephenson is probably the most famous of all British engineers. Autodidactic, prescient, entrepreneurial, and doggedly persistent, he was thirty-three years old and based at Killingworth near Newcastle when in 1814 he produced his first locomotive, the *Blucher*, which he built in his West Moor colliery workshop and which he named presumably after the Prussian field marshal Gebhard Blücher. Stephenson was familiar with the work of several of his contemporaries, including Hedley, Chapman, and Blenkinsop, and his *Blucher* is clearly indebted to their experimentations. Constructed with two cylinders, a single-flue boiler eight feet long and just under three feet in diameter, and flanged wheels running on cast-iron edge rails, the *Blucher* performed well at its trial run on July 25, 1814, laboring past Stephenson's cottage pulling eight loaded coal carriages weighing thirty tons at a speed of four miles an hour.

The demonstration, at which "hundreds if not thousands assembled to see the marvellous sight," brought Stephenson into notice and made him more convinced than ever that "I will do something in

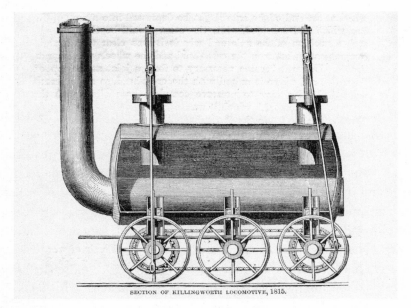

SECTION OF KILLINGWORTH LOCOMOTIVE, 1815.

THIS IMAGE of the Killingworth locomotive in 1815 was probably drawn by its inventor, George Stephenson.

coming time which will astonish all England," as he himself put it. But except in its use of friction adhesion, the *Blucher* was not an obvious advance on the Blenkinsop and Murray engines, and there were problems with it as well. It was not cost-effective in relation to horsepower. It was very noisy. It threw cinders. It was too heavy for the track. It lacked sufficient steam-raising power to keep the engine constantly working, and it was without springs and an effective method of transmitting power to the wheels, so that its progress forward was essentially a succession of jolts and jerks.[69]

Undaunted, Stephenson went back to the drawing board and within months had made a series of substantial improvements, which he incorporated into his next locomotive, the *Wellington*. At this time, Stephenson also worked to develop better rails, for he alone among the early engineers saw the problem of locomotion in its entirety, with the result that he concentrated, not just on engine design but on the crucial relationship between the train and its tracks. Entering into a partnership with the Newcastle ironmaster William Losh,

Stephenson designed rails that were so much better than previous attempts that the existing Killingworth line was ripped up and relaid with them.

By 1819, Stephenson had turned Killingworth into the center of British railway development and had advanced the locomotive to modern form in its essential features. The bigger picture was now clearly in sight. Locomotion, as Stephenson had realized for several years, was not just about moving industrial-sized volumes of coal at greater speeds and lower costs. It was about transportation far more broadly defined. The railways, he possessed the vision and the skill to see, had the potential to transform time, distance, and communication, as well as our relationship with and reliance on technology. From his workshop on the Tyne, Stephenson set in motion a commercial, mechanical, and cultural revolution that extended across Britain and then around the world, and that drove the British empire to its highest peaks of wealth and influence.

Whereas for decades colonial trade and expansion had revolved around coastal settlements, innovative steam technologies brought vast new tracts of land under British control. Powerful British steamships sailed regardless of the wind or the currents, and they voyaged farther inshore and upriver than ever before, while railways were established across the colonies and soon provided fast and safe access to resource-rich interiors that in the past had been far too hard to reach and exploit. Stephenson's inventions laid the foundation for the sophisticated international transportation network that allowed the British empire to move people, goods, and information more cheaply and dependably than ever before, that brought it previously unimaginable levels of prosperity and coherence, and that enabled it to build on successes in ways that kept it well ahead of its colonial competitors.

XII

Humphry Davy was the Regency's leading scientist and was celebrated both nationally and internationally for his groundbreaking research in areas ranging from mineralogy, geology, and agriculture, through the nature of light, heat, and electricity, to the chemistry of tanning hides and the anesthetic potential of nitrous oxide, or "laughing gas." He was, besides, an outstanding lecturer—eloquent, imaginative, and highly knowledgeable—and his crowd-pleasing talks and demonstrations at the Royal Institution greatly increased the prestige of science. In April 1812, the Regent knighted him for services to chemistry, the first knighthood for a scientist since Sir Isaac Newton more than a century earlier.[70] Shortly thereafter Davy gathered his lectures in two volumes, *Elements of Chemical Philosophy* (1812) and *Elements of Agricultural Chemistry* (1813).

Davy's most important contribution, however, came in the months following Waterloo when he invented the miner's safety lamp. The Industrial Revolution had produced an almost unappeasable demand for coal, and mines in Britain were being driven farther and farther underground, making them both more productive and much more dangerous. In May 1812, a massive explosion at the Felling Pit near Sunderland killed ninety-two miners in the most horrifying circumstances. Some were crushed by falling rocks. Others suffocated or burned to death. "In one spot were found twenty-one bodies in ghastly confusion . . . one wanted its head, another an arm." After the mass burials, forty widows, sixty girls, and twenty-six boys "were thrown upon the benevolence of the public."[71] A solution had to be found.

Following a plea for assistance from Dr. Robert Gray of the Coal Mines Safety Committee, Davy visited the Walls End colliery near Newcastle, where he discussed the situation with the chief engineer, John Buddle. Miners had to carry either a candle or an oil lamp in order to work in the darkness of the mine, but these light sources were igniting the lethal "fire-damp" gas that occurred naturally in the coal seams. What was needed was a completely reliable safety lamp. Davy dashed back to London, locked himself away in his laboratory for three months, and conducted an intense investigation using the inductive method of "observation, experiment, and analogy" that he had championed throughout his career. The "fire-damp" gas was often thought to be hydrogen, but Davy soon proved that it was methane. He then devised and rejected several forms of the safety lamp before a series of technical breakthroughs produced, in January

1816, a simple and inexpensive version in which a common cotton wick and Greenland whale oil burned within a sturdy sixteen-inch cylinder of fine wire gauze that allowed the light to pass through but absorbed the heat from the flame.[72]

It worked. One of the first examples of pure science being applied to real-world problems, the Davy Lamp unquestionably saved many hundreds of lives, and it confirmed the arrival of the modern scientific era in Britain. Davy refused to take out the patent that would have made him a wealthy man, as he did not want to profit from a device that protected lives and livelihoods, but he did accept the many honors that were showered on him, including the Regent's offer of a baronetcy. In his own account of the discovery, Davy left a detailed record of his research, not only because it was of importance to colliery owners and workers but also because it made a much larger point for all the "friends of humanity" about the relationship between the great and disinterested powers of science and the "common wants and purposes of life."[73]

The twenty-year-old Michael Faraday attended Davy's last four lectures at the Royal Institution in the spring of 1812, and within a year went to work for him as a laboratory assistant, where he learned chemistry at Davy's elbow. With Napoleon's permission, the two men set out in October 1813 on an eighteen-month tour of the major scientific laboratories in war-ravaged Europe. During their time in France, they analyzed an unknown substance that Davy recognized as analogous to chlorine and that he named iodine. "The discovery of this substance in matters so common and supposed so well known must be a stimulus of no small force to the enquiring minds of modern chemists," Faraday wrote in his travel journal. In Italy, they ignited diamonds and studied the combustion product. "According to Sir H. Davy it is probable that diamond is pure carbon," Faraday noted.[74]

Back in London, Faraday steadily took on a larger role at the Royal Institution. He worked closely with Davy during the three feverish months in which he investigated the cause of coal-mine explosions and was "witness in our laboratory to the gradual and beautiful development of the train of thought and experiments" that produced the safety lamp. For members of the City Philosophical Society, Faraday delivered a sixteen-part lecture series that treated all of inorganic chemistry. With the cutler James Stodart, he conducted his first significant original research on alloys of steel. In an 1818 essay for the *Philosophical Magazine* on the compounds of phosphorus, Davy thanked Faraday for his "useful assistance," "his accuracy," and his "steadiness of manipulation."[75] The public acknowledgment launched Faraday, who, like Davy, believed profoundly in chemistry as a force for social good and who, in Davy's Regency laboratory, readied himself for his groundbreaking work on electromagnetism and one of the most remarkable careers in all of British science.

Charles Babbage was another rising star on the scientific scene. As a disgruntled Cambridge undergraduate, he helped in 1812 to found the "Analytical Society," a pressure group that sought to introduce European mathematical methods into the conservative bastion of Cambridge. The society was dormant within two years, but Babbage played a leading role in the 1813 publication of the *Memoirs of the Analytical Society*, and he went on to produce several articles in the Regency on mathematics. In 1815, after graduating from Cambridge, he delivered a lecture series on astronomy for the Royal Institution, and five years later was one of the cofounders of the Royal Astronomical Society. The mathematician Edward Bromhead declared in 1818 that Babbage's "Genius" was "mechanical" and suggested that if he was going to be famous, he needed to invent something "strikingly useful."[76]

He did. There are a number of different versions of when Babbage first thought of devising a calculating machine—the forerunner of the modern computer—but in his autobiography he himself dates it to "1812 or 1813." In this account, Babbage describes himself as sitting one evening "in the rooms of the Analytical Society, at Cambridge, my head leaning forward on the Table in a kind of dreamy mood, with a Table of logarithms lying open before me. Another member, coming into the room, and seeing me half asleep, called out, 'Well, Babbage, what are you dreaming about?' to which I replied, 'I am thinking that all these Tables (pointing to the logarithms) might be calculated by machinery.'"[77] Before long Babbage was obsessed with this idea and had fixed on two types of "engine," as he referred to them.

The first, the "Difference Engine," was designed to solve equations and make tables of numbers. Its most obvious use was as a means of more accurately calculating navigational tables, which Britain relied on heavily as the world's preeminent naval and commercial power. The second, the "Analytical Engine," was a programmable automatic calculator. It was far more versatile and sophisticated than the Difference Engine, and it stands as the first real equivalent of the modern computer—though Babbage was never able to build one, and of course its principles were later realized electronically rather than mechanically. In conceiving of a thinking engine, Babbage grasped, perhaps before anyone else, one of the real advantages of technology to humankind. Beyond eliminating vast amounts of drudgery work, machines, he understood, could process complex calculations and large stores of information with much greater speed and far greater reliability. Babbage founded the modern discipline of computer science and is one of the most prophetic voices of the Regency. What is more, later in his career, he worked closely with Byron's only legitimate child, Ada, Countess of Lovelace, who was described by her father in *Childe Harold's Pilgrimage* as the "sole daughter of my house and heart," and who produced detailed notes on the Analytical Engine that contained ideas for what we would now call a computer program.[78]

The Regency itself, meanwhile, experienced its own information revolution. In 1812, Friedrich Koenig, a German inventor, successfully demonstrated his recently patented steam press. John Walter, owner and editor of the *Times*, was quickly sold on the new technology, and by 1814 he was using it to print his newspaper in far greater numbers and at a much lower cost. The result was a rapid and unequaled diversification and expansion in all areas of print culture. For the first time writing was produced and consumed on a mass scale, a fact that separated it from all writing that had gone before. By the end of the Regency, the new stream-press technology had driven the oral traditions of the past into a final, steep decline, and print had triumphed as the main mode of human communication. "Print has become part of our existence," Cyrus Redding confirmed in the *New Monthly Magazine* in 1821. "Like to the air we breathe, it is the medium through which we receive sound and light, every idea, and every feeling,—beyond whose influence we cannot get, and could not live."[79] In ways similar to the Internet in our own age, new technology in the Regency fundamentally altered the way people accessed information, as well as the way they interacted with one another and understood the world around them.

XIII

The doctrine of "vitalism" was at the crux of the Regency's most heated scientific debate and involved two of its most celebrated medical men, John Abernethy and William Lawrence. Abernethy spent his entire career at St. Bartholomew's Hospital in London, where as a student he came under the influence of the renowned anatomist John Hunter. In addition to a large private practice that attracted a well-heeled clientele, Abernethy was a popular lecturer, with a delivery style that was both extravagant and gruff and packed classrooms and public halls alike. In 1814, he became a professor of anatomy at the Royal College of Surgeons and delivered a lecture—inspired by the manuscript ruminations of his old teacher John Hunter—called "An Enquiry into the Probability and Rationality of Mr. Hunter's Theory of Life."

Abernethy's goal was to use Hunter's notion of a quasi-mystical "Life Force" to reconcile orthodox religious doctrine with new discoveries in science and medicine. His central claim was that there was a "subtile, mobile, invisible substance," beyond mere physical organization, that was best conceived as a kind of universal "vitality" and that was "superadded to the evident structure of muscles, or other forms of vegetable and animal matter, as magnetism is to iron, and as electricity is to various substances with which it may be connected." Abernethy, moreover, went on to declare that the work of Sir Humphry Davy endorsed this view of an analogy between "vitality" and "electricity," and indeed suggested the possibility that "life" and "electricity" were one and the same. Davy's experiments, Abernethy contended, formed "an important link in the connexion of our knowledge of dead and living matter," for they "lead us to believe, that it is electricity, extricated and accumulated in ways not clearly understood, which causes those sudden and powerful motions in masses of inert matter, which we occasionally witness with wonder and dismay."⁸⁰ From a religious standpoint, the burden of such arguments was plain. Scientific evidence pointed to the existence of a vital spark that animated human life. Theologians had known for centuries of just such a spark. They called it the immortal soul. Regency strongholds of piety and legitimacy breathed an immense sigh of relief. Religion and science, it turned out, were one.

William Lawrence categorically rejected all of this. He began his medical career as an apprentice under Abernethy at St. Bartholomew's and rose quickly through the ranks, distinguishing himself as a skillful dissector, a popular teacher, and a well-published author. A far more elegant, erudite, and cosmopolitan figure than Abernethy, he became an assistant surgeon at St. Bartholomew's in 1813 and, two years later, like Abernethy, a professor of anatomy at the Royal College of Surgeons. Lawrence's patients included Percy Shelley, who shared Lawrence's radical views on politics and religion, and who in 1815 declared that his health was "considerably improved under Lawrence's care." Rees Howell Gronow also had the "good fortune" to know Lawrence and reported that he was "allowed to have been the most scientific, as well as one of the most skilful surgeons England or Europe could boast of."⁸¹

Lawrence's skepticism, sophistication, and scholarly rigor put him on a collision course with Abernethy's mysterious life force, and in his own Royal College lectures Lawrence launched increasingly vitriolic attacks on his former tutor, who replied in kind. Life, Lawrence argued, depended entirely on complex physical organization and functionality, not, as Abernethy would have it, on some vital principle divinely bestowed by "imaginary beings." Playing Hamlet to Abernethy's Polonius, Lawrence scoffed at the vague claims and weak ideas of his adversary. "To make the matter more intelligible, this vital principle is compared to magnetism, to electricity, and to galvanism; or it is roundly stated to be oxygen. 'Tis like a camel, or like a whale, or like what you please." Science, insisted Lawrence, must be objective, fearless, and wholly independent, and he poured scorn on the way Abernethy had turned it to the service of Church and State.

THIS MINIATURE of Mary Shelley was painted posthumously by Reginald Easton but probably bears some resemblance to her shortly after she published *Frankenstein* in 1818. Easton's sources were her death mask and Edward Ellerker Williams's pencil sketch from 1821–22.

"The theological doctrine of the soul, and its separate existence, has nothing to do with this physiological question," he stated flatly. "An immaterial and spiritual being could not have been discovered amid the blood and filth of the dissecting-room."[82]

Mary Shelley's *Frankenstein* is the most powerful response to the dispute between Abernethy and Lawrence. Published in 1818 when she was just twenty years old, it is unquestionably the most famous book of the Regency, and it asks a number of questions clearly indebted to the vitalism controversy, including, most provocatively, does Victor Frankenstein's Creature have a soul? Shelley suggests a parallel to Abernethy in her representation of Victor as a misguided scientist whose work has been shaped by outmoded ideas. Equally, she draws on Lawrence, not just for his experiences amid the gore of dissecting rooms but also for his presentation of science as a radical alternative to—and wholly distinct from—Christian theology. Before the aptly named Victor conducted his experiments, God was thought indispensable to the creation of human life. After Victor, the modern world recognized a powerful new God: science.

Humphry Davy plays a prominent role in *Frankenstein*. Shelley probably met him on a number of occasions, for he was a good friend of her father, the philosopher and novelist William Godwin, to whom she dedicated *Frankenstein*. In the autumn of 1816, as she worked on the novel, she read Davy's *Elements of Chemical Philosophy*, and from him she derived her portrait of the amiable Professor Waldman, who teaches Victor chemistry at the University of Inglostadt and who gives him advice that decides his "future destiny." "Chemistry is that branch of natural philosophy in which the greatest improvements have been and may be made," Waldman tells Victor. Yet at the same time he encourages Victor to apply himself to "every branch of natural philosophy, including mathematics."[83] Thereafter, as Victor pursues his scientific studies, his ambition, eloquence, imagination, and energy repeatedly call Davy to mind.

Percy Shelley was at Mary's side from the earliest stages of the novel, and on many occasions he shared with her his passionate interest in contemporary science. As an eighteen-year-old student at Oxford, he filled his rooms with the latest gadgets and technologies. "The tables, and especially the carpet, were already stained with large spots of various hues, which frequently proclaimed the agency of fire," reported Thomas Jefferson Hogg, Shelley's closest undergraduate friend. "An electrical machine, an air-pump, the galvanic trough, a solar microscope, and large glass jars and receivers, were conspicuous amidst the mass of matter." As early as 1812, the year he met Mary,

Percy Shelley was writing on the nature of "Life," which he described as the greatest of all miracles. Two years later, he and Mary attended a London lecture by Professor Garnerin "on Electricity—the gasses—& the Phantasmagoria." Percy and Mary traveled to Geneva in the summer of 1816, where they joined Byron and his personal physician, John Polidori, at the Villa Diodati, and where Byron initiated the famous ghost-story competition that produced *Frankenstein*. On June 15, Percy Shelley and John Polidori "had a conversation about principles,—whether man was to be thought merely an instrument." It was almost certainly this discussion that provided the "circumstance" on which *Frankenstein* "rests," as Shelley put it in the "Preface" that he wrote for Mary's novel.[84]

Yet Mary Shelley was also deeply ambivalent about contemporary science. Like her husband, she recognized the immense benefits that it could deliver, and in *Frankenstein* Victor too shares their optimism as he labors to create life. "When I considered the improvement which every day takes place in science and mechanics," he states, "I was encouraged to hope my present attempts would at least lay the foundations of future success." More clearly than any of her contemporaries, however, Mary Shelley also understood that scientific exploration—that "Men Playing God"—was fraught with dangers. Victor locks himself away in his laboratory for nearly two years in order to bring his creature to life, and he selects "features" for him that are "beautiful." But Victor has been so absorbed in his task, and in thoughts of fame, that he has not been able to see what is literally right in front of him, and when he finally creates life, his immediate response is, not elation, but horror. "Beautiful!—Great God! His yellow skin scarcely covered the work of muscles and arteries beneath; his hair was of a lustrous black, and flowing; his teeth of a pearly whiteness; but these luxuriances only formed a more horrid contrast with his watery eyes, that seemed almost of the same colour as the dun white sockets in which they were set, his shrivelled complexion, and straight black lips."[85] Victor flees in terror and the Creature is left to fend for himself. As it turns out, he is the most humane and intelligent figure in the novel, but his anger at the way he has been treated, coupled with Victor's irresponsibility and egotism, eventually turns them both into monsters.

More than any other work in English literature, *Frankenstein* is a prophecy about the modern world. In addition to launching the entirely new genre of science fiction, it has had an incalculable impact on the way we imagine science. Deeply indebted to Regency speculations on electricity, anatomy, and the vital life force, the novel both anticipates and illuminates a host of moral issues in modern medicine and science, from animal cloning, stem-cell research, and genetic engineering, through organ transplants, artificial intelligence, and heterografting (the use of animal organs in human bodies), to biometrics, gene therapy, and cybernetic technologies. *Frankenstein* unnervingly reveals that scientific research has the potential to improve our lives in countless ways, but that if we deny or ignore our responsibilities, new discoveries have also the potential to pass dangerously far beyond the control of their makers and assume hideous and unpredictable forms that may betray or even destroy us. As Victor's creature resembles him, so we resemble Victor in our faith in science, our exploitation of the earth, and our failure to take care of one another. "My form," says the creature to the creator, "is a filthy type of yours."[86]

The Modern World

The Regency blazed intensely for almost a decade, but it took little time for it to seem part of a distant past. Several of its key players were soon gone. Arthur Thistlewood, who had done his best to foment insurrection during the Spa Fields riots of 1816, was convicted of high treason for his role in a plot to assassinate members of Lord Liverpool's cabinet, and he and four of his coconspirators were hanged on May 1, 1820. John Keats died in Rome in February 1821, Napoleon two and a half months later on St. Helena, and Queen Caroline, the estranged wife of George IV, in August of that same year, only a few weeks after public opinion had finally swung decisively against her, and she had failed in her bid to attend her husband's lavish coronation. Percy Shelley drowned in July 1822, and Lord Castlereagh committed suicide the following month. "Where is the world of *eight* years past?" demanded a querulous Byron in 1823. "I look for it—'tis gone, a Globe of Glass!" Changes were commonplace, he realized, but in recent years they had come with "unusual quickness." "Statesmen, chiefs, orators, queens, patriots, kings, / And dandies, all are gone on the wind's wings."[1] Less than eight months later, in April 1824, Byron himself was dead.

The reign of George IV lasted for just over ten years. He died on June 26, 1830, at the age of sixty-seven. The *Times* immediately denounced him for his "most reckless, unceasing, and unbounded prodigality," and three weeks later it laid into him again. "There never was an individual less regretted by his fellow-creatures than this deceased King," it declared. "What eye has wept for him? What heart has heaved one throb of unmercenary sorrow . . . for that Leviathan of the *haut ton*"? This view prevailed through the nineteenth century in the minds of the vast majority of Victorians, who regarded the Regency as a time of vulgarity, impiety, aggressive indifference, and vacuous extravagance, and all presided over by a man who was among the worst offenders. For William Makepeace Thackeray, most memorably, the Regent was ugly in his emptiness. "There is his coat, his star, his wig, his countenance simpering under it: with a slate and a piece of chalk, I could at this very desk perform a recognizable likeness of him. And yet after reading of him in scores of volumes, hunting him through old magazines and newspapers, having him here at a ball, there at a public dinner, there at races and so forth, you find you have nothing—nothing but a coat and wig and a mask smiling below it—nothing but a great simulacrum."[2]

Robert Peel was more generous, avoiding comment on the character of George IV but pointing out that he was "universally admitted to be the greatest patron the arts had ever had in this country." The Duke of Wellington, who received crucial support from the Regent during the fight against Napoleon, was equally generous, and he looked directly at George's character. "He was indeed the most extraordinary compound of talent, wit, buffoonery, obstinacy, and good feeling—in short, a medley of the most opposite qualities, with a great preponderance of good—that I ever saw in any character in my life." Princess Lieven, one of the powerful hostesses at Almack's, agreed. To be sure, George "was full of vanity," but "he quickly summed up persons and things. . . . He adorned the subjects he touched, he knew how to listen; he was very polished." As late as 1856, the scapegrace second Duke of Buckingham declared that "upon looking back throughout the period of the Regency, it is scarcely possible to exaggerate its importance as a portion of the modern history of the country."[3]

The more balanced view of George—among royal apologists in particular—has prevailed for much of the last century, and it is clear that as Regent he achieved much more than he did as either the Prince of Wales or as George IV.[4] His unpalatable personal habits and indefensible excesses in liquor and lust filled many with indignation, from prudish killjoys and dreary respectability-mongers all the way up to those earnestly campaigning for much higher degrees of civility in both public and domestic life, and especially in relations between women and men. But the Regent's delight in dissipation also fueled the free-spirited, healthy hedonism of Pierce Egan's *Life in London* and, more significantly, Byron's libertine epic *Don Juan*, the funniest long poem in the English language and one in which Byron exploits the promiscuities of the Regency to submit sexual double standards, identities, and experiences to the most searching interrogation they had ever received.

The Regent's spending on art collections and elegant buildings, meanwhile, infuriated Whigs, reformers, and radicals, and he became to them a potent symbol, not just of a monarchy but of an entire political system that was cruelly out of touch. The result was that opposition leaders seized on his image and his activities as a way of galvanizing support for reform, and of pushing harder than ever to ensure that Britain replaced the powers of kingship and queenship with the rights of democracy. These Regency men and women were political martyrs who spoke truth to power at a time when it too often meant loss of liberty or even of life, and their courage helped to set in place some of the fundamental principles of modern liberal states.[5] Leigh Hunt went to prison for two years for denouncing government-sponsored adulation of the Regent, but he continued to assail sycophancy and corruption from his jail cell and to defend the freedom of the press. William Cobbett and Henry Hunt pioneered civil disobedience as a strategy that sought to raise political consciousness and that brought the peaceful demands of the many right to the door of the privileged few. In *The Political House that Jack Built*, William

Hone and George Cruikshank launched a scathing attack on the government and the Regent from behind the protective barrier of satire, enabling them to expose the misjudgments and entitlements that led to the atrocities of the Peterloo Massacre. Percy Shelley wrote some of the greatest poetry of the Regency in denunciation of its political tyrannies and injustices, before leaving England for exile in Italy, from where he continued to attack the Regent and his ministers and to craft his prophecies of human freedom.

Despite his undisputed failures, the Regent fostered a climate of intellectualism, patronage, and connoisseurship. More than any other member of the royal family either before or since, he believed that novelists, poets, singers, historians, actors, painters, musicians, scientists, architects, and engineers *mattered*, and during his Regency his well-known enthusiasm for the arts and the sciences helped to energize the most extraordinary outpouring of creativity in British history. Some of it he sponsored directly. Some of it came about as a result of the huge social upheavals of the Napoleonic wars, which encouraged many of the finest minds of the age to perceive and represent the world in highly original ways. New technologies opened up vast international readerships and markets. The intense sociability of the Regency brought writers and thinkers and artists into dialogue with one another as never before, sometimes in mutually supportive coteries, sometimes in productive rivalries, and sometimes in fiercely antagonistic cultural debates.

During the Regency, John Nash planned and oversaw the construction of Regent's Park and Regent Street. With the invention of the miner's safety lamp, Sir Humphry Davy and Michael Faraday demonstrated the powers of science to improve the human condition. Charles Babbage was the first to imagine what would eventually become the modern computer. David Brewster invented the kaleidoscope, the instant and immense popularity of which revealed the burgeoning powers of consumerism, while Luddites protested business practices that brought soaring profits to owners and low-wage, dead-end misery to workers. John Clare was among the first environmental activists and wrote compellingly of the intricate interrelationship between the human and the nonhuman worlds.

Further, Pierce Egan established modern sports journalism. Robert Owen disseminated socialist thought. Percy Shelley championed secularism. Elizabeth Fry demanded the more humane treatment of prisoners. Samuel Taylor Coleridge and Thomas De Quincey were the first to detail the transient intellectual pleasure and vicious cycles of bodily pain brought on by opiate addiction. Anne Lister described her joyous experiences of same-sex love, while William Beckford and Jeremy Bentham wrote on the barbarity of punishing people for their sexual preferences. Beau Brummell made fashion statements that still influence the way men dress. Edmund Kean and Lord Byron were the first modern celebrities. Thomas Lawrence and Henry Raeburn painted the glamorous portraits that have made the Regency a byword for beauty and poise. John Constable produced timeless versions of rural England. J. M. W. Turner revolutionized British landscape art. Jane Austen wrote *Pride and Prejudice*, the most popular love story of the last two centuries, while Mary Shelley produced *Frankenstein* and John Polidori created *The Vampyre*, the two most potent horror myths of the modern age. Almost two centuries ago, the glittering world of the Regency seemed to Byron to disappear with astonishing quickness. Now it is more evident than ever that its many legacies are still all around us.

Beggars leaving Town for their Work-houses.

JOHN THOMAS SMITH engraved this image of three beggars leaving London for their workhouses.

NOTES

Abbreviations

PRIMARY SOURCES

Austen, *E*	Jane Austen, *Emma*, ed. Richard Cronin and Dorothy McMillan (Cambridge: Cambridge University Press, 2005)
Austen, *L*	*Jane Austen's Letters*, ed. Deirdre Le Faye, 4th ed. (Oxford: Oxford University Press, 2011)
Austen, *LM*	Jane Austen, *Later Manuscripts*, ed. Janet Todd and Linda Bree (Cambridge: Cambridge University Press, 2008)
Austen, *MP*	Jane Austen, *Mansfield Park*, ed. John Wiltshire (Cambridge: Cambridge University Press, 2005)
Austen, *P*	Jane Austen, *Persuasion*, ed. Janet Todd and Antje Blank (Cambridge: Cambridge University Press, 2006)
Austen, *PP*	Jane Austen, *Pride and Prejudice*, ed. Pat Rogers (Cambridge: Cambridge University Press, 2006)
Austen, *SS*	Jane Austen, *Sense and Sensibility*, ed. Edward Copeland (Cambridge: Cambridge University Press, 2006)
Ayton and Daniell	Richard Ayton and William Daniell, *A Voyage Round Great Britain*, 8 vols. (London: Longman, 1814–25)
Badcock	John Badcock, *Letters from London: Observations of a*

	Russian during a Residence in England (London: Badcock, 1816)
Ballard	Joseph Ballard, *England in 1815*, ed. Alan Rauch (New York: Palgrave, 2009)
Bamford	Samuel Bamford, *Passages in the Life of a Radical*, 2 vols. (London: Simpkin, Marshall, 1844)
Beckford	*Life at Fonthill, 1807–1822 . . . from the Correspondence of William Beckford*, ed. Boyd Alexander (London: Hart-Davis, 1957)
Bentham	Jeremy Bentham, *The Theory of Legislation*, ed. C. K. Ogden (London: Kegan Paul, Trench, Trubner, and Co., 1931)
Brunton	Mary Brunton, *Self-Control*, ed. Anthony Mandal (London: Pickering and Chatto, 2014)
Burney	*The Journals and Letters of Fanny Burney*, ed. Joyce Hemlow, Althea Douglas, Warren Derry, et al., 12 vols. (Oxford: Clarendon Press, 1972–84)
Byron, *CH*	*Byron: The Critical Heritage*, ed. Andrew Rutherford (London: Routledge and Kegan Paul, 1970)
Byron, *CMP*	Lord Byron, *The Complete Miscellaneous Prose*, ed. Andrew Nicholson (Oxford: Clarendon Press, 1991)
Byron, *HVSV*	*His Very Self and Voice: Collected Conversations of Lord Byron*, ed. Ernest Lovell (New York: Macmillan, 1954)
Byron, *LJ*	*Byron's Letters and Journals*, ed. Leslie A. Marchand, 13 vols. (Cambridge, MA: Belknap Press of Harvard University Press, 1973–94)
Byron, *PW*	Lord Byron, *The Complete Poetical Works*, ed. Jerome J. McGann, 7 vols. (Oxford: Clarendon Press, 1980–93)
Carlyle	*The Collected Letters of Thomas and Jane Welsh Carlyle, Volume One*, ed. C. R. Sanders, Kenneth Fielding, et al. (Durham, NC: Duke University Press, 1970)
Clarke	Charles Cowden Clarke and Mary Cowden Clarke, *Recollections of Writers* (London: Sampson Low, Marston, Searle, and Rivington, 1878)
Cobbett	William Cobbett, *History of the Regency and Reign of*

King George the Fourth, 2 vols. (London: Cobbett, 1830–34)

Cockburn | Henry Cockburn, *Memorials of His Time*, ed. Karl Miller (Chicago: University of Chicago Press, 1974)

Coleridge, *L* | *Collected Letters of Samuel Taylor Coleridge*, ed. Earl Leslie Griggs, 6 vols. (Oxford: Clarendon Press, 1956–71)

Coleridge, *PW* | Samuel Taylor Coleridge, *Poetical Works*, ed. J. C. C. Mays, 6 vols. (Princeton: Princeton University Press, 2001)

Constable | *John Constable's Correspondence*, ed. R. B. Beckett, 6 vols. (Ipswich: Suffolk Records Society, 1962–68)

Creevey | *The Creevey Papers*, ed. Herbert Maxwell, 2 vols. (London: Murray, 1904)

De Quincey | Thomas De Quincey, *Confessions of an English Opium-Eater and Other Writings*, ed. Robert Morrison (Oxford: Oxford University Press, 2013)

Edgeworth, *L* | *Maria Edgeworth: Letters from England*, ed. Christina Colvin (Oxford: Clarendon Press, 1971)

Edgeworth, *NSW* | *The Novels and Selected Works of Maria Edgeworth*, ed. Marilyn Butler, Mitzi Meyers, Heidi Van de Veire, Kim Walker, et al., 12 vols. (London: Pickering and Chatto, 1999–2003)

Egan, *B* | Pierce Egan, *Boxiana; or, Sketches of Ancient and Modern Pugilism*, 2 vols. (London: Sherwood, Jones, 1823–24)

Egan, *LL* | Pierce Egan, *Life in London* (New York: Appleton, 1904)

Egan, *SA* | Pierce Egan, *Sporting Anecdotes* (London: Sherwood, Neely, and Jones, 1820)

Elmes | James Elmes, *Metropolitan Improvements; or London, in the Nineteenth Century* (London: Jones, 1829)

Farington | *The Diary of Joseph Farington*, ed. Kenneth Garlick, Angus Macintyre, Kathryn Cave, and Evelyn Newby, 17 vols. (New Haven: Yale University Press, 1978–98)

Ferrier | Susan Ferrier, *Marriage*, ed. Herbert Foltinek (London: Oxford University Press, 1971)

Galt   John Galt, *Life of Lord Byron* (London: Col-
                    burn, 1830)

Granville   *Letters of Harriet, Countess Granville*, ed. F. Leveson
                    Gower, 2 vols. (London: Longmans, Green, 1894)

Greville   *The Greville Memoirs*, ed. Lytton Strachey and
                    Roger Fulford, 8 vols. (London: Macmillan, 1938)

Gronow   *Captain Gronow's Recollections and Anecdotes*, 2 vols.
                    (London: Smith, Elder, 1864–66)

Hale   William Hale, *Considerations on the Causes and
                    the Prevalence of Female Prostitution* (London:
                    Justins, 1812)

Haydon   *The Diary of Benjamin Robert Haydon*, ed. Willard
                    Bissell Pope, 5 vols. (Cambridge, MA: Harvard
                    University Press, 1960–63)

Hazlitt   *The Complete Works of William Hazlitt*, ed. P. P.
                    Howe, 21 vols. (London: Dent, 1930–34)

Hone   *The Three Trials of William Hone . . . to which is added
                    the Trial by Jury* (London: Hone, 1818)

Hunt, *A*   *The Autobiography of Leigh Hunt*, 3 vols. (London:
                    Smith, Elder, 1850)

Hunt, *DC*   *Leigh Hunt's Dramatic Criticism*, ed. L. H. Houtch-
                    ens and C. W. Houtchens (New York: Columbia
                    University Press, 1949)

Hunt, *DE*   Leigh Hunt, *Dramatic Essays*, ed. William Archer
                    and Robert Lowe (London: Walter Scott, 1894)

Hunt, *PE*   *Leigh Hunt: Periodical Essays*, ed. Jeffrey N. Cox
                    and Greg Kucich, 2 vols. (London: Pickering and
                    Chatto, 2003)

Ireland   William Henry Ireland, *Chalcographimania* (Lon-
                    don: Kirby, 1814)

Jesse   William Jesse, *The Life of George Brummell, esq.,
                    commonly called Beau Brummell*, 2 vols. (London:
                    Saunders and Otley, 1844)

Keats, *L*   *The Letters of John Keats*, ed. Hyder E. Rollins,
                    2 vols. (Cambridge, MA: Harvard University
                    Press, 1958)

Keats, *P*   *The Poems of John Keats*, ed. Jack Stillinger (Lon-
                    don: Heinemann, 1978)

Kitchener	Henry Thomas Kitchener, *Letters on Marriage*, 2 vols. (London: Chapple, 1812)
Caroline Lamb	*The Whole Disgraceful Truth: Selected Letters of Lady Caroline Lamb*, ed. Paul Douglass (Basingstoke: Palgrave, 2006)
Lamb, *L*	*The Letters of Charles Lamb, to which are added those of his sister Mary Lamb*, ed. E. V. Lucas, 3 vols. (London: Dent, 1935)
Lamb, *W*	*The Works of Charles and Mary Lamb*, ed. E. V. Lucas, 7 vols. (London: Methuen, 1903–5)
Lister	*I Know My Own Heart: The Diaries of Anne Lister, 1791–1840*, ed. Helena Whitbread (New York: New York University Press, 1988)
Lockhart, *PL*	J. G. Lockhart, *Peter's Letters to his Kinsfolk*, 3 vols. (Edinburgh: Blackwood, 1819)
Lockhart, *S*	J. G. Lockhart, *The Life of Sir Walter Scott*, 10 vols. (Edinburgh: Constable, 1902–3)
Luttrell	Henry Luttrell, *Advice to Julia*, new ed. (London: Murray, 1820)
Mitford	Mary Russell Mitford, *Our Village: Sketches of Rural Character and Scenery*, 5 vols. (London: Whittaker, 1824–32)
Moore, *J*	*The Journal of Thomas Moore*, ed. Wilfred S. Dowden, 5 vols. (Newark: University of Delaware Press, 1983–88)
Moore, *L*	*The Letters of Thomas Moore*, ed. Wilfred S. Dowden, 2 vols. (Oxford: Clarendon Press, 1964)
Moore, *LR*	Thomas Moore, *Lalla Rookh, An Oriental Romance*, 5th ed. (London: Longman, Hurst, Rees, Orme, and Brown, 1817)
Moore, *S*	*The Satires of Thomas Moore*, ed. Jane Moore (London: Pickering and Chatto, 2003)
Naples	Joseph Naples, *The Diary of a Resurrectionist, 1811–1812*, ed. James Blake Bailey (London: Swan Sonnenschein, 1896)
Owen	Robert Owen, *Observations on the Effect of the Manufacturing System*, 3rd ed. (London: Longman, Hurst, Rees, Orme, and Brown, 1818)

Police   *Report from the Committee on the State of the Police of*
                          the Metropolis (London: House of Commons, 1817)

Polidori   *The Diary of Dr. John William Polidori*, ed. William
                          Michael Rossetti (London: Elkin Mathews, 1911)

Raikes   *A Portion of the Journal kept by Thomas Raikes*, 4 vols.
                          (London: Longman, Brown, Green, Longmans,
                          and Roberts, 1856–57)

Robinson   *Diary, Reminiscences, and Correspondence of Henry*
                          Crabb Robinson, ed. Thomas Sadler, 3 vols. (Lon-
                          don: Macmillan, 1869)

Russell   Lord John Russell, *Essays, and Sketches of Life and*
                          Character (London: Longman, Hurst, Rees, Orme,
                          and Brown, 1820)

Scott, *CH*   *Scott: The Critical Heritage*, ed. John Hayden (Lon-
                          don: Routledge and Kegan Paul, 1970)

Scott, *HM*   Walter Scott, *The Heart of Mid-Lothian*, ed. David
                          Hewitt and Alison Lumsden (Edinburgh: Edin-
                          burgh University Press, 2004)

Scott, *J*   *The Journal of Sir Walter Scott*, ed. W. E. K. Ander-
                          son (Oxford: Clarendon Press, 1972)

Mary Shelley, *F*   Mary Shelley, *Frankenstein; or, the Modern Pro-*
                          metheus, ed. Nora Crook (London: Pickering and
                          Chatto, 1996)

Mary Shelley, *J*   *The Journals of Mary Shelley*, ed. Paula R. Feldman
                          and Diana Scott-Kilvert, 2 vols. (Oxford: Claren-
                          don, 1987)

Percy Shelley, *L*   *The Letters of Percy Bysshe Shelley*, ed. Frederick L.
                          Jones, 2 vols. (Oxford: Clarendon Press, 1964)

Percy Shelley, *P*   *Shelley's Prose*, ed. David Lee Clark (Albuquerque:
                          University of New Mexico Press, 1966)

Percy Shelley, *PS*   *The Poems of Shelley*, ed. Geoffrey Matthews, Kel-
                          vin Everest, et al., 4 vols. (London: Longman,
                          1989–continuing)

Simond   Louis Simond, *Journal of a Tour and Residence in*
                          Great Britain, During the Years 1810 and 1811, 2nd
                          ed., 2 vols. (Edinburgh: Constable, 1817)

Southey, *E*   Robert Southey, *Letters from England*, 3rd ed., 3
                          vols. (London: Longman, Hurst, Rees, Orme, and
                          Brown, 1814)

Southey, *S*   Robert Southey, *Journal of a Tour in Scotland in 1819*, ed. C. H. Herford (London: Murray, 1929)

Vaux   *The Memoirs of James Hardy Vaux, including his Vocabulary of the Flash Language*, ed. Noel McLachlan (London: Heinemann, 1964)

Wilson   *Memoirs of Harriette Wilson*, ed. Julie Peakman (London: Pickering and Chatto, 2007)

Wordsworth, *E*   William Wordsworth, *The Excursion*, ed. Sally Bushell, James A. Butler, and Michael C. Jaye (Ithaca: Cornell University Press, 2007)

Wordsworth, *L*   *The Letters of William and Dorothy Wordsworth: The Middle Years, Part II, 1812–1820*, ed. Mary Moorman and Alan G. Hill (Oxford: Clarendon Press, 1970)

SECONDARY SOURCES

Ashbee   H. S. Ashbee, *Bibliography of Prohibited Books*, 3 vols. (London: Jack Brussel, 1962)

Ashton, *G*   John Ashton, *The History of Gambling in England* (London: Duckworth, 1898)

Ashton, *R*   John Ashton, *Social England under the Regency*, 2 vols. (London: Ward and Downey, 1890)

Bate   Jonathan Bate, *John Clare: A Biography* (New York: Farrar, Straus, and Giroux, 2003)

Bew   John Bew, *Castlereagh: A Life* (Oxford: Oxford University Press, 2012)

Borneman   Walter Borneman, *1812: The War that Forged a Nation* (New York: HarperCollins, 2004)

Bourne   Kenneth Bourne, *Palmerston: The Early Years, 1784–1841* (London: Allen Lane, 1982)

Chandler   James Chandler, *England in 1819* (Chicago: University of Chicago Press, 1998)

Crompton   Louis Crompton, *Byron and Greek Love: Homophobia in Nineteenth-Century England* (Berkeley: University of California Press, 1985)

Cronin   Richard Cronin, *Paper Pellets: British Literary Cul-*

	ture after Waterloo (Oxford: Oxford University Press, 2010)
Dabhoiwala	Faramerz Dabhoiwala, *The Origins of Sex: A History of the First Sexual Revolution* (Oxford: Oxford University Press, 2012)
Darvall	Frank Ongley Darvall, *Popular Disturbance and Public Order in Regency England* (London: Oxford University Press, 1934)
Davenport-Hines	Richard Davenport-Hines, *Sex, Death, and Punishment: Attitudes to Sex and Sexuality in Britain since the Renaissance* (London: Collins, 1990)
Faderman	Lillian Faderman, *Surpassing the Love of Men: Romantic Friendship and Love between Women from the Renaissance to the Present* (New York: Morrow, 1981)
Gash	Norman Gash, *Mr. Secretary Peel: The Life of Sir Robert Peel to 1830* (London: Longmans, 1961)
Gatrell	Vic Gatrell, *City of Laughter: Sex and Satire in Eighteenth-Century London* (New York: Walker, 2006)
Glendinning	Victoria Glendinning, *Raffles and the Golden Opportunity* (London: Profile, 2012)
Harvey	A. D. Harvey, *Sex in Georgian England* (New York: St. Martin's Press, 1994)
Hibbert	Christopher Hibbert, *George IV*, 2 vols. (New York: Harper and Row, 1972–73)
Hitsman	J. Mackay Hitsman, *The Incredible War of 1812: A Military History* (Toronto: University of Toronto Press, 1965)
Holmes	Richard Holmes, *Wellington: The Iron Duke* (London: HarperCollins, 2002)
James	Lawrence James, *The Iron Duke: A Military Biography of Wellington* (London: Weidenfeld and Nicolson, 1992)
Johnson	David Johnson, *Regency Revolution: The Case of Arthur Thistlewood* (Compton Chamberlayne: Compton Russell, 1974)
Kahan	Jeffrey Kahan, *The Cult of Kean* (Aldershot: Ashgate, 2006)

Kelly   Ian Kelly, *Beau Brummell: The Ultimate Dandy* (London: Hodder and Stoughton, 2005)

Klingaman   William Klingaman and Nicholas Klingaman, *The Year Without Summer: 1816 and the Volcano that Darkened the World and Changed History* (New York: St. Martin's Press, 2013)

Laxer   James Laxer, *Tecumseh and Brock: The War of 1812* (Toronto: Anansi, 2012)

Linklater   Andro Linklater, *Why Spencer Perceval Had to Die: The Assassination of a British Prime Minister* (New York: Walker, 2012)

Longford   Elizabeth Longford, *Wellington: The Years of the Sword* (London: Weidenfeld and Nicolson, 1969)

Low   Donald A. Low, *The Regency Underworld* (Stroud: Sutton, 1999)

MacCarthy   Fiona MacCarthy, *Byron: Life and Legend* (London: Murray, 2002)

Macdonald   D. L. Macdonald, *Monk Lewis: A Critical Biography* (Toronto: University of Toronto Press, 2000)

Mitchell   L. G. Mitchell, *Lord Melbourne, 1779–1848* (Oxford: Oxford University Press, 1997)

Norton   Rictor Norton, *Mother Clap's Molly House: The Gay Subculture in England, 1700–1830* (London: GMP, 1992)

Parissien   Steven Parissien, *George IV: Inspiration of the Regency* (New York: St. Martin's Press, 2002)

Patten   Robert L. Patten, *George Cruikshank's Life, Times, and Art*, 2 vols. (New Brunswick: Rutgers University Press, 1992–96)

Plowright   John Plowright, *Regency England: The Age of Lord Liverpool* (London: Routledge, 1996)

Powell   Neil Powell, *George Crabbe: An English Life* (London: Pimlico, 2004)

Prebble   John Prebble, *The Highland Clearances* (Harmondsworth: Penguin, 1976)

Rendell   Jane Rendell, *The Pursuit of Pleasure: Gender, Space, and Architecture in Regency London* (London: The Athlone Press, 2002)

St. Clair — William St. Clair, *The Reading Nation in the Romantic Period* (Cambridge: Cambridge University Press, 2004)

Shanes — Eric Shanes, *Young Mr. Turner: The First Forty Years* (New Haven: Yale University Press, 2016)

Smiles — Samuel Smiles, *The Life of George Stephenson* (New York: Harper, 1868)

Smith — E. A. Smith, *George IV* (New Haven: Yale University Press, 1999)

Stott — Andrew McConnell Stott, *The Pantomime Life of Joseph Grimaldi* (Edinburgh: Canongate, 2009)

Tannahill — Reay Tannahill, *Regency England: The Great Age of the Colour Print* (London: The Folio Society, 1964)

Thompson — E. P. Thompson, *The Making of the English Working Class* (London: Gollancz, 1980)

White — R. J. White, *Waterloo to Peterloo* (London: Heinemann, 1957)

Prologue: The Regent and the Regency

1. Creevey, 1. 158.
2. Ibid.
3. Austen, *E*, lxxx; Austen, *L*, 309; MacCarthy, 161; *The Collected Works of Sir Humphry Davy*, ed. John Davy, 9 vols. (London: Smith, Elder, 1839–40), 1. 218.
4. Saul David, *Prince of Pleasure: The Prince of Wales and the Making of the Regency* (London: Little, Brown, 1998), 15.
5. Hibbert, 1. 10.
6. Byron, *PW*, 5. 520; Joanna Richardson, *George IV: A Portrait* (London: Sidgwick and Jackson, 1966), 26.
7. Hibbert, 1. 144.
8. Austen, *L*, 216–17; Thea Holme, *Caroline: A Biography of Caroline of Brunswick* (New York: Atheneum, 1980), 33.
9. *The Works of Thomas De Quincey, Volume Eight*, ed. Robert Morrison (London: Pickering and Chatto, 2001), 448.

Chapter One: Crime, Punishment, and the Pursuit of Freedom

1. John Wilson, *The New Descriptive Catalogue and Plan of the European Museum* (London: Smeeton, 1813), 10; David Hanrahan, *The Assassina-*

tion of the Prime Minister: John Bellingham and the Murder of Spencer Per-ceval* (Stroud: Sutton, 2008), 1–4; Linklater, 1–10, 216–18.
2. Hanrahan, 80–83; Linklater, 121–23.
3. "Assassination of Mr. Perceval" in *Examiner*, 5 (May 17, 1812), 315–16; Linklater, 8; "Coroner's Inquest" in *Examiner*, 5 (May 17, 1812), 318; *The Autobiography of William Jerdan*, 4 vols. (London: Hall, Virtue, 1852–53), 1. 137; Linklater, 18.
4. Linklater, 42–43; Samuel Taylor Coleridge, *Biographia Literaria*, ed. James Engell and W. Jackson Bate, 2 vols. (Princeton: Princeton University Press, 1983), 1. 212.
5. Cobbett, 1. Paragraph 128; Coleridge, *L*, 3. 410; Mrs. Warrenne Blake, *An Irish Beauty of the Regency . . . The Unpublished Journals of the Hon. Mrs. Calvert* (London: Lane, 1911), 185; *The Letters of William and Dorothy Wordsworth: A Supplement of New Letters*, ed. Alan G. Hill (Oxford: Clarendon Press, 1993), 92; Moore, *L*, 1. 189.
6. Historical UK Inflation: http://inflation.iamkate.com/; Henry Crabb Robinson, *Blake, Coleridge, Wordsworth, Lamb, etc.*, ed. Edith J. Morley (Manchester: Manchester University Press, 1922), 53; "The Trial of Bellingham" in *Examiner*, 5 (May 17, 1812), 320; "Execution of Bellingham" in *Examiner*, 5 (May 24, 1812), 335; Byron, *LJ*, 2. 177.
7. Cobbett, 1. Paragraph 133; Percy Shelley, *PS*, 1. 526.
8. H. J. Blease, *A System of British Geography* (London: Darton, Harvey, and Darton, 1820), 35, 165, 11, 10, 119.
9. Low, 8–10; *Police*, 225–26.
10. Vaux, 240; Egan, *LL*, 68; Low, 120; *1811 Dictionary of the Vulgar Tongue* (London: Bibliophile, 1984) [n.p.].
11. W. B. Gurney, *The Trials at Large of Joseph Merceron* (London: Wright, 1819), 2, 156; Low, 36–38.
12. Southey, *E*, 2. 107; Low, 69–72.
13. Low, 73, 60; *Select Committee . . . to Inquire into the State of the Police of the Metropolis* (London: Sherwood, Neely, and Jones, 1816), 112, 275; *Police*, 438–39, 540.
14. Low, 79.
15. Suzie Lennox, *Bodysnatchers: Digging up the Untold Stories of Britain's Resurrection Men* (Barnsley: Pen and Sword, 2016), 28–29; *The A to Z of Regency London*, intro. Paul Laxton (London: London Topographical Society, 1985), 50–51; Low, 91–92; Naples, 71.
16. Naples, 136, 142, 157, 173.
17. Ibid., 149, 154, 176, 166, 152–54.
18. Austen, *SS*, 239–40; Abraham Bosquett, *The Young Man of Honour's Vade-Mecum* (London: Chapple, 1817), 12; Robert Baldick, *The Duel: A History of Duelling* (London: Chapman and Hall, 1965), 102–4.
19. Percy Shelley, *L*, 1. 355; James Bieri, *Percy Bysshe Shelley: A Biography* (Baltimore: Johns Hopkins University Press, 2008), 240; "Outrage at Drury-Lane Theatre" in the *Times* (February 19, 1816), 2; "Attempted Assassination of Miss Kelly" in the *Times* (February 21, 1816), 3; Bourne, 156; Hibbert, 2. 103; Gronow, 2. 4. 168–69.

20. Judith Flanders, *The Invention of Murder* (London: Harper, 2011), 7.
21. T. A. Critchley and P. D. James, *The Maul and the Pear Tree: The Ratcliffe Highway Murders 1811* (London: Constable, 1971), 188, 79, 181, 162; Thomas De Quincey, *On Murder*, ed. Robert Morrison (Oxford: Oxford University Press, 2006), 190–96.
22. Douglas Goldring, *Regency Portrait Painter: The Life of Sir Thomas Lawrence* (London: Macdonald, 1951), 240–41.
23. Low, 1–25; David Cox, *A Certain Share of Low Cunning: A History of the Bow Street Runners, 1792–1839* (Cullompton, Devon: Willan, 2010), 30.
24. Keats, *P*, 511; Gronow, 1. 286.
25. Percy Shelley, *P*, 155; John Polidori, "On the Punishment of Death" in *Pamphleteer*, 8 (1816), 283; Samuel Romilly, *Observations on the Criminal Law of England*, 2nd ed. (London: Cadell and Davies, 1811), 3.
26. Basil Montagu, *The Opinions of Different Authors upon the Punishment of Death*, 2nd ed. (London: Longman, Hurst, Rees, Orme, and Brown, 1816), 225.
27. Cobbett, 2. Paragraph 506; Nicola Phillips, *The Profligate Son: Or, a True Story of Family Conflict, Fashionable Vice, and Financial Ruin in Regency Britain* (New York: Basic Books, 2013), 213–29.
28. Low, 43; Vaux, 198.
29. Badcock, 148; *Report from the Committee on the State of the Gaols* (London, 1814), 9; Low, 52–53.
30. Hunt, *PE*, 1. 221.
31. Hunt, *A*, 2. 144–45; Anthony Holden, *The Wit in the Dungeon: A Life of Leigh Hunt* (London: Little, Brown, 2005), 75–76; Clarke, 17; Hunt, *A*, 2. 148.
32. Byron, *PW*, 3. 88; *The Correspondence of Leigh Hunt*, ed. Thornton Hunt, 2 vols. (London: Smith, Elder, 1862), 1. 89.
33. Nicholas Roe, *Fiery Heart: The First Life of Leigh Hunt* (London: Pimlico, 2005), 184; Leigh Hunt, *The Story of Rimini* (London: Murray, 1816), 43; Keats, *P*, 32; Hunt, *A*, 2. 159.
34. *Police*, 431.
35. Edgeworth, *L*, 117; Thomas Fowell Buxton, *An Inquiry, Whether Crime and Misery are Produced or Prevented, by our Present System of Prison Discipline* (London: Arch, 1818), 113, 114.
36. Buxton, *An Inquiry*, 127; *Elizabeth Fry: A Quaker Life*, ed. Gil Skidmore (Lanham: Rowman and Littlefield, 2005), 100; Anne Isba, *The Excellent Mrs. Fry: Unlikely Heroine* (London: Continuum, 2010), xiii.
37. Gash, 11, 223–35; Keats, *L*, 1. 321–22.
38. Gash, 11.
39. Francis Charles Montague, *Life of Sir Robert Peel* (London: Allen, 1888), 17–18; Gash, 162.
40. Kyle Hughes and Donald M. MacRaild, "Irish Politics and Labour: Transnational and Comparative Perspectives, 1798–1914" in *Transnational Perspectives on Modern Irish History*, ed. Niall Whelehan (New York: Routledge, 2015), 55–56; Gash, 175.

41. William Carleton, "Confessions of a Reformed Ribbonman" in *The Vampyre and Other Tales of the Macabre*, ed. Robert Morrison and Chris Baldick (Oxford: Oxford University Press, 1997), 33–51, 260–62.
42. Prebble, 49–115.
43. Southey, *S*, 137; Prebble, 50, 79, 99, 85.
44. Plowright, 22; Darvall, 73; Byron, *CMP*, 26, 22.
45. Darvall, 115–30; George Pellew, *The Life and Correspondence of . . . Henry Addington, first Viscount Sidmouth*, 3 vols. (London: Murray, 1847), 3. 93.
46. Darvall, 158–59; C. D. Yonge, *The Life and Administration of Robert Banks, second Earl of Liverpool*, 3 vols. (London: Macmillan, 1868), 2. 444.
47. Luttrell, 71; Norman Gash, *Aristocracy and People: Britain 1815–1865* (Cambridge, MA: Harvard University Press, 1979), 76; Gronow, 1. 220.
48. Leslie Mitchell, *The Whig World, 1760–1837* (London: Hambledon and London, 2005), 15–16; Cobbett, 1. Paragraph 190.
49. John Scott, "Town Conversation" in *London Magazine*, 3 (1821), 71.
50. Jeremy Bentham, *Church-of-Englandism* (London: Wilson, 1818), 193; *James Mill: Political Writings*, ed. Terence Ball (Cambridge: Cambridge University Press, 1992), 21, 27.
51. Stanley Jones, *Hazlitt: A Life* (Oxford: Clarendon Press, 1989), 179; Hazlitt, 7. 152.
52. Keats, *L*, 1. 252; Hazlitt, 7. 274; 12. 99; 7. 115; 9. 14, 13.
53. Hazlitt, 8. 50; St. Clair, 573–75; Richard Altick, *The English Common Reader* (Chicago: University of Chicago Press, 1957), 392; Bamford, 1. 7.
54. *The Letters of Mary Wollstonecraft Shelley*, ed. Betty T. Bennett, 3 vols. (Baltimore: Johns Hopkins University Press, 1980–1988), 1. 49.
55. William Cobbett, "The Collision" in *Weekly Political Register*, 81 (August 3, 1833), 261–62; Hazlitt, 8. 50.
56. Lamb, *W*, 5. 104, 335.
57. Moore, *S*, 87, 86.
58. Moore, *S*, 153; Ronan Kelly, *Bard of Erin: The Life of Thomas Moore* (Dublin: Penguin, 2008), 313.
59. "First Trial" in Hone, 7; "Second Trial" in Hone, 8; "Third Trial" in Hone, 9; Gatrell, 523.
60. "Third Trial" in Hone, 21; "First Trial" in Hone, 35; "Third Trial" in Hone, 22; "Second Trial" in Hone, 20.
61. "Trial by Jury" in Hone, 5–6; Robinson, 2. 80; Wordsworth, *L*, 410; Keats, *L*, 1. 191.
62. Patten, 1. 110–11, 52–53; Tannahill, 10.
63. Kenneth Baker, *George IV: A Life in Caricature* (London: Thames and Hudson, 2005), 83.
64. Baker, *George IV*, 151; Gatrell, 512–13, 184.
65. Bew, 434; George Croly, "Domestic Politics" in *Blackwood's Magazine*, 8 (1820), 334.
66. Plowright, 22; Johnson, 7–8.

67. Thompson, 696; Johnson, 41.
68. "Disturbances at Dundee" in the *Times* (December 11, 1816), 3; "Riots in Bideford" in the *Times* (May 23, 1816), 3; "By the Special Commission issued to try the Ely rioters" in the *Times* (June 4, 1816), 3; "Disturbances in Norfolk and Suffolk" in the *Times* (May 23, 1816), 3; "Riots in Suffolk" in the *Times* (May 21, 1816), 3; "Riots at Littleport and Ely" in the *Times* (May 30, 1816), 3; *Particulars of the Execution and Confession of the Five Unfortunate Men . . . Who were Executed at Ely* (Ely: Orange, 1816), 1.
69. "Disturbances in Wales" in the *Times* (October 24, 1816), 3; "Riots in the West of England and in Ireland" in the *Times* (March 4, 1817), 3; White, 155–56; Thompson, 709–13.
70. W. B. Gurney, *The Trials of Jeremiah Brandreth, William Turner, Isaac Ludlam, George Weightman, and others*, 2 vols. (London: Butterworth, 1817), 1. 41, 144.
71. White, 162–75; Thompson, 722–26; Hunt, *PE*, 2. 118–21; Hazlitt, 7. 208; "Convicts for High Treason" in the *Times* (November 8, 1817), 3.
72. James Chandler, "On Peterloo, 16 August 1819": http://www.branchcollective.org/?ps_articles=james-chandler-on-peterloo-16-august-1819.
73. Bamford, 1. 207.
74. Hibbert, 2. 130; Elizabeth Longford, *Wellington: Pillar of State* (London: Weidenfeld and Nicolson, 1972), 62; Anonymous, "The Warder. No. III" in *Blackwood's Magazine*, 6 (1819), 335; Walter Scott, *The Visionary* (Edinburgh: Blackwood, 1819), 35, 50; Byron, *LJ*, 7. 81.
75. Keats, *L*, 2. 194; Chandler, 19; Hunt, *PE*, 2. 205–6; Richard Carlile, "A Letter to his Royal Highness the Prince Regent" in *The Republican*, 1 (September 3, 1819), 17, 20.
76. *Regency Radical: Selected Writings of William Hone*, ed. David Kent and D. R. Ewen (Detroit: Wayne State University Press, 2003), 203, 202, 213.
77. Percy Shelley, *L*, 1. 213; 2. 99; Stephen Behrendt, *Royal Mourning and Regency Culture: Elegies and Memorials of Princess Charlotte* (New York: St. Martin's Press, 1997), 220–36; Percy Shelley, *P*, 52.
78. Percy Shelley, *P*, 260, 259, 240; Percy Shelley, *PS*, 2. 460, 475.
79. Percy Shelley, *PS*, 1. 265, 455, 544, 546.
80. Ibid., 3. 210, 212, 190, 49, 37.
81. Ibid., 2. 495.
82. Ibid., 2. 557, 564, 589.
83. Ibid., 2. 607, 609, 610, 648.

Chapter Two: Theaters of Entertainment

1. Carlyle, 215–16; Edgar Johnson, *Sir Walter Scott: The Great Unknown*, 2 vols. (London: Hamish Hamilton, 1970), 1. 692–93; *The Letters of Sydney*

Smith, ed. Nowell C. Smith, 2 vols. (Oxford: Clarendon Press, 1953), 1. 342; Wordsworth, *L*, 572; William Wordsworth, *Sonnet Series and Itinerary Poems, 1820–1845*, ed. Geoffrey Jackson (Ithaca: Cornell University Press, 2004), 78, 110; Bew, 469.

2. Keats, *L*, 2. 237; Washington Irving, *The Sketch Book of Geoffrey Crayon, Gent.*, ed. Haskell Springer (Boston: Twayne, 1978), 355; *The Letters of Charles Dickens, Volume One*, ed. Madeline House and Graham Storey (Oxford: Clarendon Press, 1965), 382.

3. Kelly, 362; Terry F. Robinson, "National Theatre in Transition: The London Patent Theatre Fires of 1808–09 and the Old Price Riots": http://www.branchcollective.org/?ps_articles=terry-f-robinson-national-theatre-in-transition-the-london-patent-theatre-fires-of-1808-1809-and-the-old-price-riots.

4. Moore, *L*, 1. 155.

5. Charles Robert Leslie, *Autobiographical Recollections*, ed. Tom Taylor, 2 vols. (London: Murray, 1860), 2. 37; Byron, *LJ*, 3. 249; Hunt, *DC*, 88; Lamb, *W*, 1. 185.

6. Lamb, *W*, 1. 187; Hunt, *A*, 1. 241; Beckford, 271–72.

7. Stott, 229; Ballard, 57; Hazlitt, 18. 208.

8. Lamb, *W*, 1. 151; 2. 163; Hunt, *A*, 1. 237.

9. Haydon, 3. 156; Hunt, *DE*, 178; *Selected Prose of John Hamilton Reynolds*, ed. Leonidas M. Jones (Cambridge, MA: Harvard University Press, 1966), 200; Allan Cunningham, *The Life of Sir David Wilkie*, 3 vols. (London: Murray, 1843), 1. 263; Hazlitt, 18. 252.

10. T. S. Munden, *Memoirs of Joseph Shepherd Munden* (London: Bentley, 1844), 295; Lamb, *W*, 2. 149; Hunt, *A*, 1. 239; Clarke, 185.

11. *Lady Blessington's Conversations of Lord Byron*, ed. Ernest Lovell (Princeton: Princeton University Press, 1969), 140; Robinson, 2. 90; Jim Davis, *Comic Acting and Portraiture in Late-Georgian and Regency England* (Cambridge: Cambridge University Press, 2015), 196; Keats, *L*, 2. 192.

12. Farington, 11. 4151.

13. Hazlitt, 18. 196; *The Poetical Works of Percy Bysshe Shelley*, ed. Mary Shelley, 4 vols. (London: Moxon, 1839), 2. 276–77; Austen, *L*, 296.

14. Byron, *LJ*, 2. 149; Burney, 9. 445; Hunt, *A*, 1. 286; Hazlitt, 5. 375–79.

15. Hunt, *DC*, 114.

16. Hazlitt, 5. 179–80; Hunt, *DE*, 221; Austen, *L*, 268.

17. Mary Shelley, *J*, 1. 35; *The Journals of Claire Clairmont*, ed. Marion Kingston Stocking (Cambridge, MA: Harvard University Press, 1968), 50; Haydon, 1. 397; Samuel Taylor Coleridge, *Table Talk*, ed. Carl Woodring, 2 vols. (Princeton: Princeton University Press, 1990), 1. 40; Robinson, 1. 430; Byron, *LJ*, 4. 235, 115.

18. *The Collected Letters of Joanna Baillie*, ed. Judith Bailey Slagle, 2 vols. (Madison, NJ: Fairleigh Dickinson University Press, 1999), 1. 166; Raymund Fitzsimons, *Edmund Kean: Fire from Heaven* (London: Hamish Hamilton, 1976), 68; Hazlitt, 4. 77; 5. 378; *John Keats: The Major Works*, ed. Elizabeth Cook (Oxford: Oxford University Press, 2001), 346.

19. *Drury Lane Journal: Selections from James Winston's Diaries, 1819–1827,* ed. Alfred Nelson and Gilbert Cross (London: The Society for Theatre Research, 1974), 16.

20. Hazlitt, 5. 334.

21. Clarke, 15; Lockhart, *S,* 6. 41.

22. John Wilson, "Boxiana. No. V" in *Blackwood's Magazine,* 6 (1819), 280 (Wilson's authorship of this article is probable but not certain); Wilson, 98; Mitford, 1. 146.

23. Isaac Pocock, *Hit or Miss!: A Musical Farce* (London: Chapple, 1811), 37; Egan, *LL,* 189.

24. Percy Shelley, *PS,* 1. 421; Austen, *P,* 47; Greville, 1. 86; Russell, 71; Raikes, 2. 275.

25. Southey, *E,* 3. 192; Egan, *LL,* 177.

26. John Whale, "Daniel Mendoza's Contests of Identity: Masculinity, Ethnicity, and Nation in Georgian Prize-Fighting" in *Romanticism,* 14 (2008), 259–60; William Cobbett, "To the People of the United States of America" in *Weekly Political Register,* 30 (1816), 362.

27. John Ford, *Prizefighting: The Age of Regency Boximania* (Newton Abbot: David and Charles, 1971), 109–18; Simond, 1. 162–63.

28. J. C. Reid, *Bucks and Bruisers: Pierce Egan and Regency England* (London: Routledge and Kegan Paul, 1971), 12–14; Badcock, 74.

29. J. G. Lockhart, "Letter from Lord Byron" in *Blackwood's Magazine,* 7 (1820), 187 (Lockhart's authorship of this article is probable but not certain); John Wilson and William Maginn, "Boxiana. No VIII" in *Blackwood's Magazine,* 8 (1820), 64 (Wilson and Maginn's authorship of this article is probable but not certain).

30. Egan, *B,* 2. 111–14, 323–31, 305–11, 388–94; Clarke, 145; Moore, *J,* 1. 96.

31. Byron, *HVSV,* 87; Byron, *LJ,* 4. 91; Moore, *S,* 115–17, 198–207.

32. Egan, *B,* 1. iv.

33. Ibid., 1. 411–13.

34. Rob Steen, *Floodlights and Touchlines: A History of Spectator Sport* (London: Bloomsbury, 2014), 117; Egan, *SA,* 256–57; Luttrell, 18; Ashton, *G,* 191; Raikes, 2. 211; *Edinburgh Annual Register for 1813,* 6 (1815), liii–liv.

35. Ashton, *R,* 2. 328; Egan, *SA,* 30, 169; Ashton, *G,* 166.

36. Low, 127, 132; Austen, *PP,* 328; Egan, *LL,* 177.

37. Kelly, 250; Gronow, 1. 57–58; Raikes, 3. 88.

38. Byron, *LJ,* 9. 23; Gronow, 1. 57; Robert Huish, *Memoirs of George the Fourth,* 2 vols. (London: Kelly, 1831), 2. 192; Greville, 1. 79.

39. Low, 127, 142–43; Ashton, *G,* 110–11, 114, 109, 116, 115.

40. Egan, *LL,* 236, 239.

41. E. Beresford Chancellor, *Memorials of St. James's Street together with the Annals of Almack's* (London: Grant Richards, 1922), 208–34; Rendell, 86–99; Gronow, 1. 32; Raikes, 2. 240.

42. Phil Hubbard, *Cities and Sexualities* (New York: Routledge, 2012), 127.

43. Edgeworth, *L,* 15; Southey, *E,* 1. 120–21, 74–75.

44. Margaret Maria Gordon, *The Home Life of Sir David Brewster* (Edinburgh: Edmonston and Douglas, 1869), 97.
45. Austen, *L*, 272; Hazlitt, 8. 77.
46. John Feltham, *A Guide to all the Watering and Sea-Bathing Places* (London: Longman, Hurst, Rees, Orme, and Brown, 1815), 375.
47. Gatrell, 196–97, 200; Ashton, *R*, 1. 217–31.
48. Lamb, *L*, 2. 127–28.
49. Granville, 1. 9; Gronow, 1. 37; Wilma Paterson, *Lord Byron's Relish* (Glasgow: Dog and Bone, 1990), 77–88; Ralph Rylance, *The Epicure's Almanack: Eating and Drinking in Regency London*, ed. Janet Ing Freeman (London: The British Library, 2012).
50. Greville, 1. 4–5; Gronow, 1. 34, 38; Egan, *LL*, 104; William West, *Tavern Anecdotes* (New York: Forbes, 1830), 155, 185–87; Longford, 322.
51. Russell, 76; Byron, *LJ*, 9. 21–22; Scott, *J*, 217; Moore, *J*, 3. 980; Peter Virgin, *Sydney Smith* (London: HarperCollins, 1994), 123, 113, 125–28.
52. Haydon, 2. 173–76.
53. Keats, *L*, 1. 277.
54. Byron, *LJ*, 3. 206; Richard Altick, *The Shows of London* (Cambridge, MA: Belknap Press of Harvard University Press, 1978), 237, 239–41.
55. Anonymous, *The Picture of London for 1813* (London: Longman, Hurst, Rees, Orme, and Brown, 1813), 314; Ballard, 56.
56. Tannahill, 11; Anonymous, "Mr. Turner's Lectures at the Royal Academy" in *New Monthly Magazine*, 5 (1816), 60; John Gage, *J. M. W. Turner: "A Wonderful Range of Mind"* (New Haven: Yale University Press, 1987), 239; A. C. Grayling, *The Quarrel of the Age: The Life and Times of William Hazlitt* (London: Weidenfeld and Nicolson, 2000), 228.
57. Austen, *LM*, 641.
58. G. O. Trevelyan, *The Life and Letters of Lord Macaulay*, 2 vols. (London: Longmans, Green, 1876), 1. 289, 132.
59. Brunton, xx–xxi, xxxix; Alison Adburgham, *Silver Fork Society: Fashionable Life and Literature from 1814 to 1840* (London: Constable, 1983), 5–23, 320–24.
60. Austen, *L*, 244, 266, 350; Austen, *LM*, 226.
61. Austen, *L*, 287, 337; *Jane Austen: The Critical Heritage*, ed. B. C. Southam, 2 vols. (London: Routledge and Kegan Paul, 1968–87), 1. 63.
62. Carol Shields, *Jane Austen* (New York: Viking, 2001), 57.
63. Allan Bloom, *Love and Friendship* (New York: Simon & Schuster, 1993), 196–98.
64. Austen, *PP*, 215.
65. Austen, *L*, 289.
66. Francis Jeffrey, "Miss Edgeworth's *Tales of Fashionable Life*" in *Edinburgh Review*, 20 (1812), 100–101; St. Clair, 597.
67. John Wilson Croker, "Miss Edgeworth's *Tales of Fashionable Life*" in *Quarterly Review*, 7 (1812), 336.
68. Walter Scott, *Waverley*, ed. P. D. Garside (Edinburgh: Edinburgh University Press, 2007), 364, 367–83.

69. Cockburn, 270; Scott, *CH*, 75; Austen, *L*, 289.

70. St. Clair, 636–37.

71. Lockhart, *S*, 6. 159; Walter Scott, *Ivanhoe*, ed. Graham Tulloch (Edinburgh: Edinburgh University Press, 1998), 415.

72. John Scott, "The Author of the Scotch Novels" in *London Magazine*, 1 (1820), 12; Cronin, 204–06; Scott, *CH*, 144.

73. Hazlitt, 12. 129.

74. Thomas Moore, *Letters and Journals of Lord Byron*, 2 vols. (London: Murray, 1830), 1. 347; Ghislaine McDayter, *Byromania and the Birth of Celebrity Culture* (Albany: State University of New York Press, 2009), 3–4, 25–26; Tom Mole, "Introduction" in *Romanticism and Celebrity Culture*, ed. Tom Mole (Cambridge: Cambridge University Press, 2009), 1–18.

75. St. Clair, 587; Galt, 327.

76. Hallam Tennyson, *Alfred Lord Tennyson: A Memoir*, 2 vols. (London: Macmillan, 1897), 2. 69; Walter Scott, "Childe Harold's Pilgrimage, Canto III" in *Quarterly Review*, 16 (1816), 178; Pryse Lockhart Gordon, *Personal Memoirs*, 2 vols. (London: Colburn and Bentley, 1830), 2. 320; Benjamin Lease, *that wild fellow John Neal* (Chicago: University of Chicago Press, 1972), 19; Gwendolyn Davies, *Studies in Maritime Literary History* (Fredericton, NB: Acadiensis Press, 1991), 54; Byron, *CH*, 164.

77. MacCarthy, 162–63; Caroline Lamb, 78; Byron, *CH*, 35; Byron, *LJ*, 6. 127; *Medwin's Conversations of Lord Byron*, ed. Ernest Lovell (Princeton: Princeton University Press, 1966), 11; Byron, *CH*, 36; John Scott, "Living Authors. No. IV. Lord Byron" in *London Magazine*, 3 (1821), 59.

78. Byron, *PW*, 3. 158; Kahan, 50; Granville, 1. 90; *The Letters of John Murray to Lord Byron*, ed. Andrew Nicholson (Liverpool: Liverpool University Press, 2007), 267; Tom Mole, *Byron's Romantic Celebrity: Industrial Culture and the Hermeneutic of Intimacy* (Basingstoke: Palgrave, 2007), 78–97; J. G. Lockhart, *John Bull's Letter to Lord Byron*, ed. Alan Lang Strout (Norman: University of Oklahoma Press, 1947), 80.

Chapter Three: Sexual Pastimes, Pleasures, and Perversities

1. Austen, *PP*, 319, 256, 305.

2. Brunton, xxiii; Eaton Stannard Barrett, *Woman* (London: Colburn, 1818), 19; Anonymous, *"Bowdler's Family Shakespeare"* in *Christian Remembrancer*, 1 (1819), 372, 371.

3. Gatrell, 459; Walter Scott, *"Women; or Pour et Contre"* in *Edinburgh Review*, 30 (1818), 254.

4. Moore, *LR*, 323; Keats, *P*, 302, 315; Percy Shelley, *PS*, 1. 471; *The Keats Circle: Letters and Papers, 1816–1878*, ed. Hyder E. Rollins, 2 vols. (Cambridge, MA: Harvard University Press, 1969), 1. 35.

5. Constable, 2. 179; *The Love Letters of William and Mary Wordsworth*, ed. Beth Darlington (Ithaca: Cornell University Press, 1981), 229–30.

6. Keats, *L*, 2. 142, 304, 351.

7. Gatrell, 111–12; Kitchener, 2. 97.
8. Hunt, *PE*, 1. 221; Gatrell, 314; George Cruikshank, "The Court of Love" in the *Scourge*, 4 (1812), 348; *Creevey's Life and Times*, ed. John Gore (London: Murray, 1934), 274; Longford, 375; Bourne, 207–13.
9. Nicholas Suisse, *Confessions of Nicholas Suisse* (London: Jackson, 1843), 23–24, 25–26.
10. Polidori, 33.
11. Egan, *LL*, 40.
12. Rendell, 39–42; Vaux, 273; Egan, *LL*, xi–xii.
13. Egan, *LL*, 239, 246, 238, 241.
14. Ibid., 227, 229–30.
15. Egan, *LL*, 127–28; Gregory Dart, *Metropolitan Art and Literature, 1810–1840: Cockney Adventures* (Cambridge: Cambridge University Press, 2012), 107–36.
16. Austen, *LM*, 183–84; Austen, *L*, 292.
17. Kitchener, 2. 88.
18. Mitchell, 5; Creevey, 2. 199; Byron, *LJ*, 7. 169; Moore, *J*, 1. 129.
19. Byron, *LJ*, 2. 170–71; Caroline Lamb, 84, 126.
20. Galt, 187; Burney, 8. 416; Lady Caroline Lamb, *Glenarvon*, ed. Paul Douglass (London: Pickering and Chatto, 2009), 189.
21. *The Clairmont Correspondence*, ed. Marion Kingston Stocking, 2 vols. (Baltimore: Johns Hopkins University Press, 1995), 1. 24–25.
22. Byron, *LJ*, 5. 162; Daisy Hay, *Young Romantics: The Tangled Lives of English Poetry's Greatest Generation* (New York: Farrar, Straus and Giroux, 2010), 308.
23. Byron, *LJ*, 6. 237, 232; Byron, *PW*, 5. 203, 501, 154.
24. Byron, *PW*, 5. 431, 299, 71; Byron, *LJ*, 6. 105.
25. James Lawrence, *The Empire of the Nairs*, 2nd ed., 4 vols. (London: Hookham, 1811), 2. 5; Percy Shelley, *PS*, 1. 372; Hale, 13; Kitchener, 1. 180.
26. Kitchener, 1. 183; Hale, 12; Egan, *LL*, 18–19.
27. Keats, *P*, 286; David Kerr Cameron, *London's Pleasures: From Restoration to Regency* (Stroud: Sutton, 2001), 196; *Police*, 459; Anonymous, "State of Mendicity and Vagrancy in the Metropolis" in *The Anti-Jacobin Review*, 50 (1816), 66.
28. Kitchener, 2. 41–42; Harvey, 93–94; Egan, *LL*, 146, 142; *Police*, 461; Ballard, 41.
29. Bate, 135; T. A. J. Burnett, *The Rise and Fall of a Regency Dandy: The Life and Times of Scrope Berdmore Davies* (Boston: Little, Brown, 1981), 38, 36; Haydon, 1. 304–5.
30. Byron, *LJ*, 6. 108, 92; Caroline Lamb, 115; Byron, *LJ*, 8. 129.
31. Egan, *LL*, 142; Dabhoiwala, 297; Egan, *LL*, 135, 134; Rendell, 113.
32. Wilson, 26, 13, 19, 47.
33. Ibid., 433, 154.
34. Lisa O'Connell, "Authorship and Libertine Celebrity: Harriette Wilson's Regency Memoirs" in *Libertine Enlightenment: Sex, Liberty, and License in*

the Eighteenth Century, ed. Peter Cryle and Lisa O'Connell (Basingstoke: Palgrave, 2004), 163; Charles Molloy Westmacott, *The English Spy*, 2 vols. (London: Methuen, 1907), 2. 36, 54.

35. Virginia Woolf, "Harriette Wilson" in *The Essays of Virginia Woolf*, ed. Andrew McNeillie and Stuart N. Clarke, 6 vols. (London: The Hogarth Press, 1986–2011), 4. 254–58; Wilson, 316.

36. Wilson, 86; Frances Wilson, *The Courtesan's Revenge: Harriette Wilson, the Woman who Blackmailed the King* (London: Faber, 2003), 67.

37. Wilson, 220; *Confessions of Julia Johnstone*, ed. Julie Peakman (London: Pickering and Chatto, 2007), 136; Fergus Linnane, *Madams: Bawds and Brothel-Keepers of London* (Stroud: Sutton, 2005), 149; Wilson, 31, 62, 44.

38. George Paston and Peter Quennell, *To Lord Byron* (London: Murray, 1939), 157; Wilson, 443; Christopher Hibbert, *Wellington: A Personal History* (London: HarperCollins, 1997), 389–90; Wilson, 53, 66, 413.

39. Kitchener, 2. 33; Ashbee, 3. 294.

40. Harvey, 93; Thomas Harrison Burder, "On Diseases Resembling Syphilis" in *Medico-Chirurgical Journal*, 1 (1818), 7; Byron, *LJ*, 2. 56; Shanes, 431; Bate, 135.

41. Hazlitt, 5. 327; Henry Hawkins and Laetitia-Matilda Hawkins, *Sermonets* (London: Rivington, 1814), 347; [A Lady of Distinction], *The Mirror of the Graces* (London: Crosby, 1811), 96, 93.

42. Kitchener, 1. 156; Julie Peakman, *Mighty Lewd Books: The Development of Pornography in Eighteenth-Century England* (Basingstoke: Palgrave, 2003), 187; Ireland, 150.

43. Robert Southey, "To the Editor of the Courier" in *Blackwood's Magazine*, 16 (1824), 715; Gatrell, 389; Ireland, 124; Brunton, 91; Donald Thomas, *A Long Time Burning: The History of Literary Censorship in England* (New York: Praeger, 1969), 423.

44. Matthew Payne and James Payne, *Regarding Thomas Rowlandson* (London: Hogarth Arts, 2010), 366; Patricia Phagan, *Thomas Rowlandson: Pleasures and Pursuits in Georgian England* (London: Giles, 2011), 163; Parissien, 369.

45. Gert Schiff, *The Amorous Illustrations of Thomas Rowlandson* (n.p.: The Cythera Press, 1969).

46. Kurt von Meier, *The Forbidden Erotica of Thomas Rowlandson* (Los Angeles: Hogarth Guild, 1970), 159.

47. Byron, *PW*, 5. 582.

48. Colin Spencer, *Homosexuality: A History* (London: Fourth Estate, 1995), 212–16; Macdonald, 64–65.

49. Rictor Norton, "Homosexuality" in *A Cultural History of Sexuality in the Enlightenment*, ed. Julie Peakman (Oxford: Berg, 2011), 57; Christopher Hobson, *Blake and Homosexuality* (Basingstoke: Palgrave, 2000), 4–5; Norton, 91.

50. Robert Blake, *Disraeli* (London: Eyre and Spottiswoode, 1966), 14, 16.

51. Faderman, 159; Alison Oram and Annmarie Turnbull, *The Lesbian History Sourcebook* (London: Routledge, 2001), 50–52; *The Notebooks of Samuel Taylor Coleridge*, ed. Kathleen Coburn, Merton Christensen, and

Anthony John Harding, 5 vols. (Princeton: Princeton University Press, 1957–2002), 3. 4172; Park Honan, *Jane Austen: Her Life* (New York: St. Martin's Press, 1987), 186; Austen, *L*, 359–60; Matilda Betham, "Song" in *A Select Collection of English Songs*, ed. Joseph Ritson, 2nd ed., 3 vols. (London: Rivington, 1813), 1. 117; Dorothea Primrose Campbell, *Poems* (London: Baldwin, Cradock, and Joy, 1816), 127.

52. Faderman, 122–23; Lister, 210; G. H. Bell, *The Hamwood Papers of the Ladies of Llangollen* (London: Macmillan, 1930), 345.

53. Crompton, 170; Faderman, 150–51.

54. Martha Vicinus, *Intimate Friends: Women who Loved Women, 1778–1928* (Chicago: University of Chicago Press, 2004), 62–69.

55. Faderman, 152–53, 149.

56. Crompton, 161; Jeffrey Weeks, *Coming Out: Homosexual Politics in Britain, from the Nineteenth Century to the Present* (London: Quartet, 1977), 4, 13–15; Norton, 128.

57. Rictor Norton, *Homosexuality in Nineteenth-Century England: A Sourcebook*: http://rictornorton.co.uk/eighteen/1800news.htm.

58. B. R. Burg, "The HMS *Africaine* Revisited: The Royal Navy and the Homosexual Community" in *Journal of Homosexuality*, 56 (2009), 173–94.

59. Norton, 188, 199; Davenport-Hines, 91.

60. Norton, 189–91; Davenport-Hines, 75.

61. Crompton, 165–66.

62. *The Columbia Anthology of Gay Literature*, ed. Byrne R. S. Fone (New York: Columbia University Press, 1998), 212–13; Simond, 1. 470.

63. Norton, 195; Crompton, 171.

64. Davenport-Hines, 100; Arthur N. Gilbert, "Sexual Deviance and Disaster during the Napoleonic Wars" in *Albion*, 9 (1977), 112–13.

65. Byron, *LJ*, 7. 51; Charles Dickens, *Memoirs of Joseph Grimaldi*, ed. Richard Findlater (London: MacGibbon and Kee, 1968), 129; Macdonald, 63–64; Byron, *LJ*, 4. 330.

66. Farington, 8. 3148; Anonymous, *A Full Report of the Curious Trial for Libel, which took Place on Thursday, 29 June 1809* (London: M'Pherson, 1843), 8; Scott, *J*, 162; Josephine McDonagh, "De Quincey and the Secret Life of Books" in *Thomas De Quincey: New Theoretical and Critical Directions*, ed. Robert Morrison and Daniel Sanjiv Roberts (New York: Routledge, 2008), 130.

67. William Cobbett, "Horrid Punishment of James Byrne" in *Political Register*, 44 (October 12, 1822), 108.

68. Lister, 145.

69. Lister, 151; Francis Mark Mondimore, *A Natural History of Homosexuality* (Baltimore: Johns Hopkins University Press, 1996), 56; Lister, 297, 136; *The Literature of Lesbianism*, ed. Terry Castle (New York: Columbia University Press, 2003), 390.

70. Andrew Elfenbein, *Romantic Genius: The Prehistory of a Homosexual Role* (New York: Columbia University Press, 1999), 177; Coleridge, *PW*, 1. 491, 495.

71. Byron, *CMP*, 59; Byron, *LJ*, 1. 208; 2. 6, 23.

72. MacCarthy, 267; Percy Shelley, *L*, 2. 58; Byron, *LJ*, 6. 207.

73. Percy Shelley, *PS*, 2. 728; Percy Shelley, *P*, 221, 222, 223.

74. Crompton, 180; Farington, 11. 3931.

75. Timothy Mowl, *William Beckford* (London: Murray, 1998), 263–64; Norton, 223; *The Piozzi Letters*, ed. Edward A. Bloom and Lillian D. Bloom, 6 vols. (Newark: University of Delaware Press, 1989–2002), 6. 248.

76. Byron, *LJ*, 1. 210; Beckford, 271, 51, 43, 137; Norton, 229–30.

77. Bentham, 492; Crompton, 263–64, 29.

78. Dabhoiwala, 136; Bentham, 490–91.

79. Dabhoiwala, 135–38; Bentham, 493.

80. Austen, *MP*, 547; Mary Jean Corbett, *Family Likeness: Sex, Marriage, and Incest from Jane Austen to Virginia Woolf* (Ithaca: Cornell University Press, 2008), 35–37.

81. Leigh Hunt, *Foliage* (London: Ollier, 1818), 17; Percy Shelley, *PS*, 2. 171; Nathaniel Brown, *Sexuality and Feminism in Shelley* (Cambridge, MA: Harvard University Press, 1979), 212–28.

82. Byron, *PW*, 4. 74, 53, 85; Crompton, 284.

83. Benjamin Rush, *Medical Inquiries and Observations, upon the Diseases of the Mind* (Philadelphia: Kimber and Richardson, 1812), 347; Dabhoiwala, 136.

84. Alexander Peter Buchan, *Venus Sine Concubitu* (London: Callow, 1818), 67–70.

85. Thomas De Quincey, "On Suicide" in *London Magazine*, 8 (1823), 499; Ashbee, 1. 400.

86. Ashbee, 1. xliii–xliv.

87. Kahan, 96; Mitchell, 84; Anonymous, *Venus School-Mistress: or Birchen Sports* (New York: Grove, 1968), 11.

88. Anonymous, *A Plain Statement of Facts, Relative to Sir Eyre Coote* (London: Sherwood, Neely, and Jones, 1816), 27.

89. Mary Shelley, *F*, 39; Christopher C. Nagle, *Sexuality and the Culture of Sensibility in the British Romantic Era* (New York: Palgrave, 2007), 135–36.

90. Gash, *P*, 257.

Chapter Four: Expanding Empire and Waging War

1. Longford, 389.

2. *De Quincey to Wordsworth: A Biography of a Relationship*, ed. John Jordan (Berkeley: University of California Press, 1963), 160.

3. Byron, *PW*, 7. 17.

4. Austen, *L*, 200; Holmes, 161–62.

5. Haydon, 1. 239.

6. Rory Muir, *Wellington: The Path to Victory, 1769–1814* (New Haven: Yale University Press, 2013), 530; Longford, 321; Holmes, 188.

7. Holmes, 193.

8. Longford, 402; Holmes, 211–14.

9. Creevey, 1. 228.

10. Byron, *PW*, 2. 85; Holmes, 227; Vincent Cronin, *Napoleon* (London: Collins, 1971), 399; Creevey, 1. 219.

11. Longford, 419, 421.

12. James, 251–52.

13. Holmes, 233; James, 257.

14. Longford, 452.

15. Ibid., 474, 473.

16. Ibid., 489.

17. Patrick O'Leary, *Regency Editor: The Life of John Scott* (Aberdeen: Aberdeen University Press, 1983), 70; Gash, 136–37; Charlotte Anne Waldie, *Narrative of a Residence in Belgium during the Campaign of 1815* (London: Murray, 1817), 271; Austen, *L*, 342.

18. Byron, *PW*, 2. 89–92; 5. 409–11; Anthony Bailey, *Standing in the Sun: A Life of J. M. W. Turner* (New York: HarperCollins, 1998), 219; Byron, *PW*, 2. 86; *Journals of Dorothy Wordsworth*, ed. Ernest de Selincourt, 2 vols. (London: Macmillan, 1952), 2. 29.

19. Lamb, *L*, 2. 167.

20. Austen, *MP*, 140.

21. Ferdinand Brock Tupper, *The Life and Correspondence of Major-General Sir Isaac Brock*, 2nd ed. (London: Simpkin, Marshall, 1847), 280.

22. Laxer, 157.

23. Borneman, 160.

24. Laxer, 268.

25. Ibid., 274–75.

26. Hitsman, 236.

27. Borneman, 282–93; Hitsman, 236–37; Laxer, 292.

28. Alan Taylor, *The Civil War of 1812* (New York: Knopf, 2010), 419; G. C. Moore Smith, *The Autobiography of Lieutenant-General Sir Harry Smith*, 2 vols. (London: Murray, 1901), 1. 251.

29. Galt, 201.

30. Byron, *LJ*, 2. 21; Virginia Childs, *Lady Hester Stanhope: Queen of the Desert* (London: Weidenfeld and Nicolson, 1990), 139, 170.

31. William St. Clair, *Lord Elgin and the Marbles* (London: Oxford University Press, 1967), 7.

32. St. Clair, *Lord Elgin*, 267; Felicia Hemans, *Modern Greece* (London: Murray, 1817), 50; Haydon, 2. 76; Benjamin Robert Haydon, *Lectures on Painting and Design*, 2 vols. (London: Longman, Brown, Green, and Longmans, 1844–46), 1. 192.

33. Byron, *LJ*, 5. 262; Byron, *PW*, 2. 49, 48; Christopher Hitchens, *The Parthenon Marbles: The Case for Reunification* (London: Verso, 2008).

34. Tilar Mazzeo, "'Sporting Sketches During a Short Stay in Hindustane': Bodleian MS Shelley adds.e.21 and Travel Literature in the Shelley/

Byron Circle" in *Romanticism*, 4 (1998), 174–88; Maria Graham, *Letters on India* (London: Longman, Hurst, Rees, Orme, and Brown, 1814), 8.

35. *Lady Nugent's East India Journal*, ed. Ashley L. Cohen (New Delhi: Oxford University Press, 2014), xxxii, 102, 277.

36. Alexander Wylie, *Memorials of Protestant Missionaries to the Chinese* (Shanghae: American Presbyterian Mission Press, 1867), 9, 20–21; Eliza Morrison, *Memoirs of the Life and Labours of Robert Morrison*, 2 vols. (London: Longman, Orme, Brown, Green, and Longmans, 1839), 1. 513; William Milne, *A Retrospect of the First Ten Years of the Protestant Mission to China* (Malacca: Anglo-Chinese Press, 1820), 1.

37. Glendinning, 243.

38. Ibid., 99, 121, 111.

39. Ibid., 176–77, 198–99.

40. Glendinning, 218–20; Saw Swee-Hock, "Population Trends in Singapore, 1819–1967" in *Journal of Southeast Asian History*, 10 (1969), 37.

41. Klingaman, 1, 7–16.

42. *Collected Correspondence of J. M. W. Turner*, ed. John Gage (Oxford: Clarendon Press, 1980), 67, 70; Austen, *L*, 330; Coleridge, *L*, 4. 660; Klingaman, 187, 280–82.

43. Mary Shelley, *F*, 176; Byron, *HVSV*, 299; Byron, *PW*, 4. 40–41; Klingaman, 12–13.

44. *Collected Fiction of John William Polidori*, ed. D. L. Macdonald and Kathleen Scherf (Toronto: University of Toronto Press, 1994), 183.

45. James Mill, *The History of British India*, 3 vols. (London: Baldwin, Cradock, and Joy, 1817), 1. 472; Percy Shelley, *P*, 238.

46. Sydney Owenson, *The Missionary: An Indian Tale*, 3 vols. (London: Stockdale, 1811), 1. 149.

47. John Wilson, "*Lalla Rookh*" in *Edinburgh Monthly Magazine*, 1 (1817), 280.

48. Mitford, 4. 239–40.

49. Smith, 136; Hibbert, 2. 126.

50. Hibbert, 2. 125; Hazlitt, 10. 90.

51. Anonymous, *Advice to Opium Eaters* (London: Goodluck, 1823), 11; Robert Morrison, *The English Opium-Eater: A Biography of Thomas De Quincey* (London: Weidenfeld and Nicolson, 2009), 105–11, 162–65; Barry Milligan, *Pleasures and Pains: Opium and the Orient in Nineteenth-Century British Culture* (Charlottesville: University Press of Virginia, 1995), 20–28.

52. Robert Christison, *A Treatise on Poisons* (Edinburgh: Black, 1829), 528; Alethea Hayter, *Opium and the Romantic Imagination* (London: Faber, 1968), 25–35.

53. Samuel Cooper, *The First Lines of the Practice of Surgery*, 3rd ed. (London: Longman, 1813), 42.

54. Burney, 6. 610–14.

55. Moore, *LR*, 7; Keats, *P*, 369.

56. Coleridge, *PW*, 1. 514.

57. Hibbert, 2. 13; William Hague, *William Wilberforce: The Life of the Great*

Anti-Slave Trade Campaigner (London: HarperCollins, 2007), 162; Hunt, *DC*, 68; Coleridge, *L*, 4. 626; 3. 490; 4. 630.

58. *Henry Crabb Robinson on Books and Their Writers*, ed. Edith J. Morley, 3 vols. (London: Dent, 1938), 1. 187; De Quincey, 54, 75.

59. De Quincey, 73.

60. Inga Clendinnen, *Dancing with Strangers: Europeans and Australians at First Contact* (Cambridge: Cambridge University Press, 2005), 271.

61. Penelope Edmonds, *Settler Colonialism and (Re)conciliation* (Basingstoke: Palgrave, 2016), 107; Tanya Evans, *Fractured Families: Life on the Margins in Colonial New South Wales* (Sydney: University of New South Wales Press, 2015), 65–66.

62. Augustus Morris and John Byron, *New South Wales: Its Progress, Present Condition, and Resources* (Sydney: Richards, 1886), 22.

63. A. C. V. Melbourne, *William Charles Wentworth* (Brisbane: Biggs, 1934), 27; W. C. Wentworth, *A Statistical, Historical, and Political Description of the Colony of New South Wales* (London: Whittaker, 1819), 175–76.

64. Lamb, *L*, 2. 209; Ronald Coleman Solomon, *Barron Field and the Supreme Court of Civil Judicature: Law, Personality, and Politics in New South Wales, 1816–1824* (unpublished PhD thesis, University of New South Wales, 2013), 88–89.

65. Lamb, *W*, 1. 198–99.

66. Austen, *MP*, 36, 209; Byron, *PW*, 2. 19; Beckford, 136.

67. Matthew Lewis, *Journal of a West India Proprietor*, ed. Judith Terry (Oxford: Oxford University Press, 1999), 228, 42.

68. Ibid., 215, 239, 243.

69. Ibid., 203–4, 241, 110–11, 229, 249.

70. Austen, *E*, 325; [S.T.], *An Address to the Guardian Society* (London: Marchant, 1817), 17; Byron, *PW*, 2. 202; Edgeworth, *NSW*, 5. 101.

71. William Cobbett, "To William Wilberforce" in *Weekly Political Register*, 32 (November 15, 1817), 1001–2.

72. Elizabeth A. Bohls, *Romantic Literature and Postcolonial Studies* (Edinburgh: Edinburgh University Press, 2013), 75–77.

73. Malcolm Chase, *1820: Disorder and Stability in the United Kingdom* (Manchester: Manchester University Press, 2013), 53; Iain McCalman, "Anti-Slavery and Ultra-Radicalism in Early Nineteenth-Century England: The Case of Robert Wedderburn" in *Slavery and Abolition*, 7 (1986), 109; Robert Wedderburn, "The Axe Laid to the Root" in *Early Black British Writing*, ed. Alan Richardson and Debbie Lee (Boston: Houghton Mifflin, 2004), 209–10.

74. Jonathan Cutmore, *Contributors to the Quarterly Review: A History, 1809–25* (London: Pickering, 2008), 74–75.

75. Samuel Leigh, *New Picture of London* (London: Leigh, 1820), 383; Keats, *L*, 2. 95.

76. Keats, *L*, 2. 6.

77. Eleanor Anne Porden, *The Arctic Expeditions* (London: Murray, 1818), 12; Keats, *P*, 299, 358–59; Mary Shelley, *F*, 10, 170.

78. Wordsworth, *E*, 285; Chandler, 460–61, 456.
79. Prebble, 114; Earl of Selkirk, *Observations on the Present State of the Highlands of Scotland* (London: Longman, Hurst, Rees, and Orme, 1805), 162.
80. Prebble, 114; J. M. Bumsted, *Thomas Scott's Body and Other Essays on Early Manitoban History* (Winnipeg: University of Manitoba Press, 2000), 150–51; Ian Grimble, *Regency People* (London: British Broadcasting Corporation, 1972), 66.
81. Morris Birkbeck, *Letters from Illinois* (London: Taylor and Hessey, 1818), 41, 70.
82. Keats, *L*, 1. 287; 2. 9.
83. Chandler, 472; Keats, *L*, 2. 185.
84. John Barrow, "Views, Visits, and Tours in North America" in *Quarterly Review*, 27 (1822), 99; Percy Shelley, *PS*, 2. 244.

Chapter Five: Changing Landscapes and Ominous Signs

1. Ferrier, 215.
2. Wordsworth, *E*, 262; Badcock, 15; Samuel Taylor Coleridge, *Lay Sermons*, ed. R. J. White (Princeton: Princeton University Press, 1972), 169.
3. Elmes, 127–28; Tannahill, 42; Elizabeth Longford, *Wellington: Pillar of State* (London: Weidenfeld and Nicolson, 1972), 44; Haydon, 2. 282; Constable, 6. 46.
4. Jerry White, *London in the Nineteenth Century* (London: Cape, 2007), 23–26.
5. Donald Low, *That Sunny Dome: A Portrait of Regency Britain* (London: Dent, 1977), 9–11; Dana Arnold, "George IV and the Metropolitan Improvements: The Creation of a Royal Image" in *"Squanderous and Lavish Profusion": George IV, his image and patronage of the arts*, ed. Dana Arnold (London: Georgian Group, 1995), 51–56.
6. Gatrell, 81; Tannahill, 40.
7. Robinson, 2. 87; Elmes, 7; Terence Davis, *John Nash: The Prince Regent's Architect* (London: Country Life, 1966), 63–82.
8. Davis, *John Nash*, 66.
9. John Thomas Smith, *Vagabondiana, or, Anecdotes of Mendicant Wanderers through the Streets of London* (London: Chatto and Windus, 1874), v.
10. Smith, *Vagabondiana*, 24.
11. Constable, 2. 339.
12. *Thomas Lawrence: Regency Power and Brilliance*, ed. A. Cassandra Albinson, Peter Funnell, and Lucy Peltz (New Haven: Yale University Press, 2010), 217–20.
13. *Thomas Lawrence: Regency Power and Brilliance*, 228–30; Richard Walker, *Regency Portraits*, 2 vols. (London: National Portrait Gallery, 1985), 2. Plates 477–79; David Crane, Stephen Hebron, and Robert Woof, *Romantics and Revolutionaries: Regency Portraits from the National Portrait Gallery* (London: National Portrait Gallery, 2002), 84–87.

14. Kelly, 174–76.

15. Nigel Rodgers, *The Dandy: Peacock or Enigma* (London: Bene Factum, 2012), 35; Wilson, 40; Lord William Pitt Lennox, *Celebrities I Have Known*, 2 vols. (London: Hurst and Blackett, 1876), 1. 291; Jesse, 1. 70.

16. Wilson, 40; Hazlitt, 20. 153; Jesse, 2. 391.

17. *William Hazlitt: Metropolitan Writings*, ed. Gregory Dart (Manchester: Carcanet, 2005), xiv–xv.

18. Sir William Fraser, *Words on Wellington* (London: Nimmo, 1889), 203; Moore, *L*, 1. 180; *Sir Robert Peel . . . from his Private Correspondence*, ed. Charles Stuart Parker, 3 vols. (London: Murray, 1891–1899), 1. 227.

19. Charles Dickens, "First Fruits" in *Uncollected Writings from Household Words*, ed. Harry Stone, 2 vols. (Bloomington: Indiana University Press, 1968), 2. 413; Stott, 222; Patten, 1. 192, 234–36; Moore, *J*, 1. 29.

20. Jesse, 1. 15.

21. Archibald Alison, "On the Proposed National Monument at Edinburgh" in *Blackwood's Magazine*, 5 (1819), 385; John Galt, "The Ayrshire Legatees" in *Blackwood's Magazine*, 7 (1820), 266.

22. Lockhart, *PL*, 1. 43, 210–11; 3. 108–9.

23. Lockhart, *PL*, 2. 293; Duncan Thomson, *Raeburn: The Art of Sir Henry Raeburn* (Edinburgh: Scottish National Portrait Gallery, 1997), 152, 174–75, 164–65.

24. Cockburn, 163.

25. Hazlitt, 12. 365.

26. James Hogg, J. G. Lockhart, and John Wilson, "Translation from an Ancient Chaldee Manuscript" in *Blackwood's Magazine*, 2 (1817), 90; Carlyle, 114.

27. J. G. Lockhart, "On the Cockney School of Poetry" in *Blackwood's Magazine*, 2 (1817), 39; Keats, *L*, 1. 180; *The Letters of Charles Armitage Brown*, ed. Jack Stillinger (Cambridge, MA: Harvard University Press, 1966), 72.

28. Barrie Trinder, *The Making of the Industrial Landscape* (London: Dent, 1982), 128; Ayton and Daniell, 2. 11–12.

29. Wordsworth, *E*, 261, 264; Coleridge, *L*, 4. 575.

30. Owen, 4; Robert Owen, *A Supplementary Appendix to the First Volume of the Life of Robert Owen* (London: Wilson, 1858), 18.

31. Thompson, 886; Robert Owen, *Development of the Plan for the Relief of the Poor, and the Emancipation of Mankind* (London: Smeeton, 1817), 15; Hazlitt, 7. 99.

32. Southey, *S*, 261, 260, 264–65.

33. Humphry Repton, *Fragments on the Theory and Practice of Landscape Gardening* (London: Bensley, 1816), 193.

34. Austen, *MP*, 65; Thomas Love Peacock, *Headlong Hall* (London: Hookham, 1816), 35–36.

35. Powell, 133, 227; *Selected Letters and Journals of George Crabbe*, ed. Thomas Faulkner and Rhonda Blair (Oxford: Clarendon Press, 1985), 236.

36. *The Poetical Works of the Rev. George Crabbe*, ed. George Crabbe, 8 vols. (London: Murray, 1834), 1. 198; Powell, 225–26; Francis Jeffrey, "Crab-

be's *Tales of the Hall*" in *Edinburgh Review*, 32 (1819), 126; John Wilson, "Crabbe's *Tales of the Hall*" in *Blackwood's Magazine*, 5 (1819), 483, 471.

37. *George Crabbe: Complete Poetical Works*, ed. Norma Dalrymple-Champneys and Arthur Pollard, 3 vols. (Oxford: Clarendon Press, 1988), 2. 134, 329.

38. Austen, *MP*, 183; Deirdre Le Faye, *Jane Austen: A Family Record*, 2nd ed. (Cambridge: Cambridge University Press, 2004), 178.

39. Hazlitt, 18. 99; Lockhart, *PL*, 2. 260–75; Hibbert, 2. 315.

40. Nicholas Tromans, *David Wilkie: The People's Painter* (Edinburgh: Edinburgh University Press, 2007), 36, 39–42, 133.

41. Walter Scott, *The Antiquary*, ed. David Hewitt (Edinburgh: Edinburgh University Press, 1995), 247.

42. John Clare, *Poems Descriptive of Rural Life and Scenery* (London: Taylor and Hessey, 1820), 9.

43. Ibid., 132, 130, 9.

44. Constable, 1. 101; 2. 119.

45. Ibid., 2. 246.

46. G. E. Bentley, *The Stranger from Paradise: A Biography of William Blake* (New Haven: Yale University Press, 2001), 368; Constable, 3. 11.

47. Constable, 6. 100; Anthony Bailey, *John Constable: A Kingdom of His Own* (London: Vintage Books, 2007), 106.

48. Constable, 6. 78.

49. Ibid., 2. 110.

50. Ibid., 6. 108, 161.

51. Farington, 11. 3919; Constable, 3. 58.

52. Shanes, 408; Robinson, 1. 381; Robert Hunt, "Royal Academy Exhibition" in *Examiner*, 5 (1812), 363.

53. James Hamilton, *Turner* (New York: Random House, 1997), 231; Lockhart, *PL*, 2. 178.

54. Hazlitt, 4. 76; Peter Ackroyd, *J. M. W. Turner* (London: Chatto and Windus, 2005), 86–87.

55. Spencer Walpole, *The Life of Lord John Russell*, 2 vols. (London: Longmans, 1889), 1. 56; Mary Gordon, *"Christopher North": A Memoir of John Wilson* (New York: Widdleton, 1863), 139; Keats, *L*, 1. 301; Carlyle, 132; Coleridge, *L*, 4. 946.

56. Ayton and Daniell, 2. 159–61.

57. Brunton, 42; Scott, *HM*, 249.

58. William Combe and Thomas Rowlandson, *The Tour of Dr. Syntax in Search of the Picturesque* (London: Methuen, 1903), 102.

59. Ibid., 54, 30, 175.

60. De Quincey, 323.

61. Wordsworth, *E*, 261–62; Ferrier, 222; Austen, *E*, 320; Austen, *PP*, 201.

62. Henry Parnell, *A Treatise on Roads* (London: Longman, Rees, Orme, Brown, Green, and Longman, 1833), 25; Edward Berens, "Roads and Highways" in *Quarterly Review*, 23 (1820), 97; Edgeworth, *NSW*, 5. 115; Austen, *MP*, 221–22.

63. John Loudon McAdam, *Remarks on the Present System of Road-Making* (Bristol: Gutch, 1816), 32.

64. *Report from the Select Committee on the Highways of the Kingdom* (Edinburgh: Hill, 1819), 20; Mitford, 4. 288; Thomas De Quincey, "Travelling in England Thirty Years Ago" in *Tait's Magazine*, new series, 1 (1834), 802, 797.

65. Alexander Gibb, *The Story of Telford: The Rise of Civil Engineering* (London: Maclehose, 1935), 298–99.

66. Samuel Smiles, *The Life of Thomas Telford* (London: Murray, 1867), 206; W. A. Speck, *Robert Southey: Entire Man of Letters* (New Haven: Yale University Press, 2006), 177; Southey, *S*, 54; Scott, *HM*, 7.

67. Francis Trevithick, *Life of Richard Trevithick, with an account of his inventions*, 2 vols. (London: Spon, 1872), 1. 194.

68. Hunter Davies, *George Stephenson* (London: Weidenfeld and Nicolson, 1975), 47–48; Smiles, 58.

69. Thomas Summerside, *Anecdotes, Reminiscences, and Conversations of and with the late George Stephenson* (London: Bemrose, 1878), 9; L. T. C. Rolt, *George and Robert Stephenson: The Railway Revolution* (London: Longmans, 1960), 50–55.

70. Hibbert, 2. 86.

71. John Ayrton Paris, *The Life of Sir Humphry Davy*, 2 vols. (London: Colburn, 1831), 2. 72–73.

72. Sir Humphry Davy, *Elements of Chemical Philosophy* (London: Johnson, 1812), 2; Sir Humphry Davy, *On the Safety Lamp for Preventing Explosions in Mines* (London: Hunter, 1825), 118–19.

73. Davy, *On the Safety Lamp*, v, vii.

74. L. Pearce Williams, *Michael Faraday* (London: Chapman and Hall, 1965), 36, 38.

75. Bence Jones, *The Life and Letters of Faraday*, 2 vols. (London: Longmans, Green, 1870), 1. 403; Sir Humphry Davy, "New Experiments on Some of the Combinations of Phosphorus" in *Philosophical Magazine*, 52 (1818), 443.

76. Michael Lindgren, *Glory and Failure: The Difference Engines of Johann Müller, Charles Babbage, and Georg and Edvard Scheutz*, trans. Craig McKay (Cambridge, MA: MIT Press, 1990), 37.

77. Charles Babbage, *Passages from the Life of a Philosopher* (London: Longman, Green, Longman, Roberts, and Green, 1864), 42.

78. Byron, *PW*, 2. 76.

79. Cronin, 85–86; Cyrus Redding, "Blues and Anti-Blues" in *New Monthly Magazine*, 2 (1821), 223.

80. Sharon Ruston, *Shelley and Vitality* (Basingstoke: Palgrave, 2005), 24–63; John Abernethy, *An Enquiry into the Probability and Rationality of Mr. Hunter's Theory of Life* (London: Longman, Hurst, Rees, Orme, and Brown, 1814), 39, 48, 50.

81. Percy Shelley, *L*, 1. 429; Gronow, 2. 4. 61.

82. William Lawrence, *An Introduction to Comparative Anatomy and Physiology* (London: Callow, 1816), 169; William Lawrence, *Lectures on Physiology, Zoology, and the Natural History of Man* (London: Callow, 1819), 8.

83. Mary Shelley, *F*, 34, 33.

84. Thomas Jefferson Hogg, *The Life of Percy Bysshe Shelley*, 2 vols. (London: Moxon, 1858), 1. 70; Percy Shelley, *P*, 171–75; Mary Shelley, *J*, 1. 56; Polidori, 123; Mary Shelley, *F*, 8.
85. Mary Shelley, *F*, 37, 39–40.
86. Ibid., 97.

Epilogue: The Modern World

1. Byron, *PW*, 5. 488, 490.
2. Hibbert, 2. 341–42; William Makepeace Thackeray, *The Four Georges* (London: Smith, Elder, 1862), 169.
3. Smith, 265; Raikes, 1. 92; Hibbert, 2. 339; Duke of Buckingham, *Memoirs of the Court of England, During the Regency*, 2 vols. (London: Hurst and Blackett, 1856), 2. 403.
4. Parissien, 378–83.
5. Duncan Wu, *Thirty Great Myths about the Romantics* (Chichester: Wiley, 2015), 151.

ILLUSTRATION CREDITS

58 *The Dandy of Sixty*
George Cruikshank
William Hone and George Cruikshank, *The Political House that Jack Built* (London: Hone, 1819), n.p., W. D. Jordan Rare Books and Special Collections, Queen's University, Kingston, Ontario

67 *New Covent Garden Theatre*
John Summerson, Thomas Rowlandson, and A. C. Pugin, *Ackermann's Microcosm of London*, 3 vols. (London: Methuen, 1904), 3. 262, W. D. Jordan Rare Books and Special Collections, Queen's University, Kingston, Ontario

74 *Sarah Siddons*
Engraved by William Say, after Thomas Lawrence
Yale Center for British Art, Paul Mellon Collection

77 *Edmund Kean as Richard III*
Unknown artist
Yale Center for British Art, Paul Mellon Collection

82 *The Royal Cockpit*
Robert Cruikshank and George Cruikshank
Pierce Egan, *Life in London* (New York: Appleton, 1904), 176, Private Collection

84 *A Milling Match*
Thomas Rowlandson
E. Beresford Chancellor, *Life in Regency and Early Victorian Times* (London: Batsford, 1927), pp. 82–83, plate 50, Private Collection

88 *Women's Cricket Match*
Thomas Rowlandson
John Ashton, *Social England Under the Regency*, 2 vols. (London: Ward and Downey, 1890), 1. 86, Private Collection

96 *The 1814 Frost Fair*
John Ashton, *Social England Under the Regency*, 2 vols. (London: Ward and Downey, 1890), 1. 222, Private Collection

102 *Mary Linwood*
Engraved by Peltro W. Tomkins
Yale Center for British Art, Paul Mellon Collection

107 *Jane Austen*
Cassandra Austen
National Portrait Gallery, London

113 *Walter Scott*
Engraved by W. and D. Lizars, after Henry Raeburn
J. G. Lockhart, *Peter's Letters to his Kinsfolk*, 3 vols. (Blackwood: Edinburgh, 1819), 2. 350, W. D. Jordan Rare Books and Special Collections, Queen's University, Kingston, Ontario

130 *John Keats*
Benjamin Robert Haydon
Yale Center for British Art, Paul Mellon Collection

133 *Lord Yarmouth*
Richard Dighton
Lewis Melville, *The Beaux of the Regency*, 2 vols. (London: Hutchinson, 1908), 2. 182, Private Collection

136 *Life in London*
Robert Cruikshank and George Cruikshank
Pierce Egan, *Life in London* (New York: Appleton, 1904), frontispiece, Private Collection

138 *Highest Life in London*
Robert Cruikshank and George Cruikshank
Pierce Egan, *Life in London* (New York: Appleton, 1904), 245, Private Collection

138 *Lowest Life in London*
Robert Cruikshank and George Cruikshank
Pierce Egan, *Life in London* (New York: Appleton, 1904), 226, Private Collection

145 *Lord Byron*
Engraved by Henry Meyer, after James Holmes
National Portrait Gallery, London

162 *Crowd by a Gibbet*
Thomas Rowlandson
Yale Center for British Art, Paul Mellon Collection

179 *A Peep into the Blue Coat School*
George Cruikshank
The Trustees of the British Museum

185 *Arthur Wellesley, the future Duke of Wellington*
Francisco José de Goya
The Trustees of the British Museum

191 *La Haye Sainte*
Engraved by George Cooke, after Edward Nash
Robert Southey, *The Poet's Pilgrimage to Waterloo*, 2nd ed. (London: Longman, Hurst, Rees, Orme and Brown, 1816), 58, W. D. Jordan Rare Books and Special Collections, Queen's University, Kingston, Ontario

195 *The War of 1812*
George Cruikshank
John Ashton, *Social England Under the Regency*, 2 vols. (London: Ward and Downey, 1890), 1. 171, Private Collection

196 *General Isaac Brock*
   Painted by John Wycliffe Lowes Forster, after the pastel portrait attributed to William Berczy, circa 1809
   Matilda Ridout Edgar, *General Brock* (Toronto: Morang, 1904), frontispiece, W. D. Jordan Rare Books and Special Collections, Queen's University, Kingston, Ontario

226 *West India Docks*
   John Summerson, Thomas Rowlandson, and A. C. Pugin, *Ackermann's Microcosm of London*, 3 vols. (London: Methuen, 1904), 3. 219, W. D. Jordan Rare Books and Special Collections, Queen's University, Kingston, Ontario

232 *View from Morgan's Rocks of Hill River*
   Engraved by Edward Finden, after Robert Hood
   John Franklin, *Narrative of a Journey to the Shores of the Polar Sea* (London: Murray, 1823), 33, W. D. Jordan Rare Books and Special Collections, Queen's University, Kingston, Ontario

237 *Two Highland Men*
   Louis Simond, *Journal of a Tour and Residence in Great Britain*, 2 vols. (Edinburgh: Constable, 1817), 1. 395, Private Collection

249 *Priscilla of Clerkenwell*
   John Thomas Smith, *Vagabondiana* (London: Chatto and Windus, 1874), n.p., Private Collection

249 *Joseph Johnson*
   John Thomas Smith, *Vagabondiana* (London: Chatto and Windus, 1874), n.p., Private Collection

252 *Beau Brummell at Almack's*
   Lewis Melville, *The Beaux of the Regency*, 2 vols. (London: Hutchinson, 1908), 1. 242, Private Collection

255 *A Dandy*
   John Ashton, *Social England Under the Regency*, 2 vols. (London: Ward and Downey, 1890), 2. 316, Private Collection

262 *Robert Owen*
   John Ashton, *Social England Under the Regency*, 2 vols. (London: Ward and Downey, 1890), 2. 151, Private Collection

272 *Scene on the River Stour (The White Horse)*
   John Constable
   Widener Collection, National Gallery of Art, Washington, DC

277 *Borthwick Castle*
   J. M. W. Turner
   The Provincial Antiquities of Scotland, Borthwick Castle 1819; after Joseph Mallord William Turner 1775–1851; Tate, Purchased 1986; Photo © Tate, London 2018

281 *Dr. Syntax Reading his Tour*
Thomas Rowlandson
William Combe and Thomas Rowlandson, *The Tour of Dr. Syntax in Search of the Picturesque* (London: Methuen, 1903), 175, Private Collection

288 *Killingworth Locomotive*
Samuel Smiles, *The Life of George Stephenson* (New York: Harper, 1868), 168, W. D. Jordan Rare Books and Special Collections, Queen's University, Kingston, Ontario

296 *Mary Shelley*
Reginald Easton
Bodleian Library, University of Oxford

306 *Beggars Leaving London for the Workhouse*
John Thomas Smith, *Vagabondiana* (London: Chatto and Windus, 1874), n.p., Private Collection

INDEX

Page references in *italics* indicate illustrations.

343